The Origins of American Religious Nationalism

RELIGION IN AMERICA
Harry S. Stout, General Editor

Recent titles in the series:

The Origins of American Religious Nationalism

SAM HASELBY

OXFORD
UNIVERSITY PRESS

OXFORD
UNIVERSITY PRESS

Oxford University Press is a department of the University of
Oxford. It furthers the University's objective of excellence in research,
scholarship, and education by publishing worldwide.

Oxford   New York
Auckland   Cape Town   Dar es Salaam   Hong Kong   Karachi
Kuala Lumpur   Madrid   Melbourne   Mexico City   Nairobi
New Delhi   Shanghai   Taipei   Toronto

With offices in
Argentina   Austria   Brazil   Chile   Czech Republic   France   Greece
Guatemala   Hungary   Italy   Japan   Poland   Portugal   Singapore
South Korea   Switzerland   Thailand   Turkey   Ukraine   Vietnam

Oxford is a registered trademark of Oxford University Press
in the UK and certain other countries.

Published in the United States of America by
Oxford University Press
198 Madison Avenue, New York, NY 10016

© Oxford University Press 2015

Library of Congress Cataloging-in-Publication Data
Haselby, Sam.
The origins of American religious nationalism / Sam Haselby.
pages cm. — (Religion in America)
Includes index.
ISBN 978-0-19-932957-1 (hardcover : alk. paper) — ISBN 978-0-19-932958-8 (ebook)
1. Church and state—United States—History.   2. Christianity and politics—United
States—History.   3. Nationalism—United States—History.   4. Nationalism—Religious
aspects—Christianity—History.   5. National characteristics—Religious aspects—
Christianity—History.   6. National characteristics, American—History.   I. Title.
BR515.H377 2015
277.3′081—dc23
2014017353

1 3 5 7 9 8 6 4 2
Printed in the United States of America
on acid-free paper

The first religious principles must be secondary; such as may easily be perverted by various accidents and causes, and whose operation, too, in some cases, may, by an extraordinary concurrence of circumstances, be altogether prevented.
—DAVID HUME, *A Natural History of Religion*, 1757

The opinions and belief of men depend not on their own will, but follow involuntarily the evidence proposed to their minds.
—the original opening lines of Thomas Jefferson's "Statute for Religious Freedom," written in 1779, excised by the Virginia General Assembly before passage in 1786

. . . the American Bible, Sunday School, and Tract Societies, being largely patronized and aided by the public munificence, were able to supply the demand for their respective publications almost at cost, it was soon found that we could not compete with them in the market.
—Methodist General Conference, 1832

Contents

Acknowledgments

JIM STEWART, RICHARD BUSHMAN, and Herb Sloan helped shape my understanding of the eighteenth and nineteenth-century Atlantic World. At The New School, Jonathan Veitch and David Plotke made a space for me amid a lively community. My students at Eastern and Woodbourne Penitentiaries provided a model of intellectual engagement. Jon Butler helped me keep an eye on the big picture. While working on this project, I received critical support from the Mrs. Giles Whiting Foundation, the Institute for Social and Economic Research and Policy, in particular Bill McAlister, at Columbia University, the William F. Milton Fund at Harvard University, and the Faculty Support Grants program at the American University in Cairo. The Harvard Society of Fellows provided, for me, an unimagined environment in which to learn. In particular, Sohini Ramachandran, Nur Yalman, Mischa Gleimer, Andy Strominger, Bernard Bailyn, Martha Minow, Lital Levy, Leslie Dunton-Downer, and Nancy Cott exemplified this fellowship. At the Center for History and Economics at Harvard, Emma Rothschild offered the resources of the Center for History and Economics, and Julia Stephens put them to work. Shirine Hamadeh, Helga Seeden, Inanna Hamati-Ataya, and Leena Saidi made the transition from Cambridge to Beirut easy and rich. In Cairo, I could not have aked for better colleagues than the faculty and staff in the History Department at AUC. Meggan Houlihan at the AUC Library helped me gain access to much primary and secondary material.

Scholars and readers know Betsy Blackmar, Barbara Fields, and Eric Foner as accomplished scholars. I have had the great good fortune to also know them as teachers. In substance and detail, Randall Balmer, Harry Stout, and Mark Noll gave insightful and challenging critical feedback on the manuscript, for which I am grateful. Cynthia Read, Marcela Maxfield, and Charlotte Steinhardt at Oxford University Press expertly brought this book to your hands. Bruce W. Ferguson found the painting used on the cover of this book. Kent Monkman, the artist, generously granted permission for its reproduction.

Camilla Smith helped make New York home, and Curtis Brown and Diana Allan shared their lives in Cambridge and Beirut. Doris Athineos taught me much, including how to be edited. Thanks are due to Marina Rustow, Tamer El-Leithy, Marty Kenner, Evan Haefeli, Dora King, Adam Rothman, Eyal Eithcowich, and Ramzi Rouighi, for years-long discussions on history and politics. Amanda Claybaugh, Maya Jasanoff, and Martin Puchner were everywhere. Lisa and Jessica Haselby, my sisters, quicker learners, kept me working and asking questions. Radhika Philip merits special thanks, for which I do not have the words. Sonia Matthews, my mother, is a lover of books and a great storyteller. For these and other reasons, this book is dedicated to her.

*The Origins of American Religious
Nationalism*

Introduction

AMERICANS HAVE LONG looked to the War of Independence as the defining event of American nationality. Historians differ as to why it happened, what it meant, and even who led it. Yet most have shared a belief, in the words of one of its leading historians, that the "American Revolution not only created the American political nation but molded permanent characteristics of the culture that would develop within it." This book makes two revisionist claims. The first is that the War of Independence posed rather than answered the question of American nationality. The answer came with the colonization of the continent. In 1776, Adam Smith had marveled at the unique prosperity of the Anglo-American colonies, yet even this achievement, exceptional in the history of classical or early modern colonialism, could not compare with colonization of the North American interior. Patriot victory in the War of Independence freed Americans from the relative restraints imposed by British imperial considerations. The decades after independence saw the full beginning of a movement that, in a little over a century, would transform the American West from the home of 100,000 poor people to the home of 62 million rich people. The historian James Belich has described it as the most explosive growth in human history.[1]

---

1. Quote from Bernard Bailyn, *Faces of Revolution, Personalities and Themes in the Struggle for American Independence* (New York, 1992), p. 200; More recently, Gordon Wood wrote, "The American Revolution, in short, gave birth to whatever sense of nationhood and national purpose Americans have had"; see *The American Revolution: A History* (New York, 2003), p. xiii. John Ferling, "Myths of the American Revolution," *Smithsonian Magazine* (January 2010), accessed online at http://www.smithsonianmag.com/history-archaeology/Myths-of-the-American-Revolution.html, wrote, "The American Revolution and the war that accompanied it not only determined the nation we would become but also continue to define who we are." Gary Nash, *The Unknown American Revolution: The Unruly Birth of*

In the half-century following the outbreak of the war against Great Britain, nine new states—Kentucky, Tennessee, Indiana, Louisiana, Ohio, Illinois, Alabama, Mississippi, and Missouri—entered the Union. Great Britain, Germany, Italy, the Netherlands, and Belgium together could fit into the land between the original colonies and the Mississippi River Valley. With Vermont and Maine, even New England added two new states. In the same half century, the extent of territory over which the United States claimed sovereignty almost tripled. The population grew, in 1780, from less than 3 million to, by 1830, almost 13 million. In just 40 years, from 1790 to 1830, the West gained more inhabitants than had the original colonies in a century. By 1825, with the close of James Monroe's second term as president and the end of the Virginia dynasty, Kentucky and Tennessee alone had more people than Rhode Island, Vermont, Connecticut, and Massachusetts combined. The simultaneous development of Northern capitalism, the extension of the franchise to unpropertied white men, the cotton boom, the creation of the Deep South, the growth of slavery and racism, the proliferation of popular Protestantism, and the birth of mass media were all powerful, at times discordant, developments inseparable from westward expansion and growth. This movement of peoples and resources generated new ideas and institutions, and it shifted the center of American politics to the West. It also produced a new mode of nationalism, one more enduring than revolutionary-era civic republicanism, and more unruly.[2]

The major tensions of westward expansion expressed themselves as a fight within Protestantism, a fight between frontier revivalism and national evangelism. It was essentially a contest for governance of the frontier, a contest between the migrants to the periphery, mostly small farmers, who were inventing popular American Protestantism, and Northeastern elite,

---

Democracy and the Struggle to Create America (New York, 2006), and T. H. Breen, *American Insurgents, American Patriots: The Revolution of the People* (New York, 2010), dispute Bailyn's view that a small group of elites led the American Revolution, but accept the Revolution as the defining event of American nationality. Though focused on the eighteenth century, Brendan McConville, *The King's Three Faces: The Rise and Fall of Royal America, 1688–1776* (Chapel Hill, 2006), includes an epilogue about the continuing struggle in the early republic to locate American political power, pp. 313–316; David Waldstreicher, *In the Midst of Perpetual Fetes: The Making of American Nationalism, 1776–1820* (Chapel Hill, 1997), argued a still dissenting view that American nationality formed in the early republic. In Book IV, Chapter VII of *The Wealth of Nations*, Adam Smith explores the causes and consequences of the unique prosperity of the British North American colonies.

2. Charles Beard, *The Rise of American Civilization* (New York, 1931), pp. 507–509.

mostly gentry and capitalists, who represented Reformed Protestantism and a new, nationalist missionary movement. The book's second chief claim is that this conflict reshaped American nationality, resolving itself into an enduring religious nationalism. The process reached a crucial moment in the rise of Andrew Jackson. Herman Melville wrote that it was the "great democratic God. . . who didst pick up Andrew Jackson from the pebbles; who didst hurl him upon a warhorse; who didst thunder him higher than a throne!" Melville's description accords with one of the lessons of social history; great leaders are more likely to be raised than to raise. Jackson's rise, the central events of his presidency, and the role he played in expressing a new American nationality, however, are better explained by the contest between these two large, distinct movements than by the "democratic God," though Melville's theological idiom was apt.[3]

Before Jackson, American presidents were, as the historian David Potter put it, chairmen of the board–type figures, "chief executives" in the sharp sense of the phrase. Jackson was different; he was America's first truly national American political leader. Ralph Waldo Emerson, not an admirer, termed him America's "representative man." George Washington and John Adams never aspired to be America's "representative man." Even Thomas Jefferson was content to be known as a man for the people and never wished to be a man of the people. Jackson did. Both his "Common Man" campaign slogan and his war against the second Bank of the United States expressed an anti-elitist discourse developed by frontier revivalists in opposition to the missions movement of Northeastern elites. At the same time, Jackson shared the providential nationalism of the missions movement. They provided the form, a jeremiad of national history, and the main elements, a discourse of Christian paternalism and civilization, to which Jackson turned to justify his campaign of Indian removal. In describing Jackson's rise in American political culture, Melville compared him to pebble, picked up and tossed high. Rather than the pebble, this book is about the waves that, in Melville's metaphor, tossed the pebble onto the throne. The book presents the primary conflict in American religion during the early republic as one between frontier revivalism and a nationalist missions movement—in other words, not as denominational but as social and geographic. In doing so, the book offers a substantially

---

3. Herman Melville, *Moby-Dick* (San Francisco, 2011), p. 157; see also John William Ward, *Andrew Jackson: Symbol for an Age* (New York, 1962), p. 99.

new way to understand the role of Protestantism in the formation of American nationality.[4]

After the Revolution, the new republic faced two formidable nation-building challenges, the future of the Native Americans (and their land claims) and the establishment of US sovereignty over the frontier. The state was unable to address either crisis. Its organization by spartan Federalist principles, inspired by the consensus-building needs for a broad protection of religious freedom and property rights, left it constrained from taking effective nation-building measures. In short, the United States began a vast and unique continental colonization project without (in the centuries-old European sense of the terms) either "a church" or "a state." In the absence of either a national religious or sufficient state authority, two distinct Protestant movements arose. The first, frontier revivalism, came to the nation's attention in 1801, after a massive religious revival meeting at Cane Ridge, Kentucky. Rural revival meetings had long taken place in rural regions of the original colonies, but Cane Ridge brought the practice to the frontier of the early republic, where it flourished. Camp meetings became a characteristic event of the explosive growth of popular, frontier Protestantism, which involved millions of people. Out of this frontier upheaval emerged American Methodism, Baptism, Mormonism, Shakerism, the Disciples of Christ, the Millerites—and a challenge to the political order of the new American nation. The early American republic in fact was one of the most dynamic and creative periods in the history of Christianity. For generations, it has fascinated historians of America and scholars of religion. The swarming vitality of religion in the period did not come from migration. Significant religious migration to America had ended a century before the War of Independence.[5]

---

4. On Jackson as the first truly national political leader, see David Potter, *The Impending Crisis: 1848–1861* (New York, 1977), p. 7; Herman Melville, *Moby-Dick: Or, The Whale* (New York, 1851), p. 128. On the second-party system, see Richard P. McCormick, *The Presidential Game: The Origins of American Presidential Politics* (New York, 1982), esp. pp. 123–124. On Emerson and Jackson, see Lewis Perry, *Boats Against the Current: American Culture Between Revolution and Modernity* (Lanham, MD, 2003), p. 202. On the contest within early republic Protestantism, see Amanda Porterfield, *Conceived in Doubt: Religion and Politics in the New American Nation* (Chicago, 2012); James R. Rohrer *Keepers of the Covenant: Frontier Missions and the Decline of Congregationalism* (New York, 1995); Stephen Marini, *Radical Sects of Revolutionary New England* (Cambridge, MA, 1982); most important, see Nathan O. Hatch, *The Democratization of American Christianity* (New Haven, CT, 1991).

5. See Marini, *Radical Sects*, and Thomas Kidd, *The Great Awakening: The Roots of Evangelical Christianity in Colonial America* (New Haven, CT, 2009).

The philosophers David Hume and Baruch Spinoza thought that the universal attributes of hope and fear led directly to religion, and the early American republic had more than its share of both. It is one of the few societies in modern history to experience an unusual combination of demographic trends, enjoying significant economic and population growth at the same time as rising mortality rates and a crisis of malnutrition. Why exactly these typically contrary trends coincided remains unclear, but it is suggestive of the combination of freedom, social mobility, and hope, as well as violence, isolation, misery, and fear that the American experiment supported. By the end of the eighteenth century, nearly all the colonies were healthier places to live, with higher literacy rates than almost anywhere in Europe. The trade in indentured servant contracts was in long-term decline and, by 1820, over. Fertility rates were high: in 1800, the average woman bore seven children. As a result of these factors, frontier settlers in the early republic were healthier, freer, more likely to be part of a family, and less likely to have migrated for religious reasons than their colonial predecessors. At the same time, the colonization of the continent was an act of violence, more so in the United States than in Canada. In British Canada, the Crown opted for stability over rapidity and implemented strict regulations for settling new lands. In the US territories, regulation of frontier settlement was almost nonexistent. The greater value of American agricultural lands, in particular those of the Ohio River Valley and the lower Mississippi, raised the stakes, as well as intensified the competition—and the fraud. The expansion of chattel slavery, a burgeoning slave population, and afflicted and dispossessed native peoples were all common sights. Merely being white offered no protection from land speculators, who defrauded tens of thousands of settlers. Out of these conditions emerged what historians have called the "hothouse" and the "formative period" in the history of American religion.[6]

The lack of any state church or national religious authority contributed to the creativity and the chaos of religion in the early republic. Chapter 1 puts the achievement of secularism in the United States into historical context. It explains why two seemingly contradictory realities were compatible. First, disestablishment was as much the result of the strength of competing churches, rather than the weakness of religious interests.

---

6. Herman De Dijn, *Spinoza: The Way to Wisdom* (Lafayette, IN, 1996). On demographic trends in the early republic, see Herbert S. Klein, *A Population History of the United States* (New York, 2004), ch. 3.

At the same time, proponents of Christianity in American public life, especially New England Protestants, could see the US Constitution and the ascendancy of the Southern planters, especially the Virginia dynasty, as signs that the United States had betrayed the providential promise of American nationality and, instead, taken a grievous, godless course. Chapter 1 outlines what might be called the political theology of American secularism. Thomas Jefferson and James Madison saw a secular government as a core component of nationalism. Their prevailing "Virginia model," which committed the United States to limited government and rapid expansion enabled, by the 1820s, a popularization of evangelical Protestantism to an extent they had neither anticipated nor desired. They strongly disapproved of the missionary organizations as well, but these also filled a gap of governing left by a relatively weak state.[7]

Chapter 2 begins with Timothy Dwight and John Trumbull as Yale students, in the mid-1760s, writing agitprop poetry and organizing nationalist demonstrations, in New Haven, Connecticut. Dwight and John Trumbull were central figures in the Connecticut Wits, America's first literary movement. As a rule, early American literature is of greater historical than literary interest. The Wits' writings are of considerable historical interest, in good part not only because they were America's first nationalist movement, but in addition because their writings, mostly poetry, gave a full range of self-conscious symbolic expression to a vision of the American nation. They described a whole society: family life, the arts, education, labor, politics, social hierarchy, recreation, gender roles, religion, and more. Their corpus is important because, despite the Southern planters' domination of American political life in the revolutionary and early republic eras, it is in the writings of the Connecticut Wits where one finds the first fully articulated vision of American nationality. Its combination of the realized, the failed, and the forgotten is at once familiar and alien, conservative and radical.

Chapter 2 is mostly devoted to outlining their vision of American society. It is helpful to think of how it compares to that of their nemesis, Thomas Jefferson: the New Englanders imagined an America that was hierarchical, theological, and anti-racist, whereas the Jeffersonian, or

---

7. Gordon Wood, *The Radicalism of the American Revolution* (New York, 1993), writes "By the second quarter of the nineteenth century, the evangelical Protestantism of ordinary people had come to dominate American culture to an extent the founding fathers had never anticipated," p. 333.

Virginian model, of American nationality that prevailed was evangelical, egalitarian, and racist. The early and ambitious role of these Protestants in, they presumed, leading America into nationhood helps explain why they experienced the triumph of the Southern planters in American political life as a usurpation of New England's rightful role as steward of the nation, as well as as a turn away from God. A key moment comes in 1795, when, acknowledging his failure to inaugurate a national and nationalizing literature, Timothy Dwight, accepting the presidency of Yale, turns to institution building. His institution building included a historic alliance between Congregationalists and Presbyterians. With the 1801 Plan of Union, representatives of the Congregational and Presbyterian Churches, meeting in Dwight's parlor at Yale, surrendered their historic rivalry and, in essence, forged a no-competition agreement for the souls of frontier settlers. The Plan of Union represented a major change in nineteenth-century history: the progress of Christian ecumenism, a part of the significance of which is spelled out in Chapter 6. Chapter 2 concludes with the 1815 Hartford Convention, an event, at the time, conducted with a degree of secrecy and, with some success, characterized by Jeffersonians as an empty secessionist threat by ineffectual, royalist New Englanders. Seen in the context of a rich and distinctive New England version of American nationality, expressed by the Connecticut Wits, the Hartford Convention appears as a clearer and more poignant moment. It was not just the death rattle of Federalism, but the last stand, at least in US party politics, of Timothy Dwight and his imagined New English Empire.[8]

If the early republic saw American political life get away from the Northern Reformed Protestants, so too, perhaps to their even greater dismay, did American religion. Chapter 3, on frontier Methodism under Francis Asbury, and Chapter 4, on Richard McNemar in the Miami River Valley, address frontier religion. Asbury's stewardship made nineteenth-century American Methodism one of the great growth stories in the history of religion. McNemar was one of the original innovators of

---

8. For a view of the New England contribution to revolutionary-era American nationalism that emphasizes its millennialism, see Ruth Bloch, *Visionary Republic: Millennial Themes in American Thought, 1756–1800* (New York, 1988), especially p. 138–140. For an example of the millennialism component of American nationalism in New England persisting into the early republic, see Elijah Parish, *An Oration Delivered at the request of the officers, before the first regiment in the second brigade of the second division of militia in the commonwealth* (Salem, 1805), especially p. 3.

the camp meeting, the signature institution of contemporary popular religion, especially on the frontier. From his 1771 arrival in Philadelphia (from England), to his death in Spotsylvania, Virginia, in 1816, Asbury established himself as a figure as skilled in ecclesiastical government as anyone in modern history. During that time, it makes more sense to speak of Asbury's Methodists than either, singly, Asbury or the Methodists. McNemar was born in 1770, in Tuscarora, Pennsylvania. He apprenticed to an itinerant Presbyterian minister and by the 1790s had settled in the Miami River Valley, where he gained a reputation as a preacher whom the spirit visited. Crowds traveled from throughout Kentucky, Indiana, and Ohio to hear him preach. In 1805, McNemar converted to Shakerism, and he died in the Shaker Village in Watervliet, New York, in 1839. McNemar and Asbury's Methodists represent ideal types in frontier religion. Ideal types are not explanations, but descriptions, in this case of the conditions of social life on the frontier and the possibilities of frontier revivalism. The aim is to understand why so many people in the early republic, especially on the frontier, joined popular Protestant movements. For this reason, as well as others, McNemar and Asbury receive sympathetic treatment.[9]

Asbury built the Methodists into an important social force. They provided pastoral care and social regulation. Asbury's Methodists illustrate a truth about religion that has a hard time finding a hearing in liberal discourse: the fact that belief follows from action at least as often as it leads to it. Put another way, American colleges and universities, seats and generators of liberal discourse, are in this respect not well situated to understand the popularity of religion. In a college or a university, the measure of excellence is exclusion: the more people the school refuses to admit or educate, the greater it is. With religions, especially Christianity and Islam, the more people they recruit and retain, the more important they are considered. There are interesting exceptions, but as a broad rule people are loyal in their beliefs to those who take care of them. On the frontier of the early republic, no one provided more pastoral care and social regulation—certainly not any state institution—than the Methodists. In the past, historians have often asked why Americans become Methodists or Baptists or Mormons, but an at least equally important question is why Methodists or Baptists or Mormons became Americans.[10]

---

9. On ideal types, see Max Weber, *Basic Concepts in Sociology* (New York, 1968), p. 16.

10. Marc Sageman, *Understanding Terror Networks* (Philadelphia, 2004), has a fascinating discussion of how radicalization occurs: when small groups of men come together to

Whereas Asbury was an institution builder, Richard McNemar was a mystic. Thousands of settlers traveled to his revival meetings and sermons, where he displayed gifts that won him followers and enemies. Of the frontier religionists in the early republic, Asbury's Methodists (and, eventually, the Mormons) built the most dynamic and durable institutions. To thrive, religions also require spirituality, and the oratorical offers an avenue to mystical and spiritual experience. Reading a small segment of a sermon and presuming that experience compares to having heard it preached is like reading fragments of the libretto to *Don Giovanni* and presuming one has been to the Vienna Philharmonic. Scholars and other bookish types would do well to remember Benjamin Franklin's sheepish account of how the preaching of the itinerant George Whitefield, a legendary orator, charmed Franklin:

> I happened. . . to attend one of his sermons, in the course of which I perceived he intended to finish with a collection, and I silently resolved he should get nothing from me. I had in my pocket a handful of copper money, three or four silver dollars, and five pistoles of gold. As he proceeded I began to soften, and concluded to give the coppers. Another stroke of his oratory made me asham'd of that, and determin'd me to give the silver; he finished so admirably, that I empty'd my pocket wholly into the collector's dish, gold and all.[11]

David Garrick, the preeminent actor and theatrical figure of Georgian England, said that Whitefield could choose to make his audience tremble—or weep—merely by altering his pronunciation of the word "Mesopotamia." Garrick wrote that he "would give a hundred guineas, if I could only say 'O!' like Mr. Whitefield!" McNemar and his followers illustrate that some of the most powerful religious experiences are often aural rather than visual, heard rather than seen or thought. This is why, for many, the "voice of God" is a more palatable notion than

---

observe ritual and a kind of competition over purity and strictness results. Sageman calls it the "bunch of guys" theory. See also Raffi Khatchadourian, "Azzam the American: The Making of an Al Qaeda Homegrown," *New Yorker*, January 22, 2007. See also Arthur C. Brooks, *Who Really Cares: The Surprising Truth about Compassionate Conservatism* (New York, 2007), in which Brooks finds that Americans who regularly go to church and identify as conservative give more of their income to charity than do Americans who identify as liberal.

11. Benjamin Franklin, *The Autobiography of Benjamin Franklin* (New York, 1916), p. 194.

"the face of God" or "the mind of God." Martin Luther is one of the great textual exegetes in history, but German Lutheranism owed much of its popularity to his beautiful hymns (even Bach admired them) rather than Luther's hermeneutics. The point is that Whitefield and McNemar's audiences experienced something lost to mere readers, and an attempt to explain the appeal of preachers with such an order of gifts calls for a sympathetic treatment.[12]

Similarly, Francis Asbury was a mediocre preacher, but a standout and prolific hymnodist. Asbury's extensive journals are a rich historical source, but during his lifetime his literary output consisted of 42 editions of Methodist hymnals, published from 1790, until his death in 1816. Until the unprecedented print campaigns of the American Tract Society and the American Bible Society, Methodist hymnbooks were likely the most widely available religious literature in the early republic. In helping to raise worshippers to the divine, hymns played a major role in American Methodism, comparable to iconographic painting and sculpture in Catholicism. Closer to Methodism, the historian Roland H. Bainton thought that the "magnificent liturgy" of the Anglican Church, "its stately prayers and sonorous cadences," had done "more than all else. . . to endear the English church to the English people." Three qualities, together, account in large part for the phenomenal rise of Methodism in America: the appeal of its hymns; the empowering optimism of its generous, basically Arminian, theology of grace; and its innovative institutional organization, which allowed it to reach across the frontier, at once stable and flexible. It offered no theological innovations and no political content; it was rather an evangelical and social movement.[13]

The isolation and privation, the freedom and the social mobility, and the lack of government and absence of civilization that fostered frontier revivalism caused leading American nationalists concern. Benjamin Franklin, James Madison, Thomas Jefferson, and other statesmen feared that the United States would lose the frontier. The peoples of the periphery, it seemed, might join Britain, France, or Spain, or, following the Americans' own example, demand independence. There was no precedent for nationalizing diverse peoples flung across a large imperial republic.

---

12. J. B. Wakely, *The Prince of Pulpit Orators: A Portraiture of Rev. George Whitefield* (New York, 1871), p. 226.

13. Mark A. Noll, *America's God: From Jonathan Edwards to Abraham Lincoln* (New York, 2001), pp. 331–336.

The Ottoman and Austro-Hungarian examples, two contemporary models of empires extending over large geographic areas, did not rely for their legitimacy on nationalist and republican claims.

Throughout the Americas, from Canada to Peru, it was commonly believed that frontier settlers tended to be wild, degenerate, and hostile to government. As early as 1755, Benjamin Franklin had warned that "thousands" were ready to "swarm" across the Appalachians. Franklin saw no reason to presume that "our debtors, loose English people, our German servants, and slaves" would want to become Americans, and thought that "the great country back of the Appalachian mountains" was naturally distinct from "our people, confined to the country between the sea and the mountains."[14] In 1787, John Jay wrote, "I fear that Western Country will one day give us trouble." To "govern them will not be easy, and whether after two or three generations they will be fit to govern themselves," he wrote, remained an open question. Jay was not alone in fearing that the frontier imperiled the fragile American experiment, that what Madison called "the country beyond the mountains" was too distant from education, civilization, law, and government. "Shall we not fill the wilderness with white savages," he asked, "and will they not become more formidable to us than the tawny ones which now inhabit it?" Even Hector St. John de Crèvecoeur, America's great agrarian nationalist, thought the first wave of frontier settlers "no better than carnivorous animals" who represented the "most hideous parts of our society." It was financial imperative, however, as much as imperial ambition, that drove US expansion. In debt to Dutch bankers from the costs of the War of Independence, the sale of Western lands served as the federal government's primary source of income.[15]

---

14. In Benjamin Franklin's 1755 "A Plan for Settling Two Western Colonies," Franklin proposed organizing civilian militias as a colonial avant-garde and marching them "under the conduct of the government to be established over them," into the interior; see Leonard W. Labree, ed., *Papers of Benjamin Franklin* (New Haven, CT, 1962) V, pp. 457, 462, 458. In the spring of 1786, James Monroe, chairman of the congressional committee charged with turning Jefferson's 1784 Land Ordinance into the 1787 Northwest Ordinance, wrote to James Madison about his worries that a misstep would "separate these people" west of the Appalachian Mountains "from the federal government & perhaps throw them into the hands. . . of a foreign power"; Monroe quote in Harry Ammon, *James Monroe: The Quest for National Identity* (New York, 1971), pp. 55–56. On the frontiers of the Americas, see J. H. Elliott, *Empires of the Atlantic World: Britain and Spain in America* (New York, 2006), pp. 275–276.

15. Jay to Jefferson April 24, 1787, in Julian O. Boyd, ed., *Papers of Thomas Jefferson* (Princeton, NJ, 1955), vol. 11, pp. 313–314; Jay quoted in Michael Allen, "The Mississippi River Debate, 1785–1787," *Tennessee Historical Quarterly* (Winter 1977), pp. 447–467, quote

To address the problem, Congress passed the Northwest Ordinance. Even as the Ordinance adopted means from the British example, such as the extension of the common law, its choice of the word "territory" signaled an original, homegrown discourse of empire. Its formula for establishing territories, turning territories into states, and admitting them to the Union on equal terms was new. Still, after the passage of the Northwest Ordinance, in 1788, Thomas Jefferson wrote to Madison, asking what to do if Westerners "declare themselves a separate people." We "are incapable of a single effort to retain them," he warned. Claims today that the interior, the Midwest and the South, embody "real" America are so familiar that it can be odd to remember that this now popular answer to nationality was once a worrisome question. Seen in historical perspective, the creation of American nationality in the early republic appears at least as unlikely as either the patriots' victory against the British, or, with the ratification of the Constitution, the birth of the republic.[16]

The historian Harry S. Stout has written about how Americans understood the carnage of the Civil War as a consecration, a baptism in blood, of the nation. Without question, the Civil War was the great nationalizing event in US history. The fact that for many members of the Northern political and business classes, the Union had already become sacred, strongly informed their resolve to preserve the Union. Chapter 5 shows that liberal Protestants from the New England gentry, even Unitarians, also turned to missionary nation-building work. Despite real differences, and much squabbling between (and among) elite Northeastern Protestants, their shared commitment to the nation, to missionary nation building, and to a national, ecumenical ideal, gave them something foundational in common, something that distinguished them from frontier revivalists. Like their more conservative cousins, these Protestant elites found popular frontier religion a serious threat.[17]

---

from p. 461; Hector St. John de Crèvecoeur, *Letters from an American Farmer* (Mineola, NY, 2005), p. 28 (originally published in 1782).

16. Anders Stephanson, "A Most Interesting Empire," unpublished essay that shows the historical novelty of the American method of continental imperialism and presents a typology of American imperialism, over the course of US history; cited with permission of author. Jefferson to Madison, January 30, 1787, in Julian O. Boyd, ed., *Papers of Thomas Jefferson* (Princeton, NJ, 1955), vol. 11, p 93.

17. Harry S. Stout, *On the Altar of the Nation: A Moral History of the Civil War* (New York, 2007).

The current literature depicts frontier revivalism as a "democratizing" force in the early republic, but contemporary elites did not see it that way. Frontier lay ministers claiming the authority to interpret the scriptures, sometimes by divine revelation, outraged or scandalized ministers from established Protestant Churches. Whether priest or ministers, respectable and responsible men agreed that sound textual exegesis required specialized skills. They agreed that the age of revelation was over. A Presbyterian missionary sent to Missouri, for example, described Campbellism as a dangerous deception and false religion, a "cunning system" that aped godliness for base worldly reasons. "I have no hesitation in saying that in my opinion Campbellism is the great curse of the West," he wrote. It is "more destructive and more injurious to the cause of religion than avowed Infidelity itself." At the same time, the nationalism of the Northeastern Reformed Protestants bound them to the frontier settlers. To these nationalists, the atheism of European intellectuals was a distant threat. As William White, an Episcopal minister, told the Domestic and Foreign Missionary Society in 1832, the "sound of the Gospel must be heard" by the "progeny of the [frontier] settlers" because the settlers and their children were "our fellow members of the same communion."[18]

A theological, and etymological, perspective helps to clarify this important development. One of the original meanings of "salvation," in the classical Greek, is "making whole." In an existential sense, for Christians, the theological event of salvation is the "making whole" of the individual through her harmonious reunion with the true community of believers. The mid-twentieth-century Anglican theologian John MacQuarrie described salvation as a delicate alignment between the individual and the community. "Too much stress on decision and commitment," wrote MacQuarrie, "tends to overemphasize individual salvation, and to lose sight of the fact that there can be no genuine salvation for an individual apart from the true community of faith." In a theological sense, pure individualism is deeply un-Christian. Even in Protestantism, wrote MacQuarrie, "the agency by which the Spirit works in the world"

---

18. Martin E. Marty, *Pilgrims in Their Own Land: 500 Years of Religion in America* (Boston, 1984), p. 169. For an establishment Protestant view of frontier religion, see, for example, Dwight, *Travels in New-England and New-York* (London, 1823), vol. III, p. 25. AHMS missionary quoted in William Warren Sweet, *Religion in the Development of American Culture, 1765–1840* (New York, 1952), p. 224; William D. White, "Of the Increase of the Church, A Sermon," reprinted in *Proceedings of the Domestic and Foreign Missionary Society of the Protestant Episcopal Church* (Philadelphia, 1832), pp. 84–85.

has generally been held to be the community, the true community of faith, not the individual. In the early republic, many frontier Christians—this book looks primarily at Methodists, Baptists, and Shakers—were still looking for salvation as Christians historically had, through their church or religions.[19]

At the same time, growing Anglo-American political power led many Protestants, especially those in the Reformed traditions, to identify nation or empire as the sacred community. The historian C. A. Bayly has described the Reformed Protestants' self-assertion on a global scale, including the historic mobilization of Protestant missions, which resulted as "imperialist evangelization." In this book, the American missionaries are called national evangelists and their movement national evangelism. Almost every Protestant in nineteenth-century America was evangelical, but the missionary movement, in the original sense of the word "evangelist"—"bearer of good news"—went to the frontier, and around the world, to spread the "good news" of the nation as the true and sacred political community. The missionaries did not pair the words "national" and "evangelism" into self-designation, but the phrase was a minor imposition. The nation was the most important concept around which their work cohered, and they often compared their efforts to those of the original evangelists.[20]

Interestingly, the original intention of the early missions movement was to convert Native Americans. The Massachusetts Missionary Society, founded in 1799, for example, stated its original purpose as diffusing "the knowledge of the gospel among the heathens. . . in the remote parts of the country." The field experience of the Society's missionaries, however, who reported that the poor white settlers were degenerating to a state of barbarism, provoked a crisis. In 1804, the Massachusetts Missionary Society amended its constitution to identify poor white people as the primary object of the mission: "The object of this society is, to diffuse the gospel among the people of the newly-settled and remote parts of our country."[21] Similarly, also in 1804, a missionary from the Northern Missionary Society of the State of New York, working among the Oneida Indians, reported to the Northern Missionary Board on three months spent trying

19. John MacQuarrie, *Principles of Christian Theology* (New York, 1966), pp. 298–299.

20. C. A. Bayly, *The Birth of the Modern World, 1780–1914* (Malden, MA, 2004), p. 330.

21. Constitutions of the Massachusetts Missionary Society reprinted in Francis Wayland, *A Memoir of the Life and Labors of the Rev. Adoniram Judson, D. D.* (Boston, 1854), vol. 1, p. 44.

to convince the Indians to give up alcohol, to adopt European agricultural practices and systems of property rights, and to accept the Christian God. It was an unequivocal failure. He requested, and the Board agreed, to change his appointment to make him a missionary to "the white inhabitants in the vicinity of the Oneida nation." In brief, the American missions movement set out to Christianize Native Americans and ended up instead nationalizing poor white settlers.[22]

Based primarily on records and publications of the American Tract Society, the American Bible Society, and the American Board of Commissioners for Foreign Missions, Chapter 6 puts this movement into historical context. Historians have not paid much attention to these organizations since the mid-twentieth century, when a pair of influential works presented them as little more than formalized statements of bourgeois class ideology. Chapter 6 argues they were much more that than, and focuses on how they served in the United States as novel nation-building organizations. They played an important role, establishing an ecumenical ideal, diminishing differences between established Protestant Churches, and, in several senses, serving as some of the first truly national institutions in the United States. Though they soon became forces helping to drive the globalization of Protestantism, their primary reasons for being were to counter the perceived threat of deism and infidelity and to nationalize, and they were self-professedly counter-Enlightenment measures. Their nationalism was evident not only in their theological homogenization, but in their impressive array of schools, associations, and publications aiming to make manners and people more alike, more, in general terms, middle-class and modern. In quantitative terms, their literary output was astonishing, amounting to hundreds of millions of pages, not just of scriptures but also of pamphlets and tracts. In all of these ways— their ecumenical ideal, their nationalism, their emphasis on education and literature, and the leading role that Reformed, Northeastern clergy

---

22. *Report of the Northern Missionary Society of the State of New York* (Troy, NY, 1804), quote on p. 2; the same switching of the assignment of a missionary from Native Americans to poor white settlers is described in *Report of the Trustees to the Hampshire Missionary Society at Their Meeting in Northampton* (Northampton, 1803), pp. 8, 6, 10. On the missionaries' attempts to Christianize Indians, only to be taken up in the cause of civilizing the poor white settlers of the frontier, see Ruth H. Bloch, "Battling Infidelity, Heathenism, and Licentiousness: New England Missions on the Post-Revolutionary Frontier, 1792–1805," in Frederick D. Williams, ed., *The Northwest Ordinance: Essays on Its Formulation, Provisions, and Legacy* (East Lansing), 1989, pp. 39–60. For the American Bible Society reporting the same discovery, see *Seventh Report of the American Bible Society* (New York, 1823), p. 26.

played—the missionary organizations were direct descendents of the Connecticut Wits. With their expansive bureaucracies, centralized authority, ambitious print media campaigns, and extensive scale of operations, these associations were comparable to modernizing nineteenth-century nation-states, what the historian Christopher Bayly has called "empires of religion." Chapter 6 touches on all of these aspects of the national evangelist organizations, including their notable departure from the Wits' anti-racism. It shows that the missionary organizations were actually the first prominent Americans to maintain that slavery was a "positive good," because, their literature explained, it Christianized Africans. The promotion of racism, and the corresponding de-emphasis of religious difference, especially among Protestants, epitomized the nation-building function of the organizations.

Northeastern missionaries saw themselves as worthy successors to Matthew, Mark, Luke, and John, the original evangelists. Frontier revivalists found different analogies more apt, ranging from Johann Tetzel, the seller of indulgences who moved Martin Luther to protest, to the horseleech. Many frontier revivalists found the missionaries' wealth, fund-raising techniques, and worldly ambitions to be un-Christian. Their money, their intrusions into the lives of others, and their disdain for local ways helped give shape, on the frontier, to the stereotype of the arrogant and meddlesome Yankee. A popular association developed between the missionaries and the Bank of the United States, regarded by some as another Yankee class interest project. The Bank was not especially popular on the frontier, especially following the Panic of 1819, which brought hard times to many in the United States, in particular to poor rural people trying to pay off land debts. Chapter 7, the final chapter, reveals how the missionaries aggravated these class antagonisms. In Jackson's campaigns, Westerners aggrieved by Yankee missionaries and banks found at the same time an outlet for their anti-elitism and an inlet to nationalist politics.

Chapter 7 shows how the creative contest between national evangelism and frontier revivalism informed the defining events of Jacksonsonian politics: in particular, his war with the Second Bank of the United States and his dispossession of the Southeastern Indians. Jackson presented his opposition to re-chartering the Second Bank of the United States as a move on behalf of equality and independent producers, especially smallholders, and as a blow against capitalism, privilege, and fraud. This agrarian critique of capitalism was not new, but neither was its popularity to be taken for granted. Over a decade before Jackson focused it on the Bank, frontier revivalists had popularized a very similar, potent attack against another signature institution of the Northeastern elite: the missions. Aggrieved by their encounters with missionaries and missionary literature, they had attacked the missions as an exploitative class interest project designed to enrich the Eastern elite at the expense of Western farmers. On the other hand, when he dispossessed the Southeastern Indians, Jackson turned to a discourse of the Eastern elite, of the missions movement. For decades, the missions movement had been refining and promoting a narrative of a providential, Christianizing nation, overseen by paternalistic leaders. The historian Wesley Frank Craven called it "the legend of the Founding Fathers," and gave most of the credit to early nineteenth-century New Englanders. To rationalize the dispossession of the Southeastern Indians, Jackson appropriated this discourse, putting it to contrary ends, that of exclusion.

America's eighteenth-century revolutionaries spoke (at least for men) a universal language of inalienable rights. Their exclusions violated their own theories. Jackson presented himself as a common man, while speaking of innate differences in culture, religion, and race of those to be excluded. The contrast captures much of the change that came with the popularization of nineteenth-century American nationalism: from gentlemen speaking the language of universal rights to a commoner, a man of the people, presenting racialist theories of exclusion. Such justifications remain familiar, and they originated in the reformation of American nationality that took place in the early republic.

In both the veto of the Bank re-charter and the dispossession of the Indians, Jackson invoked the sovereign authority of the people, as invested in the president, to defy the other branches of government. It was an unprecedented use of the executive branch, rationalized on nationalist grounds. Jackson portrayed new policies with new justifications as fulfillments of original intentions. He did not invent this mode of national discourse out of whole cloth. Though they were not exclusive to these contemporary Protestant movements, frontier revivalism did as much to popularize frontier anti-elitism, aimed at the Northeastern elite, as any movement in the early republic. At the same time, no one did more than the national evangelists, the missionary organizations, to promote the jeremiad and the sacred national founding. These two Protestant movements at once represented and reformed the political landscape of the early republic. Some of their distinguishing qualities came together in

Jackson's presidencies in ways that illuminate real, and enduring, changes in American religious and political authority between the revolutionary and the Jacksonian eras.

In the half century following independence, the democratization of politics, the popularization of Protestantism, the appearance and proliferation of the Northeastern missionary movement, and the nationalization of the frontier all took place. It is difficult to posit a simple cause and effect relationship between these four processes, but the strong claim of this book is that these changes coincided in such a way as to be best understood together. In the context of classic interpretations of American nationality, the approach has the interest of showing how Perry Miller's emphasis on the missionary "errand into the wilderness" and Frederick Jackson Turner's focus on the frontier are not incompatible. The claim that these processes helped generate a religious nationalism is predicated on three considerations. First is the general historical pattern that nationalisms change, following the formation of the state, when they are popularized. Second, the scale of quantitative growth and change in the early republic gave these religious movements a formative role. Third, the idea that exclusions from the political community, especially ones violating established principles—and Jackson's Christian justification for Indian removal was such a violation and exclusion—leave deep and lasting imprints on a society. This approach places this book somewhere between more recent postcolonial and culture histories, and their interest in modes of discourse and representation, and older and more established histories emphasizing political and economic processes.[23]

A word on terminology may be helpful. The practice of American religious nationalism is familiar, even if the phrase is not. Forty years ago, in a classic essay, following Rousseau's *The Social Contract*, the sociologist Robert N. Bellah described a national "collection of beliefs symbols, and rituals with respect to sacred things and institutionalized in a collectivity." The strong tendency of Protestantism to idealize its origins contributes to the sacred quality of things, especially texts, associated with

---

23. See, for example, Gauri Viswanathan, *Outside the Fold: Conversion, Modernity, and Belief* (Princeton, NJ, 1998). Frederick Jackson Turner wrote, "The triumph of Andrew Jackson marked the end of the old era of trained statesmen for the Presidency"; see Turner, "Contributions to American Democracy," in *The Frontier in American History* (Tucson, AZ, 1986) pp. 254–255; Uday S. Mehta, "Liberal Strategies of Exclusion," in Frederick Cooper and Ann Laura Stoler, eds., *Tensions of Empire: Colonial Culture in a Bourgeois World* (Berkeley, 1997).

the American Revolution. The Declaration of Independence, the United States Constitution, and the Bill of Rights, for example, are spoken of as containing timeless truths that merit vigilant conservation. They barely exist in a secular way in American political culture.[24] The national shorthand for the American revolutionaries, the "Founding Fathers," suggests the "sacred source" dimension of American religious nationalism. Though the phrase was coined in the twentieth century (in 1916, by Warren G. Harding), the revered status of the revolutionaries is older. In 1838, for example, Abraham Lincoln asked Americans to practice fidelity to the revolutionaries as the *political religion of the nation.*" Reverence for American revolutionaries, he said, should be "breathed by every American mother to the lisping babe. . . taught in schools, in seminaries, and in colleges;—let it be written in Primmers [*sic*], spelling books, and in Almanacs;—let it be preached from the pulpit, proclaimed in legislative halls." Fidelity to the Revolution, Lincoln said, should "become the *political religion* of the nation; let the old and the young, the rich and the poor, the grave and the gay, of all sexes and tongues, and colors and conditions, sacrifice unceasingly upon its altars."[25]

The sacralization of origins, especially in print form, and the subsequent understanding of history as a process of degradation, is a distinctively Protestant historical consciousness. Martin Luther inaugurated it when he held up his reading of the scriptures to demonstrate the Church's degeneration. To Luther and his followers, showing declension conferred authority to the defender of the foundational text, the purported restorer of the original promise. In historical consciousness, those who revere the US Constitution, in particular its originalists, are the sectarian heirs of Martin Luther, or at least his mode of authority. The same Protestant consciousness is evident in the extent to which the matter of whether proposals or programs are "constitutional" predominates in the American political discussion, often in lieu of whether they are effective

---

24. Robert N. Bellah, "Civil Religion in America," *Daedalus*, vol. 96, no. 1 (Winter 1967), pp. 1–21, quote from p. 8. Sydney G. Fisher, "The Legendary and Myth-making Process in the Histories of the American Revolution," *Proceedings of the American Philosophical Society*, vol. 51, no. 204 (April–June 1912), pp. 53–75, presents a fascinating summary of scholarly, and popular, writings about the American Revolution from the nineteenth and early twentieth century; The American Revolution Center, "American Revolution: Who Cares?" (Philadelphia, 2009), esp. pp. 5–7.

25. Abraham Lincoln, "Address to Young Men's Lyceum," in *Selected Speeches and Writings* (New York, 1992), pp. 17–18. Italics in original.

or counterproductive, wise or foolish, ethical or immoral. When it comes to politics, Americans are textual exegetes and a people of the word.[26]

In the jeremiad, the sacred origins and its foundational text have their own rhetorical ritual, one that joins public exhortation with spiritual renewal with social reform. The literary scholar Sacavan Bercovitch has demonstrated the enduring power and prevalence of the jeremiad, especially its "rhetorical continuities," in American political discourse. The practice encourages reformers, Andrew Jackson and Abraham Lincoln, for example, to do so in the name of continuity, as a return to original principles.[27] A simplified civil theology, a premium placed on religious toleration, the sacralization of the American Revolution, and the dominance of the jeremiad in American political discourse are the main components of American religious nationalism. The final element concerns the prevalence of theology, in the literal sense of "God talk," as a conspicuous and enduring feature of American political life. While the form (though not the content) of jeremiad is a legacy of the Reformation and New England Puritans, and the content of national evangelism a solution to the crisis of the frontier, the nineteenth century also saw the theological center of American political discourse shift from God to Jesus. The turn from God-talk to Jesus-speak resulted from the popularization of Protestantism as well as the social action emphasis of the national evangelist associations.[28]

---

26. Anthony Kemp, *The Estrangement of the Past: A Study in the Origins of Modern Historical Consciousness* (New York, 1991); Lewis P. Simpson, "The Act of Thought in Virginia," *Early American Literature*, vol. 14, no. 3 (Winter 1979–1980), pp. 253–268. See also Daniel Lazare, *The Frozen Republic: How the Constitution Is Paralyzing Democracy* (New York, 1996).

27. Sacvan Bercovtich, *The American Jeremiad* (Madison, 1978) and *The Rites of Assent: Transformations in the Symbolic Construction of America* (New York, 1993), especially chs. 3 and 4. David W. Noble, *The End of American History: Democracy, Capitalism, and the Metaphor of Two Worlds in Anglo-American Historical Writing, 1880–1980* (Minneapolis, 1985), acknowledges the continuity of the jeremiad, but emphasizes its rejuvenation, after the pessimistic conclusions of Turner's "Frontier Thesis," through the new naturalizing and universalizing laws of economic development, i.e., deliverance through an American-led globalization of capitalism, at the beginning of the twentieth century. Here the emphasis is on the changes to the content of the jeremiad caused by the colonization of the continent and the appearance of a national political community. The phrase "rhetorical continuities" is from Bercovitch, *The Puritan Origins of the American Self* (New Haven, CT, 1975, p. 186. For a study on how rhetorical patterns can shape thought, see Albert Hirschman, *The Rhetoric of Reaction: Perversity, Futility, Jeopardy* (Cambridge, MA, 1991); On the unnaturalness of the present US national political geography, see Joel Garreau, *The Nine Nations of North America* (New York, 1989).

28. Stephen Prothero, *American Jesus: How the Son of God Became a National Hero* (New York, 2004), passim; Boyd Hilton, *The Age of Atonement: The Influence of Evangelicalism on Social and Economic Thought, 1765–1865* (New York, 1986), p. 5.

A fight within Protestantism over the colonization of the continent is not a complete explanation for these features of American nationalism. Imagining a past golden age seems to be part of human nature. As the last moment in history when the political, intellectual, and literary leaders of a large society could be the same people, and so long as a golden age is presumed to be an age of heroes, the late eighteenth century makes for a good golden age. Reverence for the "founding fathers" also allows identification with an underdog, a compelling if long-expired model for an American national symbol. The United States is a large and in many respects unnatural nation. Making the American Revolution sacred contributes to set of shared presumptions. Recently, the American Revolution Center, a Philadelphia-based organization dedicated to commemorating the Revolution and educating Americans about its accomplishments, elaborated on this idea: "We are a nation united not by blood, land, or religion, but rather by the great Founding principles expressed in the Declaration of Independence and the Constitution of the United States." The statement reveals misgivings: other nations might have as their foundation "blood, land or religion." The United States, it claims, has principles expressed in texts. It is in fact not any particular principle in the Declaration of Independence or the Constitution, but their mythology, and that of the American Revolution, which unites Americans. They are myths not in the sense of being false, but in that their meaning is never fixed. Americans will continue to debate their political and moral lives through these eighteenth-century texts. The result is sometimes grand, often awkward.

American religious nationalism is a set of conventions, derived in part from religion, oriented around the way the Revolution functions in American political discourse. It provides a set of necessary conventions. Dominant American ideas about politics, economics, the role of the United States in the world, the relationship of the state to society, and much more, differ in important respects from those of half a century ago, much less from more than two centuries ago. By depicting change as a return to original principle, American religious nationalism renders unsettling history as a friendly past. The most familiar instance in nineteenth-century America is the "Gettysburg Address," a symbolic act of inclusion. In the "Gettysburg Address," Abraham Lincoln reinvented the Declaration of Independence as a promissory note on emancipation. Over three decades earlier, in his 1830 State of the Union Address, Andrew Jackson pioneered American religious nationalism. Jackson's Address used the same conventions of the sacred founding and obligations to original intention, but in order to exclude. For this reason, among others, it is less remembered, but Jackson's Address deserves remembrance, especially by historians, if only to remind that neither the American Revolution nor the founding fathers offer the answers. I understand, for example, that when Americans debate Thomas Jefferson's ideas, or his character, they are, usually, in fact, talking about what kind of nation the United States of America should be. On the balance, however, my view is that this myth, and its rituals and habits, inhibit thought and limit choice, and that questions of the founders often cause thought to flounder.[29]

Finally, historians of the United States might find a few more words on terminology helpful. Certain key words in the literature on the history of American religion will not be found. The "church-state relations" model has little to do with the development of American religious nationalism. As James Madison pointed out, the vocabulary of "church-state relations," came into existence in a European context and referred to a form of "political and civil organization" that did not exist in the United States. By the late 1820s, American political democracy had generated a more subtle and complex relationship, which Madison described as a "line" separating "religion and the Civil authority." Madison saw that "it may not be easy, in every possible case, to trace the line of separation between the rights of religion and the Civil authority with such distinctness as to avoid collisions."[30] When one stops presuming that Jefferson's "wall of separation" existed and approaches the early republic with Madison's more accurate description in mind, the problem of religion and politics in early nineteenth-century America begins to look more interesting. Rather than courts and state legislatures performing periodic masonry work on an imaginary wall, the conflict between a popular, anti-elitist frontier revivalism and a bourgeois and nationalist metropolitan missionary emerges as the main contest.[31]

---

29. The phrase "the legend of the founding fathers" comes from Wesley Frank Craven, *The Legend of the Founding Fathers* (New York, 1965); The American Revolution Center, "The American Revolution: Who Cares?" (Philadelphia, 2009), p. 5. I have been influenced on this question by Carolyn Marvin and David W. Ingle, *Blood Sacrifice and the Nation: Totem Rituals and the American Flag* (New York, 1999) and George Kateb, *Patriotism and Other Mistakes* (New Haven, CT, 2008).

30. Madison's letter to the Rev. Jasper Adams, reprinted in John F. Wilson and Donald L. Drakeman, eds., *Church and State in American History: The Burden of Religious Pluralism* (Boston, 1987) pp. 80–82.

31. Ibid. My critique of the vocabulary of "church-state relations" in regard to the United States comes from Sidney E. Mead, "Neither Church nor Sate: Reflections on James

Nor does this work use the "awakening" paradigm. As the social anthropologist Ernest Gellner wrote, the "awakening" is (in many languages) a keyword of nationalism.[32] Calling the extreme religious situation of the early republic the "Second Great Awakening" is to naturalize both religion and nationalism. In the context of the history of American religion, a comparably ideological act of naming would be to replace references to "Christians" and "God" with "Christers" or "the Christers' Sky God." By offering the previous absence of religious belief or nationalism as the very "proof" of their eternal existence, the "awakening" model is a good illustration of the historian David Potter's observation that the primary ideological function of the twentieth-century historian was to justify the existence of the nation-state.[33] The earliest use of the phrase that I have been able to find is from 1867, in *The Edinburgh Review.* In an approving notice of John Hill Burton's nationalist *History of Scotland*, the reviewer noted that the work lent credence to the idea that the Protestant Reformation was the "second great awakening" of Scottish national life. From the start of its career, therefore, the "second great awakening" device has worked to enlist religion in the service of nineteenth-century nationalism. A more objective approach treats widespread religious dissidence as an abnormal state of affairs.[34]

Madison's 'Line of Separation,' " *A Journal of Church and State*, vol. X (Autumn 1968) no. 3, pp. 349–363.

32. Ernest Gellner, *Nationalism*, ch. 1. Jon Butler's article, "Enthusism Described and Decried: The Great Awakening as Interpretative Fiction," *Journal of American History*, vol. 69 (1982), pp. 305–325, suggests the problem of the awakening model, especially in the manner that its critics sought to substantiate the contributions of evangelicals to American nationalism. See, for example, Frank Lambert, "The First Great Awakening: Whose Interpretive Fiction?" *The New England Quarterly*, vol. 68, no. 4 (Dec. 1995), pp. 650–659; James F. Cooper Jr., "Enthusiasts or Democrats? Separatism, Church Government, and the Great Awakening in Massachusetts," *NEQ* (June 1992), pp. 265–283; George W. Harper, "Clericalism and Revival: The Great Awakening in Boston as a Pastoral Phenomenon," *NEQ* (December 1984), pp. 554–566; Mark A. Noll, "The American Revolution and Protestant Evangelicalism," *Journal of Interdisciplinary History* (Winter 1993), pp. 615–638; John F. Wilson, "Religion and Revolution in American History," ibid., pp. 597–613.

33. David M. Potter, "The Historian's Use of Nationalism and Vice Versa," *The South and the Sectional Crisis* (Baton Rouge, 1968), pp. 34–83. More basically, "awakening" as a synonym for a human realization or epiphany probably derives from a repeated suggestion in the Hebrew scriptures that the experience of time is a basic difference between man and God: men sleep, and though God "rested" after creating the universe, He does not appear to slumber. For example, "Behold, he that keepeth Israel shall neither slumber nor sleep" (Pslams 121:4, King James).

34. Sydney Smith, review of *The History of Scotland*, *The Edinburgh Review*, vol. 126 (Edinburgh, 1867), p. 251; Bruce Lincoln, "Conflict," in Mark C. Taylor, ed., *Critical*

Whereas "awakening" is a fundamentally ideological term, "evangelical" and "evangelicalism" are merely not very useful. It is difficult to find a Christian in nineteenth-century America who cannot be described as an evangelical. The term does not accommodate the difference between frontier revivalism and national evangelism, both of which, despite frequent mutual animosity, were evangelical movements. To better represent the division, I have called the frontier upstarts "frontier revivalists" and the missionaries "national evangelists." Though "revivalism" presents the same denotative problems as "awakening," it lacks the ideological career of the latter term and presents the signal advantage of common contemporary usage. Finally, the breadth of religious movements and the range of strange and compelling figures in the early republic, as well as their engagement with almost every cultural and political issue of the day, gives the era a kaleidoscopic quality. This book addresses the problem in the spirit of Clifford Geertz's advice to social scientists—"seek complexity and order it"—and without any pretense to be a thorough portrait of religion in the era, much less a complete one.[35]

Terms for Religious Studies (Chicago, 1998), pp. 56–57; Sacvan Bercovitch, *The Rites of Assent: Transformations in the Symbolic Construction of America* (New York, 1993), pp. 147–148.

35. See, for example, Mark A. Noll, David W. Bebbington, George A. Rawlyk, eds., "Introduction," in *Evangelicalism: Comparative Studies of Popular Protestantism in North America, the British Isles, and Beyond, 1700–1900* (New York, 1994), where evangelicalism is defined as a form of Protestant Christianity that emphasizes biblicism, crucicentrism, activism, and conversionism; Clifford Geertz, *The Interpretation of Cultures* (New York, 1973), p. 34.

I

The Powers of the Earth

SECULARISM AND AMERICAN NATIONALISM

IN SPITE OF its cultural and intellectual pretensions, New England was the heart, not the head, of early American nationalism. Chesapeake plantation society, Virginia in particular, gave more shape and direction to American thought. In addition to plantation slavery and its peculiar racism, Virginia gave America the Constitution, its first and greatest dynasty of presidents, and, in Parson Weems, its first national mythologist. It was also in Virginia that James Madison and Thomas Jefferson won a historic, and in some ways unlikely, victory for secularism. The term "secularism" would not be not coined until the mid-nineteenth century, by an English bookseller supporting the Italian Risorgimento; at the same time, the body of doctrine and practice that would come to be known by the term gained momentum and authority in revolutionary-era America, particularly in Virginia. The immediate consequences, in Virginia, of Thomas Jefferson and James Madison's political victories on behalf of secularism were complex. Nonetheless, with what became the 1786 Virginia Statute for Religious Freedom, Thomas Jefferson contributed a classic statement of Enlightenment secularism, though James Madison was the more consistent and creative thinker on the matter. The depth of historical transformation since the eighteenth century has meant that the substance of secularism in America changes and requires scrutiny, but its formal ideals have remained remarkably enduring.[1]

---

1. Edmund Morgan, *American Slavery, American Freedom* (New York, 2003); Jack N. Rakove, *James Madison and the Creation of the American Republic* (New York, 1990); David Armitage, *The Declaration of Independence: A Global History* (Cambridge, MA, 2008); Jack P. Greene, *Pursuits of Happiness: The Social Development of Early Modern British*

Until relatively recently, secularism was usually taken for granted as a simple, straightforward phenomenon. In his 1976 *Keywords*, for example, Raymond Williams did not see reason to include an entry for "secular" or "secularism." Secularization actually includes at least three distinct processes. Secularists usually want religion to be separate from the state. In the American vocabulary, separation was called "disestablishment." Social scientists call it "differentiation." Differentiation or disestablishment involves a mix of legal, economic, and political considerations. In Virginia, only a skillful exploitation of unusual circumstances made differentiation possible, and even then, barely so. First, many dissenting churches resented Anglican establishment. Opposition to Anglican privilege led many of the acutely religious and evangelical in Virginia to support disestablishment, not because they were secularists but because they preferred no state church to an Anglican one. Second, the Anglican alliance with Britain during the War of Independence had left the established church vulnerable. Even with a motivated opposition and a weakened established church, disestablishment required James Madison's deft legislative stewardship and political manipulation in order to prevail. Far-reaching consequences followed. The advent of what would become a renowned model is the most familiar, but it also brought more mundane results. In 1802, for example, disestablishment resulted in Virginia's confiscation of the Episcopal glebes (farmlands). Until Emancipation, liquidation of Virginia's Episcopal glebes was the largest state seizure of private property in US history.[2]

Second, secularists want religion to privatize. To some extent, privatization is obviously contingent upon the changing, and ideological, demarcation between public and private. Generally, however,

---

Colonies and the Formation of American Culture (Chapel Hill, NC, 1988); Sydney G. Fisher, "Myth-Making Process in the Histories of the American Revolution," *Proceedings of the American Philosophical Society*, vol. 51 (April–June 1912), pp. 53–75; Lewis P. Simpson wrote that the "drama of the spiritualization of the secular in New England is not as fundamental in shaping the motives of the emerging American nation-state as the more intangible and less coherent drama of the secularization of spirituality" in Virginia, see "The Act of Thought in Virginia," *Early American Literature*, vol. 14, no. 3 (Winter 1979–1980), pp. 253–268.

2. Thomas E. Buckley, "Evangelicals Triumphant: The Baptists' Assault on the Virginia Glebes, 1786–1801," *William and Mary Quarterly*, vol. 45 (January 1988), pp. 33–69; George Jacob Holyoake, a veteran of the socialistic and cooperative Owenite movement and a London bookseller, coined the term "secularism" in 1851. See Eric S. Waterhouse, "Secularism," *The Encyclopedia of Religion and Ethics* (New York, 1921), vol. 11, p. 348. In its entry for "secularism," *The Encyclopedia of Religion and Ethics* does not mention the American Revolution, though it does credit Tom Paine as an early progenitor of the concept; Raymond Williams, *Keywords: A Vocabulary of Culture and Society* (London, 1976).

privatization means that religion must restrict itself to the pastoral care of individuals and abstain from challenging public morality, especially in matters regarding the state and markets. Of course, religions often have a lot to say about political and social life. As a result, religionists can see the privatization imperative of secularism as, in essence, the impious or the heretical telling them that attempts to observe some of the sacred duties of their religion are inherently illegitimate. The directive that religion belongs in the private sphere is a secular discourse in the same way that talking about "religion" as such is. The devout tend to conceive of God, or Jesus, or Allah, or the Bible, or the Quran—something divine—as an incomparable, unique authority. Talking in a generic way about "religion" and its general place in society is a deeply secular discourse, and its prevalence in the United States is probably the greatest triumph of American secularism. Finally, secularists often want religious belief and activity to decline. Secularists often claim that they really want to protect religion from politics, so that it can thrive. Though sometimes sincere, the point presumes a secular view of political life and, as was the case with Jefferson and Madison, the claim can also be disingenuous.[3]

The acute Protestants of revolutionary-era New England were not secularists. To say that they saw society and religion as symbiotic would be insufficient. Symbiosis is a mutually beneficial relationship between two separate organisms. To them, a moral society and Reformed Protestantism were not symbiotic because they were inseparable. Christian grievances with secular America are therefore as old as the United States. Timothy Dwight, for example, denounced the godless US Constitution, attributing the political troubles of the 1790s to the fact that "we commenced our national existence under the present system without GOD." Thus already by the 1790s, in Dwight's view, America had become *a smoke in the nostrils of JEHOVAH.*[4]

---

3. Jonathan Z. Smith, "Religion, Religious, Religions," in Mark C. Taylor, *Critical Terms for Religious Studies* (Chicago, 1998); Talal Asad, *Formations of the Secular: Christianity, Islam, Modernity* (Palo Alto, CA, 2003), esp. chapter 1, argues that the practice of the secular, in the modern sense, predated its formulation into a doctrine regarding the relationship of religion to civil government. For the three components of secularization, see Jose Casanova, *Public Religions in the Modern World* (Chicago, 1994). For a more philosophical view, see Charles Taylor, *A Secular Age* (New York, 2007).

4. "We formed our Constitution without any acknowledgement of GOD; without any recognition of his mercies to us, as a people, of his government, or even of his existence. The Convention by which it was formed, never asked, even once [sic], his direction, or

In contrast, in his 1843 essay "On the Jewish Question," Karl Marx wrote that disestablishment in the United States led to the "perfect Christian state." By building a state that "relegates religion to a place among the other elements of civil society," wrote Marx, Americans had enabled the nation-state to express and represent the most basic human needs. Competition for ultimate loyalty from religious groups was thus minimized, and the state, in Marx's phrasing, assumed a position in relation to civil society that is "just as spiritual as the relations of heaven to earth." America, Marx observed, had become "pre-eminently the country of religiosity." Disestablishment, religious freedom, and political democracy, he thought, had combined to demonstrate the limitations of the political state. Insulated from most religious passions, this set of circumstances allowed religion, in what Marx called "North America," to thrive. In his view, this was an important shortcoming of the political state. Nonetheless, Marx saw the Americans' achievement as a step in right direction, as progress toward the social state.[5]

Madison and Jefferson understood that disestablishment would protect the state from implication in sectarian passions. In their role as secular nationalists, their relationship to religion has been more influential, and was more creative, than that of their pious New England opponents. The most familiar words in the history of American secularism are a monument from the contest between the Virginia secularists and the New England Christians. Even outside the United States, the phrase "a wall of separation between church and state" is known as a pithy expression of a secular ideal. Though sometimes presumed to be from the US Constitution, the words are from an 1802 letter that President Thomas Jefferson sent to the Danbury Baptist Association of Danbury, Connecticut. Opposed to the state support for the Congregationalist Church, and concerned that Connecticut's religious establishment, known as the Standing Order, would seek more penalties or prohibitions on dissenting groups, the Danbury Baptist Association wrote to Thomas Jefferson, offering their congratulations on his election as president and expressing approval of his support for religious freedom.[6]

---

his blessing, upon their labours. . .. [thus we have become] a smoke in the nostrils of JEHOVAH." Dwight quoted in Kenneth Silverman, *Timothy Dwight* (New York, 1969), pp. 138–139.

5. Karl Marx, "On the Jewish Question," in Robert C. Tucker, ed., *The Marx-Engels Reader* (New York, 1978).

6. Peter S. Field, *The Crisis of the Standing Order: A History of Congregationalist Ministers in Massachusetts* (New York, 1993).

In the disorderly and contested election of 1800, state delegations cast 36 ballots for president. In those 36 ballots, Connecticut did not cast a single vote for Thomas Jefferson. Connecticut was the home of Timothy Dwight, perhaps the nation's most preeminent anti-Jeffersonian. State taxes supported the Congregationalist Church. Along with Massachusetts, it was the center of Christian Federalism. Moreover, as president, Jefferson had no legal authority over the establishment of state churches or religions, a fact that the Danbury Baptists acknowledged: "Sir, we are sensible that the President of the United States. . . cannot destroy the Laws of each State." Instead, their letter presented Jefferson with a political opportunity, which he seized. In a January 1, 1802, reply, he wrote to the Danbury Baptist Association, insisting that religion is a matter that lies solely between "man & his God," citing his "sovereign reverence" for the First Amendment, which he characterized as "building a wall of separation between Church & State." In an even more liberal interpretation, he added that the First Amendment expressed the "supreme will of the nation in behalf of the rights of conscience." He implied that religious establishments were a violation of natural rights: "I shall see with sincere satisfaction the progress of those sentiments which tend to restore to man all his natural rights." Sending this letter into the heart of Christian, Federalist New England was a political act. Jefferson had no authority over Connecticut state law, he was unpopular there, and, at best, his interpretation of the First Amendment was eccentric. In effect, Jefferson was using the platform of the presidency to try to nationalize an ideal version of the First Amendment and his 1786 Virginia Statute for Religious Freedom. The Danbury Baptists expressed hopes for an even more ambitious, millennial outcome: "our hopes are strong that the sentiments of our beloved President. . . like the radiant beams of the Sun, will shine and prevail through all these States and all the world till Hierarchy and Tyranny be destroyed from the Earth." Jefferson's alliance with the Danbury Baptists was one of convenience, an opportunity to make a statement of principle, and (he no doubt realized) to make it in the front yard of Timothy Dwight and the Standing Order. In an important way, the Baptists had more in common with their Congregationalist opponents than they did with their champion in the White House. Like the Connecticut Congregationalists, the Baptists wanted not only a Christian nation, but also a Protestant one. Jefferson and other secular rationalists explicitly did not.[7]

---

7. For the correspondence between Jefferson and the Danbury Baptist Association, see Merrill D. Peterson, ed., *Thomas Jefferson: Writings* (New York, 1994), pp. 510–511, and

By accepting the nation as a sacred community, nationalism brought New England Protestants a crisis of community, one they meant to address by strengthening political associations with religion. For Jefferson and Madison, too, the nation was sacred, but they wanted to weaken religion. Different responses to secular victories illustrate the conflict. Whereas the secular US Constitution infuriated Timothy Dwight, Virginia's secular Statute for Religious Freedom brought the usually cautious and restrained James Madison jubilation. He wrote to Thomas Jefferson, in 1786: we have "in this country extinguished forever the ambitious hope of making laws for the human mind." Jefferson and Madison's hopes for secularism in Virginia, and in the United States, came to partial success. Eventually (Connecticut disestablished its state church in 1818, Massachusetts in 1833) differentiation (or disestablishment) established its authority. Though under consistent attack from religionists, their view that religion should remain private—in the secularists' sense of private as remote from political power—remains perhaps the core ideal of American secularism.[8]

The birth and proliferation of popular American Protestantism is proof of the failure of American secularism, at least of Jefferson's ideal version of secularism. The dramatic rise, rather than decline, in religious belief and activity in the early republic followed, in part, as a result of an expansionist, slaveholder's republic. The prospect of the United States assuming a place "among the powers of the earth," as the Declaration of Independence put it, depended on plantation slavery. Plantation slavery in the United States required strong protection for private property and

---

Daniel L. Dreisbach, *Thomas Jefferson and the Wall of Separation Between Church and State* (New York, 2002), p. 48. My understanding of the political context and meaning of the fight for disestablishment and the Statute for Religious Freedom in revolutionary-era Virginia owes much to the work of Thomas E. Buckley, S.J., "Reflections on a Wall," *William and Mary Quarterly*, vol. 56 (October 1999), pp. 795–800, and "After Disestablishment: Thomas Jefferson's Wall of Separation in Antebellum Virginia," *The Journal of Southern History*, vol. 61 (August 1995), pp. 445–480, and *Church and State in Revolutionary Virginia, 1776–1787* (Charlottesville, 1977). Buckley, however, concludes that "to treat Jefferson as a herald of twentieth-century secularism is to read him dogmatically and falsely," whereas I see Jefferson precisely as a herald of modern secularism; see too the influential work of Sidney E. Mead, *The Old Religion in the Brave New World* (Berkeley, CA, 1977), p. 92, and *The Lively Experiment: The Shaping of Christianity in America* (New York, 1963), pp. 58–64. For a different view of the Danbury letter, see Johann N. Neem, "Beyond the Wall, Reinterpreting Jefferson's Danbury Address," *The Journal of the Early Republic*, vol. 27 (Spring 2007), pp. 139–154.

8. See Ralph Ketcham, ed., *Selected Writings of James Madison* (Indianapolis, IN, 2006), p. 21.

a relatively weak federal state—a state that the three-fifths clause almost turned over to the planter class. The same weak state surrendered the governance of the frontier to the popular Protestant upstarts and the Northeastern missionaries. In New England, in contrast, strong church, town, and state governments were normal, crucial components of social and political life. But it is Virginia, where religion existed, and flourished, between society and a weak state, that became the American norm. In this ironic manner, disestablishment in Virginia contributed to the proliferation of popular religion in the United States.[9]

To understand the bitter hostility that some Christians felt for secular America, as well as the even stronger nationalist bond that most Christian and secular Americans share, it is helpful to appreciate the triumphs and defeats of secularism and the extent to which its proponents borrowed from religion to foster nationalism. To this end, a brief look at the intellectual history and political context of three moments in the early formation of American secularism is instructive. James Madison's "Memorial and Remonstrance Against Religious Assessments," Thomas Jefferson's "Bill for Establishing Religious Freedom," and the Declaration of Independence are three documents that all help illuminate an early, formative moment in the interdependent history of religion, secularism, and American nationalism. They show that secularism in revolutionary-era Virginia developed as a strategic arrangement between civil and religious authority designed to fortify American nationalism. Nationalism was the road by which both secularizing Virginia deists and acute New England Protestants meant to assume, as the Declaration of Independence states, a place "among the powers of the earth." Most Americans presumed that religion was essential to a just and right-thinking society, and many elite New England Protestants knew that the religion must be Reformed Protestantism. Among the political elite, the destination was nationhood. Everyone understood that the powers of the earth were nation-states, not religions.[10]

Recently, among some historians, James Madison's "Memorial and Remonstrance Against Religious Assessments" enjoyed a reputation

---

9. For a recent debate on this matter, see William J. Novak, "The Myth of the 'Weak' American State," *American Historical Review*, vol. 113 (June 2008), pp. 775–772, and the subsequent exchange, John Fabian Witt et al., AHR Exchange: "On the 'Myth' of the 'Weak' American State," *American Historical Review*, vol. 115 (June 2010), pp. 768–778

10. On the federal state as either pro-slavery or weak until its capture by the Radical Republicans, see Barrington Moore, "The American Civil War: The Last Capitalist

as the inspiration behind Federalist No. 10.[11] The misperception of the "Memorial and Remonstrance" as the dress rehearsal for Federalist No. 10 is unfortunate, as the latter had no influence in revolutionary-era America, and the "Memorial and Remonstrance" did. According to this story, James Madison's most original revision of classical political theory was his answer to the classical maxim that republics degenerate over time. His counterintuitive solution, in Federalist No. 10, proposed that the competition of many factions would result in contingent and temporary majority alliances, protecting the rights of the minority and ensuring the preservation of liberty and virtue. In other words, contrary to centuries of political theory, virtuous large republics were more, not less, viable. Madison said this idea derived from the "Memorial and Remonstrance." The actual relationship between the two is worth clarifying. It reveals that this secular victory in American history came neither from a point of principle nor from popular support, but resulted from Madison's manipulation of sectarian animosity.[12]

As the "Remonstrance" in the title suggests, the "Memorial and Remonstrance" was designed to oppose. Madison wrote the "Memorial and Remonstrance" to oppose Governor Patrick Henry's "Bill for Establishing a Provision for Teachers of the Christian Religion," introduced to the Virginia Assembly in October 1785. Henry had first gained prominence in colonial Virginia, in 1758, arguing the controversial "Parson's cause," which aimed to give Virginia's vestry squires greater control over Anglican ministers, at the expense of the Crown. Religious matters also first brought Madison into Virginia politics, 15 years later, when Anglican suppression of Baptist revivalists moved Madison, in

---

Revolution," in *Social Origins of Dictatorship and Democracy: Lord and Peasant in the Making of the Modern World* (Boston, 1966), and Eric Foner, *Reconstruction: America's Unfinished Revolution* (New York, 1988); David W. Noble, "Revocation of the Anglo-Protestant Monopoly: Aesthetic Authority and the American Landscape," *Soundings*, vol. 79 (1996), pp. 149–168.

11. Gordon Wood, *Creation of the American Republic* (Chapel Hill, NC, 1998), pp. 606–615; Lance Banning, *The Sacred Fire of Liberty: James Madison and the Founding of the Federal Republic* (Ithaca, NY, 1995), pp. 4, 6, 99, 103. Following Arthur Bentley's *1908 The Process of Government: A Study of Social Pressures* (Cambridge, 1908) on interest group politics, Wood makes a case for the centrality of Federalist No. 10 to revolutionary-era politics. In fact, however, Federalist No. 10 had no impact on late eighteenth-century politics and was not cited in a Supreme Court case until 1974.

12. Gary Wills simply calls the "Memorial and Remonstrance" the "best defense of religious freedom," see Wills, *James Madison* (New York, 2002), p. 3; Ralph Ketcham, *James Madison: A Biography* (Charlottesville, VA, 1990), pp. 163–167.

1773, to action. Virginia Anglicans had jailed several "well-meaning" (Madison's phrase) Baptist ministers for publishing tracts that Madison described as "in the main. . . very orthodox." The affair outraged Madison. He wrote to his friend William Bradford that, to their "eternal Infamy," it was the "Imps" from "the Clergy" and their "Diabolical Hell conceived principle of persecution" maligning the Baptist ministers. This religious persecution, he wrote, "vexes me the most of any thing whatever."[13]

In 1776, when Virginia held its own convention to declare independence from Britain, Madison convinced the more established Henry to propose an amendment to Article Sixteen of George Mason's Declaration of Rights. As submitted, Mason's Article Sixteen read: "all men should enjoy the fullest Toleration in the Exercise of Religion according to the Dictates of Conscience." Madison's amendment read: "no man or class of man ought on account of religion to be invested with peculiar emoluments or privileges." Madison's proposed change amounted to the disestablishment of Christianity, which Henry, no secularist, seems not to have initially realized. Madison's proposed change was withdrawn.[14]

Nearly a decade later, Henry was serving as champion of a bill for the establishment of Christianity in Virginia. The 1785 bill actually drew its impetus from a grassroots campaign by Virginians, who had sent to the House petitions calling for the state support of Christianity. Henry placed the petitions before the House, which endorsed them by a vote of 47 to 23. House members Richard Henry Lee and John Marshall voted in favor of the general state assessment on behalf of Christianity. George Washington let it be known that he supported the measure. A similar resolution, calling for the "incorporation of all societies of the Christian

---

13. In 1774, Madison wrote his friend William Bradford a dismal assessment of the effects of religion on Virginia society: "Poverty and luxury prevail among all sorts: Pride ignorance and Knavery among the Priesthood and Vice and Wickedness among the laity. This is bad enough. But it is not the worst I have to tell you. That diabolical Hell conceived principle of persecution rages among some and to their eternal Infamy the Clergy can furnish their quota of Imps for such business. This vexes me the most of any thing whatever. There are at this [time?] in the adjacent County not less than 5 or 6 well meaning men in close Gaol for publishing their religious Sentiments which in the main are very orthodox. I have neither patience to hear talk or think of any thing relative to this matter, for I have squabbled and scolded abused and ridiculed so long about it. . . I am without common patience. So I [leave you] to pity me and pray for Liberty of Conscience [to revive among us].

14. Ibid., pp. 5–7.

religion," introduced three weeks later by another delegate, passed by an even larger majority, 67 to 23.[15] Before any of these resolutions could become law, they had to be introduced as a proper bill. Henry, however, had just been elected governor. Nonetheless, he had transformed the petitions into a bill that called upon the state of Virginia to legally recognize Christianity as the one "true religion," by, among other means, a mandatory tithe to be paid to the government by each citizen—in tobacco. In addition to state funds of Christianity, Henry's bill also proposed that the state of Virginia officially recognize that Heaven and Hell exist, that the Old and New Testaments were of divine origin, and that the Christian God be publicly worshipped. Most of the bill had been taken from an even stronger South Carolina measure, requiring prospective officeholders to recognize Protestantism as the only true religion.[16] Henry, however, erred in not seeing the bill through committee before leaving the House for the governor's office. In the resulting delay, Madison moved against the measure. "The bill for a religious assessment has not yet been brought in," he wrote to James Monroe. "Mr. Henry, the father of the scheme, is gone up to his seat for his family, and will no more sit in the House of Delegates,—a circumstance very inauspicious to his offspring." Madison's description of Henry's bill as a "scheme" was more telling than fair.[17]

Madison addressed the Virginia House, asking for postponement. There are no reports of his speech before the House, only a short outline scrawled in tiny script on the back of a torn letter.[18] Madison was not an orator and the occasion was difficult. He was attempting to turn the House against a measure that enjoyed popular support, which they had already twice approved in principle, and that was a pet project of the new governor. By combining argument and political arm-twisting Madison won an unlikely reprieve. He also resorted to a bit of parliamentary legerdemain, waiting until the last day of the legislative session, December 24, 1784, to bring before the House a motion postponing consideration of Patrick Henry's establishment bill until the following spring. The motion

15. The legislative story of the origins of Henry's bill, and Madison's parliamentary measures to delay it, in William C. Rives, *The History of the Life and Times of James Madison* (Freeport, NY, 1970), vol. 1, pp. 599–610. Originally published in 1859.

16. Patrick Henry's "A Bill Establishing a Provision for Teachers of the Christian Religion," reprinted in Edwin Scott Gaustad, ed., *Religious Issues in American History* (New York, 1968), pp. 67–72. Hereafter cited as *Religious Issues*.

17. Madison to Monroe quoted in Rives, p. 606.

18. Madison's speech notes reprinted in Rives, p. 605.

prevailed (45 to 38), probably aided by the Christmas Eve holiday, giving opponents of the state establishment of Christianity a chance to take their case to the people of Virginia. It was in this context that Madison composed his "Memorial and Remonstrance," to be circulated alongside Henry's bill (as well as many other broadsides on the matter), among the people of the state of Virginia.[19]

The "Memorial and Remonstrance" carries all the freight of the difficult circumstances in which it was born. Though it has been described as a great statement in the history of religious freedom, the "Memorial and Remonstrance" did not win religious freedom, or make a case for secular government, on grounds of principle or progress. Rather, the "Memorial and Remonstrance" helped bring into existence an awkward, fragile coalition that defeated state support of Christianity in Virginia. The "Remonstrance" presented 15 arguments, in numbered paragraphs, as to why Virginians ought to "remonstrate against" state support of Christianity. Although a secularist may find several of the 15 points compelling, no one could find all of them so. Some points argue that establishment will make the state too strong. Other points argue that establishment of a state church will enervate the state. Some points argue that the state must not be allowed to theologize. A few points, however, rely on explicitly theological claims in order to rally opposition, for example, that to legislate matters of conscience would constitute an "offence against God." As political theory, the "Memorial and Remonstrance" amounts to less than the sum of its parts. As a strategic intervention to ally the devout in revolutionary Virginia against state support for Christianity, however, it was a well-crafted effort.[20]

The "Remonstrance" is inconsistent in the logic of its appeals, but deliberately so. The purpose of the broadside was neither innovation nor consistency in political theory, but rather to cast a net widely, and deftly, enough to catch all those who might have been convinced, in Virginia during the spring of 1785, to oppose, for any possible reason, the legal establishment of Christianity. To that end, it was predicated upon Madison's knowledge of the ambitions, hopes, and fears of Virginia's

---

19. Rives provides a detailed account of the establishment bill's political origins and its course through the Virginia House. He also provides an account of Madison's parliamentary maneuvering to kill it, pp. 599–610 and 629–634, but he does not analyze either Henry's Bill or Madison's "Memorial and Remonstrance."

20. Madison's "Memorial and Remonstrance" reprinted in *Religious Issues*, pp. 72–79.

religious sects.[21] It sought to enlist as many sects and factions as possible, by one rationale or its opposite, against Henry's establishment bill. Madison referred to it as the "divide and rule" strategy. Writing to Jefferson, he explained that he had strategized with dissenters: "At the *instance of some of its adversaries*," he wrote, "*I drew up the remonstrance* herewith enclosed." The primary, though not exclusive, aim was to upend a coalescing pro-establishment alliance between Presbyterians and Episcopalians. His efforts, he wrote, had helped push the Presbyterians into opposing the state establishment of Christianity: "The Presbyterian clergy have at length espoused the side of the opposition, being moved either by *a fear of their laity or a jealousy of the Episcopalians*." He rallied this opposition, he wrote, by fanning the flames of the sects' mutual animosity. "The mutual hatred of these sects has been much inflamed," he wrote, and "I am far from being sorry for it, as a coalition between them could alone endanger our religious rights, and a tendency to such an event has been suspected."[22]

Jefferson later recalled this political fight, to disestablish the Church of England, and make into law the principles of his "Bill for Religious Freedom," as the "severest contests in which I have ever been engaged."[23] He described how the defeat of the establishment bill owed much to the fact that the Anglicans had "shown their teeth and fangs," thereby inadvertently rallying dissenters against establishment. It was not only that the Christians' "mutual hatred was much inflamed," as Madison put it, which made their disestablishment victory possible. Identification with Britain had weakened the Anglican Church, the established church.

---

21. Some points argue that establishment would ultimately destroy the law. Other points insist that establishment will render the law tyrannical. Some points argue that religion and religious societies are wholly exempt from the legislative authority. In the same legislative session, however, Madison subjected a religious organization to legislative authority when he helped broker a deal that allowed for the state incorporation of the Episcopal Church so that the Anglicans might retain what, under colonial rule, had been state property; so religious societies were demonstrably not exempt from legislative authority. Finally, Madison argued that society as a whole, much less its "viceregent" the legislature, lacked the authority to enact Henry's bill. Yet in another point of the Memorial, Madison claimed that such a measure ought be imposed only upon "clearest evidence that it is called for by a majority of citizens." Such clear evidence, Madison claimed, was simply lacking.

22. Madison to Thomas Jefferson, August 20, 1785, Gaillard Hunt, ed., *The Writings of James Madison* (New York, 1901), vol. II, pp. 163–164. Hereafter cited as WJM.

23. Miller, *The First Liberty* (New York, NY, 1986), p. 11. For Jefferson on the contest in the Virginia legislature to legalize freedom of religious worship and disestablish the Anglican Church, see Paul L. Ford, ed., *The Works of Thomas Jefferson* (New York, 1904), vol. I, p. 62.

Many Anglican clergy had fled, or had been chased out of, Virginia during the war. Before the Revolution, the state had supported 91 Anglican clergy, but by the close of the war, Virginia was home to only 28 Anglican ministers. The Anglicans' dubious nationalist credentials, and the depletion of their ministerial ranks, helped make disestablishment possible.[24]

Evangelical opposition to Anglicanism played a more important role. Madison's Memorial won 1,552 signatures. Another, evangelical petition to oppose Anglican incorporation garnered 4,899 signatures. Of the state's 72 counties, 48 contributed petitions to the House on the matter of Henry's establishment bill; 41 opposed the measure. In total, the House received over 10,000 signatures in opposition and only about 1,200 in support of the assessment on behalf of Christianity. The aggregate opinion in Virginia had not changed; a majority of Virginians still supported the state establishment of Christianity. At the same time, Madison and his allies had reshaped the political landscape relating to the issue, changing it from a general endorsement of Christianity to a referendum on state support for the Episcopal Church. Since its introduction the previous October, the legislative fortunes of the bill on behalf of assessment had reversed.[25]

The explanation for the reversal, noted the historian Norman Risjord, offered one of the most important political insights of the time. Madison and his allies had shown that the popular voice "could be artificially expanded in volume in order to manipulate the system." It was, Risjord wrote, the first step in the transformation of political parties from simple assembly interest groups into organizations that, with policy goals in mind, set out to shape public opinion. It also exemplified an enduring role of religion in the landscape of American politics: its ability not to create political causes, but to amplify and distort, sometimes grossly, existing issues. In the context of the history of secularism and freedom

---

According to Jefferson, the ferocity of the contest derived from the fact that "although the majority of our citizens were dissenters. . . a majority of the legislature were churchmen," as well as the aversion "to risk innovations" such as disestablishment of church and state, pp. 63, 64. The former statement was an exaggeration, the latter perhaps more true. Hereafter cited as WTJ.

24. Jefferson quoted in Miller, *The First Liberty: Religion and the American Republic,* pp. 39–40; Finke and Stark, "How the Upstart Sects Won America, 1776–1850," *Journal for the Scientific Study of Religion,* vol. 28 (March 1989), p. 34.

25. Ibid.

of religion, the lesson was also political. Politically, the evangelicals, particularly the Baptists, made possible disestablishment in Virginia.[26] They were not against Christianity. They championed disestablishment because it disestablished the Episcopalians. Evangelicals' victory against their Episcopal rivals encouraged them to pursue other measures of state support for Christianity. In the years immediately following disestablishment, Virginia's evangelicals succeeded in passing legislation against working on the sabbath, in recognition of days of prayer and fasting, as well as changes to Virginia marriage law, based on the Book of Leviticus. In essence, Madison had seized upon sectarianism to further secularism—the same strategic alliance that crystallized between Thomas Jefferson and the Baptists of Danbury, Connecticut. It is not too much to say that it was the support of dissenting Protestant evangelicals that made the historic achievements of secularism in the early United States possible.[27]

If any overriding logic can be found in Madison's "Memorial and Remonstrance Against Religious Assessments," it is that religion might weaken the state in more ways than it might strengthen it. On the need for their separation, Madison was radical and uncompromising. He opposed the Bank of the United States because he feared it set a precedent by which churches or missionary enterprises too could secure a federal charter. As president, political pressures over the unpopular War of 1812 compelled him to make two religious pronouncements (the second because the deistic gentility of the first caused it to backfire). After his presidency, he called these, his own pronouncements, "doubly wrong." He opposed congressional and military chaplains on the grounds that clerics paid by the government amounted to federal sponsorship of religion and therefore violations of the Constitution. He supported what he called the principle of "pure religious freedom." Each step short of the principle of pure religious freedom, he wrote, "will be found to leave crevices at least thro' which bigotry may introduce persecution; a monster, that feeding & thriving on its own venom, gradually swells to a size and

---

26. Nicholas Miller, *The Religious Roots of the First Amendment* (Oxford, 2012), passim.

27. Norman K. Risjord, *Chesapeake Politics, 1781–1800* (New York, 1978), pp. 208–210; Buckley, "After Disestablishment: Thomas Jefferson's Wall of Separation in Antebellum Virginia," pp. 448–449; Daniel L. Dreisbach, "A New Perspective on Jefferson's Views on Church-State Relations: The Virginia Statute for Establishing Religious Freedom in Legislative Context," *American Journal of Legal History*, vol. 35 (April 1991), pp. 172–204.

strength overwhelming all laws divine & human." In this rigorous view of separation between religion and government, Madison held a minority position.[28]

James Madison's opposition to mixing religion with government, as well as his clarity and ingenuity, contributed to historic achievements in legislative politics, state-building, and political theory. His legislative victory for disestablishment, for which he composed the "Memorial and Remonstrance," was predicated on a native's knowledge of Virginia's political and religious landscape. As a figure in the history of religion and the development of American nationalism, Madison is a more satisfying figure than Thomas Jefferson. As a champion of religious liberty, Madison was at least the equal of Jefferson, whose role in the complex history of religion and the development of modern nationalism is less coherent and more provocative. For this reason, however, Jefferson is perhaps a more important figure than Madison, a better representation of the continuing ambivalence between religion and nationalism.[29]

Scholars have variously depicted Jefferson as everything from a crypto-Unitarian with a deep love of Jesus to a priest-baiting infidel. My own view is that the latter comes closer to the truth, but, more important, he was helping to invent something new: American nationalism. His contributions to American nationalism are unique. In the two-party system, the two long-established political parties have both taken their names from Jefferson's Democratic-Republicans. No one wrote more eloquently about freedom, nor did anyone do more to expand slavery and authorize racism. No American president was more closely associated with Europe, yet none did more to foster American exceptionalism. In the Declaration of Independence, he authored the Revolution's most important contribution to world political literature. He knew both the state of scientific and religious learning of his time better than any subsequent president has known either one. Despite the fact that it has never been an accurate description of the relationship between American religious and civil authority, his phrase "wall of separation between church and state" continues to serve, for many in and outside the United States, as an ideal. In the story of religion and the development of early American nationalism, Jefferson was a kind of nationalist mystic. In terms of intellectual history,

---

28. Elizabeth Fleet, "Madison's 'Detached Memoranda,'" *William and Mary Quarterly*, vol. 3 (October 1946), pp. 554–555.

29. Gary Wills, *James Madison*, p. 164.

at a time when the Enlightenment was replacing angels with geniuses, Jefferson may be best understood as an angel of the Enlightenment. The contradiction of the phrase makes it more, not less, fitting.[30]

The political content of Jefferson's Declaration of Independence was not unique. In the War of Independence, which was also a civil war between Anglo-Protestants who had for generations lived together as British subjects, patriots from South Carolina to Massachusetts issued dozens of declarations of independence. American towns and counties in fact issued over 90 different declarations of independence, many of which preceded Jefferson's.[31] It was Jefferson's eloquence, and the authorization of Congress, not the singularity of his political ideas, that made his effort "the" Declaration of Independence. The Declaration drafted by Jefferson, and revised by a congressional committee, contains a turn of phrase that captures a bit of the mysticism, and a trace of theology, that nationalism requires. "We hold these truths to be self-evident," proclaims the Declaration. The peculiar act of declaring as "self-evident" matters that were anything but such had a history. Readers of Locke knew the tactic from Locke's defense of Christianity, which relied upon the doctrine of self-evidence. Locke argued that Jesus was Christ because of his miracles, and that the truth of the Christian religion and its obligations and rights was therefore "self-evident."[32]

To proclaim truths "self-evident" (or "sacred and undeniable," as Jefferson's first draft read) is to announce that one is not willing to debate the matter. This "proof" was not intended to convince skeptics, much less opponents, but to strengthen the bonds among believers. Benedict Andersen has called nations "imagined communities," but "communities of faith" may be as accurate a description of the material with which nationalists work. Because nations are impossible to experience in any direct, tangible way, they depend on faith, in the scriptural sense. Patriots must believe in the "evidence of things not seen, the substance of things

---

30. Philip Hamburger, *Separation of Church and State* (Cambridge, MA, 2002); David Armitage, *The Declaration of Independence: A Global History* (Cambridge, MA, 2007); Adam Rothman, *Slave Country: American Expansion and the Origins of the Deep South* (Cambridge, MA, 2005); Joyce Appleby, *Thomas Jefferson* (New York, 2003); Barbara J. Fields, "Of Rogues and Geldings," *American Historical Review*, vol. 108 (December 2003), pp. 1397–1405; Darrin M. McMahon, "Genius and Geniuses in the Eighteenth Century," talk delivered to the Harvard Colloquium for Intellectual and Cultural History, September 17, 2009.

31. Pauline Maier, *American Scripture: Making the Declaration of Independence* (New York, 1997).

32. Morton White, *The Philosophy of the American Revolution* (New York, 1978), ch. 2.

hoped for," as the scriptures define faith. The bonds of belief among nationalists are vital, especially early in nationalist movements. This mystical quality inherent within "We hold these truths to be self-evident" helps account for its status as a patriot proverb. It does not represent an argument, or even an idea, but a statement of belonging to what Ernest Renan called the "spiritual family" of the nation.[33]

Importantly, the problem of slavery brought forth perhaps the most notable appearance of religion in Jefferson's writing. This instance, in *Notes on the State of Virginia*, differs from the playful pirating of theological concepts and mystical invocations of nationalist bonds of the Declaration. It comes in Query 18, on "Manners," and it is also a bizarre moment (the historian Lewis P. Simpson called it "chilling") in the only book Jefferson published: inconsistent, angst-ridden, and fantastic. Consideration of the manners, or character, of Virginians brings Jefferson to the influence of slavery. The subject propels him into imagining supernatural interference, a just God reaching down and turning slaves into masters and masters into slaves. One can see Jefferson losing, regaining, and again losing his Enlightenment bearings. In a deistic work, meant to foster the authority of natural science over that of religion, the specter of divine intervention in human affairs hits an odd note:

> And can the liberties of a nation be thought secure when we have removed their only firm basis, a conviction in the minds of the people that these liberties are of the gift of God? That they are not to be violated but with his wrath? Indeed, I tremble for my country when I reflect that God is just: that his justice cannot sleep forever: that considering numbers, nature and natural means only, a revolution of the wheel of fortune, an exchange of situations, is among possible events: that it may become probable by supernatural interference! The Almighty has no attribute which can take side with us in such a contest.

---

33. Hebrews 11:1; Yi-Fu Tuan, *Topophila: A Study of Environmental Perception, Attitudes and Values* (Englewood Cliffs, NJ, 1974), wrote that the modern nation "as a large, bounded space is difficult to experience in any direct way," p. 100. Late eighteenth-century thinkers, Rousseau for example, thought that to make a nation meant changing human nature, taking "recourse to an authority of another order. " The nation-builder must "attribute their own wisdom to the Gods" and "make the Gods speak," see Jean-Jacques Rousseau, *The Social Contract* (Harmondsworth, UK, 1968), p. 87. In "What is a Nation?" Ernest Renan wrote, "A nation is a spiritual principle, the outcome of the profound complications of history; it is a spiritual family not a group determined by the shape of the earth." Renan's essay reprinted in Geoff Eley and Ronald Grigor Suny, eds., *Becoming National: A Reader* (New York, NY, 1996), pp. 43–44.

Jefferson begins by reconsidering the secular achievement of the Revolution, an achievement he cherished, as a reckless gambit. He wonders about divine justice, veers suddenly back to rational criteria ("numbers, nature, and natural means only"), only to get carried away by fears of a vengeful God reaching down to turn the planters into slaves ("by supernatural interference!"). In this short section, interestingly, on "Manners"—as opposed to the more obvious homes for the subject in the sections on "Population" or "Manufactures"—slavery pushed him into manifold contradiction. In addition, just before this fearful fantasy of supernatural justice, Jefferson referred to Virginia's slaves as "citizens." With "what execration should the statesman be loaded," he wrote, "who permitting one half the citizens thus to trample on the rights of the other," thereby corrupts the moral fiber of the masters as he subjugates the slaves. Slaves in Virginia were not citizens, of course. With nationalist measures, Jefferson seemed in command of his mystical and theological maneuvers. When the subject of slavery arose, however, it pushed him into a different engagement with religion, that of the fantastic and supernatural.

The fact that *Notes on the State of Virginia* is essentially an extended essay on natural history makes Jefferson's mention of divine intervention more notable. Modern readers sometimes find its chapters, organized as "Queries" ("Rivers," "Sea-Ports," "Mountains," "Cascades," and "Productions Mineral, Vegetable and Animal") perplexing. They were Jefferson's response to a prejudice, fashionable among European intellectuals, and popularized by the influential French naturalist and mathematician the Comte de Buffon, known as creolean degeneracy theory. "In America," wrote Buffon in his *Natural History: General and Particular*, "animated Nature is weaker, less active, and more circumscribed in the variety of her productions." Jefferson included tables, "A Comparative View of the Quadrupeds of Europe and North America," for example, providing the respective weights of hedgehogs, shrew mice, otters, and other animals in North America and Europe. He also described, in detail, mineral deposits, river currents, soil composition, and arboreal life. Natural history writings were a favorite genre of Enlightenment intellectuals, one especially consonant with the practice of sophisticated plantation agriculture. The empirical, scientific approach of natural history transformed God's creation, or the wilderness, into the natural world. The natural history perspective challenged core claims of Christianity to the organization of time. At times, such as in Jefferson's explanation of the origin of the Blue Ridge Mountains and the

Shenandoah Valley, the challenge to the Christian account of creation was almost explicit:

> The first glance of this scene hurries our sense into the opinion, that this earth has been created in time, that the mountains were formed first, that the rivers began to flow afterwards, that in this place particularly they have been dammed up by the Blue ridge of the mountains, and have formed an ocean which filled the whole valley; that continuing to rise they have at length broken over at this spot, and have torn the mountain down from its summit to its base. The piles of rock on each hand, but particularly on the Shenandoah, the evident marks of their disruptive and avulsion from their beds by the most powerful agents of nature, corroborate this impression.[34]

The words "this earth has been created in time" and "the most powerful agents of nature" were not subtle code phrases. Jefferson's acutely Christian political opponents, mainly New England Federalists, responded to *Notes on the State of Virginia* with accusations of immorality and irreligion. "Howling atheist" and "confirmed infidel" were among the verdicts. Jefferson complained, "O! that mine enemy would write a book! has been a well known prayer against an enemy. I had written a book and it furnished matter of abuse for want of something better."[35] James Madison had tried to dissuade Jefferson from publishing *Notes*, warning, "Perhaps an *indiscriminate gift* might offend some *narrow minded parents*." Jefferson however was undeterred and, one senses, incorrigible before the prospect of contributing a natural history of Virginia to the causes of American equality and science.[36]

As a composition of natural history, Jefferson's *Notes on the State of Virginia* is part of an inherently anti-supernatural genre. It replaces the supernatural creation story with an account of natural generation. Jefferson could, however, enlist Adam and Eve in the service of

---

34. Thomas Buckley, "Reflections on a Wall," *The William and Mary Quarterly*, vol. 56 (October, 1999), n2 and n3, pp.795–796; cite some Christian responses to Notes; Jefferson, *Notes on the State of Virginia*, William Peden, ed., *Notes on the State of Virginia* (New York, 1982), p. 19.

35. Ibid., p. xxiv.

36. Madison quoted in Thomas Jefferson, *Notes on the State of Virginia*, p. xvii, n20. On natural history as a genre, see Steven Shapin, *The Scientific Revolution* (Chicago, 1996), pp. 87–90, 110–111.

democratic nationalism, such as, when he wrote a friend that he would like to see the world cleared for Adam and Eve to seed the cause of republican freedom. "I would have seen half the world desolated," he wrote, in 1793, "were there but an Adam and Eve left in every country and left free, it would be better than it is now."[37] It is characteristic of Jefferson's complex role in the historical development of American nationalism that he brought religion to nationalism while subjecting religion to rationalism. He learned Greek to write *The Life and Morals of Jesus of Nazareth*, though he never published the book. The book's title, and its last lines, tells much of the story: it pointedly does not confer the Christ appellation. Instead, Jefferson depicted Jesus as a man, one of a certain time and place—Nazareth—whose life has passed but remains instructive because of his moral example. In Jefferson's book, Jesus was a moral man and a great teacher, but not divine, not the son of God. Because miracles were an impossible transgression of natural law, *The Life and Morals of Jesus of Nazareth* offers none. Nor did "Jefferson's Bible" offer any resurrection. "There laid they Jesus," concludes the work, "and rolled a great stone to the door of the sepulchre, and departed." Historians should leave it to Christians to decide who is and who is not a Christian. At the same time, if words are to have any meaning, it is difficult to see how someone who did not think that Jesus was Christ should be called a Christian.[38]

For the inscription on his tombstone, Jefferson chose three accomplishments: the Declaration of Independence, the founding of the University of Virginia, and Virginia's 1786 Statute for Religious Freedom. Each of these achievements is related to the problem of religion and nationalism. In the Statute for Religious Freedom, Jefferson characteristically brought high rationalism to the subject of religion and poetry to the scientific spirit. His testimony to the power of truth and free inquiry, closing the first section

---

37. Jefferson to William Short, January 3, 1793, in Koch and Peden, eds., *The Life and Writings of Thomas Jefferson* (New York, 1944), pp. 321–322. In *Common Sense*, Tom Paine also enlisted Christianity in the cause of democratic nationalism. In *The Rights of Man*, too, for example, Paine invoked the creation story as a possible origins story for natural rights, writing, ". . . it may be worth observing, that the genealogy of Christ is traced to Adam. Why then not trace the rights of man to the creation of man?" See Edmund Burke and Thomas Paine, *Two Classics of the French Revolution: Reflections on the Revolution in France and The Rights of Man* (New York, 1989), p. 303. Paine and Jefferson's impulse to place the origins of democratic nationalism within the context of the Christian creation story is not just wordplay, but indicative of a sense of the sacred nature of nation-states.

38. Thomas Jefferson, *Life and Morals of Jesus of Nazareth* (St. Louis, MO, 2008), p. 164. See also Edwin S. Gaustad, *Neither King nor Prelate: Religion and the New Nation, 1776–1826* (New York, 1993), pp. 101–103.

of the statute, is the very essence of the Enlightenment: "Truth is great and will prevail if left to herself," wrote Jefferson: "She is the proper and sufficient antagonist to error and has nothing to fear from the conflict unless, by human interpolation, disarmed of her natural weapons, free argument and debate—errors ceasing to be dangerous when it is permitted freely to contradict them." Madison's deft stewardship through the Virginia House of Delegates made the bill into law, and he wrote to Jefferson exulting that we "have in this country extinguished forever the ambitious hope of making laws for the human mind." Jefferson concurred, replying that "kings, priests, & nobles" had for centuries conspired to keep man in ignorant subordination. It was Virginia's great honor "to have produced the first legislature who had the courage to declare that the reason of man may be trusted with the formation of his opinions."[39] In the context of early modern political philosophy, to state that the reason of man may be trusted with the formation of his opinions was another way of stating the radical content of "all men are created equal." The famous phrase did not mean that men possessed equal physical or intellectual capacities. It meant that all men could reason and were capable of acting as responsible, and accountable, moral agents. It was, and remains, a radical idea.[40]

Disestablishment and freedom of religion amounted to historic secular achievements, but Jefferson and Madison had intended them as simply creating the conditions of possibility, as the first steps, toward a secular society. Positive measures must follow. The most important were founding schools and libraries, educating qualified teachers, and providing the people with rudimentary scientific and literary education, especially in philosophy. Scientific and philosophical education was necessary to replace the moral influence, social programs, and historical teachings of the churches. So Jefferson proposed alternatives to Christian institutions. In the 1785–1786 session of the Virginia Assembly, his "Bill for Establishing Religious Freedom," was bill number 82 of 126 proposed bills. Bills 79, 80, and 81 were also Jefferson's. These bills proposed to create a nonreligious school system, organized by county and providing free education through the elementary grades; to sever the College of William and Mary's church ties and make it a republican college; and to establish a

---

39. Madison and Jefferson quoted in Miller, *The First Liberty*, pp. 43, 76.

40. Morton White, *The Philosophy of the American Revolution*, esp. ch. 2; see also Colin Kidd, "Civil Theology and Church Establishments in Revolutionary America," *The Historical Journal*, vol. 42, no. 4 (1999), pp. 1007–1026.

public library system built around science, philosophy, and civics. An ally of Jefferson's aptly described the ambition of the measures. They "propose a simple and beautiful scheme, whereby science. . . would have been 'carried to every man's door,'" he wrote. Emphasizing the need to reach and, through education, change the public, he wrote: "Genius, instead of having to break its way through the thick opposing clouds of native obscurity, indigence, and ignorance, was to be sought for through every family in the commonwealth." Churches would have been the big losers of this "systematical plan," but their opposition was not the only reason it failed to materialize. The nature of Southern plantation society did not permit potential alternatives, such as state-run school systems, to planter authority. Slavery was simply more important to American nation-building than secularism. The planters, however, cannot be held uniquely responsible. With notable exceptions, for example the French state education system, secularists generally failed to build institutions that offered alternatives to Christian social, political, and personal morality.[41]

Instead, it would be the frontier revivalists, in particular the Methodists, who would pioneer, on the western periphery of the early republic, carrying their message from door to door. By the 1820s, the sons of the Northeastern elite, following the Methodists and working for an array of Protestant missionary and moral improvement associations, would follow, bringing a different message of bourgeois nationalism "to every man's door." Their system of Protestant auxiliary societies, ladies' societies, libraries, and schools—not the republican and scientific system that would have been provided for by Jefferson's Bills 79, 80, and 81 from the 1785–1786 session of the Virginia Assembly—would flourish across the frontier. Jefferson would be left with the University of Virginia, to which, after his retirement from the presidency, he devoted extraordinary energies. He refused to hire a professor of divinity, urging the College of Columbia, in Columbia, South Carolina, to follow his example and instead hire professors of geology and mineralogy. In defiance of long-standing architectural practice, in which the church stood at the center of a college campus, Jefferson made the library the central feature of the University of Virginia. The University of Virginia did not even have a chapel until 1889, when the university built Newcomb Chapel. UVA's neo-Gothic

---

41. Ibid., p. 48; see too Jonathan Israel, review of Emmet Kennedy, *Secularism and Its Opponents from Augustine to Solzhenitsyn, American Historical Review*, vol. 115, (April 2010), pp. 502–503.

Newcomb Chapel fit the idealizations of medieval Europe that late nineteenth-century Americans loved, particularly for their college campuses, but it could hardly be more at odds with Jefferson's neo-Palladian campus, which honors the Italian Renaissance.[42]

Amid the proliferation of upstart Protestants in the early republic, Jefferson's countermeasures amounted to symbolic resistance. He found the birth of popular Protestantism a foreboding development, writing to a friend in 1822, "The atmosphere of our country is unquestioningly charged with a threatening cloud of fanaticism, lighter in some parts, denser in others, but too heavy in all." Jefferson had expected that disestablishment would weaken religion, especially revealed religion. He believed, as Immanuel Kant put it, "if only freedom is granted, enlightenment is sure to follow." Into the 1820s, John C. Calhoun and Thomas Jefferson were still predicting that America was well on its way to becoming a Unitarian country. "There is not a young man now living in the United States," Jefferson wrote in 1822, "who will not die an Unitarian." It was an absurd prediction. For Jefferson, Madison, and other genteel rationalists, democracy in religion had proven less sanguine than democracy in politics. If some supernatural act, comparable to the one Jefferson had imagined switching American masters and slaves, offered to replace the frontier of Millerites, Baptists, and Methodists with a periphery of Anglicans, the proposition might have given them pause. Decoupled from Federalism, which had by then imploded for its own reasons, and in contrast to the hothouse of sectarians, visionaries, and millenarians that were flourishing across the frontier, the Anglicans, whose church Madison and Jefferson had battled so hard to disestablish in the 1780s, would have had been more welcoming to their Enlightenment dreams.[43]

In conclusion, the Virginia model, which the historian Lewis P. Simpson called "the secularization of spirituality" in America, is an ambiguous affair, but some pertinent conclusions emerge. First, secularism and religious freedom in Virginia were political battles, realized by an

---

42. Dell Upton, *Architecture in the United States* (New York, 1998), pp. 19–33.

43. Jefferson to Dr. Thomas Cooper, November 2, 1822, see Paul L. Ford, ed., WTJ, vol. XII, pp. 270–271; Immanuel Kant, *Foundations of the Metaphysics of Morals, and What Is Enlightenment?* (New York, 1990), p. 88; Jefferson to Benjamin Waterhouse, June 26, 1822, see Ford, ed., WTJ, vol. XII, p. 243; Drew McCoy, *The Elusive Republic: Political Economy in Jeffersonian America* (Chapel Hill, NC, 1980), chs. 9–10; Elizabeth Fleet, ed., "Madison's 'Detached Memoranda,'" *The William and Mary Quarterly*, vol. 3 (October, 1946), pp. 534–568; Gordon Wood, "Evangelical America and Early Mormonism," *New York History*, vol. 61 (October 1980), p. 363.

alliance between a small but politically skilled faction of elite freethinkers and a large group of evangelicals. These two groups came to share a position in support of disestablishment and religious liberty, but with contrary purposes. The deists saw disestablishment and religious freedom as steps to human freedom. Some conservative planters joined the fight, hoping to strengthen state control over churches, while an energetic group of evangelicals gave support for sectarian reasons. For the freethinkers, the Virginia model of secularism and religious freedom, which became the American one, was a distinctly partial victory. Seen in light of the aspirations of leading deists, who led the fight for disestablishment and religious freedom through the thickets of Virginia politics, the results were mixed.[44]

Some leading secularists, Jefferson and Madison among them, had also hoped for a state-run education program, consisting of libraries and schools teaching science, philosophy, letters, and the arts. They understood that religion brought a world of ideas, and sometimes a whole social life, as well as political opportunity, to Virginians rich and poor. Most people would not turn their backs on this world of religion simply out of political principle. The secularists would have to offer real alternatives: schools, libraries, ideas, stories, forms of community, an active and ongoing presence in the lives of Virginians. Jefferson knew this, and in *Notes on the State of Virginia*, he proposed a system of public schools that would replace sacred history with profane history. The schools were to be free, for everyone, for three years. Examinations would find the best students among "those whose parents are too poor to give them further education." These students could receive more schooling, paid for by the state, through William and Mary College. "By this means," Jefferson wrote, "the best geniuses will be raked from the rubbish." The object, wrote Jefferson, was "provide an education adapted to the years" for citizens, rich and poor alike, "directed to their freedom and happiness" and suited to everyone's natural ability. "Instead of putting the Bible and Testament into the hands of the children, at an age when their judgments are not sufficiently matured," he noted, children should instead receive educations in "Grecian, Roman, European, and American history," Latin,

---

44. The idea that the American nation, or patriot political class a whole, held fast to principled secularism because they realized it fostered a salubrious Christianity, or an ideal form of religious freedom, can be found in Steven Waldman, *Founding Faith: How Our Founding Fathers Forged a Radical New Approach to Religious Liberty* (New York, 2009).

Greek, mathematics, and the sciences. No law, he wrote, was "more important, none more legitimate," than one to provide secular arts and sciences education for the people at large. It would, he wrote, make them effective "guardians of their own liberty."[45]

Second, in the realm of political theory, Thomas Jefferson and James Madison struggled to leave religion behind. Unable to disentangle religion from techniques of governing and nation-state building, they turned to mystical and theological techniques for help in inventing modern nationalism. The depth of their drive to implement political separation itself suggests the potential affinity between religion and nationalism, which have been the two large cultural systems legitimating political authority in the West over the past few centuries. This is not to suggest that religion and nationalism are somehow the same. The British historian Lewis Namier was wrong when he wrote, "religion is a 16th-century word for nationalism." Jefferson and Madison borrowed from religion in hopes of leaving it behind, a fact that makes the possibility of a more sincere alliance between the two easy to imagine.[46]

Though in Virginia disestablishment and religious freedom were hard-won and important political accomplishments, they initiated rather than solved the problem of religion in the early republic. Most Americans presumed that an enlightened nation was by definition a Protestant nation, but Protestantism offered no clear model for enlightening the peoples of a large and expanding republic. The Puritans, who had never been democrats, much less secularists, were not nation-builders. Eighteenth-century Anglican missions had reaped at best modest results. Rational religion had always been an upper realm, a preserve for the educated elite. Did democracy require the proliferation of rational religion? Could ordinary people be inoculated against religious fanaticism? No clear answers presented themselves. Even Immanuel Kant, in his 1784 essay "What Is Enlightenment?" maintained that freedom of speech and freedom of religion required a wise and benevolent monarch. "A republic could not dare"

---

45. See Jefferson, *Notes on the State of Virginia*, Query 14, Laws.

46. The description of religion and nationalism as the two successive large cultural systems legitimating political authority in the past several centuries of Western history is from Benedict Anderson, *Imagined Communities: Reflections on the Origins and Spread of Nationalism* (New York, NY, 1991); Alexander Stille, "Historians Trace an Unholy Alliance: Religion as the Root of Nationalist Feeling," May 31, 2003, *New York Times*; Roger Friedland, "Religious Nationalism and the Problem of Collective Representation," *Annual Review of Sociology*, vol. 27 (2001), pp. 125–152.

enact the ideal of freedom of conscience, wrote Kant.[47] Pro-American partisans shared Kant's misgivings. Confidence that the precarious republican experiment could withstand what Crèvecoeur called "the rage, the malice of an ignorant, prejudiced public" was shaky. In *Letters from an American Farmer*, Crèvecoeur warned that it would be "these country saints" from the "obscure parts" who, raised by the Revolution, "have assumed the iron sceptre and from religious hypocrites are to become political tyrants." Indeed, the colonization of the continent was undertaken with a degree of desperation, amid considerable disorder, and stewarded by a government described by the historian John Murrin as a midget institution in a giant land. To many, the situation threatened to bring Crèvecoeur's prediction of tyranny or chaos to pass. Some notable New Englanders had strong views on these matters. They saw American nationality and empire not as a political possibility, but as a providential opportunity, one in which they claimed a proprietary stake. They were convinced that all depended on the spread of Reformed Protestantism and strong state institutions, the New England way.[48]

Finally, disestablishment and religious freedom were Virginia accomplishments, not valued by many acutely Protestant Northerners, especially among New England's Reformed Protestant elite. However partial, these real secular victories were achieved by a deist-evangelical alliance that grew out of a very different society from that which New England's Christian Federalists represented. The New England Christians and the Virginians were simply at odds over the nature of American society and nationality, not just the role of religion. Given the depth and breadth of these differences, it is not difficult to understand why New England would consider secession, or turn, in their search for a regenerate political community, from politics to missions. The depth of these differences turns attention back to the remarkable nature of the nationalism that had brought New England and Chesapeake plantation society together.

47. Peter Gay, *The Enlightenment* (New York, NY, 1995), p. 528; David W. Noble, "Revocation of the Anglo-Protestant Monopoly."

48. Crèvecouer, *Letters from an American Farmer and Sketches of Eighteenth-Century America* (New York, NY, 1981), p. 422; John Murrin, "The Great Inversion, or Court versus Country: A Comparison of the Revolution Settlements in England (1688–1721) and America (1776–1816)," in J. G. A. Pocock, ed., *Three British Revolutions* (Princeton, NJ, 1980), p. 425.

2

"The Songs of a Nation"

THE CONNECTICUT WITS AND THE NEW ENGLISH EMPIRE

See where her Heroes mark their glorious way,
Arm'd for the fight and blazing on the day
Blood stains their steps; and o'er the conquering plain,
'Mid fighting thousands and 'mid thousands slain,
Their eager swords promiscuous carnage blend,
And ghastly deaths their raging course attend.
Her mighty pow'r the subject world shall see;
For laurel'd Conquest waits her high decree.

—JOHN TRUMBULL, member of the Connecticut Wits,
"An Essay on the Use and Advantages of the Fine Arts,"
delivered at the Yale College commencement, 1768

IN THE MID-1760s, a small group of literary intellectuals, based at Yale College, emerged as America's first nationalist movement. Calling themselves the Connecticut Wits, they envisioned the United States as a modestly prosperous agrarian and commercial society of dissenting Protestants, a family-based republic of saints. In essence, they imagined the United States of America as an idealized version of revolutionary-era New England, especially Connecticut and Massachusetts, writ large. Timothy Dwight and John Trumbull, as Yale students and tutors, were the founding members of the Wits. They embodied its nationalist agenda and gave the group its distinctive literary style. David Humphreys, Joel Barlow, Noah Webster, Theodore Dwight, as well as others, moved in and out of the group or its immediate influence.[1] The Wits'

---

1. Samuel Adams is said to have been a supporter of American independence by 1768. Dwight and Trumbull seem to have been American nationalists by 1767, perhaps earlier, and their Wits were a movement. See John K. Alexander, *Samuel Adams: America's Revolutionary Politician* (Lanham, MD, 2002), p. 65.

writings, mostly poetry, elaborate a rich social and cultural vision. In contrast to the evangelical, egalitarian, and racist Jeffersonian, and later Jacksonian, nationalism that became the dominant American political culture, the Wits imagined a theological, hierarchical, anti-racist American society. When, in the early republic, Federalism, as a force in US party politics, imploded, the Wits' immediate descendants abandoned the present prospect of making the New England way the American way. Reinventing themselves as a missions movement, they went across North America, and abroad, in search of new political communities through which to regenerate the world.[2]

In search of authority for this new missionary enterprise, New England Protestants rewrote the history of religion in America. Commissioned by the American Board of Commissioners for Foreign Missions, Joseph Tracy's *History of the American Board of Commissioners for Foreign Missions* (1842) offered John Eliot as the face of New World Protestantism. Tracy neglected to mention John Winthrop, the central figure in the settlement of Puritan New England. Tracy's *History* began: "The first settlement of New England was a missionary enterprise," a fundamental misrepresentation. In essence, Puritans were excluders, not missionaries. The Trotskyites of early modern European Protestantism, Puritans were too concerned with fine-grained assessments of human goodness to undertake the comparatively coarse good work of missions. For a people who moved across the Atlantic, they maintained, even in their physical world, a remarkable inwardness. A 1635 Massachusetts law forbade the construction of any house farther than half a mile from the meetinghouse. They filled their towns, as one historian noted, with "hedges, walls and fences, all of them, frontiers of exclusion." In contrast to the Spanish, who, within a generation, planted settlements deep in the interior of South America, the Puritans, for almost two centuries, remained in their coastal towns, facing east toward the sea.[3]

To find adventurers and missionaries in the early modern Americas, one looks not to New England but to New Spain. As early as 1559, 802 Spanish Franciscan, Dominican, and Augustinian missionaries had established 160 religious houses in New Spain. By the early eighteenth century, the Jesuit-run *reducciones* of Peru and Paraguay were home to

---

2. On the political culture of American democracy, see Sean Wilentz, *The Rise of American Democracy* (New York, 2005).

3. Joseph Tracy, *History of the American Board of Commissioners of Foreign Missions* (New York, 1842), p. 1; J. H. Elliott, *Empires of the Atlantic World*, p. 48.

perhaps 150,000 Guaraní Indians. In contrast, at their peak in the 1670s, John Eliot's New England "praying towns" never held more than 1,600 American Indians. Of these, only about 15 percent, a percentage comparable to other churchly Bay Colony towns, were "elect" members of the Church. That means that Eliot's 14 "praying towns" held about 240 full members of the congregation. Moreover, in the seventeenth-century Anglo-American world, Eliot was a quixotic and unpopular figure. His "praying towns" attracted Massachusett, Nipmuck, and Pennacook Indians, members of weak tribes who hoped that converting to Christianity would win them the protection, either of the New English or their God, from rival tribes. In fact, however, in 1675, during King Philip's War, New Englanders turned on and killed many of the native converts to Christianity.[4]

Why did Joseph Tracy and the American Board of Commissioners of Foreign Missions put forth John Eliot's praying towns as indicative of the New England past? Why did they claim as representative an atypical experiment that, moreover, had ended in a grisly slaughter? The awkward selection of Eliot resulted from a search for a usable past, a past preferred to the present political disappointments that, more than Eliot's legacy, drove the missions movement. In their construction of a past to serve the present, the New England missionaries resembled the grandchildren of the defeated Aztecs, who, in the late sixteenth century, had explained their grandparents' defeat to the Spanish by claiming that their ancestors had thought that the Spanish were gods. A similar reluctance to call defeat by its name led the founders of the missions movement to emphasize their tenuous link to Eliot's mixed legacy. It was better to talk about Eliot than to acknowledge that the United States had rejected them.[5]

The founders of the American missions movement were the immediate descendants of the Connecticut Wits, America's first nationalist movement. In the War of Independence, New England, especially Massachusetts and Connecticut, had offered ferocious and uncompromising resistance to Britain. These were the New Englanders of whom Edmund Burke

---

4. On Spanish missions, see Elliott, *Empires of the Atlantic World*, p. 69, 186. On John Eliot, see Alan Taylor, *American Colonies*, pp. 197–198, and James Axtell, "Some Thoughts on the Ethnohistory of Missions," *Ethnohistory* (Winter 1982), p. 36.

5. Tracy was not the only one to make the analogy. See also *The Connecticut Evangelical Magazine*, vol. III, no. 10 (April 1803), pp. 361–374. *The New-York Missionary Magazine and Repository of Religious Intelligence*, vol. II, 1801, reprinted Cotton Mather's hagiography of John Eliot. See Camilla Townsend, "Burying the White Gods: New Perspectives on the Conquest of Mexico," *American Historical Review*, vol. 108, no. 3, June 2003.

spoke, in 1775, when he had warned Parliament that the Americans would not acquiesce. They are, Burke said, the kind of Protestants "most adverse to all implicit submission of mind and opinion." Their religion, he said, "is a refinement on the principle of resistance; it is the dissidence of dissent, and the Protestantism of the Protestant religion." Not only had the Wits been the first champions of an independent United States, they had written some of the most popular literature of the Revolution. They had emerged from, and after the Revolution were preparing to lead, America's best schools. They expected that in the new nation, they would assume the role of a kind of republican elect, smiths of American culture. They did not dream of shaping school curriculums in the Sandwich Islands, but of guiding a global US empire. They did not imagine that they, the sons of New England, who had defeated the British Empire, would lose the contest for the United States to yeoman farmers and Southern slaveholders. To apprehend their unusual role in American history, the basis of their grand expectations, the poignancy of their failure, it is necessary to appreciate their place in American society and to glimpse the scale of their ambitions. The picture that emerges is at once foreign and familiar, of provincialism and worldly ambition, of real radicalism and a state conservatism that never became part of the national political tradition.[6]

Poets of Empire and Nation

The words "empire" and "imperial" meant something a little different in the late eighteenth and early nineteenth century. The first *Encyclopaedia Britannica*, published in 1771, defined empire as "a large extent of land under the jurisdiction or government of an emperor." In an attempt to revise this age-old association between empire and monarchy, Thomas Jefferson, in an 1809 letter, wrote that no nation had ever been so well positioned for "extensive empire & self government" as the United States. In the same letter, Jefferson found a more enduring phrase when he described the United States as an "empire of liberty." Jefferson's phrase-making resulted from the implied contradiction, for many, between "empire" and freedom, as advocates of republican government understood it. "Empire," however, could also mean simply a sovereign polity. This is the sense of the word George Washington used in 1783, when

---

6. On New England in the American Revolution, see Kevin Phillips, *The Cousins' Wars: Religion, Politics, Civil Warfare and the Triumph of Anglo-America* (New York, 1999).

he called the United States of America a "rising empire." It is the same sense of the word James Madison invoked in the Fourteenth Federalist (1787), when he wrote of the United States as "one great, respectable, and flourishing empire." In this sense, the United States was an empire before it was a nation. Noah Webster put it clearly, in 1785, writing, "America is an independent empire, and ought to assume a national character." Despite the small problem of historical semantics, it is fair to say that the underlying imperial process that had brought all peoples of European and African descent to the Western hemisphere not only continued, but accelerated in the early American republic.[7]

Nonetheless, there was nothing natural or inevitable about the political geography that the United States has assumed, the now familiar band across the middle of the North American continent. Bearing in mind the contingency of US continental colonization is important in understanding the missionary movement in the early republic and, in turn, the formation of American religious nationalism. It is more important, however, to grasp the meaning of Noah Webster's implied question: America has always been an empire; the question was, would it become a nation? American patriots wondered. One supporter of the Constitution said it gave the United States a federal roof without national walls. Pelatiah Webster, a Philadelphia political economist and patriot, came up with a more prosaic image: "Thirteen staves, and ne'er a hoop, can not make a barrel." In opening his 1782 *Letters from an American Farmer*, Hector St. John de Crèvecoeur presumed that the North American interior would give rise to different nations, explaining the importance of his subject by the fact that North America would be "the cradle of future nations." Twenty years later, John Bradbury, an English naturalist who spent

---

7. Samuel Johnson, *A Dictionary of the English Language*, defined "empire": "1. Imperial power, supreme dominion; 2. The region over which dominion is extended. 3. Command over anything." See Johnson, *Dictionary of English Language* (London, 1792), n.p.; in his American *Dictionary*, Noah Webster followed suit, defining empire as simply "imperial power or government," see Webster, *A Dictionary of the English Language* (Hartford, CT, 1817), p. 111. Webster's reference to the United States as an empire but not a nation is from his essay "Improving the Advantages and Perpetuating the Union," reprinted in Homer D. Babbidge, ed., *Noah Webster: On Being American, Selected Writings, 1783–1828* (New York, 1967), p. 43. The word "imperialist" was not used in its present sense until the late nineteenth century; before then, it meant "the adherent of an emperor or of an imperial form of government." See Raymond Williams, *Keywords: A Vocabulary of Culture and Society* (New York, 1983), p. 159; see also Fred Anderson, *The Crucible of War*, passim. See also Woody Holton, "The Ohio Indians and the Coming of the American Revolution in Virginia," *The Journal of Southern History*, vol. 60, no. 3 (August 1994), pp. 453–478.

1809–1811 on an expedition throughout the American West, wrote that the population west of the Alleghenies was not a people. Rather, they were "compounded of a great number of nations." It would, wrote Bradbury, be "absurd to expect that a general character could now be formed, or that it will be for many years to come." Twenty years after Bradbury's tour, Alexis de Tocqueville, despite his generalizations of America and Americans, thought the states akin to separate nations, and referred to them as such in his notebooks. During his tour, Tocqueville wrote to a friend in France that America lacked the requisite cultural foundations for nationality. "All of these peoples," he wrote, "have different languages, beliefs and opinions." It was, continued Tocqueville, "a society without roots, memories, biases, routines, shared ideas or national characteristics."[8]

In *Common Sense*, Tom Paine had claimed that the social relations formed by the pursuit of reasoned self-interest, through free commerce, would bind Americans to one another. Like Paine, Tocqueville was optimistic about American nationality, and he was following Paine's manner of announcing the triumph of what he called this new social theory as a suitable foundation, over more conventional hallmarks of culture, for a nation. Nonetheless, leading members of the American political class envisioned political geographies that never happened as necessary to the survival of American nationality. During the War of 1812, Thomas Jefferson wrote that the conquering of Canada "will be a mere matter of marching." Jefferson's expectation proved misguided; Canadians did not, as he predicted, welcome the "invaders as liberators." In 1820, John C. Calhoun advocated armed invasion of Cuba "at the first possible opportunity." It was not just Southern slave owners who hungered for Cuba. In 1823, Secretary of State John Quincy Adams, as principled an anti-slavery man as any in early national politics, wrote that Puerto Rico and Cuba were "natural appendages" to the continent and that a "multitude of considerations" made the acquisition of Cuba of "transcendent importance." Adams called the annexation of Cuba "indispensable to the continuance and integrity of the Union itself."[9]

As inevitable as the incorporation of Canada and Cuba seemed to many, other annexations that have happened were unexpected. The fact the United States traverses the Rocky Mountains and runs from the Atlantic to the

---

8. Leo Damrosch, *Tocqueville's Discovery of America* (New York, 2010), pp. 100, 140.

9. For these and other examples, see D. W. Meinig, *The Shaping of America: A Geographical Perspective on 500 Years of History*, vol. 2 (New Haven, CT, 1993), pp. 47, 35.

Pacific Ocean would have surprised Missouri senator Thomas Hart Benton, for example. One of the most enthusiastic of early nineteenth-century American expansionists, Benton presumed that the Rocky Mountains formed a natural western boundary to the United States. Massachusetts senator Daniel Webster, another champion of westward colonization, likewise saw the Rockies as a political terminus. Webster thought it inevitable that an independent "Pacific republic" would develop on the Western coast.[10] In addition to uncertainty about American nationality, and dashed ideas of the shape the nation might take, political leaders of the early republic did not speak about empire the way that one might imagine such great imperialists ought to have. There was no (and never has been) any grassroots movement for "empire." No president, or any serious candidate for the presidency, ever campaigned promising to "expand the empire" or celebrating empire as such. In fact, empire has never been a popular political issue, and sometimes it has been a very unpopular one.[11]

To find Americans in the early republic speaking as one might imagine imperialists ought, it is necessary to turn to the Christians. More specifically, the Protestant literary intellectuals of New England articulated grandiose visions of empire. One can in vain scour presidents' annual messages to Congress, for example, or decades of congressional speechifying, for any statement approaching Timothy Dwight's 1813 sermon to the American Board of Commissioners for Foreign Missions (ABCFM). Dwight saw himself as engaged in the work of creative destruction, and Dwight's chiliasm was saturated with nationalistic and geopolitical concerns. America, Dwight told the American Board, would unleash a wave of cleansing violence that would regenerate the world:

> How amazing must be the change, when the *Romish* cathedral, the mosque, and the pagoda, shall *not have one stone left upon another, which shall not be thrown down*: when the *Popish, Mohammedan, Hindoo, and Chinesian*, worlds shall be created anew; and the voice of angels exclaim concerning each, JEHOVAH *bless thee,*

10. Jefferson also thought Montreal (and Quebec) a "plum ready for the picking," as did John Quincy Adams. See Meinig, p. 47; later in the nineteenth century, even Walt Whitman thought it only a matter of time before Cuba and Canada became states; see Arthur Schlesinger, Jr., "The American Empire? Not So Fast," *World Policy Journal* (Spring 2005), pp. 43–46.

11. "Imperialist" and "imperialism" are words that would not be in use until late in the nineteenth century; see Schlesinger, ibid., and Raymond Williams, *Keywords*, pp. 159–160.

O habitation of justice, O mountain of holiness. . . when *Europe* shall no longer convert her wide domains into a stall of slaughter; nor offer herself as a voluntary holocaust upon the altar [*sic*] of *Moloch*: when the human wolves, which have so long prowled the *American* deserts, shall assume the innocence and meekness, of the lamb.. . . But we are not to be confined in our reasearches to *Hindostan*, to *Asia*, or to the Eastern Continent. We are to range the World.. . . This rank and baneful crop is everywhere to be weeded out. Truth and righteousness are every where to be sown, and to produce their golden harvest of comfort, peace, and joy.. . . Churches are every where to be gathered: and minds are every where to be born of God.[12]

The millennium did not materialize, but the global reach of American Protestantism did.

By 1840, the ABCFM would support missionary endeavors in India, Ceylon (Sri Lanka), China, Burma, Singapore, Siam (Thailand), the Sandwich Islands (Hawaii), Athens, Beirut, Persia, Cyprus, Syria, Liberia, Sierra Leone, and among the Zulus in Southern Africa. The American Board of Commissioners for Foreign Missions would become, probably, the greatest transnational enterprise of nineteenth-century America. With the US Supreme Court case *Worcester v. Georgia*, Samuel Worcester, an ABCFM missionary among the Georgia Cherokee, would become the face of a political and legal battle, opposed by President Andrew Jackson, to incorporate Native Americans into US political society. Like many of the hundreds of other religious voluntary societies that pursued missionary and philanthropic goals, founded by New Englanders in the early republic, the ABCFM would serve as an important site of class consolidation for the Northeastern bourgeoisie. In the context of the history of religion, they would help affect a consolidation of authority and a bureaucratization that were perhaps as historic as the consolidation that turned the 13 colonies into the United States of America. All of these aspects of the American missionary movement are distinct from but related to the important role they would play in the formation of religious nationalism in the United States.[13]

---

12. Timothy Dwight, *A Sermon. . . .. Before the American Board of Commissioners for Foreign Missions, at their Fourth Annual Meeting* (Boston, 1813), pp. 26–27, 30, 31.

13. Theda Perdue and Michael D. Green, *The Cherokee Nation and the Trail of Tears* (New York, 2008), ch. 2; C. A. Bayly *The Birth of the Modern World, 1780–1914* (Malden, MA 2004), pp. 325–363.

The unprecedented proliferation of Protestant missions that followed the American Revolution—New Englanders alone founded 933 Protestant missionary or moral improvement societies between 1787 and 1827—can be placed in historical contexts from the Reformation to the Louisiana Purchase. Nationalism, along with uncertainty about American nationality, however, was a major force behind the American missions movement. A mid-eighteenth century movement of nationalist literary intellectuals offers the most economical origin point. They were known, variously, as the Connecticut Wits, the Wicked Wits, or the Hartford Wits.[14] They shared Yale, a position in notable New England families, great literary ambitions, and a profile as some of the earliest agitators for American independence. At various times, members or affiliates of the Wits included the editor and Federalist Congressman (and secretary of the secessionist 1814 Hartford Convention) Theodore Dwight, the poet and diplomat Joel Barlow, the American lexicographer Noah Webster, George Washington's aide-de-camp and entrepreneur David Humphreys, the Litchfield, Connecticut, physician Lemuel Hopkins, and others. Barlow, who would become the apostate of the group, was the most interesting, but Timothy Dwight (Yale class of 1769) and John Trumbull (class of 1767) were the most important and prolific Wits. Trumbull and Dwight were probably two of the "3 or 4 dissensients" behind a student-led demonstration at Dwight's 1769 Yale commencement. To protest the 1767 Townshend Acts, which had imposed taxes on British goods in America, some colonists had stopped buying British manufactures. To show that they saw the Townshend Acts as a violation of their rights, the entire Yale class of 1769 appeared at commencement wearing homemade clothes, also known as homespun. "We were put to some difficulty," recalled one participant, "to obtain all the articles of American manufacture. Inspired with a patriotic spirit, we took pride in our plain coarse republican dress."[15]

It was not the first protest the Yale class of 1769 had seen. As students, Dwight and Trumbull had been involved in attempts to reform the Yale curriculum, petitioning for the addition of modern British writers to

---

14. Alexander Cowie, *John Trumbull*, pp. vii–viii, 210–111; Charles E. Cunningham, *Timothy Dwight, 1752–1817: A Biography* (New York, 1942), pp. 21–22, 30–31, 36, 39, 95; Henry A. Beers, *The Connecticut Wits and Other Essays* (New Haven, CT, 1920), pp. 7–30; Samuel Bernstein, *Joel Barlow: A Connecticut Yankee in an Age of Revolution* (Portland, ME, 1985), pp. 40, 113–115, 119.

15. David McClure, *Diary of David McClure Doctor of Divinity, 1748–1820* (New York, 1899), p. 19.

the established study of classical languages, theology, mathematics, and astronomy. A contemporary described the curriculum as "almost monastic." In the context of mid-eighteenth century Connecticut Puritanism, Trumbull and Dwight's championing of modern British literature was provocative and brought forth a spirited contest. Still, it was not the most dramatic instance of activism they witnessed during their time as Yale students. In the spring of 1765, dissatisfaction with the college had taken a violent turn. Angry over President Thomas Clap's "autocratic" style and the poor physical condition of the college, students and townspeople stormed Clap's home, smashing 30 windowpanes, prying off clapboards, and carrying away the president's front gate. The following March, threats of further violence caused the tutors to flee the campus. When the tutors could not be convinced to return, the Yale Corporation effectively canceled the remainder of the spring 1766 semester. In this climate, Dwight and Trumbull's campaign for modern literature, and their preference for petitions and homespun, marked them as moderates.[16]

The unrest brought some fast changes. President Clap resigned and in the summer of 1766 the Yale Corporation voted to begin listing the incoming class rosters alphabetically, instead of by social rank. Dwight and Trumbull's reaction to this egalitarian move is not known. Seeing themselves as agents of progress, they probably approved, despite their own estimable social rank. Trumbull was born in 1750, in Watertown, where the Trumbulls were to Connecticut what the Mathers were and Adamses would be to Massachusetts. The Trumbulls claimed descent from King William's secretary of state; in just a few generations in America, they produced a historian, a philologist, an artist, a general, and three governors. John's father, also John Trumbull, was a Congregationalist minister. When a few members of Trumbull's congregation converted to Anglicanism, he bought their farms to encourage them to move. Dwight was born in 1752, in Northampton, the eldest of 13 children. His father, also named Timothy Dwight, a successful merchant and large landowner, was known as the first citizen of Northampton. His mother, Mary, was the daughter of the eminent Puritan divine Jonathan Edwards, which made Dwight a prince of both the New England merchant and intellectual classes. Trumbull and Dwight both would feel themselves to be among the natural leaders of the new nation, a kind of republican elect. The fact

---

16. Alexander Cowie, *John Trumbull: Connecticut Wit* (Chapel Hill, NC, 1936), pp. 34–34, 41–43.

that they never acquired the national status, or commanded a natural following—both of which they presumed was their due—was difficult for them to understand and brought Dwight in particular considerable pain.[17]

From a young age, both Dwight and Trumbull had been precocious, especially in regard to languages and literature. By age four, Dwight was reading the King James Bible; by six, he read Latin. At eight, he passed the Yale entrance examination, which required sight translation of Virgil and Cicero and New Testament Greek. Trumbull had passed the same exam three years earlier, when he was seven. In both cases, their parents held them out of college until age 13, Trumbull beginning at Yale in 1763 and Dwight in 1765. Where Trumbull and Dwight both experienced the upheaval that roiled the Yale student body, Dwight also underwent a more personal trauma. In 1772, his second year as a tutor, in an attempt to normalize the "clearness of apprehension" that study sometimes brought him, Dwight began to reduce the amount of food that he consumed. In an era in which gout and drunkenness were common among men of his class, Dwight veered sharply in the other direction. He gave up meat and he restricted himself to one meal a day, dinner, at which he consumed no more than "twelve mouthfuls" of vegetables or potatoes. He studied, principally the works of Isaac Newton, every day from dawn until midnight while continuing to perform his duties as tutor. After over a year of this regimen, an emaciated Dwight, suffering severe attacks of "bilious colic," began to lose his eyesight. Still, he would not accept that his ascetic life was bringing him physical harm. When he could no longer study, his friends contacted his father, who removed him to Northampton. A year of convalescence restored much of his health, though his eyesight had suffered permanent damage.[18]

National glory, of which Dwight would paint a vivid picture in his 1813 sermon to the ABCFM quoted above, was the driving force behind their work, even before they came together as the Connecticut Wits. His 1777 poem "Columbia! Columbia! To Glory Arise," written while serving as a chaplain in the Revolutionary Army, became popular as a song among patriot soldiers. Its verses proclaim that the "empire shall rise" until it "dissolve with the skies." The "splendors shall flow" to America and "earth's little kingdoms. . . shall bow." America, he wrote, would send her fleets "to all regions" and even the ocean would obey her. Joel Barlow's *Vision*

---

17. Cowie, pp. 9–10.

18. Cunningham, pp. 43–46.

of Columbus (1787) was the first American bestseller after the Revolution, and it made the author the first American to receive fair pay for writing a book. Two decades later, Barlow expanded it into *The Columbiad* (1807), which, like its predecessor, he wrote, "is a patriotic poem; the subject is national and historical." David Humphreys wrote "Address to the Armies of the United States of America" (1780), "The Future Glory of the United States of America" (1782), "A Poem on the Happiness of America" (1785), and "The Industry of the United States of America" (1802). Trumbull wrote "Prospect of the Future Glory of America" (1770) and the "Genius of America; An Ode" (1777). In Dwight's *Conquest of Canäan* (finished in 1775, but not published until 1785), he portrayed America as the new Holy Land. His "Columbia! Columbia!" was an early (1777), and his greatest, literary success.[19]

The Wits wrote about nationalist violence with a glee that still jars. What is at least as unusual, however, is that they wrote about it at all. Its primary perpetrators preferred more subtle and sophisticated language. Over 40 years before Dwight's sermon to the ABCFM, Trumbull, in an address quoted in the epigraph to this chapter, spoke of "thousands and 'mid thousands slain" and predicted that Americans' "eager swords promiscuous carnage blend." Speaking at the Yale commencement of 1770, at which he received his master's degree, Trumbull versified about how America would "Rush big with death and aim th' impending blow." He foresaw the day the world would tremble at the advance of the United States: "ev'ry realm, that hears the trump of fame / Quake at the distant terror of her name." America's "Heroes mark their glorious way" while "[b]lood stains their steps." The "raging course" would be marked by "ghastly deaths" but would end in "mighty pow'r" and "laurel'd Conquest." Trumbull described "our future glory," always, defined by the twin rise of arms and letters:

> *Her glories spreading to the boundless skies:*
> *Of ev'ry fair, she boasts th' assembled charms;*
> *The Queen of empires and the Nurse of arms. . .*
> *The first in letters, as the first in arms.*[20]

---

19. American National Biography.

20. John Trumbull, *An Essay on the Use and Advantages of the Fine Arts* (New Haven, CT, 1770), p. 14.

Before reciting his verse, Trumbull gave an oration in which he called for strict observance of boycotts on British manufactures. "I cannot but hope, notwithstanding some dangerous examples of infamous defection," he said, "that there is a spirit remaining in these Colonies, that will invariably oppose itself to the efforts of usurpation and perfidy, and forbid that Avarice should betray us to Slavery." In the summer of 1770, many colonists, especially New Englanders, were observing the boycott of British manufactures. In the manner typical of the American revolutionaries, Trumbull spoke of malevolent conspiracies against the colonists' liberties and the prospect of their enslavement. Trumbull's 1770 address is, however, notable for his near call for national independence. Five years later, in July 1775, Dwight lamented that even his Whiggish associates were still responding with contempt and hostility to his arguments for "absolute independence."[21]

Most Americans remained loyal to King George III until 1776. Benjamin Franklin, one of several eighteenth-century Americans to have been called "the first American," did not become an American nationalist until 1774. Dwight claimed that he began his nationalist epic (it is 11,000 lines long), *The Conquest of Canäan*, in 1771 and completed it by 1775.[22] Trumbull's "An Elegy on the Times," which he began in late 1773, following the Boston Tea Party (December 16, 1773), and published in 1774, is a clear call for a nationalist revolution. Arguably, so was his 1770 Yale commencement address. It is difficult to convey how early these calls for independence are; it was somewhat like coming out against the Vietnam War in 1953, when President Eisenhower sent military advisors. By any measure, the Wits came to believe in American independence very early. Addressing the Yale class of 1776 at commencement, Dwight told the graduates that the achievement of American national independence would bring about the millennium. If they were "to act for the empire of America," they would help see the day when "we may laugh at the impotent malice of other nations, and look forward with rapture to the superlative grandeur and happiness of our own." Here in America, he said, they would catalyze "the last thousand years of the reign of time." It was July

---

21. Cunningham, p. 53.

22. On Franklin, see H. W. Brands, *The First American: The Life and Times of Benjamin Franklin* (New York, 2000). On Dwight's claim to have completed *The Conquest of Canäan*" by 1775, see June 6, 1788, letter to Noah Webster, reprinted in Theodore A. Zunder, "Notes and Queries: Noah Webster and the Conquest of Canäan," *American Literature*, vol. 1, no. 2 (May 1929), pp. 201–202.

1776, and many Americans had finally caught up with their support for national independence. Dwight and Trumbull felt themselves visionaries. Trumbull, in some of his more felicitous lines, wrote, "Prophets and poets were the same, / And all the praise that poets gain / Is for the tales they forge and feign."[23]

Like some of their contemporaries, Dwight and Trumbull believed that Britain was in decline. Of course, the opposite turned out to be true. For the Wits, however, the purported decline of Britain meant not only the emergence of the United States as a world leader, but also the opening of a place in the world of letters. In his 1770 Yale commencement address, Trumbull told listeners, "Polite Letters at present are much on the decline in Britain," where "luxurious effeminacy. . . hath caused a decay of genius." Trumbull made the same point in verse: America was "[h]iding in brightness of superior day / The fainting gleam of Britain's setting ray." He again picked up the cause of modern English literature that he and Dwight had tried to carry to the Yale curriculum:

> The unaffected ease of Gay and Prior, the spirited wit of Congreve, the delicate fancy of Parnelle, the dramatic powers of Otway, Southern and Rowe, the cervantic humour of Arbuthnot, with the pointed satire and strong imagination of Young. These writers will convey the English glory to the most distant ages of posterity.

John Gay (*The Beggar's Opera*), Matthew Prior ("Alma"), and William Congreve (*The Way of the World*) are still read, but, like the Connecticut Wits, the rest of Trumbull's pantheon did not make it into the canon.[24] In the case of the Wits, their poems are unread because they are unreadable: bombastic, full of predictable rhymes, wooden characters, platitudinous sentiments, stiff neoclassicism, heavy-handed pedantry, and showy erudition.[25]

That they were not great writers, and often not good ones, does not change the fact that the Connecticut Wits were America's first literary

23. On Trumbull's "An Elegy on the Times," see Cowie, p. 131; Dwight's 1776 "Valedictory" reprinted in Noah Webster, *Instructive and Entertaining Lessons for Youth* (New Haven, CT, 1835), quotes from pp. 198, 200.

24. See Stephen Greenblatt et al., eds., *The North Anthology of English Literature* (New York, 2006).

25. These are some of the judgments of Trumbull's admiring biographer Cowie, who also called his odes and elegies "extremely dull" and full of "tinsel and fustian and tedious

movement. They are, however, more important figures in the history of American nationalism than in national literature. As a shorthand guide to the political content pushing the missions movement into being, they are invaluable. Much more than the Transcendentalists, for example, the Wits made their association and mutual admiration a matter of record. In *The Columbiad* (1807), Joel Barlow praised his mentor: "For Dwight's high harp the epic Muse sublime / Hails her new empire in the western clime." Barlow also paid tribute to David Humphreys's turn from military service to poetry: "See Humphreys glorious from the field retire, / Sheathe the glad sword and string the soothing lyre." In turn, Humphreys ("On the Future Glory of the United States of America") wrote of waking the lyric giants slumbering in his friends: "Why sleep'st though, Barlow, child of genius? / Why see'st thou, blest Dwight, our land in sadness lie? / And where is Trumbull, earliest boast of fame?"[26] Trumbull, in fact, was praising Dwight and Barlow, in his "Lines Addressed to Messrs. Dwight and Barlow" (1775) writing, "Pleased with the vision of a deathless name, / You seek perhaps a flowery road to fame."[27] Not to be outdone, Dwight (*Greenfield Hill*, 1794) compared Trumbull to Raphael, "Such forms, such deeds on Rafael's tablets shine, / And such, O Trumbull, glow alike on thine."[28]

The Wits shared more than Yale and mutual admiration. They all thought poetry, particularly epic poetry and to a lesser extent lyric poetry, the highest mode of artistic expression. Neoclassicism was their basic style. Their neoclassicism resounds with the events and characters of the scriptures, particularly the Hebrew scriptures, and was written in dialogue with modern British literature. By these means, they tried to Christianize and modernize the classical epic. They wrote and published a good amount, and they shared a common purpose of advancing American national glory. In fact, they self-consciously tried to produce a national literature. They did so not only with a Christianized neoclassicism, but also with a limited range of subjects: satires of Loyalists and freethinkers, idealizations of New England town life, heroic renderings of figures in the

heroics"; see Cowie, *John Trumbull*, pp. 62–63. Cowie's assessment of Trumbull's comic verse is much better.

26. Joel Barlow, *The Columbiad* (London, 1809), p. 277. Originally published 1807.

27. John Trumbull, "Lines Addressed to Messrs. Dwight and Barlow," reprinted in *The Poetical Works of John Trumbull* (Hartford, CT, 1820), p. 105. Republished in 1968.

28. Timothy Dwight, *Greenfield Hill: A Poem in Seven Parts* (New York, 1794), p. 164.

American past, from Columbus to George Washington. They shared an anxious presumption that they were to be American Virgils, revered poets and national tastemakers, smiths of a new American culture. This expectation could lead to moments of unintentional self-parody, such as when Trumbull cited, as evidence of their visionary abilities, the fulfillment of his own prediction that British critics would disapprove of Timothy Dwight and Joel Barlow's work.[29]

At the time the Wits wrote, "culture" still meant agriculture, as when, in 1800, Thomas Jefferson wrote, "The greatest service which can be rendered any country is to add an [sic] useful plant to its culture."[30] It is therefore a bit of an anachronism to characterize the Wits as the cultural program of New England Federalism, particularly its Christian branch. In the language of early modern writers, rather than culture, they spoke of "taste" and "manners." In 1817, Benjamin Silliman, a professor of chemistry at Yale, recalled the Wits as the ones who "overthrew the dominion of false taste."[31] Occasionally, instead of manners or taste, they would speak of "the arts." Trumbull, for example, called his 1769 Yale commencement address, which was a call for nationalist revolution and imperial glory, "An Essay on the Use and Advantage of the Fine Arts." History, he said, proved that "Learning and Glory walk hand in hand through the world." Only if they followed the example of antiquity, in which, according to Trumbull, the "whole nation" became "encouragers of science, and every person a judge of literature," could Americans seize the opportunity to make the nation "famous throughout the world" and imitated by "all posterity." For the Wits, ancient Greece and Rome reached the summit of civilization and "Britain alone can claim the glory of an equality with Greece and Rome." Like many patriots, the Wits were sure that the crisis with the

---

29. For a different perspective on letters and politics in the early republic, see Bryan Waterman, "The Bavarian Illuminati, the Early American Novel, and the Histories of the Public Sphere," *The William and Mary Quarterly*, vol. 62, no. 1 (January 2005), pp. 9–30. For Trumbull's view on how the British reviews of their work ironically confirmed their abilities, see Trumbull, *The Poetical Works of John Trumbull* (Hartford, CT, 1820), pp. 107–108. Republished in 1968.

30. Jefferson quoted in Daniel J. Kevles "An American Passion Revealed," review of Philip J. Pauly's *Fruits and Plains: The Horticultural Transformation of America, New York Review of Books*, vol. 57, no. 8 (May 13, 2010), p. 54. Akira Iriye, "Culture," *The Journal of American History*, vol. 77, no. 1 (June 1990), pp. 99–107, writes, "In the study of international relations, culture may be defined as communication, and the cultural approach as a perspective that pays particular attention to communication within and among nations," p. 99.

31. Benjamin Silliman, *A Sketch of the Life and Character of President Dwight* (New Haven, CT, 1817), p. 6.

colonies indicated a rot within British society. Unlike most patriots, however, their theological and literary consciousness pushed them to build a grand America that stood poised to be the fourth great empire in history. In its ascendancy, the arts would "ennoble the soul, purify the passions, and give the thoughts a better turn."[32]

To appreciate the place of the Connecticut Wits in American history, one must understand how tight a needle they were trying to thread. Fame, glory, and worldly power sit in some tension with Christianity. Dwight and Trumbull and their cohort were not just Christians, they were the proud bearers of one of the most radical enduring forms of Reformed Protestantism. In their Puritan tradition, worldly riches and empire, as well as fame and earthly power, were blandishments of the hated and feared Catholics, or those, the Anglicans for example, who had made peace with the great enemy. Nonetheless, the Wits' hunger for all of these worldly things was irrepressible. A well-established interpretation views the Connecticut Wits as reactionaries. "The nineteenth-century was knocking at their door, but they would not open it," wrote the historian Vernon L. Parrington, "they hated new ways with the virtuous hatred of the well-to-do." This view, however, is an inheritance of the Jeffersonians' anti-Federalist propaganda. In fact, the Wits are difficult to place on the political spectrum, but trying to do so helps illuminate some of the complexity of political life in the early republic. To begin with, Trumbull and Dwight's ancestors would not have agreed that the Wits were conservatives. In 1700, using some of the same scriptural allusions that Dwight invoked in his 1813 sermon to the ABCFM, Cotton Mather had prophesied that too much worldly engagement would pollute and destroy the purity of the gathered. He warned that losing the sense of distinction between the church and the world, the sacred and the profane, would delude even "the most Conscientious people" of New England into thinking "themselves concerned to gather Churches out of Churches." Cotton Mather would have thought that the Wits had lost their way.

Without question, a change had taken place. At the beginning of the seventeenth century, the Separatists, finding the Church of England too polluted to even live in the country in which it enjoyed state establishment, had fled across the Atlantic Ocean. By the late eighteenth and early nineteenth century, their descendants would be leaving New England, in Dwight's words, to range the world, so that they might purify Hindus,

---

32. Trumbull, pp. 12, 11, 14.

Jews, and Muslims, as well as heathen American Indians. The point is not to place the Wits in a Puritan declension narrative, but to show how for them the national empire became the community through which one sought salvation. They had reinterpreted Christianity to sanctify nationalism, and there was nothing conservative about nationalism. In this sense, the Wits did not close the door on the nineteenth century, they led the way into it.[33]

Trumbull's oration "On the Use and the Advantages of the Fine Arts" also challenges a durable view of the Wits as conservatives, or even reactionaries. New England was known for theology, a theology that viewed sculpture, opera, architecture, and painting (though they held Benjamin West in the highest esteem) as suspect. The fine arts were associated with the life of the European royal court, which the New England churchly saw as prurient, effeminate, and decadent, a product and producer of irreligion. As the historians J. G. A. Pocock, Bernard Bailyn, and others have shown, in a long Anglo history in which "Country" and "Court" represented opposing political traditions, New England was all "Country," and the fine arts were decidedly "Court." No one looked to America, much less New England, for the fine arts. The most ambitious American artists of the eighteenth century—John Singleton Copley, Charles Wilson Peale, Benjamin West, and Gilbert Stuart—went to London.

Trumbull's claim that America, with New England leading the way, would become a great nursery of the fine arts was provocative and, in the context of Puritan history, even wild. With the exception of their turn to the nation as the new community of salvation, and their anti-slavery stance, this view of a society freed from Puritan and Yankee misgivings about the fine arts was the Wits' most radical act. If nationalism was waging a war on centuries of Protestant theology, the Wits were too busy joining many of the battles to see that war. They accepted nationalism without reflection, as an absolute value. Their first battle, even before the elevation of America, was for the nationalization of the New England way. In ways that would prove decisive, the nationalization of the New England way was as counterintuitive as the Yankee championing of the fine arts. In terms of population growth, the Middle States and the frontier territories

33. Dwight's *Conquest* quoted in Harris, p. 205; see also Silverman, p. 133. On the Mathers, see David D. Hall, *The Faithful Shepard: A History of the New England Ministry in the Seventeenth Century* (Chapel Hill, NC, 1972), pp. 276–277, 275. Dwight's ancestors, Hooker and Stoddard, took more liberal positions on the scope of the Church mission than the Mathers, though neither as expansive as Dwight's vision; see Hall, pp. 164–166, 206–207.

were more dynamic societies than New England. In the Deep South, cotton would soon drive a boom that not only fortified the control which the slave power held in American politics, but would make the Southern planters the richest ruling class in the world. In terms of political and economic power, New England was a junior partner in the new republic, and was becoming more junior. In raw economic power, it took a back seat to the South and the rising bourgeoisie of New York City; at the same time, its factories in Lowell, Massachusetts, the global reach of its maritime commerce firms in Boston and Providence, and its innovations in corporate practice and law made pioneering contributions to the development of American capitalism.[34] When it came to culture and ideas, New England punched above its weight. Its concentration of colleges and the depth of its theological and literary production were unique. With his popular geography textbooks, especially *American Geography* (1789), Jedidiah Morse, another Connecticut born and Yale-educated Congregationalist minister, taught Americans continental geography. By and large, the writing of American history was left to New Englanders, or those educated in its institutions. As late as 1903, enough of New England's dominance in history-writing still remained to compel the Yale historian Ulrich B. Phillips, a Georgia native educated in Madison, Wisconsin, to complain, "The history of the United States has been written by Boston and largely written wrong. . . New England has already over done its part."[35]

Its preponderance of cultural power prevented many New Englanders, including the Wits, from grasping the consequences of their relative political weakness. But they seem to have sensed the discrepancy, and it contributed to a frequent shrillness. Noah Webster's *Ten Letters to Dr. Joseph Priestly* (1800) offers an example. In 1799, Joseph Priestley, a renowned British chemist (one of the discoverers of oxygen), grammarian, theologian, and outspoken political radical, had published *Letters to the Inhabitants of Northumberland*, in which he argued on behalf of deism

34. Joyce Appleby, Lynn Hunt, and Margaret Jacob, *Telling the Truth about History* (New York, 1994), pp. 241–242; Peter Dobkin Hall, *"Inventing the Nonprofit Sector" and Other Essays on Philanthropy, Voluntarism, and Nonprofit Organizations* (Baltimore, MD, 2001); Morton Horowitz, *The Transformation of American Law, 1780–1860* (Cambridge, MA 1979), esp. ch. 4.

35. On Jedidiah Morse, see James King Morse, *Jedidiah Morse: Champion of New England Orthodoxy* (New York, 1929), chs. 1–2; Phillips quoted in Peter H. Wood, "Circles in the Sand: Perspectives on the Southern Frontier at the Arrival of James Oglethorpe," in Phinizy Spalding and Harvey H. Jackson III, eds., *Oglethorpe in Perspective: Georgia's Founder after Two Hundred Years* (Tuscaloosa, AL, 1989), p. 5.

and the affinity of the American and French Revolutions. Webster opened his reply by complaining that Priestley had neglected New England opinion: "You say, you *see* almost all the News papers in Philadelphia; it is to be wished, Sir, that you would *learn* the opinions of the Inhabitants of New England before you assert things that have not the least foundation."[36] Webster reminded Priestley that, "New England, sir, contains about a million of inhabitants." Priestley had lived in America since 1794, when mob violence and state persecution had compelled him to flee Britain and seek asylum in the new republic whose Revolution he had defended. Despite Priestley's residence of six years, and his pro-American credentials, Webster attacked him as one of the "foreigners and aliens" whose "pestiferous disputes" and "arrogant pretensions" were polluting America. Had Priestley even tried to engage in "correspondence with men of correct information," that is, the New England sages, he would have learned that, in contrast to the Jacobins and the followers of "French principles," New Englanders still believed in "religion and law."[37] Priestley represented a rationalist movement that many New England Protestants despised. In immigrating to Pennsylvania, Priestley had hoped to start a Unitarian congregation, a community of "rational Christians," and to head a college in America. Diminishing religious persecution in England (enabling his partners to stay), and the unexpected hostility of Americans to his heterodoxy, upended these plans.[38]

Dissenting Protestants could be prickly and righteous. Faced with perceived threats, they moved quickly to aggressive defenses, which often helped Jeffersonians to portray New England Federalists as "monocrats," anti-republican elitists bent on restoring monarchy. New England Federalists did not want to restore monarchy, but they did not hesitate to express unpopular ideas about social hierarchy. The Puritan tradition of the elect, those who had demonstrated saving grace, had contributed to an unapologetic view of the elite. For example, despite the fact that Priestley had written the most influential English grammar textbook of the eighteenth century, and that he read or spoke 10 languages, Webster explained to him the "true" meaning of the word aristocracy: "The word *aristocracy*,"

---

36. Noah Webster, *Ten Letters to Dr. Priestly* (New Haven, CT, 1800), pp. 3, 4. Italics in the original.

37. Ibid., pp. 5, 9, 8.

38. Robert E. Schofield, *The Enlightenment of Joseph Priestley: A Study of His Life and Work from 1733 to 1773* (University Park, PA, 1997), pp. 274–275.

wrote Webster, "has been perverted in Europe" to denote rule by "the richest men and men of noble rank" who are often "the *worst* men." Its real meaning, Webster wrote, was "government by the *best or most excellent men.*" This true aristocracy "still exists" in New England, where rule by men of property and education, "*learned, aged, experienced. . . men*" prevailed and formed a "true *patriarchal government.*" These "venerable counselors" and "venerable clergy" and "venerable men" comprised a "*personal and adventitious aristocracy.*" Thus the New England aristocracy, an aristocracy in "the true sense of the word," Webster wrote, had produced a society where people enjoyed "a longer period of uninterrupted freedom" than any "spot on the globe."[39]

If America followed the New England way, aristocracy may yet resume "its true primitive signification" in the nation at large, wrote Webster. The fostering of a true aristocracy, one of learning, piety, and wisdom, was, he claimed, essential to the preservation of republican society. The danger to republicanism came from the other states, he wrote. "New England," wrote Webster, "if insulated from the all world, might enjoy a republic system. . . for centuries." Other states, however, with their "free admission of foreigners" and their "too liberal extension of the right of suffrage" threw the American experiment into peril. Government by people of "little property, education, or principle," wrote Webster, "laid the foundation of evils that half a century will not cure." The fact that New England was "attached to sister states" adopting such ill-considered practices, wrote Webster, put her historic achievements at risk. Webster's defense of "true aristocracy" and his analysis of regional differences in American society contained much insight and interest. At the same time, in a democratizing American society, such arguments made New England Federalists easy political targets.[40]

Assessing Webster's boast that New England elites had produced the freest society in the world depends on what kind of freedom one values. If freedom means libertarian freedom from state regulation, the claim was absurd. Though it was part of their seventeenth-century past, Massachusetts had executed Quakers, and, also in the seventeenth century, Connecticut had allowed, among other punishments, the boring of their tongues, a procedure for which the law required the Quakers to pay. Into the nineteenth century, both Massachusetts and Connecticut

---

39. Webster, *Ten Letters to Dr. Priestley*, p. 30. Italics in original.

40. Ibid., pp. 28–29. Italics in original.

claimed the right to take children judged by selectmen to be "ignorant" from their parents and "put them into better hands." Massachusetts forbade anyone "not worth £200" from "wearing gold or silver or lace or buttons or bone lace above 2s. per yard, or silk hoods or scarfs." Massachusetts and Connecticut both prohibited travel on the Sabbath, which began at Saturday sundown. As late as 1804, Massachusetts arrested judges for traveling in Maine on a Sunday. Massachusetts allowed "any person or persons to apprehend, without a warrant, any Jesuit, priest, missionary, or Roman ecclesiastic." Playing cards, as well as "dice. . . shuffleboard, billiards" and several other games, was illegal throughout New England. As late as 1812, the justice of the peace in North Haven, Connecticut, arrested seven young men for card playing. They were prosecuted, convicted, and fined $3.34 each, plus $1.27 costs. In eighteenth-century Connecticut, it was illegal to fly a kite. In short, a broad range of individual expression was not a premium part of the kind of freedom cherished by New England Federalists, including the Wits.[41]

In other ways, Webster's boasts that New England was an unusually free, stable, and egalitarian society were true. Eighteenth-century New England, for instance, was one of the most literate societies in human history. "Beneath New England's burning Protestantism and consequent universal male literacy," wrote the historian Kenneth A. Lockridge, "Anglo-America was a world in which literacy moved glacially at a middling level." From seventeenth-century levels that had been no higher than those in England, literacy in eighteenth-century New England rose steadily. Only Scotland and Sweden, beginning late in the seventeenth century, had enjoyed a comparably rapid spread of literacy as eighteenth-century New England. Like Scotland and Sweden, New England was a small and relatively homogenous society with a strong Protestant influence. By 1750, 70 percent of New England men and 45 percent of women were literate, unusually high figures for the time. In France, for example, male literacy was no more than 50 percent.[42]

Eighteenth-century New England knew poverty and social strife. As with literacy, both were on the rise. Unlike England, however, New England had

41. Walter F. Prince, "An Examination of 'Peters's Blue Laws,'" *Annual Report of the American Historical Association* (1898), pp. 97–138, examples taken from pp. 111, 113, 108, 107, 116.

42. Kenneth J. Lockridge, *Literacy in Colonial New England: An Enquiry into the Social Context of Literacy in the Early Modern West* (New York, 1974), pp. 87–93, 5; Elliott, *Empires of the Atlantic World*, p. 216.

no large, illiterate, and subordinated laboring class. Unlike the Chesapeake, the Caribbean colonies, and Spanish South America, it also lacked a mass of enslaved laborers. The colonial New England economy was not based on industrialism or plantation agriculture or natural resource extraction, all of which required a brutalized and dispossessed labor force and tended to produce a small, very rich elite. The small-scale agriculture, husbandry, and merchant commerce that formed the base of the New England economy not only allowed for widespread literacy, it produced, by the standards of the early modern Atlantic world, relative social equality. It would be decades before Massachusetts senator Charles Sumner would inveigh against the "lords of the loom" and the "lords of the lash," the alliance of British industrialists and Southern planters, but the conditions that allowed great British industrialists and grand Southern planters to establish themselves and flourish did not exist in New England. In addition, the modern reader tends to place the emphasis in Sumner's phrases on "loom" and "lash," but to New Englanders of the eighteenth or nineteenth century, the indictment would have been "lords." In all of these ways, Webster's claim that New Englanders "are independent landholders, free and accustomed to manage their own local concerns" was true.[43]

Webster was also referring to New Englanders' rejection of primogeniture. New Englanders considered the fact that they had always been able to distribute their property as they saw fit a significant step in the history of freedom. Adam Smith agreed, and in *The Wealth of Nations*, Smith noted that New Englanders adhered to "the Mosaical law," where "the oldest has only a double share." Smith saw the absence of primogeniture "in the three provinces of New England" as a significant factor inhibiting "the engrossing of land" which "is the greatest obstruction to its improvement." He described the resulting "movable" condition of land titles in New England as one of the "principal causes" of their "rapid prosperity," especially compared to the New World colonies of Spain, Portugal, and France, where "estates go all to one person" or the "largest estates of the country" are tied up in "noble tenures." The departure from the European practice of primogeniture exerted a strong influence on the social structure. It reinforced other tendencies to freedom and egalitarianism, it broadened participation in civic life, and, as Smith noted, it made labor

---

43. On New England distinctiveness, see J. H. Elliott, *Empires of the Atlantic World*, pp. 156, 250.

a "greater and more valuable" activity. Virginia would not abolish primogeniture until 1785, and New York not until 1786.[44]

In addition, New England, along with Pennsylvania and New York, were unusual for having been the only parts of the New World settled by families, instead of by single men. From the beginning, women constituted half the population. The early presence of traditional family structures contributed to social stability and obviously altered the character of social life. Along with many others, Ralph Waldo Emerson would later mythologize colonial New England town government, writing that "the whole population of the town" attended town meetings and had a "voice in the affair," which was not true. In Emerson's own Concord, Massachusetts, during the eighteenth century, less than 50 percent of freemen attended town meetings. In colonial New England overall, only 10 to 25 percent of eligible voters regularly went to the polls, and a turnout of 50 percent was rare. Nonetheless, over the course of the eighteenth century, New England civic life exhibited notable vibrancy and stability. Its characteristic event, the town meeting, has become an American political ritual. In brief, whether the frame of reference was the North Atlantic, the New World, or the North American colonies, New England was a distinct and unusual society.[45]

The most fanciful aspect of the Wits' ambition to nationalize, even globalize, all these odd regional characteristics may have been their intention to affect this transformation through literature. Literary faith, however, can run deep and many writers, major and minor, have shared the Wits' belief in the almost limitless power of poetry and prose. They had a near-contemporary exemplar in the English man of letters Samuel Johnson, whom Noah Webster quoted ("The chief glory of a nation arises from its authors") in the "Preface" of his 1828 *American Dictionary*.[46] In 1776 and 1777, during their service as chaplains in the Continental Army, Dwight and Barlow were already expressing, in almost exactly the same words, an almost magical view of literature. When he entered his army

44. On New England and primogeniture, see Richard B. Morris, "Primogeniture and Entailed Estates in America," *Columbia Law Review*, vol. 27, no. 1 (January 1927), pp. 24–51; Adam Smith, *The Wealth of Nations*, Book IV, ch. 7, para. 41.

45. J. H. Elliott, *Empires of the Atlantic World*, p. 336. On colonial New England voter participation rates, see Michael Schudson, *The Good Citizen: A History of American Civic Life*, pp. 17–18.

46. Andrew O'Hagan, "The Powers of Dr. Johnson," *New York Review of Books*, vol. 56, no. 15 (October 8, 2009), p. 7; Webster's "Preface" to the 1828 *An American Dictionary of the*

chaplainry, Barlow said he would be able to do "more for the cause" as a poet than as a chaplain and promised to continue writing, to use his poetry to "encourage the taste" of the soldiers. "I have great faith in the influence of songs," Barlow said, "One good song is worth a dozen addresses or proclamations." Dwight, who from 1777 to 1778 served as chaplain in General Samuel H. Parsons's First Connecticut Brigade, which spent the winter breaking ground at the fort that would become West Point, liked to tell his fellow soldiers, "Let me write the songs of a nation, and you may make its laws." Barlow's best-known effort (he and Dwight and Trumbull suggested that they did not claim authorship of all the patriotic songs they wrote during the war) was "The Burning of Charlestown," written in response to the June 1775 Battle of Bunker Hill. In it, he compared the British to Cain, "who madly spilt his brother's blood" and warned Lord North and General Thomas Gage to "dread the day" and the "dire torments" that God's vengeance would bring:

> *Yes, there's a God, whose laws are still the same,*
> *Whose years are endless, and whose power is great:*
> *He is our God: Jehovah is his name:*
> With him we trust our sore oppressed State.[47]

Just over a year later, while he was still serving as chaplain to General Parsons's Brigade, Dwight wrote "Columbia! Columbia!" The poem would be reprinted in readers well into the nineteenth century and its best-known lines—"Columbia! Columbia! To glory arise / The queen of the world, and child of the skies!"—were familiar to generations of Americans. In the poem, Dwight expressed the eager expectation of literary glory that was characteristic of the Wits: "New bards and new sages unrivalled shall soar / To fame, unextinguished when time is no more." The new American writers, he envisioned, would win distinction for the content and the form of their work: "Nor less shall thy fair ones to glory ascend / And genius and beauty in harmony blend." Because they had "virtue's bright image enstamped on their mind," their "sweetness unmingled" and their "manners refined" would combine in work bound to bring joy to "all nations."[48]

English Language, reprinted in Robert E. Spiller, *The Roots of National Culture: American Literature to 1830* (New York, 1949), quote from p. 447.

47. J. T. Headley, *The Chaplains and Clergy of the Revolution* (New York, 1864), p. 208, 188.

48. "Columbia! Columbia!" reprinted in Headley, pp. 186–187.

Written in 1777, "Columbia! Columbia!" would mark the height of Dwight's literary success. The same year, the Yale Corporation almost offered Dwight the presidency of the college. He was twenty-five. Instead, they chose Ezra Stiles, who developed an aversion to Dwight's yearning for glory, writing: "He meditates great Things & nothing but great Things will serve him—& every Thing that comes in the Way of his preferment must fall before him. Aut Caesar, aut nullus." To be Caesar, or be nothing, to be consumed with worldly ambition, was, from one Puritan to another, a damning estimation. Others, however, helped to carry the torch of Dwight's literary fame. As late as 1828, Noah Webster promoted Dwight as one of the Americans whom the Revolution raised to historic stature. "I do not indeed expect," wrote Webster in his *Dictionary*, "to add celebrity to the names of Franklin, Washington, Adams, Jay, Madison, Marshall, Dwight." Of course, adding celebrity was what Webster aimed to do.[49]

Outside New England, the Wits were likely to be seen as provincial as much as polarizing. A contemporary critic described their patriot songs as "psalms and hymns adapted to the taste of Yankee rebels."[50] The Wits may have been provincials, but they were right that their province enjoyed real cultural resources, including America's most important church and greatest schools. Though almost wholly confined to New England, at the close of the Revolutionary War, Congregationalists formed the largest and most powerful religious body in the United States. Congregationalism began the nineteenth century with at least 700 churches in New England. Many Congregationalist ministers had played conspicuous roles as sup-porters of the American Revolution, and the Church enjoyed distinction in letters and, in particular, in the law. Some historians have claimed that American constitutionalism descends from the Congregational cov-enant tradition. In Massachusetts and Connecticut, the Church enjoyed state protection, a status that bolstered the Wits' confidence and which helped make nearly every Congregationalist a Federalist, and the Church was a stronghold of Federalism. By 1795, a Massachusetts newspaper, the *Salem Gazette*, complained that Congregationalist ministers' political activity was so unceasing and pointed that more and more people were

---

49. On Dwight and presidency of Yale, see Kenneth Silverman, *Timothy Dwight*, pp. 94–96; Stiles quoted in Peter K. Kafer, "The Making of Timothy Dwight: A Connecticut Morality Tale," *WMQ*, vol. 47 (1990), pp. 195–196; John R. Fitzmier, *New England's Moral Legislator* (Bloomington, IN, 1998), p. 231; Webster quote from *Preface* to the *American Dictionary* (1828), reprinted in Stiller, p. 447.

50. Quote taken from Headley, p. 209.

coming to see them as "party managers rather than spiritual teachers." The Federalist perspective is evident even in the Wits' earliest, most radical work.[51]

John Trumbull's *M'Fingal* was the most successful of any of the Wits' writings. As with Dwight's "Columbia! Columbia!" but on a greater scale, the triumph came early. After leaving John Adams's Boston law office, where he worked after being admitted to the bar, Trumbull moved to New Haven, where he wrote *M'Fingal* in the latter half of 1775. *M'Fingal: A Modern Epic Poem* was published in January 1776. After its publication, it quickly went through 30 editions. No other American poem sold 30 editions until Henry Wadsworth Longfellow's *Evangeline: A Tale of Acadie* did so in 1847, when America's population exceeded 20 million. Trumbull's *M'Fingal* accomplished the feat in a country of 3 million. A nineteenth-century critic said it "penetrated into every farm-house and sent the rustic volunteers laughing into the ranks of Washington and Greene." It made Trumbull the most widely read American poet until Longfellow. The Jeffersonian freethinker Philip Freneau may have been the poet of the American Revolution, but John Trumbull's *M'Fingal* was the poem of the Revolution. It was one of the most widely read works of any kind in revolutionary America. In contrast to the grandiosity that afflicts most of the Wits' poetry, its tone is relatively light. It has its share of awkward references to Homer ("As that famed weaver, wife t'Ulysses") and gratuitous footnotes ("*So says Milton"), but in contrast to the Wits' other poems, the Oxford English Dictionary moments are relatively rare, though there are a few, such as when a patriot accuses a loyalist of being "stuff'd with choler atrabilious."[52]

M'Fingal satirizes the misadventures of its eponymous hero as he attempts to sway New Englanders to the Loyalist position. M'Fingal is a Scotsman ("His fathers flourished in the Highlands / Of Soctia's fog-benighted islands") residing in a small New England town. Because Americans, and New Englanders in particular, often saw themselves as the conservatives, as the defenders of religious orthodoxy and prerogatives guaranteed by an ancient English constitution against corrupt

51. William Warren Sweet, *Religion on the American Frontier, 1783–1850*, vol. III, *The Congregationalists* (Chicago, 1939), pp. 5–12.

52. Cowie, *John Trumbull*, p. 167; John Nichol, *American Literature: An Historical Sketch, 1620–1880* (Edinburgh, UK, 1882), p. 89; Editor, *Harper's New Monthly Magazine*, vol. LII, December 1875 to May 1876 (New York, 1876), p. 407; John Trumbull, *M'Fingal: A Modern Epic Poem* (Hartford, CT, 1856), pp. 26, 31, 54.

British usurpers, Trumbull characterizes M'Fingal as intent "to raze, as nuisance. . . church and state the Constitutions." In addition to his support for a plan to "Enslave th' Amer'can wildernesses, / And rend the province in pieces," M'Fingal holds unorthodox religious views. Trumbull later described the poem as an example of one of the Wits' writings that were "supposed, at the time" to "have checked and intimidated the leaders of disorganization and infidel philosophy." M'Fingal's religious unorthodoxy is of the silly kind; he claims psychic powers. In the Scottish Highlands, wrote Trumbull, "gain'd our 'Squire two gifts by right, / Rebellion and the Second-sight." In Trumbull's hands, M'Fingal's "Scottish gift of second-sight" brings the Scot to one error after another: "So gain'd our 'Squire his fame by seeing / Such things, as never would have being." Depicting M'Fingal as a Scot who claimed "second-sight" was a satirical personification of the Scottish Enlightenment. The Wits thought heretical the view that human intelligence, through science, could make sense of aspects of the world long held accessible only to divine reason. Trumbull's personification of the Enlightenment as a Loyalist Scot boasting clairvoyant powers was perhaps the inaugural instance of the their numerous attacks on deistic European philosophers. Hume was a favorite target, as was Voltaire. Such attacks would also feature in the literature of the nineteenth-century Anglo-American missionary organizations.[53]

Trumbull's poem begins at a New England town meeting, with a debate between the patriot Honorius and the "hero" M'Fingal. With Honorius and M'Fingal, Trumbull later claimed to have done justice to both the Tory and the patriot positions, but if that were true the poem would not have won its great popularity in America. M'Fingal, for instance, invokes the divine right of kings to admonish his audience, a group of New England Dissenters gathered in a church, that to be good Christians they must submit to the King. When God, through the King, "means to send you pain, / You toss your foreheads up in vain; / Your way is, hush'd in peace, to bear it, / And make necessity a merit." For his part, Honorius gets all the popular arguments. His claim that Britain, with the Quebec Act, by which Parliament granted freedom of religion to Quebec Catholics, has "Set wide for Popery the door, / Made friends with Babel's scarlet whore"

---

53. Trumbull's claim that the Wits' writings succeeded in checking infidelity are found in the prefatory author's memoir, *M'Fingal*, p. 19; quotes from pp. 25, 27. Peter Millican, "Introduction," in David Hume, *An Enquiry Concerning Human Understanding* (New York, 2007), pp. ix–x.

appealed to New Englanders' deep anti-Catholicism.[54] Raising grievances felt across the colonies, Honorius criticizes Britain for bullying, mistaking rights for privileges, and, during the Seven Years' War, for treating Americans like Indians rather than like Englishmen:

> *For she, her case grown desperater*
> *Mistook the plainest things in nature;*
> *Had lost all use of eyes or wits,*
> *Took slavery for the bill of rights;*
> *Trembled at whigs and deem'd them foes*
> *And stopp'd at loyalty her nose;*
> *Styled her own children, brats and caitiffs*
> *And knew us not from th' Indian natives.*[55]

Continuing the parent-child metaphor that informed much discourse between Britain and America, M'Fingal compares the colonists to spoiled and vicious children. He calls them "Ungrateful sons! A factious band, / That rise against your parent land!" He castigates the patriots as "Ye viper race, that burst in strife / The genial womb that gave you life." In essence, he tells them that the debt they owe Britain from the Seven Years' War is a legitimate one, accusing them of "scorn the debt and obligation, / You justly owe the British nation."[56]

Trumbull casts his hero as a bumbler whose pro-Loyalist arguments only insult and raise the colonists' ire. M'Fingal, for example, reminds the patriots of their debt of gratitude to Archbishop Laud, widely regarded as a tyrant. M'Fingal, however, says it was "the deeds of England's primate" that drove "your fathers to this climate." Laud's "jails and fines and every ill" had forced the colonists to "good against their will." M'Fingal credits the hated measures of Laud and Charles II for establishing the American religious landscape: "Who'd seen, except for these restraints,/ Your witches, quakers, whigs, and saints,/Or heard of Mather's famed *Magnalia,*/If Charles and Laud had chanced to fail you?" It was Charles II and Archbishop Laud, he continues, who did not hesitate to "send you. . . their missionary crew, / To teach you law and gospel too." Now, in the revolutionary crisis, Britain again brought liberty to the colonies. This liberty

54. Trumbull, *M'Fingal*, p. 33.

55. Ibid., p. 34.

56. Ibid., p. 56.

came, according to M'Fingal, in the form of quartering British soldiers, and he asked the colonists, "When fear and want at once invade, / Can you refuse to lend them aid?" These references to the hated Quartering Acts of 1765 and 1774, which in essence gave the British Army the right to take over colonists' homes, of course only hurt M'Fingal's cause. His assurance that the British "sent their troops t'establish law, / And with gunpowder, fire and ball, / Reform your people, one and all" were also unlikely to have swayed many patriots.[57]

M'Fingal's wide contemporary readership merits comparisons with better known works of the American Revolution, Tom Paine's *Common Sense* and Thomas Jefferson's "Declaration of Independence." In some ways, Trumbull's poem may be a more accurate representation of the forces that pushed the colonists to revolution. In contrast to the jaunty confidence of Paine's *Common Sense* or the distillation of high principles that dominate the opening of the Declaration, *M'Fingal*, despite its satirical, burlesque qualities, bristles with anger and fear. Trumbull lingers on British slights to the colonists, as when M'Fingal tells the New Englanders that "Ye're cowards, every mother's son; / And if you offer to deny, / We've witnesses to prove it by." In particular, the poem picked at old wounds of honor from the Seven Years' War. Despite the triumph of British and colonial forces over the French, the experience of the war opened a fissure between Americans and the British. Colonists' discovery, in military service, that the British did not consider them equals caused real offense. This grievance, combined with a widespread feeling that the British failed to pay proper due to Americans' military contributions, were two of the few things that colonists, as a people, shared. Citing reports from the British officers in the Seven Years' War, M'Fingal argues that the patriot cause is doomed because Americans are cowards. Jeffrey Amherst, former governor of Virginia and governor general of North America, reports M'Fingal, "swore that with five thousand foot / He'd rout you all." Other British officers, including "the mighty Colonel Grant" have testified "against your courage." They have affirmed "your universal failure / In every principle of valor." In Britain, M'Fingal continues, it is well known that Americans are such "scamperers" and "so swift" that they outran French bullets. Because Americans, "by native instinct run away," further escalation with "that grim old beast, the British Lion" could be calamitous. If the colonists yet chose to fight, to face the British

57. Ibid. pp. 58–59.

"storm," however, they at least might eventually get to see their "troops in uniform." This jibe concerned American troops' and officers' lack of uniform dresses, which, in the Seven Years' War, explained Trumbull, "was a constant theme of ridicule with the British." Given American grievances over their military experience in the Seven Years' War, M'Fingal's arguments that Americans were cowards and bumpkins appealed less to colonists' humor than their pride and anger.[58]

Unlike pure satire, Trumbull's *M'Fingal* stoked colonists' fears. In particular, the hero foresees the colonists suffering gruesome retribution at the hands of Native Americans and slaves. Britain would "set at work all engines / To spirit up the native Indians." The "tawney band" would unite behind the leadership of "her duplicate of Guys," Guy Carleton, the governor of Quebec, and Guy Johnson, the British superintendent of Canadian Indians. With Americans preoccupied by coastal attacks from the powerful British Navy, the Indians would descend "on your backs" with hatchets and "with scalping knives, / And butcher children and your wives." Britain would pay her Indian allies with "your scalps" while boasting "again with vanity, / Her English national humanity." In the parlance of the British Empire, M'Fingal explained, "This term, *humanity*, comprehends / All things of which, on this side hell, / The *human mind* is capable."[59]

While exciting the Indians to depredations against the colonists, Britain would also join forces with American slaves. She would "rouse your slaves to cut your throats," paying "your blacks" with "her notes." Not only would Britain emancipate "your blacks in Carolinas" and "your slaves at Boston," she would give them military honors, "Emboss'd with regimental red; / While flared the epaulette, like flambeau, / On Captain Cuff and Ensign Sambo." They would be "accounted then" among General Gage's "very bravest men." Vanquished patriots would not be executed. Britain would preserve their lives so that they may serve their former slaves, newly enfranchised by virtue of seized patriot property: "While Confiscation at command / Shall stalk in terror through the land." Britain would "give all whig-estates away." Dispossessed and enslaved, colonists would perform manual labor for a ruling class of Tories and freedmen: the "Whigs subdued, in slavish awe, / Our wood shall hew, our water draw." Seeds of this arrangement had already been planted, "For since our leaders have decreed, / Their blacks to join us, shall be freed."

---

58. Ibid., pp. 61–63, 80.

59. Ibid., pp. 63–65.

In a particularly New England twist to this fantasy vision, after receiving military honors, Americans' emancipated slaves would fill the Anglican Church. Colonists would be forced to watch "the New England bishop's see grow, / By many a new-converted negro." A resurgent Anglican Church, having "turn'd many an Afric to a tory," would establish a bishopric in America. Of course, M'Fingal foresaw "this formidable league rose / Of Indians, British troops, and negroes" crushing the rebels. It's "no war, each mortal knows, / Where one side only gives the blows." Resuming the parent-child metaphor, he concluded, "On reflection / The most we call it is correction."[60]

Trumbull's M'Fingal was one of the most popular writings of the revolutionary and early national era. Few works, certainly none of the Wits' writings, rivaled its wide readership. It merits attention not just because it was the poem of the American Revolution, but also because it expresses a social philosophy out of which the missions movement emerged and that it never fully left behind. The anti-Anglican and anti-Catholic sentiments in the poem, though not likely to surprise those familiar with the history of religion and politics in early America, nonetheless suggest how the national evangelists wanted to propagate the right kind of Protestantism. What the Wits, in the early modern fashion, called "manners" and "taste" could be almost indistinguishable from the right kind of Protestantism. Manners and taste, in this deep sense, grew out of a social life. The social life that the Wits idealized was that of the New England elite, that which Noah Webster had claimed was an aristocracy in the original sense of the word, rule by the most excellent and virtuous men. Their view of themselves as a natural and just elite, a true aristocracy, stood in contrast to their negative view of the British aristocracy. Some later editions of M'Fingal bore the subtitle A Swiftian Satire on British Society and Politics, but the subtitle is misleading. The patriot Honorius, M'Fingal's debating opponent, levels derisive attacks on Britain that never reach the level of satire. His contempt for British society is that it is an unnatural, decadent aristocracy, peopled by "ten thousand bastards" and "the left-handed progeny of their kings." They dominate and corrupt British politics, buying opponents with titles, "banners," and "ducal tassels." If they prevailed in America, Thomas Hutchinson would become the Earl of Massachusetts and "Knights, viscounts, barons, shall ye meet, / as thick as pebbles in the street." Because Anglicanism and the Catholic Church,

---

60. Ibid., pp. 65–67, 88, 89, 74.

with their bejeweled prelates and ornate mitres, were complicit with the decadent British aristocracy, bishops and even cardinals would arise and spread across America. The country would fall into decay. Like the European empires, it would become, in Timothy Dwight's words, "a world despoiled, for luxury and gold." In brief, the Wits held antipathy for the political consequences of European aristocracy.[61]

Because of its association with capitalism, some leading scholars of modern nationalism prefer to speak of "bourgeois nationalism." Despite their key role as pioneering nationalists, the Wits' social vision was not, in the proper sense of the word, bourgeois. If the nation provided the form of the Wits' sacred social metaphysic, middle-class, Federalist Protestantism formed the content. Completed in 1794, and dedicated to dedicated to "John Adams, Esquire, Vice-President of the United States," Timothy Dwight's 1794 poem, *Greenfield Hill*, gives the fullest expression of the Wits' social vision. It is for this reason the most important of their works. As poetry, it ranks above two of Dwight's more ambitious works, *The Conquest of Canäan* (1785) and *The Triumph of Infidelity* (1788). The grandiosity of the former, a self-conscious attempt to fashion a Protestant, American version of *The Aeniad*, is suggested by the umlaut. *The Conquest of Canäan* intersperses events from the Hebrew scriptures with battles of the American Revolution; the Israelites become the Americans, the Egyptians become the British, and Joshua and George Washington alternate as the hero. At times Washington and Joshua appear to be one and the same. It was Dwight's most ambitious work and one of the great failures in the history of American literature. It is 11 books, nearly 10,000 (9,678) lines long, and there may not be a soul alive who can quote one of the lines.

The Triumph of Infidelity suffers from the fact that it is more abusive than satirical. For example, *The Triumph of Infidelity* includes a sarcastic tribute to "Mons. De Voltaire," in which Dwight acknowledges Voltaire's "shining talents" while noting his choice to devote his "industrious" life to the "single purpose" of elevating himself above God. Dwight castigates Voltaire for "sophistry, contempt, obloquy," for setting the perverse example of a life, "the chief end" of which "was to slander his God, and abuse him forever." Reasoning, writes Dwight, "is an unhappy engine to be employed against Christianity; as, like elephants in ancient war, it usually, in this case turns upon those who employ it."[62] Eventually, the

---

61. Trumbull, *M'Fingal*, pp. 59–50, 86–87.

62. Timothy Dwight, *The Triumph of Infidelity* (Hartford, CT, 1788).

counterattack against the deists and freethinkers would take the form of missionary organizations, rather than poetry. In *The Triumph of Infidelity*, the success of the American Revolution banishes Satan from the United States. Forced to fly across the Atlantic, Satan spends time playing whist with Voltaire and David Hume. An English reviewer, not knowing that Dwight actually existed, found the "malignant spirit, which is breathed out in these lines against all those who do not bear the badge of orthodoxy" so sulfurous that he wondered if "Timothy Dwight, D.D." might be a deist plant designed to discredit orthodoxy.[63] "Probably there can now be left for us on this planet," wrote the literary scholar Moses Coit Tyler, "few things more provocative of the melancholy and pallid form of mirth, than that presented by the laborious efforts of the Reverend Doctor Timothy Dwight to be facetious at the expense of David Hume, or to slay the dreadful Monsieur de Voltaire in a duel of irony." The poem was not a success.[64]

Repeated failure had dimmed Dwight's expectation that he would be, in Trumbull's words, "our American poet." *Greenfield Hill (1794)* was his final attempt to establish a great literary reputation. While it did not win Dwight renown as a poet, *Greenfield Hill* is a simpler, better, and readable work. Opening with the poet standing atop a hill in his Connecticut parish, it describes in detail the social conditions and habits of the country, while recounting its history, warning of perils, and predicting a great future. Though it contains some ascensions and Satan has a speaking part, in contrast to Dwight's earlier work, *Greenfield Hill* is earth-bound, mundane. When it, too, failed, Dwight in effect abandoned his literary ambitions. In 1795, at age 43, a year after the publication of *Greenfield Hill*, Dwight accepted an offer to become president of Yale.[65]

Henry Adams described Dwight as "a man of extraordinary qualities, but on whom almost every other mental gift had been conferred in fuller measure than poetical genius." By all accounts, institution building was one of Dwight's gifts. By the time he accepted the Yale position, he had already succeeded in building an impressive academy in Fairfield, Connecticut, that had attracted students from as far away as France. Yale presented him with greater resources, which he was eager to marshal. Since the 1788 publication

---

63. Colin Wells, *The Devil and Doctor Dwight: Satire and Theology in the Early Republic* (Chapel Hill, NC, 2002).

64. Moses Coit Tyler, *Three Men of Letters: George Berkeley, Timothy Dwight, Joel Barlow* (New York, 1895), p. 92.

65. On Dwight as Yale president see Silverman, pp. 97, 111–113, 132. On Dwight and America, see passim, but especially chs. 4–5.

of his *Triumph of Infidelity*, the threat and stature of the deists had grown. Dwight saw Yale as a haven for irreligion, which was not true, though Ezra Stiles, Dwight's predecessor at Yale, was cut from a different bolt of Puritan cloth. Despite his Calvinist Christianity, Stiles had supported the French Revolution. He had once stopped a New Haven lawyer on the street, and exclaimed, "Have you heard the news? The French have entered Holland— they have planted the Tree of Liberty before the Stadtholder's palace. They will plant it before the palaces of all the princes of Europe. The people will live under its shade—I rejoice at it—I am a democrat—yea, I am a Jacobin—I glory in the name."[66] Some saw Dwight's 1794 pamphlet, *Discourse on the Genuineness and Authenticity of the New Testament*, as a brief on behalf of his candidacy for the presidency of the college. Dwight accepted the popularity of deism at Yale as a challenge. His heroes were George Washington and John Calvin, and with a program at once modernizing and Christianizing, he set out to transform Yale—and America.[67]

Upon his arrival, Dwight changed the language of publication for the college bylaws from Latin to English. He put the rules through a republican updating. When Dwight assumed office, underclassmen were still required to doff their hats within 5, 8, and 10 rods (one rod equals approximately 16.5 feet) of a faculty member, the exact distance varying with the faculty member's rank. Freshmen were allowed to speak when spoken to and, literally, served the seniors as hewers of wood and drawers of water. In the spirit of republicanism, Dwight began a long campaign, over the objections of the faculty, to do away with many aspects of this code. He expanded the curriculum, augmenting in particular the study of chemistry, mathematics, literature, philosophy, and theology. He successfully petitioned the legislature for £900 for the purchase of books by "modern authors" and won large donations from the Connecticut politician Oliver Wolcott, among others, for the library. During his presidency, the library more than doubled in size, to over 7,000 volumes.[68]

Dwight generated a national profile for Yale, and under his tenure the school produced two generations of professors, congressmen, and missionaries. Horace Bushnell claimed that "a very large share of the

---

66. Stiles quoted in Edmund Morgan, *American Heroes: Profiles of Men and Women Who Shaped Early America* (New York, 2009), p. 33; see also idem., "Ezra Stiles and Timothy Dwight," *Proceedings of the Massachusetts Historical Society* (Oct. 1957—Dec. 1960), pp. 101–117.

67. Cunningham, pp. 247, 302.

68. Ibid., pp. 247–248, 256.

colleges in our nation draw their lineage, not from Harvard. . . but from Yale." Bushnell specified Dartmouth, Princeton, Williams, Middlebury, Hamilton, Western Reserve, Jacksonville, and Athens University in Georgia as "planned. . . or in principal degree manned, by the graduates of Yale College and the sons of Connecticut." Princeton's first three presidents were Yale men. Yale graduates under Dwight's tenure ranged from Lyman Beecher to John C. Calhoun, both of whom counted Dwight as a mentor. Calhoun (class of '04) told a visitor to Congress that he "had seen the time when the natives of Connecticut, together with all the graduates of Yale College there collected, wanted only five of being a majority of that body." Well into the nineteenth century, Connecticut contributed to Congress a share of representatives and senators considerably larger than the proportion of her population.[69] The conspicuous role of Connecticut men in Congress and among America's college faculty resulted from the powerful machinery of the state school system, not just Yale. Yale, however, was the apex of Connecticut education, and Timothy Dwight, in addition to being its president, was the most well-known educator in America. Indeed, one of his admirers would later recall that in the two decades from 1790 to 1810, Dwight was "the most conspicuous man in New England, filling a larger space in the public eye, and exerting a greater influence than any other individual." Save for Daniel Webster that was true.[70]

Jeffersonians were given to imagining Dwight as the force behind great anti-egalitarian conspiracies. In 1800, the *Philadelphia Aurora*, a Jeffersonian newspaper, attacked the Federalists as "New England Illuminati united" to implement "hierarchy and aristocracy" and "a monarchy, controlled by Dr. Dwight." In 1801, *The American Mercury*, another Republican paper, alleged that Dwight had pushed Yale "into the hands of a party" and that he was scheming to consolidate "all power, both civil

---

69. In 1843, for example, 18 congressmen were native-born sons of Connecticut. Including those who were born out of state to emigrants from Connecticut, the number was 47. Massachusetts had 17. In proportion to its population, Massachusetts should have had 42. Nine congressmen were native-born to New Jersey. Proportionate to its population, it should have had 21. See Horace Bushnell, *Work and Play* (New York, 1881), vol. I, pp. 219–221. Six graduates of Yale, and one of Harvard, founded The College of New Jersey, later Princeton, and Yale gave Princeton its first three presidents. See Francis L. Broderick, "Pulpit, Physics, and Politics: The Curriculum of the College of New Jersey, 1746–1794," *William and Mary Quarterly*, Vol. 6, (January 1949), p. 46.

70. Cunningham, pp. 253, 255; Robert J. Imholt, "Timothy Dwight, Federalist Pope of Connecticut," *The New England Quarterly*, vol. 73, no. 3 (September 2000), pp. 386–411.

and ecclesiastical." In the late eighteenth and early nineteenth century, the *Philadelphia Aurora* and the *American Mercury* published dozens of attacks on Dwight and his alleged plots to gain power. The *Mercury* wrote that Dwight's students became missionaries so that they might hide their true designs behind the ministerial cloth and that they were in fact "political pimps." Dwight's missionaries went to the frontier to "gain a larger see," wrote the *Mercury*, for the Federalist Pope Timothy. To see the truth behind Yale religion, reported the *American Mercury*, one need only follow the money to reveal that they were "speculators" whose missionaries "received great wages," working for organizations that had accumulated "more capital than the biggest bank." Of the many charges leveled against Dwight's political program, the attack on the closeness of the missionary organizations and the bourgeoisie, in the form of the banks, was one of the most accurate, though it was hardly Dwight's sole doing.[71]

Dwight also provoked those within New England Protestantism. David Austin, a Congregationalist minister who had been a student at Yale during Dwight's time as a tutor, thought that Dwight's opposition to deists and freethinkers had led him astray. Austin charged that Dwight's obsession with Voltaire and the philosophes had caused him to lose sight of the true enemy, Catholic Rome. In the freethinkers' attacks, Austin hoped, Rome would suffer and Protestantism would gain. Dwight, he alleged, had mistaken the enemies of Satan for his servants. The New Milford, Connecticut, Congregationalist minister Stanley Griswold thought Dwight too political, too worldly. In an 1801 pamphlet, *Infidelity not the Only Enemy of Christ, or Hypocrisy and Antichrist Exposed*, Griswold chastised Dwight for caring more about what president a man believes in than what savior. John C. Ogden, a Princeton-educated Episcopalian, attacked Dwight's theology, his close relationship with Connecticut politicians, his administration of Yale, his imperious manners, and his patronage of missionary societies. Ogden even singled out Dwight's clothing as too ornate. The "ruffles. . . [and] garnet coloured coat and white under-dress" in which Dwight gave his sermons, wrote Ogden, gave away Dwight's papal ambitions. Austin and Ogden charged Dwight with "Calvinistic Popery," denounced his "caeseropapism," and enjoyed some success in tagging Dwight as "Pope Timothy" or the "Federalist Pope." Attacking Dwight's influence over the Connecticut clergy and press, Ogden wrote

---

71. John R. Fitzmier, *New England's Moral Legislator* (Bloomington, IN, 1998), pp. 64–65; Imholt, p. 403.

(mocking Dwight's *Greenfield Hill*) that in Connecticut, "no man can preach or speak but by permission of the Pope of Greenland."[72]

In fact, because it was so widely shared, Dwight's most radical political and religious act escaped his critics' censure. On July 4, 1798, for example, Dwight delivered an anti-libertarian sermon to the citizens of New Haven. He said that a US war with France had been predicted in the Book of Revelation and that it would usher in the millennium. It is worth comparing Dwight's sermon with his grandfather Jonathan Edwards's 1741 sermon "Sinners in the Hands of an Angry God." Both used the structure of the jeremiad to dramatize that salvation, though elusive, remained within reach. How to achieve salvation, what theologians call soteriology, had changed. In Edwards's sermon, "the souls of wicked men" were accountable to an omnipotent God, and the souls were individual souls. Edwards neither told congregants the fate of their individual souls nor consigned them to a collective fate. He speculated that if "some that are now present should. . . be in hell in a very short time," it would not be a "wonder." Edwards also told his congregants that "the souls of people at Suffield," a neighboring congregation and a different unit of church governance, were just as "precious" as their own.[73]

In Dwight's sermon, nations are the agents, and they have souls, which are either wicked or virtuous. France, Germany, Belgium, Spain, Portugal, and the Italian city-states had been corrupted by "unclean teachers, or teachers of unclean doctrines," principally the philosophes and the Jesuits, and were together conspiring "against the kingdom of God." The operative voice is the nationalist's first-person plural; in contrast to Edwards's sermon, individual agency has diminished, while responsibility to the collective has increased. Faithful Americans now find grace through obedience to the national mission. History, he said, evinced "glorious and wonderful proofs of divine protection" for America, and with these favors came responsibility. Since few citizens "can be concerned in settling systems of faith, moulding forms of government, regulating nations, or establishing empires," Dwight told listeners that they could contribute through "personal obedience and reformation." Individual moral behavior amounted to the "sum, of all national worth and prosperity." After all, Abraham had been "a simple husbandman"

---

72. Imholt, pp. 387–389, 397, 392, 394.

73. Jonathan Edwards, "Sinners in the Hands of an Angry God," reprinted in Clarence H. Faust and Thomas H. Johnson, eds., *Jonathan Edwards: Representative Selections, with Introduction, Bibliography and Notes* (New York, 1962), pp. 158, 170, 172, 171.

and his contributions to world history could not be doubted. With "union among ourselves, and unshaken adherence to the existing government," and perhaps "great sacrifices of property, of peace, and of life" in a holy war with France, " 'he who seeketh to save his life shall lose it, and he who loseth it. . . shall find it'. . . beyond the grave."[74] Borrowing Paine's famous words from *Common Sense*, he called the sermon "The Duty of Americans, at the Present Crisis," a choice that enraged Connecticut Democrats.[75]

In the early national period, Dwight was the face of establishment New England Protestantism and a polarizing figure. The charges against him ran a broad gamut and came from divergent quarters. The *American Mercury* and the *New London Bee* even charged that Dwight, who was an American nationalist before most any of the founding fathers, was a monarchist and a crypto-Tory who wanted to bring about reconciliation with Britain.[76] Along with Tom Paine and Aaron Burr, Dwight belonged to a small group of contemporary public figures who had the propensity to unhinge their opponents. The fact that he never held elected office probably helped some imagine that Dwight had developed grand conspiratorial designs or that he had already achieved vast, secret influence. In politics, Dwight was basically an old-fashioned Federalist, with a millennial inflection and an enthusiasm for American expansion. Though his influence never reached the systemic levels that some feared, it was real and broad, and included the missions movement. The bourgeoisie, not ministers or college presidents, would run the most important American missions, including the American Board of Commissioners for Foreign Missions, the American Bible Society, the American Tract Society, and others. Nonetheless, Dwight served as a bridge between establishment Protestantism and the missionary organizations. He inspired, and guided, many young men into missionary work. He expressed in some detail the social philosophy behind the missionary movement. For these reasons, *Greenfield Hill*, which is the fullest articulation of that social philosophy, is the most important of the Wits' writings.

Greenfield Hill has many pleasing and clever lines and some beautiful ones. Though brief in comparison to *Conquest of Canåan*, it is still a long

---

74. Ibid., pp. 29, 30, 17, 16, 25–26; Gellner, "Nationalism and High Cultures," in Hutchinson and Smith, eds., *Nationalism*, p. 63.

75. Dwight, *The Duty of Americans, at the Present Crisis, Illustrated in a Discourse, Preached on the Fourth of July, 1798* (New Haven, CT, 1798), pp. 7, 8–11; Silverman, pp. 69–80.

76. Imholt, p. 401.

poem (168 pages). There are also, however, moments such as Dwight's description of Horace as "desipient Horace," which provoked an otherwise friendly nineteenth-century critic to lament, "It might be supposed that in the whole range of English poetry there was no descriptive epithet so ludicrously pedantic." The pedantry of *Greenfield Hill* also makes it a richer document of the Federalist cultural program. The poem, for instance, makes liberal use of the unpoetical footnote, in which Dwight explains his literary references, expounds on his ideas, or provides substantiating evidence to political points. In one footnote, he compared "national honour," which was probably his life's concern, to a "soap-bubble." National honor, Dwight explained, was both as beautiful and as delicate as a soap bubble. What "powers suffice," he asked, that could imbue America with the finest beauty of which she was capable? She already has it, answered *Greenfield Hill*, in some of her "sacred institutions. . . mild laws. . . pure religion. . . morals uncorrupt. . . plain and honest manners." He asked Americans to "thyself revere! / Look not to Europe, for examples just." Instead, they need only look to Connecticut ("Hail, O hail / My much-loved native land! New Albion hail!") In another footnote, he explained that the success or failure of America's honor depended on the establishment of "national manners." He predicted that the nationalization of New England manners was imminent. "Negro slavery," he allowed, had enabled the plantation society of Virginia and South Carolina to also develop distinctive manners. There could, however, be no mistake, wrote Dwight, that the manners of New England were superior to those made possible by plantation society. Like many, Dwight believed slavery would decline and disappear, and he wrote movingly of that prospect:[77]

> Few objects more demand the attention of men of influence, in this country, than the establishment of national manners. There are but two, or three countries, in the United States, in which the manners have any thing like a general uniformity: the low country of Virginia, the low country of South Carolina, and New England. The manners of Virginia and South Carolina cannot be easily continued, without the continuance of the Negro slavery; an event, which can scarcely be expected. The manners of New England appear to be rapidly spreading through the American republic. When the enterprize, industry, oeconomy, morals, and happiness, of New

---

77. Dwight, *Greenfield Hill*, pp. 9–11.

England, especially of Connecticut, are attentively considered, the patriotic mind will perhaps find much more reason to rejoice in this prospect, than to regret it.[78]

Dwight detailed the bases for the superior manners of New England, describing them as "The noblest institutions man has seen." He listed the supremacy of law ("beholding no superior, but the law"), Protestant religiosity ("piety to God"), the commitment to education ("the nurturing school; in every village" and "Education opens, spreading far / Through the bold yeomanry"), and material comfort ("Thy granaries, and thy cellars" are "stor'd / With all the sweets of life").[79]

Dwight singled out for repeated praise New England's social equality, which he attributed to the lack of primogeniture. "No entail / The first-born lifting into bloated pomp," he wrote. Without a class of decadent and idle oldest sons, Dwight wrote, New England had been spared the "lust, and sloth, and pride, and rage" that afflicted European, and Southern, social relations. New England also lacked a class of dispossessed and desperate younger sons whose on-the-make errands fueled imperialist violence. Dwight described these younger sons as "hissing death," and hurrying "to gain a wigwam, built on Nootka Sound, / Or Falkland's fruitful isles." To Dwight's mind, the consequences of primogeniture on the social structure were difficult to exaggerate. It produced "wealth enormous" and "enormous want," making both "lazy sinecures" and "suffering toil" prevalent. It generated great landlords, who wore a "robe of useless pride" while "shivering thousands want beside." Because of primogeniture, Europe "in one palace sinks a thousand cots; / In one manor drowns a thousand lots." The extremes of wealth and poverty brought in its train "silly pomp" and trained men to adore "meanness." The decadent court society spawned both "lordly churches" and courtiers who spouted "phrenzied unbelief." It led to the idolatrous preeminence of fashion in Europe, the "frippery" by which men came to fall down before "a new head-dress" and to "worship" not God but "barbers, milliners, / Taylors, mantua-makers."[80]

Dwight devoted much of *Greenfield Hill*'s seven "books" to detailing the society of New England, primarily Massachusetts and Connecticut,

78. Ibid., pp. 170–171.

79. Ibid., pp. 33, 14–15.

80. Ibid., p. 19.

as a counterexample to Europe and the American South. Given the Reverend Dr. Timothy Dwight's deserved reputation as a figure in the history of American religion, his vivid and often-articulated sense of an active and purposeful God, and his frequent focus on "manners" and "taste," it is worth clarifying that, like other elite late eighteenth-century American intellectuals, his thought was rooted in political economy. Though the national evangelist perspective granted a central, indispensable place to religion, their vision was in the proper sense a social philosophy, growing out of political economy. Dispensing with the verse, Dwight made this clear in the unpoetical footnotes. "The peculiar prosperity of New England in general, and particularly of Massachusetts and Connecticut," he wrote, "arises from the equal division of property." He wanted the poem to "to exhibit the blessings, which flow from an equal division of property." The equal division of property was not for the national evangelists the order of equality that would become renowned through nineteenth-century socialism and communism. It simply meant that repudiating primogeniture would help every free, white man claim the fruits of his own labor. This, too, Dwight made clear in the footnotes:

> Wherever an *equal division of property* is mentioned, in this Work, the Reader is requested to remember, that that state of things only is intended, in which every citizen is secured in the avails of his industry and prudence, and in which property descends, by law, in equal shares, to the proprietor's children.[81]

From this "heav'n-laid foundation," which included the "universal establishment of schools, and their peculiar manner of supporting the gospel," *Greenfield Hill* rendered in verse the most just and promising society in history.[82]

Without the circumspection that characterized the way members of the political class spoke about American empire, *Greenfield Hill* explained that America would top the greatest empires the world had seen. She would outshine the French, British, Ottoman, and Spanish empires, as well as India and Persia:

---

81. Ibid., pp. 171–172.

82. Ibid. p. 15.

Round the mild year, let Albion's verdure run;
Let Gallia's opening vines allure the sun;
O'er brighter realms, the Turkish crescent rise,
Wash'd by fair seas, and warm'd by vernal skies;
Let richer Ind, and prouder Persia, tell
The diamond cavern, and the pearly shell;
Peruvia vaunt her streams, in silver roll'd,
And sunny Darien lift her hills of gold.
Here the best blessings of those far-fam'd climes,
Pure of their woes, and whiten'd from their crimes,
Shall blend with nobler blessings, all my own;
Here first th' enduring reign of Peace be known.[83]

A generation before Thomas Hart Benton and Daniel Webster envisioned a United States that stretched to the Rocky Mountains, Dwight wrote about the United States incorporating California. But Dwight imagined California not as a western endpoint, but as a launching pad by which to take Asia:

All hail, thou western world! By heaven design'd
Th' example bright, to renovate mankind.
Soon shall thy sons across the mainland roam;
And claim, of far Pacific shores, their home;
Their rule, religion, manners, arts, convey,
And spread their freedom to the Asian sea.[84]

New England was the nursery of this superior empire. Aided by the equal descent of property, it was, Dwight thought, united in equality: "Here every class (if classes those we call, / Where one extended class embraces all / All mingling, as the rainbow's beauty blends / Unknown where every hue begins or ends)." New Englanders recognized the supremacy of rule by law over the tyranny of rule by men: "The voice of scepter'd Law wide realms obey." Only in New England had the diffusion of education and religion produced an enlightened general population: "Refinement of the heart / Illumes the general mass," wrote Dwight.[85]

---

83. Ibid., p. 151.

84. Ibid., p. 52.

85. Ibid., pp. 36, 151, 16.

In contrast to Europe's rapacious princes and predatory landlords, Dwight envisioned an American empire ruled by a simple, practical, and civic-minded middle class. Protestant ministers, businessmen, doctors, and lawyers would direct a more just and egalitarian empire:

> *Divines, and lawyers, hence,*
> *Physicians, statesmen, all with wisdom fraught,*
> *And learning, suited to the use of life,*
> *And minds, by business, sharpen'd into sense,*
> *Sagacious of the duty, and the weal,*
> *Of man, spring numberless; and knowledge hence*
> *Pours its salubrious streams, through all the spheres*
> *Of human life. Its bounds, and generous scope,*
> *Hence Education opens, spreading far*
> *Through the bold yeomanry, that fill thy climes,*
> *Views more expanded, generous, just, refin'd,*
> *Than other nations know.*[86]

Their middle-class affinity for education meant that America would lift, rather than oppress, the "mass of man" falling under its dominion. China and South America would convert. The triumph would be God's, and the world would unite in peace:

> *From the long torpor startled China wake;*
> *Her chains of misery rous'd Peruvia break;*
> *Man link to man; with bosom bosom twine;*
> *And one great bond the house of Adam join:*
> *The sacred promise full completion know,*
> *And peace, and piety, the world o'erflow.*[87]

The redeemer nation and the millennial empire faced threats, but they were not what one might expect. Other than lending more credence to the charge of some Connecticut Protestants that he had become blind to the continued threat of their historic enemy, it is difficult to know what

---

86. Ibid., p. 16.

87. Ibid., pp. 52–53.

to make of the fact that in *Greenfield Hill*, "Rome" is the classical Roman Empire, not the Vatican.[88]

In Dwight's view, the US mission faced two threats. Both had the power to turn the nation into a fundamentally different society from that embodied by Connecticut and Massachusetts. The first was the plantation slavery of the South. Slavery in the North was wrong, too, but it did not approach the barbarism of that found in the South and the West Indies. In New England, a slave:

> *toils, 'tis true; but shares his master's toil;*
> *With him, he feeds the herd, and trims the soil;*
> *Helps to sustain the house, with clothes, and food,*
> *And takes his portion of the common good.*[89]

Dwight wrote that slaves in New England received better treatment than those on plantations, who were "dragged, with. . . galling chain" and "hung. . . on th' infernal crane." Plantation slaves wore "memorials hellish of the marking brand" and were deformed and tortured with "pincers" and "scalding oil." He condemned all slavery as the "laurel of the Infernal mind, / Proud Satan's triumph over lost mankind." Perhaps thinking of his nemesis Jefferson, Dwight called any defense of slavery "gangrene of the reasoning mind." In a footnote, Dwight contended that it was slavery that degraded people of African descent: "The black children are generally sprightly and ingenious, until they become conscious of their slavery. This usually happens, when they are 4, 5, or 6 years of age," he wrote. "From that time, they usually sink into stupidity, or give themselves up to vice." Moreover, slavery, but especially plantation slavery, degraded everyone involved, falsely elevating masters and gratuitously subjugating laborers. Unlike the West Indies and the American South, New England offered a society, "Where none are slaves, or lords; but all are men."[90]

Greenfield Hill gave three reasons that slavery was wrong. First, it separated work from its benefit, denying the man, or woman, the right to the fruit of his or her labor. Second, slavery distorted the natural equality of all men before God, their common descent from Adam, and their

---

88. See, for instance, pp. 77, 93, 157.

89. Ibid., p. 37.

90. Ibid., pp. 37, 38, 173, 153.

shared, sinful human nature; all men were by nature depraved, all men's hearts were black, Dwight maintained. Finally, slavery led to gross violence. Because Dwight wrote *Greenfield Hill*, as he put it, to move "many persons, who would scarcely look at a logical discussion," the grotesque physical abuses of slavery received the most attention. He hoped the revulsion to slavery would therefore be "more deeply felt, and more lastingly remembered" by more people.[91] Some of the scenes did indeed depict a memorable gruesomeness; Dwight's description of a slave forced to eat his own flesh, for instance, and that of a domestic who had her throat cut for spilling gravy on a guest:

> *Why shrinks yon slave, with horror, from his meat?*
> *Heavens! 'tis his flesh, the wretch is whipp'd to eat.*
> *Why streams the life-blood from that female's throat?*
> *She sprinkled gravy on a guest's new coat!*[92]

In a footnote, Dwight wrote that he was reporting, not inventing, these episodes of grisly sadism. In sum, *Greenfield Hill* has over 14 pages of footnotes. Perhaps nothing more simply betrays the mistrust Dwight had in literature than the dozens of footnotes explaining, justifying, elaborating, and substantiating. The poem also has headlines summarizing the contents of the verse, many of which, *"Public Property employed for the Public Benefit"* and *"Penal Administrations improved by Benevolence,"* for example, suggest a policy paper rather than a poem. Neither Dwight's relationship to poetry, nor his vision of his role in America, was as simple as his prefatory remark, "'Allow me to make the Songs of a nation,' said a wise man, 'and who will may make their Laws,'" would have it. His ambitions were too broad, and his sense of the possibility in the historical moment too urgent for him to feel truly confident with poetry. Though he spent 20 years trying to nationalize Americans through poetry, he must also have possessed some inchoate understanding that neoclassical verse would be neither the way to effect change in nineteenth-century America nor the genre of its people.[93]

Understanding the essential incompatibility between Dwight's literary and political ambitions helps show the continuity of purpose in his turn

---

91. Ibid., p. 7.

92. Ibid., p. 40.

93. Ibid., p. 148.

from poetry to institution building. *Greenfield Hill* also reveals an irony in how this turn unfolded, at least in regard to the mission movement. The slave society that Dwight described as a threat to America would in fact become powerful, dominating American politics until 1860. But Dwight also feared the bourgeoisie. In *Greenfield Hill*, he made clear that they were also an internal threat to the triumph of the New England way. Though Dwight was not a great poet, he could be a very acute social observer. Like the planter class, the bourgeoisie would prosper in nineteenth-century America. In fact, they would run the most important missionary organizations, enterprises that began as Dwight's dream, not theirs. *Greenfield Hill* portrays their class as immoral and degenerate, exerting a ruinous influence on almost every aspect of society. The rich evaded their responsibilities to the common good. Addressing the New England farmer and merchant, Dwight wrote, "Thou pay'st the tax, the rich man will not pay; / Thou feed'st the poor, the rich man drives away." The rich connived for wars but lacked the courage to fight them: "Thy sons, for freedom, hazard limbs, and life, / While pride applauds, but shuns the manly strife." The rich held in contempt the simple joys of life: family, hospitality, neighborliness, piety: "Yes! let the proud despise, the rich deride / These humble joys, to Competence allied." Again a footnote put the matter in plain prose instead of verse: "Men in middling circumstances appear greatly to excel the rich, in piety, charity, and public spirit; nor will a critical observer of human life hesitate to believe, that they enjoy more happiness."[94] The "Noblest manners" belonged to the middling men and women, those who were neither poor nor rich and were "competent," that is, dependent on neither man nor market. "Where Competence, in full enjoyment, flows," wrote Dwight, "Where man least vice, and highest virtue, knows." No one, not even Jefferson, cast the small farmer and independent tradesman in as vital a role as Dwight, who wrote, "And every joy, to Competence allied" and "O Competence, thou bless'd by Heaven's decree." He who lived "the calm, the meek, the useful life" was by nature "the friend of man, the foe of strife." The repeated message of *Greenfield Hill* was that a society dominated by middling types was the only just kind. America's historic opportunity derived, in part, from the fact that "the good, the humble, thrive, / And in *this sweet republic* live." The poem provides dozens of such expressions on the moral superiority of the middling classes to the rich.[95]

---

94. Ibid., pp. 32–33, 173.

95. Ibid., pp. 151, 153, 33–34, 76.

When depicting either a just and vibrant society of middling types or a degenerate society dominated by the rich, both Dwight and Trumbull found women's roles powerful shorthand. Europe's rot was evident in her "brothels, circling, with their tainted walls" and her "Unnumber'd female outcasts." European society supported, "in countless herds, the mistress vile." Such was the hypocrisy of the rich that the mistresses lacked the decency to be ashamed and instead affected "matron sanctity."[96] On the other hand, Dwight wrote that New England women "are inferior to none, in the world. They blend the useful, and the pleasing, the refined, and the excellent, into a most delightful, and dignified union." Women's social roles and the mode in which men and women interacted "form a very respectable branch of our national manners."[97] In turn, some of Trumbull and Dwight's most vivid attacks on bourgeois society took the form of contempt for the social power that bourgeois domestic life could accord women. In 1771, Trumbull criticized the influence that "ladies of a certain age" held over what he called "tea table" society. Trumbull's "Advice to Ladies of a Certain Age" alleged that the "subject world obey, / Obsequious to thy sovereign sway."[98] Slander and malign gossip, wrote Trumbull, stemmed from the jealousy of aged women for the beauty of youthful ones:

> *Those haughty airs of face and mind,*
> *Departed beauty leaves behind.*
> . . .
> *The jealous glance of rival rage,*
> *The sourness and the rust of age.*[99]

They spoke "venom," he wrote, because they wished to drown out the sound of "the croaking raven's throat." The raven's note was loud because "death's dire omens swell the note."[100] Driven by envy of the young and fear of death, the "ladies of a certain age" held court in parlors, where their gossip slandered the innocent and destroyed reputations:

---

96. Ibid., p. 18.

97. Ibid., pp. 182–183.

98. John Trumbull, "Advice to Ladies of a Certain Age," *The Poetical Works of John Trumbull*, pp. 175, 178.

99. Ibid., p. 172.

100. Ibid., pp. 175, 173.

> *Now at tea-table take thy station,*
> *Those shambles vile of reputation,*
> *Where butchere'd characters and stale*
> *Are day by day exposed for sale:*
> *Then raise the floodgates of thy tongue,*
> *And be the peal of scandal rung;*[101]

From their idle domestic life, perhaps addled by drink ("She takes her glass; before her eyes / Imaginary beauties rise"), they succumbed to character assassination:

> *While malice tunes thy voice to rail,*
> *And whispering demons prompt the tale—*
> *Yet hold thy hand, restrain thy passion,*
> *Thou cankerworm of reputation;*
> . . .
> *Let other's faults and crimes alone,*
> *Survey thyself and view thine own.*[102]

He lamented that in this society the "foes" to the ladies of the tea table were "so feeble and so few." Trumbull advised a different course. They should "avoid the sland'rous tongue" and turn from judging others to self-examination while assuming a bland, pleasant outward demeanor. "Let soft good humour, mildly gay," he wrote, "Gild the calm evening of your day." It would be more becoming, he wrote, if they took a quiet, inconspicuous exit from life: "Go, sink, unnoticed and unseen, / Forgot, as though thou ne'er hadst been." At the time he wrote "Advice to Ladies of a Certain Age," Trumbull was 21 years old. This impulse to tell people three or four times their age what to do helped bring many young men with an authoritarian streak into the missionary ranks.[103]

Dwight's *Greenfield Hill* expressed the same fear of and contempt for what Trumbull called the "sovereign sway" that well-to-do ladies could hold over society. Dwight versified on the matter under the header: *"What is not, and what is, a social female visit."* A healthy "social female visit" is

---

101. Ibid., p. 175.

102. Ibid.

103. Ibid., p. 178.

a bit ambiguous, but Dwight portrayed it as youth engaged in innocent, outward activity: "Yon cheerful group of females passes by!" Their "hearts, attun'd to social joy," focused on a "friendly visit to some neighbouring fair." They moved in a "lovely train" from which "neatness glistens." The overall impression was one of inimitable "Bright charm!"[104] Trumbull had named the tea table as the crucible of bourgeois social life and called them "ladies of a certain age." Dwight set their reign in "the drawing room" and called them "dames of dignified renown" who were "Rever'd alike in country, and in town." He described their drawing room domain as at best stifling: "To sit, to curb, to toss, with bridled mien, / Mince the scant speech, and lose a glance between." More likely than simple discomfort, however, drawing room society led one into immoral activity both painful and destructive.[105] In perhaps *Greenfield Hill's* most visceral writing, Dwight described domestic life in bourgeois society permitting an unnatural, cruel assessment of individuals. In contrast to the Puritan tradition of self-examination, the ladies' concerns remained superficial. Filling out the almost diabolical scene, the "revered dames" held court over Chinese tea and card games:

> Or sit, in silent solitude, to spy
> Each little failing, with malignant eye;
> Or chatter, with incessancy of tongue,
> Careless, if kind, or cruel, right, or wrong;
> To trill of us, and ours, of mine, and me,
> Our house, our coach, our friends, our family,
> While all th' excluded circle sit in pain,
> And glance their cool contempt, or keen disdain:
> T' inhale, from proud Nanking, a sip of tea,
> And wave a curtsey trim, and flirt away:
> Or waste, at cards, peace, temper, health and life,
> Begin with sullenness, and end in strife,
> Lose the rich feast, by friendly converse given,
> And backward turn from happiness, and heaven.[106]

---

104. Dwight, *Greenfield Hill*, p. 48.

105. Ibid., pp. 30, 48.

106. Ibid., p. 49.

"Stiff brocade" and the "pink'd beau" lady were the symbols of this degenerate society. A lady in full dress, wrote Dwight, could not be happy.[107]

Happy women, in a healthy society, wore humble, simple clothes. "I do not remember ever to have seen a lady, in full dress," he wrote, "who appeared to be so happy, or to behave so easily, and gracefully, as when she was moderately dressed." The highly artificial formal attire of well-to-do women symbolized luxury and insincerity. More alarmingly, character grew to fit the dress: "Toil, taste, and fancy, are put to exertion, to contrive, and to adjust, the dress, which is expected highly to ornament the person; and the same exertion, appears to be used in contriving, and fashioning, manners, which may become the dress." Happily, New England remained a bastion of virtue, its women could "not yet tell a diamond, from a spade."[108]

Twenty-five years before he published *Greenfield Hill*, while a tutor at Yale, Dwight had helped lead the class of 1769 to wear homespun at commencement. In 1794, about to become president of Yale, he again turned to its symbolic potential. In a just, Christian society, young women would not be gusseted in frilly bows and stiff brocades. They would be working at home, producing homespun for the whole family:

> *Your daughters find a sweet employ,*
> *And, singing, turn the wheel with joy:*
> *With homespun rich the loom be gay;*
> *Your households clad in bright array;*
> *And female toil more profit yield,*
> *Than half the labours of the field.*[109]

Women should also excel at small-scale husbandry. "White are the swine; the poultry plump and large," he wrote, "For every creature thrives, beneath her charge." Dwight versified about the New England wife's cider and flax production, her maintenance of a rich granary and ample woodpile, her attentive cleaning of the furniture and dishes, her regular shining of the pewter, and her keeping the "linen white. . . to assure the traveler a refreshing night." She would be rewarded in the afterlife, "For

---

107. Ibid., p. 48.

108. Ibid., pp. 174, 45.

109. Ibid., p. 128. See also p. 132.

heaven will always toils like these regard," while her husband, from her efforts, "daily saw his wealth increase." A lively debate exists among historians about the relationship of such home production to the development of a capitalist economy and a market society.[110]

From a theoretical perspective, the society dominated by middling types engaged in some kinds of home production, the kind of society idealized by Dwight and the Wits, is a short step away from a bourgeois, market economy. The trust, discipline, and order of such a society also helps enable the formation of market relations.[111] In social life, however, small differences can make a big difference, and to the Wits a market society was neither desirable nor just. Dwight advised farmers to take the first profitable price they found. He compared playing the market to a dog chasing its shadow:

> *When first the market offers well,*
> At once your yearly produce sell.
> *A higher price you wait in vain,*
> *And ten times lose, where once you gain.*
> *The dog, that at the shadow caught,*
> *Miss'd all he had, and all he sought.*[112]

Time and again, he turned to women, more specifically women's social roles, as symbolic of the vices that accompany riches. Women must be turned from "fashions, cards, and plays." If these "vile forms" and "idle follies" were not repudiated, men and women alike would become "victims" to "show, to flattery."[113] To "fix the heart" of both boys and girls, Dwight wrote, Americans should raise girls to hate high fashion and love plain virtue. Young women must be taught:

> *The peacock's gaudry to despise,*
> *And view vain sports with parents' eyes.*

---

110. Ibid., pp. 45–46; Winifred Rothenberg, "The Invention of American Capitalism: The Economy of New England in the Federal Period," in Peter Temin, ed., *Engines of Enterprise: An Economic History of New England* (Cambridge, MA: Harvard University Press, 2000).

111. Robert L. Heilbroner, *The Worldly Philosophers: The Lives, Times, and Ideas of the Great Economic Thinkers* (New York, 1999), pp. 18–42.

112. Dwight, *Greenfield Hill*, p. 128.

113. Ibid., p. 165.

On things of use to fix the heart,
And gild, with every graceful art.
Teach them, with neatest, simplest dress,
A neat, and lovely mind t'express.[114]

The Wits wanted to bring the "good news" of their America to the rest of the nation and to the world, to evangelize the nation. Their America was an idealized version of Massachusetts and Connecticut (two states which, in 1790, ranked fourth and eighth out of 16 states in population).

The contours of life in the Wits' empire were clear enough. It was a parochial vision. There would be no primogeniture, no planter class, no slavery, no aristocracy, and no bourgeoisie. Its citizenry would consist of middle-class Reformed Protestants, independent men and hard-working women, who eschewed fashion, theater, cards, and other vices. Social equality resulting from broad property ownership, universal literacy, an educated populace, and strong civic participation would be the distinguishing features. Their support for the Alien and Sedition Acts demonstrated to the world what their writings, as well as the history of New England, had already made clear: they did not hold a broad range of individual freedom of expression to be of primary importance. Nor did they take criticism very well. They were pompous and pedantic in ways that could work within certain hierarchical relationships—teacher-student, minister-congregation, master-apprentice—but that made it very difficult for them to sustain a friendship with someone from whom they differed. The shine of their righteousness was often clouded by self-righteousness. Their immense pride in the social equality of New England did not preclude them from also being elitists of a type now so discredited as to challenge the imagination. When, in 1797, for example, Vermonters elected to Congress Irishman Matthew Lyon, who had arrived in America in 1765 as an indentured servant, the Wits verified: "This beast within a few short years / Was purchased for a yoke of steers; / But now wise Vermonters say / He's worth six hundred cents a day." Their elitism was perhaps most clearly on display in their writings on the War for Independence. The Wits were visionary nationalists; six of them were veterans of the Continental Army. David Humphreys received a sword from Congress, for bravery at Yorktown. They wrote a lot about war, including battles and their heroes. The consummate symbol of modern nationalism is military—the tomb of

---

114. Ibid., p. 132.

the Unknown Soldier. Many nations have such moments. The anonymity of the soldier's remains helps to represent the mystical substance inside all members of the nation. It never occurred to the Wits, however, to render the common soldier in monumental or representative terms. All their heroes were presidents or officers, preferably generals.[115]

On the other hand, they were also serious and honest men given to self-examination. They brought a vital drive to everything they did. While Trumbull's *M'Fingal* may have drawn on stereotypes about Native Americans and people of African descent, the Wits, unlike their Jeffersonian (and later Jacksonian) opponents, were not racists. That is, they did not find in the discourse of race a solution to the challenge that profound inequality posed to American ideals.[116] In this respect they were out of step with the American nineteenth century. While pro-slavery men ransacked scriptures for threads out of which to spin separate origins stories for white and black men, and anti-slavery men conceded natural differences but argued for mitigations in the cruelty of slavery, the Wits held to the common origin, and the inherent sinfulness, of all mankind. In his epic poem, *The Columbiad*, Joel Barlow has Hesper, a guardian genius guiding Columbus to America, warn Columbus against the notion that there were multiple Adams. Columbus asks Hesper if the "war painted chiefs" he sees in the Americas "boast a lineage with the race of man," if "these forgotten shores and useless tides / Have form'd them different from the world besides?" Hesper disabuses Columbus of the error of separate origins or unequal fates. "Think not," he answers, "in all the range of man, / That different pairs each different cast began." It would be equally wrong to conclude, continues Hesper, that "tribes distinct, by signal marks confest, / Were born to serve or subjugate the rest." In Barlow's view, "a common source all nations claim" and that "tints of face / In different lands diversify the race." Hesper then takes several hundred lines, most of Book II of *The Columbiad*, telling an elaborate, alternative creation story by which mankind emerged from classical Greece

---

115. On M. Lyon, see F. Sheldon, "The Pleiades of Connecticut," *The Atlantic Monthly*, (Boston, MA, 1865), vol. XV, p. 191; Anderson, *Imagined Communities*, pp. 9–10. John Adams is the only founding father mentioned in Barlow's "Vision of Columbus."

116. Barbara J. Fields, "Slavery, Race, and Ideology in the United States of America," New Left Review and "Of Rogues and Geldings," *American Historical Review*, vol. 108, no. 5 (December 2003), 1397–1405.

and in which the European conquest of the Americas involved historic depredation and slaughter.[117]

To explain the degraded condition of the enslaved and of Native Americans, the Wits did not resort to race. Rather, they maintained, oppression begat immorality. Dwight even thought that the ascendant secular vocabulary obscured the true cause of social ills: poverty, he wrote, was "only another name for disgrace," that is, the want of saving grace. Attaining grace, becoming proper Christians, would admit anyone to full equality. The "greatest obstacle to Christianizing the Indians," wrote Dwight, "is now, as it has usually been, their riveted persuasion, that the British Colonists, have aimed at. . . the acquisition of their lands." Unfortunately, Dwight wrote, the Indians' aversion to the Anglo way of life was "founded on too unequivocal and shameful proof" of Anglo-American deceit and destruction.[118]

Dwight made harsh observations about the pathetic state of American Indians, writing that the Indian "leads the life, not of a man, but of a snail; and is rather a moving vegetable than a rational being." He added, however, that their "calamity" would afflict "all other people in like circumstances." Their "minds," he wrote, "are natively of the same structure with those of Frenchmen or Englishmen." Their degradation derived "from the want, not of capacity, but of inclination" and they lacked inclination because Americans had thrown them into a degraded state. The fact that they were not proper Christians set in motion a pernicious cycle of immorality to which their oppressors then pointed as justification for continued abuse. In regard to slavery, Dwight took the same stand. Enslavement, he said, made for a life of "sloth, prodigality, poverty, ignorance, and vice." Responsibility to right this wrong, he said, lay with the children of slaveholders. They had it in their power to give to the enslaved "knowledge, industry, economy, good habits, moral and religious instruction, and all the means of eternal life." People of African descent, he told an audience at a Connecticut school for Negro girls, were the victims of slaveholders' sin; they were not "weaker, or worse, by nature." In 1788, Dwight purchased a slave, Naomi. True to his word, Dwight employed her as a domestic until

---

117. On Hesper's revelation to Columbus, see Barlow, *The Columbiad*, Book II, quotes from pp. 40, 41, 45.

118. Dwight, *Travels in New-England and New-York*, vol. III (London, 1823), p. 20; Dwight, *Greenfield Hill*, p. 177.

her work had repaid her purchase price, then manumitted her. He was an early and consistent supporter of the Connecticut anti-slavery society.[119]

It is not hard to see the beginnings of abolitionism in the Wits' combination of anti-slavery, self-scrutiny, and sense of divine justice. Later in life, Philip Freneau would become an abolitionist, but well after the Revolution (1792) the Jeffersonian poet and newspaper editor was still accusing political opponents, including Federalists, of plots to enslave Americans. Tom Paine's *Rights of Man* outraged Federalists, Freneau wrote, because it upset their "royal plan." Their alleged plan, Freneau wrote, was to establish a hereditary aristocracy that would, for most Americans, amount to slavery:

> *Thus briefly sketched the sacred RIGHTS OF MAN,*
> *How inconsistent with the ROYAL PLAN!*
> *Which for itself exclusive honor craves,*
> *Where some are masters born, and millions slaves.*[120]

The Wits were American exceptionalists, too, but, for them, the contingency of exceptionalism was more likely to turn on what Americans did about the millions who were actual slaves. Barlow's *Columbiad* identified slavery as the potentially fatal contradiction at the heart of the republic. Freneau had claimed that so long as it was "without a king," America would remain "the guardian of the Rights of Man." Barlow thought that the question of Americans' relationship to "the rights of man" revolved around slavery and stood poised between hypocrisy and opportunity: "Ah, would you not be slaves, with lords and kings, / Then be not masters; there the danger springs." Ending chattel slavery, wrote Barlow, was in Americans' own interest because "tyrants are never free" and "all masters must be tyrants soon or late."[121]

The vitality of the Wits' hatred of slavery flowed neither from any argument about self-interest, nor from liberal ideas about the right to own the fruits of one's labor, but from simple moral outrage. Whereas the Haitian Revolution filled Southern planters with fears of their annihilation as a

---

119. Ibid. pp. 23, 24; n.a., "Political Correctness Runs Amok at Yale University," *The Journal of Blacks in Higher Education*, vol. 37 (Autumn 2002), p. 44.

120. Philip Freneau, *Poems Written and Published during the American Revolutionary War* (Philadelphia, 1809), vol. II, p. 295.

121. Joel Barlow, *The Columbiad* (Washington City, 1825), p. 279.

class, Barlow imagines American slavery provoking the destruction of both American continents. In *The Columbiad*, Atlas, the guardian genius of Africa, castigates Americans for hypocrisy, calling them "a strange ungenerous race, / Enslave my tribes, and each fair world disgrace." Barlow may have become, in the view of other Wits, a pagan, but for him "disgrace" retained its theological potency. Atlas accuses Americans of timidity: "the bolt [of freedom is] ill placed in thy forbearing hand" and warns that continued hypocrisy may deliver "wide vengeance on their lawless land." Invoking Tom Paine, Barlow's Atlas calls on Americans to match their deeds to their words:

> *Enslave my tribes! Then boast their cantons free,*
> *Preach faith and justice, bend the sainted knee,*
> *Invite all men their liberty to share,*
> *Seek public peace, defy the assaults of war.*
> . . .
> *Enslave my tribes! What, half mankind imban,*
> *Then read, expound, enforce the rights of man!*[122]

His admonitions ignored, masculine Atlas appeals to a personified, feminine Earth. Together, Earth and Atlas deliver awful destruction on North and South America. Atlas stokes subterranean fires and the Earth swells a massive wave out of her "wallowing womb." The wave descends on the Western Hemisphere, folding rocks as if they were paper and destroying "your curst continent. . . scattering wide / Rocks, mountains nations, o'er the swallowing tide." When the cataclysm has subsided, the Atlantic and the Pacific have united to bury the Americas: "Two oceans dasht in one!" The new ocean "climbs and roars, / And seeks in vain the exterminated shores." Barlow describes a lone "bald eagle" flying above where the Americas used to be. She "skims alone the sky" before finding a "cavern'd crag, her solitary rest," an on outcropping of Pambamarca, an Ecuadorian mountain that has escaped total submersion.[123]

To Barlow, the annihilation of the Americas was not a grandiose punishment for American slavery. He believed that slavery presented Americans with a test as important to world history as that which the forbidden fruit had to Adam and Eve. By the time he rewrote *The Vision of*

---

122. Steven Blakemore, *Joel Barlow's Columbiad: A Bicentennial Reading* (Knoxville, TN, 2007), pp. 229–233.

123. Barlow, *Columbiad*, pp. 276, 277.

Columbus (1787) into *The Columbiad* (1807), Barlow had become the apostate of the Connecticut Wits. In *Columbiad*, therefore, the modern version of the Fall of Man and the destruction of Paradise come about at the hands of classical, pagan figures of Atlas and Earth, rather than by the Christian God. Barlow had been a minister licensed by the state of Connecticut and a chaplain in the Continental Army. In 1788, he accepted a position as a land agent, an assignment that took him to Paris. Two years later, in England, under the tutelage of Tom Paine, Mary Wollstonecraft, Joseph Priestley, and others, Barlow abandoned the Wits' blend of Protestantism and Federalism and embraced deism and revolution. From Europe, he became a foe of both the Washington and Adams administrations. After two years in England, he returned to Paris, where he made a fortune in securities speculation, was made a citizen of the French Republic, and became a friend and patron of Robert Fulton, the inventor of steamships. In 1793, he introduced Jacobins on the Continent to an English song satirizing "God Save the King." It has sometimes been wrongly attributed to Barlow. The tune, which became popular among Continental radicals, promised that "great George's poll / Shall in the basket roll." It looked forward to the day when "all the world, like France, / O'er tyrants' graves shall dance." It was called "God Save the Guillotine" and it began:

> *God save the guillotine!*
> *Till England's king and queen*
> *Her power shall prove;*
> *Till each anointed knob*
> *Affords a clipping job*
> *Let no rude halter rob*
> *The guillotine.*[124]

While Paine was imprisoned in France, Barlow worked to help Paine's *Age of Reason* get published. He also wrote and published *Advice to the Privileged Orders* (1792), in which he called for abolishing religion, primogeniture, the death penalty, standing armies, colonies, property requirements for the franchise, and hereditary privileges. A "general revolution" of "irresistible" force, he wrote, was already underway and it would lead to a new age of equality and happiness among men. Some critics have

---

124. Benson John Lossing, *The Pictorial Field-Book of the War of 1812* (New York, 1869), p. 94.

called *Advice to the Privileged Orders* a more concise and literary version of Paine's *Age of Reason*. It won more favor, in Europe, than his poetry ever did in America. Later, when Paine's reputation in America was low (1809), Barlow showed some courage in writing for publication that Paine had possessed "an uncommon share of original genius" and been "among the brightest and most undeviating luminaries of the age."[125]

Assisting the much-hated Paine in advancing irreligion was not the bitterest pill Barlow delivered to his erstwhile Connecticut brethren. At the end of 1795, James Monroe, the American ambassador to France, sent Barlow to Algiers, as consul, in order to negotiate a treaty with the Barbary states. Proving himself an adept diplomat, Barlow secured the release of American prisoners and produced the Treaty of Tripoli. Article 11 included the historic statement, "the Government of the United States of America is not, in any sense, founded on the Christian religion." President John Adams signed the treaty and sent it to the US Senate, where, in June 1797, it passed unanimously. For Dwight, it was all too much. He made his own translation of the Psalms to replace that of his wayward protégé and, with ceremony, removed portraits of Barlow from Yale.[126]

Though his Jacobinism and deism made it hard for the Wits to appreciate the continuities, Barlow's radicalism bore clear stamps of Connecticut Congregationalism. *The Columbiad*'s denunciation of slavery, as grand and scathing as any in American letters to that time, was more consistent with Christian Federalism than with Jeffersonian nationalism. *The Columbiad* also describes a global future that is one of the strangest pieces of writing from the early republic, an atheistic millennium presided over by a world government. It would be catalyzed by Americans ("thy swelling pinions led the trackless way") who, somewhat like New Englanders, promoted commerce, shipping, engineering, civic works, and the arts. Order would prevail: "One centered system, one all ruling soul / Live through the parts and regulate the whole." The "tongues of nations" would "blend" until "one pure language through the world extend." A great council of elderly married men, "long rows of reverend sires sublime," would rule in benevolent and unchallenged sovereignty, presided over by a Washington-like "sire elect shining in peerless grandeur." The august committee would hold their sessions in

---

125. A. L. Ford, *Joel Barlow* (New York, 1971) pp. 109–115.

126. Blakemore, *Joel Barlow's Columbiad*, p. 235. In 1784, when Connecticut leaders' nationalism led them to abandon the English Congregationalist Isaac Watts's translations

Mesopotamia in a "sacred mansion" with soaring golden spires and a solar fire in the center:

> *On rocks adamant the walls ascend*
> *Tall columns heave, and sky-like arches bend;*
> *Bright o'er the golden roof the glittering spires*
> *Far in the concave meet the solar fires;*
> *Four blazing fronts, with gates unfolding high,*
> *Look with immortal splendor round the sky.*

Envoys from around the world would travel to the mansion's central court. There, beneath a statue of the Genius of the Earth, each envoy would lay an "idol," a symbol of "all destructive things." These idols, Barlow wrote, included a sword, a crown, a crescent, and a cross. Even as a radical, Barlow wrote about an imperial reign on a cosmic scale, and with a level of social and technical detail unlike any in American politics or letters, save for the visions of the Connecticut Wits.[127]

Elements of *The Columbiad*'s imperial program could have been found in Trumbull and Dwight's Yale commencement addresses of four decades earlier, or in Dwight's *Greenfield Hill*. The "state of the arts and sciences" were the finest and final measure of a society. In both, education was the unavoidable path to achievement. Nations, wrote Barlow, "are educated, like a single child. They only require a longer time and a greater number of teachers." Barlow praised Harvard, Yale, Columbia, Dartmouth, Princeton, Brown, and William and Mary, and foresaw American scientists and artists uniting with the "torch of science flaming" and the "canvas and the lyre" in hand. Together, this "sapient band" of American scientists and artists would embark to "world after world" where they would "lead, light, and allure" mankind, raising colleges "on every shore." They would teach the importance of civic technology, in particular canals, and bring with them advanced "medical and political knowledge." Everywhere, they would work toward the "advancement of physical and moral science." An

---

of the Psalms for an American vernacular version, Dwight and other members of the Connecticut establishment successfully backed Barlow for the position of American translator and editor of the Psalms; see Bernstein, *Joel Barlow*, pp. 30, 131–133. On Dwight and Barlow at Yale, see Silverman, pp. 96–98, 148.

127. Barlow, *The Columbiad*, pp. 362, 361, 358, 360.

American economy based on agricultural production and maritime commerce would power the new world order. Experience had proven that "the pursuit of industry at home and the free exchange of. . . productions abroad" formed the happiest social foundation. Though his move to radical politics and religion had caused bitter estrangement from his erstwhile New England brethren, Barlow's social philosophy and his anti-racism were still theirs.[128]

Who would implement this social philosophy? During the last third of the eighteenth century, the answer seemed clear: the federal state. As Dwight wrote in *Greenfield Hill*:

> *See the wide realm in equal shares possess'd!*
> *How few the rich, or poor! how many bless'd!*
> *O happy state! the state, by Heaven design'd*
> *To rein, protect, employ, and bless mankind.*

Dwight admitted that his view included a "despotic" role for the law. "There is no country," he wrote, "in which law has a more decided, (and if I may be allowed to use the expression) despotic power, than in Connecticut." Dwight made a distinction between the despotic power of the law and despotism. In his view, however, the structure of society did not allow the despotic power of the law to turn to despotism. Since the force of the law, he wrote, rests "wholly on. . . the people at large," in practice it served to produce and to preserve not despotism but "all their happiness." This is why the political economy, the social order, and the manners he described in *Greenfield Hill* were so important. With an educated people, living amid social equality, in a Christian society of farmers, artisans, and tradesmen, they would ensure that just laws prevail. To be a just and righteous nation, the country would have to transform. Then, in making the New England way into the American way, the Wits simply imagined that the federal state would assume most if not all of the analogous social and civic functions held by the New England town and state governments.[129]

The Wits envisioned an America long lost from memory, except perhaps to professional historians. They thought of the social changes as a refinement of manners. "Amend, refine, complete," wrote Dwight. The scale of

128. Barlow, pp. 123, 432, 424; Blakemore, p. 241.

129. Dwight, *Greenfield Hill*, p. 153.

the project seemed a task fitting for the descendants of New England's fore-fathers, who had secured them a providential place in history, and the sons of the founding fathers, who gave them the world as a stage. Dwight compared their role to that of a silversmith making a fine bowl: "He sees the ductile mass refine, / And in a beauteous vessel shine." Instead of refining America, history gave them a series of challenges, beginning with what their Jeffersonian opponents called the revolution of 1800. The rise of Jefferson's Democratic-Republicans, and the Virginia Dynasty, put the US government in the hands of men whom the Wits tended to see not just as opponents, but also enemies—heretics, anarchists, and immoral slavers whose hypocrisy and reckless politics would squander a providential opportunity.[130]

The New Englanders' alienation from the direction of American democracy led directly to the Hartford Convention, an event that New England Federalists would spend years trying to explain. "Thousands of persons," complained the *New England Magazine* two decades later, "have denounced the Convention as a nefarious assemblage, got up for sedition and treason." Thomas Jefferson, for one, saw the Hartford Convention as an act of treason, and he found the New Englanders' religious identification especially irksome. "These reverend leaders of the Hartford nation," Jefferson wrote in 1815, "it seems then are now falling together about religion, of which they have not one real principle in their hearts." The Hartford Convention consisted of 26 leading members of New England Society, Federalist politicians and intellectuals from Massachusetts, Connecticut, Rhode Island, and New Hampshire. Jefferson compared them to pious prostitutes. "Like bawds," he wrote, "religion becomes to them a refuge from the despair of their loathsome vices. They seek in it only an oblivion of the disgrace with which they have loaded themselves, in their political ravings, and of their mortification at the ridiculous issue of their Hartford convention." He encouraged identifying the participants as traitors and rejoiced in their failure: "Under any other [constitution] their treasons would have been punished by the halter." What was the alleged treason of the Hartford Convention? Many believed, with the Hartford Convention, that leading New England Federalists had threatened to secede from the United States. New Englanders would spend

---

130. Dwight was among the leaders of a strenuous effort by Federalist clergy to defeat Jefferson. For other examples, see John Mitchell Mason, *Voice of Warning, to Christians, on the Ensuing Election of a President of the United States* (New York, 1800), and William Linn, *Serious Considerations on the Election of a President: Addressed to the Citizens of the United States* (New York, 1800).

years insisting, unconvincingly, that allegations of secessionism were baseless.[131]

The War of 1812 was the immediate cause of the Hartford Convention. The war was unpopular in New England, in particular with many Reformed Protestants, who envisioned the United States and Britain as Protestant brethren engaged in a joint project of world regeneration. "The war," noted the *New-England Magazine*, "was much against the wishes of the leading men and the people." For New Englanders, however, the crisis had been brewing since the 1807 Embargo Act, the first of a series of commercial restrictions, supported by the Jefferson and Madison administrations that aimed to chasten Britain and France, especially Britain, for violations of US neutrality. The restrictions inaugurated by the Embargo Act proved unpopular and difficult to enforce, while bringing particular hardship to the maritime commercial interests that underlay the New England economy. Defending the Hartford Convention, a New England Federalist described these measures as *"eight years, fellow citizens, of bondage and servitude!"* The Convention, he wrote, was merely a measure toward "the preservation of their resources from total ruin." The writer for the *New-England Magazine* asked Americans to realize that "a great body of the people. . . living, and acting, and suffering. . . could not know when the evils they endured would come to an end." Defending the Convention, he wrote, that it comprised "some of our best and purest men. . . who generously risked" the current of world affairs to defend liberty.[132]

Of the 26 New Englanders who met in Hartford, Connecticut, in December 1814 to January 1815, Connecticut contributed seven delegates. The lawyer and judge Roger M. Sherman was, for decades, one of Dwight's closest friends. Senator James Hillhouse, the head of the Connecticut delegation to the Convention, was Dwight's former student, and Dwight had helped bring him to saving grace. Under Dwight's presidency, Hillhouse became the long-serving treasurer of Yale. Congressman Theodore Dwight, a secondary member of the Wits, and Timothy Dwight's younger brother, was the secretary of the Convention. Dwight's protégé Noah Webster had organized it. All seven of the Connecticut delegates had been

---

131. See n.a., *The New-England Magazine* (March 1834), p. 24; Thomas Jefferson to Benjamin Waterhouse, October 13, 1815, in Paul Leicester Ford, ed., *The Works of Thomas Jefferson: Correspondence and Papers, 1808–1816*, vol. XI (New York, 2010), pp. 491–492.

132. Theodore Lyman, *A Short Account of the Hartford Convention* (Boston, 1823), pp. 7,9; n.a., *The New-England Magazine* (March 1834), p. 193.

Dwight's students or friends at Yale. Of the Massachusetts delegates, Harrison Gray Otis, Timothy Bigelow, George Bliss, and others would serve as board members or important contributors to the American Board of Commissioners for Foreign Missions. Others would go on to support the American Bible Society, the New England Tract Society, and other missionary organizations. In brief, the Convention may have been the end of Federalism, but it was an early expression of the American missions movement.[133]

The real cause of the Convention was the declining political power of New England Federalism, or, conversely, the ascendancy of the Southern planters. From initial settlement, important differences had separated New England and Chesapeake elites. In the revolutionary era, and into the 1790s, a shared commitment to national independence, and then in a federal government capable of fostering American nationality, brought them together, but differences remained. In the nineteenth century, as the republic became richer, as it expanded westward, as the population grew and property requirements for voting lowered, these differences re-emerged in competition for support from settlers, immigrants, and, especially, small farmers. In essence, control of nineteenth-century US politics was decided by this contest between Southern planters and Northeastern capitalists for the loyalty of small farmers. As the new republic moved into the nineteenth century, the planters began to dominate. In 1800, Thomas Jefferson won the presidency without winning a single electoral vote from New England. In 1803, the Jefferson administration's Louisiana Purchase more than doubled the size of the United States, further weakening the political power of New England in the Union. In 1804, when Jefferson won re-election, the only state he lost was Connecticut.[134]

The Hartford Convention made six demands, a series of proposed constitutional amendments, all of which revealed New Englanders'

133. Dwight, *Greenfield Hill*, pp. 20, 136. On the Hartford Convention, see George Dangerfield, *The Awakening of American Nationalism, 1815–1828* (New York, 1965), pp. 23–24. On Sherman and Hillhouse, see Cunningham, pp. 222, 257, 315, 336. On the members of the Convention, see Lyman, *A Short Account of the Hartford Convention*, pp. 22–23. On leading New Englanders' sense of the region and its history as exceptional and as the source of the best qualities of America, see Wesley Frank Craven, *The Legend of the Founding Fathers* (New York, 1956), especially pp. 35–36, 38.

134. On the long and complex relationship between New England and Chesapeake elites, see Kevin Phillips, *The Cousins' Wars*, esp. chs. 2–4. On nineteenth-century US politics as

increasing sense of alienation from the political process, and that aimed, in their view, to restore the balance of power in American politics. They sought to limit presidents to one term and to prohibit the election of any president "from the same State two terms successively." Both prohibitions were designed to check the power of the planters, especially the Virginians. Recognizing that Federalism and the New England way were not proving popular on the frontier, they asked that the ability of Congress to admit new states be restricted. Perhaps the most radical proposal of the Convention addressed the three-fifths clause of the US Constitution. The three-fifths clause had basically given Southern planters 66 votes for every 100 slaves they owned, thereby securing their domination of the US government. The Convention wanted it removed.[135]

The changes the Convention wanted to make would have reshaped American politics. If they were unlikely to find wide support in the United States under the best of circumstances, their future, and the ignominy of the Hartford Convention as well, were sealed three days after the Convention closed, before it had a chance to present its demands. On January 8, 1815, Andrew Jackson's unlikely victory in the Battle of New Orleans secured for the United States a respectable peace in the War of 1812. In essence, the representatives of the Hartford Convention arrived in Washington, D.C., to protest, in very strong terms, a war that their country had just won. Even without such unpropitious timing, the New Englanders had made a political miscalculation. As Jefferson's 1815 letter castigating the Hartford Convention assured Benjamin Waterhouse, outside New England, particularly on the frontier, the Convention would further alienate people from the New Englanders: "We let them live as laughing stocks for the world, and punish them by the torment of eternal contempt. The emigrants from the Eastern states are what I have long counted on." The Convention had also asked for a constitutional amendment restricting "the capacity of naturalized citizens, to hold offices of trust, honour, or profit." The Convention, wrote Jefferson, illustrated his opponents' "religious & political tyranny." The "effects of this squabble," he concluded, "cannot

---

a contest between Northeastern capitalists and Southern planters, see Barrington Moore, *The Social Origins of Dictatorship and Democracy: Lord and Peasant in the Making of the Modern World* (New York, 1966), ch. 3, esp. pp. 111–132.

135. See *Secret Journal of the Hartford Convention*, reprinted in Theodore Lyman, *A Short Account of the Hartford Convention*, pp. 29–30.

fail to be good." It would "drive the oppressed to milder associations," in other words, to his Democratic-Republicans. Indeed, the Hartford Convention was a political disaster for the Federalist Party, but in fact the current of history had for some time been running against the New England way.[136]

During the 1790s, Tom Paine, the philosophes, and the leaders of the French Revolution, though all embattled, had been generating an intellectual excitement and energy that New England Federalists, even with all their cultural resources, could not rival. With old enemies on the rise, and new ones appearing, the Wits, their students, and their followers would make peace with the bourgeoisie. The new alliance, between New England Protestant intellectuals and members of the New York and Philadelphia commercial class contains, in essence, the transformation of American Federalism into Whiggism. In this transition, more liberal New England Protestants also played an important role, as did Elias Boudinot, a prominent politician and Philadelphia-born lawyer who did a lot of legal work in New Jersey and New York. First, however, it is necessary to look at the rise of popular American Protestantism, from the interior of the North American continent, which presented a strange new threat. To these New Englanders it promised to pervert Protestantism, the core of the New England way, from within.[137]

---

136. Proposal to restrict immigrants' rights in *Secret Journal of the Hartford Convention*, reprinted in Lyman, *A Short Account of the Hartford Convention*, p. 31; Jefferson to Benjamin Waterhouse, in Ford, ed., *The Works of Thomas Jefferson*, vol. XI, pp. 491–492.

137. F. Sheldon, "The Pleiades of Connecticut," *The Atlantic Monthly* (Boston, MA, 1865), vol. XV.

3

To Raise a Holy People, Wear No Slouched Hat

THE METHODIST SETTLEMENT OF THE FRONTIER

*Many years ago. . . before the bloody scenes of Lexington
or Bunker Hill were enacted; before these states were
declared independent, and before there was a President
in the chair of the Union; when all the western country
was a waste, howling wilderness. . . the pioneer Methodist
preacher might have been seen urging his way along the
war-path of the Indian, the trail of the hunter, or the
blazed track of the backwoodsman, seeking the lost sheep
of the house of Israel in these far-off, distant lands.*
—THE REV. JAMES B. FINLEY, *Sketches of Western Methodism,*
1857

MINISTERS GOVERNED THE frontier of the early American republic.
Often they were itinerant ministers, and many were lay ministers as well.
Sometimes they were frontier Presbyterians, but most often they were
Baptists or Methodists. Methodist circuit-rider biographies and autobi-
ographies abound with claims resembling those of William (ancestor
of Adlai) Stevenson to be "the first Protestant preacher. . . to preach on
Texas and Oklahoma soil." William Winans, a cobbler's son from western
Pennsylvania, claimed to have participated in the Whiskey Rebellion (as
a six-year-old) before finding God and becoming a Methodist preacher
in the Natchez District of the Old Southwest. In 1785, at age 22, Hope
Hull fled an apprenticeship as a house carpenter in Baltimore to become
a "pioneer of Methodism" in the Old Southwest. In many parts of what
is now western Georgia and eastern Alabama, Hull was the first preacher
people ever saw. Shadrach Bostwick was born in Maryland, in 1767. As

a young man, he abandoned his medical studies to spend 14 years as a Methodist itinerant, riding circuits that included upstate New York, western Massachusetts, and what is now Ohio. Bostwick stopped riding in 1803, settling in Pittsburgh, where, he claimed, he was the first minister to preach regularly.[1]

Jesse Walker was born in western North Carolina, during the American Revolution. When he was a boy, his family moved to Tennessee, where he learned how to dress animal skins. He worked as a "skin-dresser" until 1802, when he joined the ranks of the Methodist itinerants. Walker claimed to have organized the first camp meeting in Illinois, in 1803. Born on a small family farm in Fauquier County, in the Virginia Piedmont, Daniel Hitt spent four years, 1793 to 1797, on horseback west of the Alleghenies. During that time, he carried the "gospel where it had not before been preached, or where its institutions were not yet established." After a year preaching in the Virginia Tidewater, Hitt went west again, riding circuit from 1798 to 1801 in what is now Ohio. Elijah Sabin was born in 1776, in Tolland, Connecticut. Two months later, at the Battle of Trenton, his father was fatally shot in the head. Sabin's two older brothers both soon succumbed to illness and Sabin went, at eight years of age, to work on a farm in western Vermont. In 1796, at 22, he began preaching in Vermont. He died at age 42, and had spent his adult life riding circuits from Georgia to Canada.[2]

In one sense, William Winans, Shadrach Bostwick, Elijah Sabin, Jesse Walker, and Daniel Hitt were typical. These men, and others like them, constituted the great corps of Methodist circuit-riders. This body of men was to American Protestantism what monks were to late antique Christianity, a small group of eccentrics who helped make their faith a mass religion. The early Methodists, almost to a man, came, in the words of one itinerant, from families whose "advantages were very limited." In the early American republic, becoming a Methodist itinerant gave young men from the lower orders the kind of opportunity that joining the armed services gives working-class Americans today. Both also require surrendering control over some basic aspects of life, and subjecting oneself to

1. On William Stevenson, see Walter N. Vernon, *William Stevenson: Riding Preacher* (Dallas, TX 1964), p. 3. On William Winans, see Ray Holder, *William Winans: Methodist Leader in Antebellum Mississippi* (Jackson, MS, 1977). On Bostwick, see William B. Sprague, *Annals of the American Pulpit: Methodist*, vol. VII (New York, 1861), p. 200.

2. On Hull, Hitt, Walker, and Sabin, see Sprague, *Annals of the American Pulpit: Methodist*, vol. VII, pp. 113, 200, 185, 381, 307.

trying physical challenges, in exchange for modest pay and a certain kind of respectability.[3]

For their knight-errant existence in the wilds and their notorious asceticism, the prolific historian of Christianity Kenneth Scott Latourette compared the early North American Methodists to medieval Franciscans or Dominicans and called them a "kind of Protestant order." Certainly North America, and maybe even Protestantism, had never seen anything quite like the Methodists before. They were fully Protestant, but unlike the Puritans in a dozen ways, including their lack of formal education, their embrace of man's potential for free will, their Arminian theology, and their inclusive, evangelistic ethos. At the same time, like the New England Puritans, they brought a resolute self-seriousness to life at the periphery of empire. As systems-builders on the imperial frontier, they also resembled the seventeenth-century Spanish Franciscan and Jesuit missionaries, who established a large missions civilization from Amazonia through Meso-America and California. The Spanish Catholic missionaries and the North American Methodists may have both served as the thin end of the wedge of empire, but their relationships to their respective empires differed. Catholicism was the head and heart of the Spanish empire, and Spanish Catholic missionaries served as proud representatives of an empire that, in comparison to Anglo-American settlement in the New World, was bureaucratized and centralized. Anglo-American settler colonialism, in contrast, was a laissez-faire enterprise and North American Methodism a late byproduct. It began to take shape in the late eighteenth and early nineteenth centuries, coalescing from a volunteer assembly of laborers and farmers and apprentices, cast-offs or adventurers who had emerged from the unregulated and disorderly European immigration to North America, and American migration into the interior of the continent. In the colonization of the North American interior, the Methodists were the human variant of the honeybee. Native to Europe, honeybees were not seen west of the Mississippi until 1797. Typically, they appeared about 100 miles ahead of the frontline of white settlement, earning them, from Native Americans, the sobriquet "the white man's flies." The Methodists were the honeybees, as well as the "white man's flies," of the Anglo-American colonization of the frontier.[4]

---

3. On the general lack of advantages among early Methodist ministers, see Sprague, p. 434.

4. In part for their asceticism, Latourette described Methodist itinerants as "a kind of Protestant order," one that was "fully Protestant in faith and spirit," yet committed to "the three rules of the Roman Catholic monastic bodies—chastity, poverty, and obedience,"

James B. Finley's words, which serve as the epigraph to this chapter, capture the Methodists' early precedence on the nineteenth-century North American frontier, though with one misrepresentation. The early Methodists were more likely to see the frontier as bountiful and as God's country rather than as a "waste, a howling wilderness." They were not, as Finley implied, waiting for the American Revolution. A couple of notable exceptions notwithstanding, the Methodist Episcopal Church was indifferent to the United States of America, as a nationalist project. The Emperor of China, who in 1817 asked an official to prepare a report on the republic on the other side of the Pacific, showed more formal interest in the United States than did Francis Asbury, the leader of early North American Methodism.[5] This indifference is remarkable because Methodism was not just any movement. Under Asbury's stewardship, North American Methodist membership increased from 1,200 in 1773, to 50,000 in 1793, to 214,000 at his death in 1816. In contrast, it took the first Christians a century to recruit about 10,000 people. Asbury also left Methodism in good stead: by 1850, almost 2.7 million Americans were Methodists. It was one of the most phenomenal instances of sectarian growth in the history of Christianity and the largest social movement in US history until the Civil War. Methodism was not a nationalist movement. It pioneered the settlement of the frontier for religious reasons. Its goals were spiritual and social, not political. Early American Methodism, especially on the western periphery where it flourished, does not so much emerge out of US history as it develops adjacent to American national history, a related but distinct movement. Its rise both challenged and changed the American national project.[6]

---

especially the Franciscans and Dominicans. See Kenneth Scott Latourette, *A History of the Expansion of Christianity*, vol. 4 (New York, 1941), pp. 185–186, 188; J. H. Elliott, *Empires of the Atlantic World: Britain and Spain in America, 1492–1830* (New Haven, CT, 2006), pp. 268–271. On the honeybees, see John Bradbury, *Travels in the Interior of North America, in the Years 1809, 1810, 1811* (Liverpool, 1817), pp. 33–35.

5. Xiong Yuezhi, "Difficulties in Comprehension and Differences in Expression: Interpreting American Democracy in the Late Qing," *Late Imperial China*, vol. 23, no. 1 (June 2002), p. 3.

6. On Methodist growth figures, see Edwin Scott Gaustad and Philip L. Barlow, eds., *New Historical Atlas of Religion in America* (New York, 2001), p. 219, except the middle figure (50,000 in 1773), which is from Elmer E. Clark, ed., *The Journal and Letters of Francis Asbury* (Nashville, TN, 1958), vol. II, p. 156, and the 1850 figure, which is from Roger Finke and Rodney Starke, "How the Upstart Sects Won America: 1776–1850," *Journal of the Scientific Study of Religion* (March 1989), pp. 27–44. A large and high-quality body of scholarship exists on the history of Methodism; see John H. Wigger, *Taking Heaven by Storm: Methodism and the Rise of Popular Christianity in America* (New York, 1998); Dee. E. Andrews, *The Methodists and Revolutionary America, 1760–1800: The Shaping of an*

The scale of Methodist growth and the prolific activity of early Methodists have brought the movement to the attention of generations of scholars of American, British, and Canadian history. E. P. Thompson's treatment has been influential. Thompson's *The Making of the English Working Class* suggested that whether Britain was to follow France into revolution was a question that fell to the Methodists, who balked. In the words of another historian, however, seeing Methodism as so close to the center of the nationalist politics, or as a movement inclined to modern political revolution, is "an optical illusion." Early Methodism was a social and religious movement; it was not averse to political revolution but, without democratic or nationalist aspirations or a structural sense of politics or society, incapable of it. It was anti-elitist, but anti-elitism, the historian of Britain E. R. Taylor pointed out, is "not a social theory." Taylor concluded that Methodism "had no social theory," which is not to suggest that Methodists lacked ideas. Methodist publications from the early republic overflow with ideas, but ideas are not a social theory either. In contrast to both the Puritan and the republican intellectual traditions, North American Methodism lacked the institutional and intellectual resources required to establish (much less promulgate) a social theory, which in the proper sense of the term implies a degree of rigor and systematization. Instead, Methodism brought a moral anthropology (a view of human nature, man's place in the world, and right and wrong), a theology of sin and forgiveness, and a vital energy to the American frontier. As Taylor put it, Methodism "set men's hearts on fire with hatred for oppression." It also built an institutional structure, based on members' participation, which proved both stable and dynamic. In the competition of sects, these factors put Methodism in a good position on the North American frontier, where, in the words of the historian of Canada J. I. Little, the "various religious denominations represented virtually the only institutions of local self-governance."[7]

Unlike that of the seventeenth-century Puritans or eighteenth-century Quakers, John Wesley's theology was not explicitly political. The avowed

---

Evangelical Culture (Princeton, 2000); David Hempton, *Methodism: Empire of Spirit* (New Haven, CT, 2005); Lynn Lyerly, *Methodism and the Southern Mind, 1770–1810* (New York, 1998). I have been most influenced by Russell E. Richey, *Early American Methodism* (Bloomington, IN, 1991).

7. E. P. Thompson, *The Making of the English Working Class* (New York, 1991); Roy Porter, *English Society in the Eighteenth Century* (New York, 1982), p. 193; E. R. Taylor, *Methodism and Politics, 1791–1851* (Ann Arbor, MI, 1935), p. 97. In a review of Russell E. Richey's *Early*

purpose of Wesleyan Methodism was "an attempt to think clearly concerning how to live the Christian life"—in other words, a social code.[8] Social codes travel more lightly than political systems, and Wesleyan Methodism was in this way suited to thrive on the North American borderlands. *The Doctrines and Discipline of the Methodist Episcopal Church*, published annually from 1784 through the first half of the nineteenth century, codified the permissible and impermissible beliefs and behavior for society members, as well as the means of the society for conducting others' conduct. The Methodists called themselves a "Society," rather than a Church, and it is a better term. Across the frontier, their little book was known simply as *The Discipline*. It was to nineteenth-century North American Protestantism what Mao's "Little Red Book" was to twentieth-century Chinese communism. It offered at first dozens, quickly growing to hundreds, of rules and maxims. Many had nothing to do with theology, but were simply rules for a moral and orderly life: "Beware of clownishness (either in speech or in dress)," warned the first edition, in 1784. It continued, advising members: "Wear no slouched hat." Jewelry and dancing were forbidden, as were "lace, ruffles" and "enormous bonnets." To go with its moral anthropology, Methodism also brought this social code, replete with rules about how to live. In spirit, they ranged from the sophistic, petty bourgeois nature of John Wesley's "Mend your clothes, or I shall never expect you to mend your lives," to honorable admonitions about giving charity, to neighbors and strangers alike, without inquiry. Max Weber would cite Wesley's "Earn all you can, save all you can, give all you can" as an instance of the Calvinist spirit driving capitalism, but it is hard to imagine John Calvin approving of John Wesley—or either one of them approving of modern capitalism.[9]

The Discipline also reveals the Society correcting itself, in small but revealing ways, to adapt to the nineteenth century. For example, the

---

American Methodism, Dee Andrews criticizes Richey for making a similar argument about the lack of theoretical sophistication in Methodism; see *Journal of American History*, vol. 79, no. 3 (December 1992), p. 1140; J. I. Little, *Borderland Religion: The Emergence of an English-Canadian Identity, 1792–1852* (Toronto, ON, 2004), p. x.

8. On the relative political vacancy of Wesleyan theology, despite Wesley's vocal anti-liberalism, see Theodore R. Weber, *Politics in the Order of Salvation: Transforming Wesleyan Political Ethics* (Nashville, TN, 2001), passim, but especially pp. 17–38. On Wesleyan Methodism as a social code, see Emory Stevens Bucke et al., *The History of American Methodism*, vol. 1 (Nashville, TN, 1964), pp. 11–24.

9. 1784 edition of *The Discipline and Doctrines of the Methodist Episcopal Church*, reprinted in Robert Emory, *History of the Discipline of the Methodist Episcopal Church* (New York, 1843), quote from p. 53; John Wesley quoted in Porter, *English Society in the Eighteenth*

century that sees the rise of capitalism began on a properly symbolic note when, in the 1800 edition of *The Discipline,* the Methodists changed the phrasing from paying substitute preachers "for their trouble" to reimbursing them "for their time."[10] Such little accommodations to the rise of time management and middle-class culture did not come with a politics of any sophistication or any strong orientation to encourage bourgeois or even commercial life. They simply encouraged fair play among members; if anything, *The Discipline* sought to limit the role of the market in members' lives. Some Methodists did become radicals, but most did not. The precepts of Methodism were too supple and ambiguous, and the society also simply became too large, to ensure any simple or clear position on divisive political issues. There was no Methodist principle or worldview forceful enough to counter the politics of slavery, for example, which split the Church. In 1844, members simply decamped to separate pro- or anti-slavery organizations, taking their Methodism with them.[11]

In essence, Methodism in the early republic was a North American Protestant (in the original "protest" sense of the name) and freedom movement. It was protesting the disorder and loneliness that accompanied the colonization of the continent, while it utilized the freedom of poor and uneducated people to organize and theologize and the freedom of religion from state regulation.[12] The historian Russell E. Richey has written about the continental orientation of Methodism in the early republic, and its lack of a concept of the nation. The fact that it was not a patriotic movement raises interesting questions about the role of popular religion and changing class relations in the development of American nationality. If, for example, the most dynamic portion of the largest social movement in America was not a nationalist movement, when did it become nationalized, and why?[13]

Century, p. 193; see Donald Frey, "The Protestant Ethic Thesis," eh.net (Economic History Association website), http://eh.net/encyclopedia/article/frey.protestant.ethic, viewed on April 28, 2013.

10. Emory, *History of the Discipline of the Methodist Episcopal Church,* p. 327.

11. Donald G. Mathews, *Slavery and Methodism: A Chapter in American Morality, 1780–1845* (Princeton, NJ, 1965), esp. ch. 4.

12. On North America between the Appalachians and the Rocky Mountains as outside the "world wide web" until after 1800, see J. R. McNeill and William H. McNeill, *The Human Web: A Bird's-Eye View of World History* (New York, 2003), p. 174.

13. Russell E. Richey, *The Methodist Conference in America* (Nashville, TN, 1996), ch. 14; see also Richey, *Early American Methodism,* ch. 3.

Early North American Methodism encouraged a set of ideals based on agrarian life and the Bible, and it provided society. Francis Asbury's 1788 instructions to itinerant ministers to visit settlers' homes and talk to them was typical: "If possible visit from house to house, and that regularly. . . for no other purpose to speak to each in the family about their souls." Keep the sermons brief and pertinent, Asbury told itinerants, do not press abstract systems but rather "life and application in the heart." The 1801 edition of the *Doctrines and Discipline of the Methodist Episcopal Church* also emphasized the pastoral and the social: approach the world home by home—"preaching and visiting from house to house." Methodism "is not deep," stated *The Discipline*, and it will be "superficial, partial, uneven till we spend half as much time in this visiting, as we do now in talking." It did not claim to be democratic either; but rather to bring vitality, action, order, and, again in Asbury's words, "fervency" and "warm hearts" to the North American frontier. Methodist geography was theological, not political. Sometimes the Methodists spoke in global terms. In 1818, for example, the inaugural issue of *The Methodist Magazine* explained its purpose as to "harmonize, improve, and sanctify the human species." Sometimes, its sense of community seemed to be North Atlantic, as when Bishops Thomas Coke and Asbury, in 1796, declared, "We are but one body of people. . . whether in Europe or America," remarks that the General Conference of 1800 approved and for years republished.[14] Usually, physical geography exerted its influence and led the Methodists to view their community as continental: "we humbly believe," proclaimed the 1801 edition of *The Discipline*, "that God's design in raising up the preachers called Methodists. . . was to reform the continent."[15]

Methodist talk about their continental mission was not just talk. Their circuits extended deep into Canada, where between 1790 and 1812, the Church supported 72 circuit riders. "Our whole plan is to raise a holy people," stated the *Discipline*. In this mission, the North American Methodists changed the role of the bishop, stripping it of its historical prerogatives of property and political power while retaining its churchly authority. For many American Protestants, the concept of a bishop

14. Asbury quoted in Noll, *America's God*, p. 333; Appendix to *The Discipline*, reprinted in Robert Emory, *History of the Discipline of the Methodist Episcopal Church* (New York, 1843). The year 1796 is given on p. 281, the "one body of people" and "to raise a holy people" remarks, p. 309.

15. "Introductory Address," *The Methodist Magazine*, vol. 1, 1818, p. 3; *The Doctrines and Discipline of the Methodist Episcopal Church* (Philadelphia, 1801), pp. 23, 34, iii.

suggested monarchism and European court life, and American critics of Methodism sometimes pointed to its adoption of bishops as evidence of its monarchical, un-American character. In fact, the role of the bishop in early American Methodist society had no neat precedent. Asbury's power over the lives of Methodist itinerants was as great as that of any Anglican or Catholic bishop over the lives of his ministers or priests; in contrast to those churches, however, it was by the will of those ministers that Asbury served as bishop. Differing from the sumptuous life of Anglican or Catholic bishops, which were, and are, rooted to a particular place, a bishopric, Asbury lived a labor-filled life of itinerant poverty. The preeminent bishop of Methodism worked as hard, for as little pay, and traveling more than as any minister in American history. *The Discipline* reminded readers "the property of the preaching-houses is invested in the trustees," that is, not the bishops. In explaining why "our American bishops have no probability of being rich," the Society did not turn to republican fears of concentrated power or suspicions of ecclesiastical property. They explained the change as necessary for a Church based on itinerancy, suitable to the expansive North American landscape, and as a way of acknowledging the unique character of "Mr. Wesley's authority." The result was something new, a blending of Protestant and Catholic characteristics: ascetic but activist, egalitarian but authoritarian, churchly and social but not political.[16]

In addition to bringing about a change in who owned society property, the great North American continent led John Wesley to allow a less-educated clergy. In a 1784 letter to "our North American brethren," Wesley acknowledged that the isolation faced by settlers in North America was very different from the situation in Britain. "No one," he wrote, "either exercises or claims any ecclesiastical authority at all." In America, wrote Wesley, "there are none for some hundred miles. . . to baptize or to administer the Lord's supper. Here, therefore, my scruples are at an end."[17] It was the power of this North American geography that led to the rise of the circuit-rider, one of the most identifiable social figures of nineteenth-century America. Some of the notable differences between British and American Methodism derived not from ideology but

---

16. Christopher Adamson, "God's Continent Divided: Politics and Religion in Upper Canada and the Northern and Western United States, 1775–1841," *Comparative Studies in Society and History*, vol. 36, no. 3 (July 1994), p. 434; Noll, *America's God*, p. 342.

17. Wesley's letter reprinted in Emory, p. 24.

from geography. British Methodism flourished among the new laboring classes packed together in squalor, serving the furnaces of British industry. Francis Asbury grew up among them, in Birmingham, England. He escaped a life as a servant to a newly rich family before immigrating to North America, where Methodism served overwhelmingly rural peoples, living in small, independent homesteads, from Upper Canada to the Mississippi Delta.[18]

From its beginnings in North America, organized Methodism expressed a continental consciousness. The contrast between the first edition of the American *Discipline*, in 1784, and the Church's English *Minutes* of the same year is instructive. Both editions pose a question: "What may we reasonably believe to be God's design in raising up the preachers called Methodists?" The English edition answers, "Not to form any new sect; but to reform the nation, particularly the Church; and to spread Scriptural holiness over the land." The North American *Discipline*, however, answers the same question: "To reform the continent, and to spread Scriptural holiness over these lands."[19] Its social ideal was what historians call "competency," or freedom from dependencies. Dependency on an employment market, the primary features of which were wage labor and a cash economy, was especially suspect. Moral life took place primarily within the family and its relations, though morality (as was one's relationship to God) was individual. The Methodist ideal of competency and the importance of modesty and virtue coincided with republican precepts. Its emphasis on the individual as the moral agent was more consistent with liberal principles. The Methodists' mission in the early republic, however, unfolded on its own terms, obviously in a world that could be understood according to Atlantic world political theories, but the Methodist church

18. John Wesley, "To Dr. Coke, Mr. Asbury, and our Brethren in North America," reprinted in Emory, p. 23.

19. North American *Discipline* and the English Minutes, and "Large Minutes," discussed and compared in Emory, pp. 9–27. According to Emory, the Wesleys had been writing the General Rules for Methodists since 1743, and those General Rules began to be adopted by conferences in 1744. Methodists began activities in North America in 1766 and began having conferences in 1773, at which time the North American Methodists put forth the *Doctrines and Discipline* as the "sole rule of their conduct." The "peculiar circumstances" of the North American situation necessitated some differences from the English Minutes. Basically, between the 1773 commencement of Methodist conferences in North America and the 1784 establishment of North American Methodists into a separate church from British Methodism, one has to compare the North American Annual Minutes with what Methodists called the Larger Minutes, or English Minutes, in order to see the differences between the North American and British churches.

was not much interested in Atlantic world political theory, and certainly unconcerned with consistency in such matters. They played a lead role in building a society on the American frontier, one that, depending on where one looks, can appear either republican or liberal, but should also be understood on its own terms, as simply Methodist.

Methodist society owed much of its growth to opportunity, a generous free-will theology, and a detailed social code codified in *The Discipline*. The fact that the indefatigable Francis Asbury, like the Mormon prophet Joseph Smith, was an organizational genius played an important role.[20] Skill in building and running a Church proved more valuable than presence in the pulpit, which Asbury lacked. During the 1780s, to compensate for his lack of oratorical gifts, Asbury traveled with Harry Hosier, a "small, very black, keen-eyed" Philadelphia rag picker who became a sensation as a Methodist preacher. Benjamin Rush once called Hosier the greatest natural orator he had ever heard. Hosier's preaching was so moving that Asbury, his fellow Bishop Thomas Coke, and the prominent Methodist preacher Freeborn Garretson, all, at various times, traveled with Hosier as their featured preacher.[21]

Asbury's preeminence in North American Methodism resembled that of John Wesley's in British Methodism. In Wesley and Asbury, Methodism on both sides of the Atlantic enjoyed long-serving, authoritarian, and peripatetic leaders. They also shared proximities to revolutions. For the British, it was the Industrial Revolution and the nearby French Revolution. If British historians have enjoined the Methodists to explain why Britain did not have a political revolution, historians of the United States used to be preoccupied with explaining how popular Protestantism influenced the revolution they did have. The most ambitious attempt was Alan Heimert's 1966 *Religion and the American Mind*. Its central argument was that evangelical Protestantism encouraged liberal individualism, which in turn led to support for the American Revolution. The historian Edmund Morgan described this claim as dependent on the

---

20. Richard L. Bushman, *Joseph Smith: Rough Stone Rolling* (New York, 2007), claims that Smith's organizational acumen was a decisive factor in the growth of Mormonism. In 1810, a young and admiring itinerant remarked of Asbury's preaching: sententious, dry, and unimpressive, never rating high in "general estimation." See Ray Holder, *William Winans: Methodist Leader in Antebellum Mississippi* (Jackson, MS, 1977), p. 17.

21. On Harry Hosier, see Carter G. Woodson, *The History of the Negro Church* (Washington, DC, 1921), pp. 57–58 and Clark, ed., *Journal and Letters of Francis Asbury* (hereafter cited as *JLFA*) vol. I, pp. 380, 424, 434.

author's maintaining that "words or actions mean the opposite of what they seem to mean" or that "the author of them is the opposite of what he seems to be." Maintaining that evangelical Protestantism led to the American Revolution, Morgan concluded, "partakes more of fantasy than of history."[22]

In 1977, with what he termed "civil millennialism," the historian Nathan Hatch made the most persuasive and compelling case for a link of significance between religion and the political thought of the American Revolution. In 1992, Hatch argued that the real story about the role of evangelicalism in the era was to be found on the other side of the Revolution, in the early republic. Hatch's *The Democratization of American Christianity* portrayed the upstart evangelicals of the "Second Great Awakening" as the true inheritors of the more egalitarian impulses of the American Revolution. According to this argument, the hothouse of religious activity in the early republic coheres by virtue of the upstarts (most notably the Methodist and Baptists) applying the more democratic of revolutionary principles to the doctrines and institutions of American Christianity. Methodism, however, owed more to the United Kingdom and the North American frontier, John Wesley's social code, and the nature of life on the frontier, than to the political ideas of the seaboard colonies.[23]

While New England clerics warned that the degeneracy of the frontier would imperil the republic, Asbury and his fellow frontier ministers saw their churches and influence grow. Traveling through Tennessee in October 1803, he marveled at the flow of migrants, as well as their poverty. On a road he described as the worst on the whole continent, he passed "four or five hundred. . . men, women and children. . . almost naked paddling bare-foot and barelegged along. . . [with] little or nothing to eat." He saw opportunity: "I was powerfully struck with the consideration, that there were at least as many thousand emigrants annually from east to west: we must take care to send preachers after these people." At the Western Conference annual meeting that year, the Methodists did just

---

22. Alan Heimert, *Religion and the American Mind, from the Great Awakening to the American Revolution* (Cambridge, MA, 1966); Edmund Morgan, *William and Mary Quarterly*, vol. 24, no. 3 (July 1967), pp. 454–459.

23. Hatch, *The Democratization of American Christianity*; see also Dee E. Andrews, *The Methodists and Revolutionary America, 1760–1800*, pp. 218–221. For an exception to this interpretation, one that stresses the independence of the early Methodist Church, see Russell Richey, *Early American Methodism*, ch. 3. For a good critique of Hatch's democratization thesis, see Stephen J. Stein, "Radical Protestantism and Religious Populism," *American Quarterly*, vol. 44 (June 1992), pp. 262–270.

that, assigning more circuit-riders to the West. The next year, observing a similar procession, he remarked, "It is wonderful to see how Braddock's Road is crowded with wagons and pack-horses carrying families and their household stuff westward. . . [to places] calculated for poor industrious families." In 1812, he observed with equanimity, "Old Virginia, because of the great migrations westward, and deaths, decreases in the number she gives the Methodists; but new Virginia gains." For Asbury, serving the poor was remaining faithful to John and Charles Wesley's charter for their American church. He saw westward migration without any of the consternation that informed the views of many leading contemporary American nationalists, from Benjamin Franklin to Timothy Dwight.[24]

Among westward-looking Methodist officials, Asbury's lack of interest in the political life of the new nation was not exceptional. Methodist perseverance into the remote parts of North America gained wide recognition. A nineteenth-century saying, popular during violent thunderstorms, had it that "there's nobody out tonight but crows and Methodist preachers." The preacher did not always find his way inside. In a cold Louisiana winter of 1815, the itinerant Richmond Nolley was found frozen to death by the side of the road, near Harrisonburg, in Catahoula Parish. In *A Week on the Concord and Merrimack Rivers*, an account of a camping trip into the White Mountains, Henry David Thoreau told of encountering a farmer who protected his remote melon patch with a deadly trap, a gun rigged to a tripwire. "He was a Methodist man," explained Thoreau, "who. . . by his own tenacity, held a property in his melons, and continued to plant."[25] In *The Confidence Man*, Herman Melville gave a Methodist lay-minister a distinctive supporting role. The novel takes place on a New Orleans–bound Mississippi steamboat, full of a *Canterbury Tales* assortment of soldiers, slaves, "farm-hunters and fame-hunters," "men of business and men of pleasure," "modish young Spanish Creoles, and old-fashioned French Jews," "English, Irish, German, Scotch, Danes. . . Sioux chiefs solemn as high priests" and a "Methodist minister . .. a tall, muscular, martial-looking man." Melville's "soldier-like Methodist" and "brave Methodist" confronts the conman on the steamboat, grabbing and throwing him to the deck "like a nine-pin" while goading, "You took me

---

24. Clark, ed., *JLFA.*, vol. II, pp. 411, 443, 694.

25. Richard Hofstadter, *Anti-Intellectualism in American Life* (New York, 1963), p. 96; On Nolley, see Sprague, *Annals of the American Pulpit*, p. 443; Henry David Thoreau, *A Week on the Concord and Merrimack Rivers*, reprinted in Robert F. Sayre, ed., *Henry David Thoreau* (New York, 1985), p. 237.

for a non-combatant, did you?" The passengers gather around, crying out in approval of the "church militant!"[26]

The Methodists' reputation for combining wildness and austerity crossed the Atlantic. In the 1790s, Zachary Macaulay, the governor of the British colony of Sierra Leone and father of the historian Thomas Macaulay, complained that the Methodists in the colony made his job much more difficult. They took their "dreams, visions, and the most ridiculous bodily sensations," he wrote, as "incontestable proof" of divine approval for their program of "pure democracy." Their influence threatened to upend British progress and drag the colony, and its inhabitants, wrote Macaulay, into a "wretched state of barbarism." Half a century later, in denigrating the radical French Revolutionary Maximilien de Robespierre, whom he described as a "rabid triviality. . . without head, without heart, or any grace, gift, or vice beyond common," the historian Thomas Carlyle concluded that Robespierre had been "meant by Nature for a Methodist parson of the stricter sort."[27]

Methodist ministers were more written about than writers. The Church forbade them from publishing their own writings. A mid-nineteenth-century nostalgia for the early Methodist circuit-rider brought numerous journals and autobiographies onto the market. As a rule, these works lack interest in worldly affairs, are consumed by factional Church politics and doctrinal debate, and are given to homiletic stories of good over evil or stoic accounts of misfortune. They typically lack introspection, erudition, or style. The itinerants' many followers left numerous accounts of camp-meetings, sermons, and conversions, but they tend toward clichéd exclamation and require a sympathetic, interested reader. They found such a reader in William James, whose *Varieties of Religious Experience* draws on accounts of Methodist camp-meetings; but, in brief, the itinerants' status as legendary social figures is not intelligible from their own writings or those of their followers. American literature in the early republic is of primarily historical interest, and the Methodists were not known for their literary prowess. Despite their appearances in the writing of Thoreau and Melville, it was not until Lillian Smith described

---

26. Herman Melville, *The Confidence Man: His Masquerade* (New York, NY, 1949), pp. 21–25.

27. Thomas Carlyle, *Critical and Miscellaneous Essays*, vol. IV, (Boston, 1860), p. 90; Catherine Hall, "An Empire of God or of Man? The Macaulays, Father and Son," in Hilary M. Carey, ed., *Empires of Religion* (New York, 2008), p. 69; see also John Clive, *Macaulay: The Shaping of the Historian* (New York, 1973), pp. 3–4, 6.

her childhood in late nineteenth-century Georgia that the legend of the Methodist itinerant found full and able exposition. By Smith's time the itinerant system had transformed beyond recognition from the early republic. The figure of the circuit-rider, his role in rural society, and the nature of his appeal, which drew Smith's greatest interest, had changed less.[28]

Smith's description of the Methodist itinerants, and their place in the rural society of nineteenth-century America, is the best American litera-ture offers. "Church," wrote Smith, "was our town—come together not to kneel in worship but to see each other." Attending services excited not so much a "profound reverence for the Unknown" as an excitement at "looking at each other's clothes or watching the veins swell out on old Mr. Amster's neck as he sang. . . or staring at little Mr. Pusey as he led the tenors." For children, church was "more interesting than school" because grown-ups attended and "one's eyes could not get enough of their movements, their quick glances, the sudden stiff droop of those who fell asleep." Baynard Rush Hall, the president of Indiana Seminary in the 1820s, also reported that many pioneers went to the "religious meetings in the wooden world" out of "secular motives." Hall claimed that sharing news and searching for stray livestock were the most common reasons for attending revival meetings.[29] Smith was more sympathetic. She remem-bered the wonder, for children, of seeing grown men in the throes of the spirit: "I shall never forget how I suffered with these strong men of our town. . . as they knelt there sobbing like children." Sunday school meant gilded books, mite boxes, and stories of lions, slingshots, and floods. It was not theology that brought people to church, but the sight and sound of strong men sobbing at confession, a stage topped with a calliope and a piano, town and country people gathered in the best clothing they could make or buy, and the honor of the visiting minister.[30]

Even into Smith's childhood, in the early twentieth century, the Methodist itinerant cut a distinctive profile. Wherever they went, the "crossroads saloon keeper vied with the pillars of the church for the privi-lege of putting them up for the night." Respect was more forthcoming in the South, especially in Georgia, than in New England. Elijah Sabin, who

---

28. On the ban on itinerants' publishing, see *The Doctrines and Discipline of the Methodist Episcopal Church* (New York, 1813), p. 207.

29. Carlton, p. 119.

30. Lillian Smith, *Killers of the Dream* (New York, 1994), pp. 99, 102, 106.

rode circuit for nearly 20 years, from 1799 to 1818, found that "in Georgia, and at the South generally," Methodists "ranked among 'respectable' people." In New England, however, Sabin was once knocked from his horse by a whip. On three other occasions, Sabin found himself threatened by New England mobs. Once, he was sure, he escaped death only because of "the interposition of a neighbour" of the mob-leader. Certainly they were "brave men," Smith wrote, "these circuit riders, who could kill a rattler or swamp panther or wild turkey with casual accuracy or throw a drunken bully out of their meeting with no more than a comma's pause in their sermon." They brought excitement to rural settlements characterized by "loneliness, ignorance, and isolation." Settlers and townspeople were "hungry for news" of the world and the revivalist brought with him both "enormous terror and at the same time a blessed respite from monotony." To many in rural North America, the circuit-rider or revivalist brought, first, not theology, but terrifying entertainment and hot-cold pleasure, a "brief surcease from the gnawing monotony that ate our small-town lives away."[31]

Smith recalled the revivalists as gripping and flawed moral figures. The men who flourished in this ministry had "powerful instincts of sex and hate." Their lust and rage were "woven together into a sadism that would have devastated their lives and broken their minds had they acknowledged it for what it was." Such breaking may have happened more than Smith had realized. As early as the first edition of *The Discipline*, in 1784, the Church addressed an apparent problem, asking, "What reason can be assigned why so many of our preachers contract nervous disorders?" Smith saw the itinerants as trying to bind their lust and rage into "verbal energy and with this power of the tongue" drive "men in herds toward heaven." In doing so, they tended to be "sincere if ham actors," the best of whom "touched greatness now and then."[32]

Their most distinctive quality may have been their willingness to pursue terrors into tender places of the human psyche. They were "unafraid to explore the forbidden places of man's heart," recalled Smith. A life amid the arts had acquainted her with "few artists today who would dare probe so ruthlessly the raw sores of our life as did these evangelists." Smith thought that they instinctually understood the power of "buried memories quite as much as Freudians do." Combined with an often

31. Smith, pp. 99–105. On Sabin, see Sprague, *Annals of the American Pulpit*, p. 308.

32. The first *Discipline*, reprinted in Emory, quote from p. 48.

"very shrewd. . . use of mass psychology," the itinerants knew how to move a man and a mass of men and, even more so, women. Many were guests in Smith's home, and she remembered them as "remarkable storytellers, with a warm near-riotous sense of humor, brilliantly adept with words, soft and gentle with children, and courteous and considerate" of the hostess. For children, they were "full of games and animal stories." They knew how to shrink sin "to a stature that our small egos could cope with." In the revival meetings, however, they revealed "monstrosities that Mr. Barnum would not have dared exhibit." Queer "misshapen vices, strange abnormal sins, were marched out before our young eyes, titillating us as no circus could do." It was in these meetings that young people learned about "lush pleasures" and how "scarlet women dangle before men's eyes." Words "we had never heard in our homes and would not dare repeat" flew through the air. Adolescents whose parents had been unable to explain where babies come from "sat on the edge of benches, wet-lipped and tense, learning rococo lessons in Sin." How exactly the Methodist itinerant, "who seemed magnificently experienced in such matters," had come to such forbidden knowledge was not asked. Smith remembered how the sermon "titled *For Men Only* lifted the lid from the flaming pit of things one should not know." Even "little girls and their mamas" waiting safe at home hoped for "bits of ash that might fall from the big fire" of such sermons.[33]

The itinerants were not wise men. They were "indifferent to cultural patterns." They could in fact "turn into stupid foolish men when confronted with questions that ask 'Why?'" Their talents and skills could scare and move and soothe people, but also left the itinerants speechless when confronted with the "problems of poverty, of race segregation, unions, wages, illness and ignorance, war. . . or to the old question of human freedom." Indeed, in 1813, a minister asked Church officials, "Why is it that the people under our care are not better?" The "chief" reason, answered the Church, is "because we are not more knowing and holy."[34] They embodied and popularized a religion "too narcissistic to be concerned with anything but a man's body and a man's soul." These evangelists "were in love with Sin" in the way a child was "in love with his own image" or the way that an invalid was "in love with his disease." They loved sin, wrote Smith, so deeply and simply that they "believed they had

33. Smith, p. 108.

34. *The Discipline* (1813), p. 68;

created it themselves." To them, sin was holy, an "immaculate conception" that sprung from the souls of men. Sin accounted for all that was wrong or bad in the world, and discussions of society or politics or exploitation were merely excuses for a failure to look inside and confront individual sin. Men listened to them because they preached on the "sins that tough frontier men committed: drinking, fighting to kill, fornication, self-abuse, gambling, and stealing." With their passion and eloquence, they "made these sins of heroic size." For "more than a century," she explained, "they shaped and gave content to the conscience of southerners, rich and poor."[35]

They were, recalled Smith, "twisted men, often fanatics, but they were delightful companions." The best possessed what Smith called the two essential qualities of leadership: "They were free of personal anxiety and close to their instinctual feelings." People, she explained, knew that the circuit-riders were "pioneering for God" because they saw them take death and danger "as quietly as they took sleep." Nothing, Smith remembered, "but a lynching or a race-hate campaign could tear a town's composure into as many dirty little rags or give as many curious little satisfactions" as one of their revival meetings. The great revivalists were "like political demagogues," in that they "enjoyed people" and "won allegiance by bruising then healing a fear deep within men's minds." They loved God but they "feared Him far more than they loved Him." They preached "asceticism but they preached it with the libertine's words." As they preached, "they looked as unlike an ascetic as you can imagine." Some twentieth-century historians would later claim that early nineteenth-century popular ministers' gender ambiguity was consistent with the "feminization of American culture." Smith made a strong contrary claim. "These were potent men—anyone is wrong to think otherwise," she wrote, "who used their potency in their ardent battle for souls." They were often "fine looking men, strong, bold, with bodies of athletes."[36]

Even a sensibility as unsympathetic to popular frontier Protestantism as the Boston Brahmin and Mariolatrist Henry Adams recognized the important role of rural ministers in the early republic. In his *History of the United States*, Henry Adams noted that while it was true that the New England clergy's "police authority" had withered in the wake of the Revolution, clericalism still predominated in the countryside, where

35. Ibid., pp. 102–104.

36. Smith, pp. 105–106.

ministers retained an "autocratic" rule.[37] Instead of college-trained clergy, the frontier generated lay-ministers, prophets and scriptural autodidacts, circuit-riders, camp-meeting leaders, and revivalists. Baynard Rush Hall, a Princeton-trained minister who took up the cause of civilization by emigrating to take over Indiana Seminary in 1820s, called the frontier revivalists "profoundly ignorant, vain, empty, conceited, self-confident, and snarling fanatical preachers." He warned Americans that if they failed to send proper missionaries, the "New Purchasers" would be "abandoned" to a set of ignorant imposters. Hall wrote a version of what he called the frontier preachers' "apostolic creed," a mocking account, in dialect, of an ignorant and proud lay minister:

> Yes, bless the Lord, I am a poor, humble man—and I doesn't know a single letter in the ABC's, and couldn't read a chapter in the Bible no how you could fix it, bless the Lord!—I jist preach like old Peter and Poll, by the Sperit. Yes, we don't ax pay in cash nor trade nither for the Gospel, and arn't no hirelins like them high-flow'd college larned sheepskins—but as the Lord freely give us, we freely give our fellow critturs.[38]

Hall's satire contained some truths. The Methodists did favor the spirit over knowledge, itinerants and their followers were poor, and they did deride the learned as full of soulless erudition. Knowledge of the early history of Christianity might have tempered Hall's derision: the early Christians required a century to convert 50 literate men. In 1844, Peter Cartwright estimated that fewer than 50 (of 4,282) of his fellow itinerants had more than a grade school education. If the emphasis on feeling—that ran into disdain for learning, which frontier preachers of the early republic exemplified—was, at least in its popularity, a new phenomenon, it was also one that was not going away. The valorizing of individual spirit struck

---

37. Henry Adams, *The United States in 1800* (Ithaca, NY, 1960), p. 56; John M. Murrin made the same observation as Adams, but more generally and without geographical distinction, "Religion and Politics in America from the First Settlements to the Civil War," in Mark A. Noll, ed., *Religion and American Politics from the Colonial Period to the 1980s* (New York, 1990), pp. 26–36. On the Christian nationalism of New England clergy, see David Brion Davis, *The Problem of Slavery in the Age of Revolution* (Ithaca, NY, 1975), pp. 255–306, and Ruth H. Bloch, *Visionary Republic: Millennial Themes in American Thought, 1756–1800* (New York, 1985), passim.

38. Robert Carlton (Baynard Rush Hall), *The New Purchase: Or, Seven and a Half Years in the Far West* (Princeton, NJ, 1916), p. 59, 121. Originally published in 1843.

a deep chord with Protestantism. In contrast to Catholicism or Judaism, which try to combine erudition and esoteric knowledge with institutional authority, Protestantism encourages believers to come to their own relationship to the truth. In such a fashion, the Methodists, as well as the Baptists, called Hall and other educated men of God "man-made ministers," as opposed to their own kind, who were "God-made."[39]

In the absence of state authority and institutions, frontier ministers in the early republic exercised broad authority.[40] What Edmund Burke had in 1775 called the Revolutionary New England clergy's "dissidence of dissent," the spirit with which Burke said the patriots exemplified "the Protestantism of the Protestant religion," also passed from the New England clergy to the frontier revivalists, at least in matters of religion and spiritual truth. While important details of continental imperialism often put American nation-builders at odds, they found a common ground on the necessity of placing the West under colonial rule. From their perspective, the Northwest Ordinance extended civilization into the wilderness. From the perspective of some on the periphery, the founders' marshaling of force to quell both Shays' Rebellion and the Whiskey Rebellion demonstrated the teeth in Jefferson's apparently magnanimous remark, in his 1801 Inaugural, "We are all Federalists, we are all republicans." The frontier ministers were often neither. They did not necessarily conceive of

---

39. Keith Hopkins, *A World Full of Gods*, p. 83; Finke and Stark, "How the Upstart Sects Won America, 1776–1850," pp. 35–36; Alistair McGrath, *Christianity's Dangerous Idea: The Protestant Revolution—A History from the Sixteenth Century to the Twenty-First Century* (New York, 2008).

40. Here, as throughout the work, I have drawn on Michel Foucault's insights in his investigations of governance and sovereignty as related but distinct concepts. Foucault is convincing that tools of modern state sovereignty came into being by borrowing techniques of governance from many sources, including religious practice and doctrine, and that the "double movement. . . of state centralization, on the one hand, and of dispersion and religious dissidence, on the other" produced the conditions with which the "the art of government" contended. These related processes combined to help pose the problem, in Foucault's words, "with peculiar intensity, of how to be ruled, how strictly, by whom, to what end." Neither Adams's characterization of the early nineteenth-century rural ministers as exercising "police authority," nor important elements of Foucault's terminology are impositions into the vocabularies of the late eighteenth- and early nineteenth-century American ministers and nationalists. Studying a body of early modern literature on the "art of government," Foucault proposed a series of definitions of governance and government. One of these definitions of governance, the development of systematized modes by which to "conduct others' conduct," describes the role and aspiration of frontier ministers and churches well. Foucault wishes to show that modes of knowledge are as essential to the reality and survival of the state as its functions. See Michel Foucault, "Governmentality," in James D. Faubion, ed., *Power* (New York, 2000), pp. 201–222, quotes from pp. 201, 202.

justice and governing in the language of Anglo-American rights talk. They did, however, govern—mediating disputes, regulating conduct in matters from money lending and borrowing to hiring practices, marriage, and appropriate attire. With the camp meetings, they organized perhaps the largest public gatherings of the early republic.[41] William Warren Sweet, a prolific mid-twentieth-century historian of American religion, called the churches of the early republic the "moral courts" of the frontier. Even when church membership constituted a small proportion of the local population, he wrote, the churches "set the moral standards and patterns of conduct." Individuals routinely "submitted to the extra-legal action of the churches in their attempts to regulate his life and conduct." According to Sweet, "no religious body ever maintained a more rigid supervision in respect to morals and conduct" than the Methodists. The evident exaggeration should not obscure the point that as representatives of justice and morality, the Methodist itinerants played an important role.[42]

No two individuals represent the intertwined but distinct worlds of frontier religion and the American nation better than Francis Asbury and George Washington. Born in 1745, in Handsworth, England, and having been ordained a Wesleyan minister in 1767 at age 22, by John Wesley, Asbury immigrated to Philadelphia in 1771. By the early nineteenth century he was already known as "The Prophet of the Long Road." In the words of a contemporary, Asbury, "in his locomotive faculty, [was] a sort of Sinbad on land." Though officially based in Baltimore, Asbury spent his life traveling through the original 13 colonies and into the interior of the North American continent, preaching, organizing, and performing ministerial intercessions in the lives of the poor, whom he considered his, and

41. On the problem of frontier justice and vigilantism, see Thomas P. Slaughter, "The Friends of Liberty, the Friends of Order, and the Whiskey Rebellion: A Historiographical Essay," in Steven R. Boyd, ed., *The Whiskey Rebellion: Past and Present Perspectives*, (Westport, CT, 1985), pp. 9–30; see also Alan Taylor, *William Cooper's Town: Power and Persuasion on the Frontier of the Early American Republic* (New York, 1995), pp. 183–198. On the similarities and differences between Federalist and republican theories and practices of the state more generally, see Bethel Saler, "An Empire for Liberty, A State for Empire: The U.S. National State Before and After the Revolution of 1800," in Peter Horn et al., eds., *The Revolution of 1800: Democracy, Race, and the New Republic* (Charlottesville, VA, 2002), pp. 360–378. On the "internal oligarchic character" of nineteenth-century US colonialism, see Jack Ericson Eblen, *The First and Second United States Empires: Governors and Territorial Governments, 1784–1912* (Pittsburgh, 1968), and Gordon T. Stewart, "The Northwest Ordinance and the Balance of Power in North America," in Frederick D. Williams, ed., *The Northwest Ordinance: Essays on Its Formulation, Provisions, and Legacy* (East Lansing, MI, 1989), p. 30.

42. William Warren Sweet, *Religion in the Development of American Culture, 1765–1840* (New York, 1952), pp. 145, 143.

God's, "people." The "Prophet of the Long Road" spent over four decades on horseback, traveling 300,000 miles. He crossed the Alleghenies over 60 times. Between 1784 and 1815, he traveled from the Northeast to the South 30 times.[43] When he preached in the then brand-new Washington, D.C., in 1793, he was billed as *this man that rambles through the United States.*[44] He saw far more of the interior of the continent and its peoples than probably any dozen of the delegates to the Constitutional Convention combined. In his wandering life, Asbury (though on a scale commensurate with the North American continent) carried on the tradition of John Wesley. To "speak the rough truth" about the dangers of luxury and the beauty of holiness and morality, Wesley rode 25,000 miles on horseback, and preached 40,000 sermons. Perhaps no one in Great Britain had better utilized the new system of English roads.[45]

One of the provisions of Asbury's will stipulated that each child named after him receive a Bible. The executor of his (otherwise nonexistent) estate recalled that he had to "distribute several hundred copies of the scriptures to persons bearing the name FRANCIS ASBURY, and it is quite likely that we did not obtain knowledge of the half." Earlier generations of denominational historians referred to him as a "Minister of State," a play on words that indicates some truth about Asbury's role among the thousands of settlers who had embarked into the wilderness.[46] By the mid-twentieth century, historians writing articles with titles such as "Asbury Knew Washington" had created for Asbury a place in nationalist mythology. In fact, Asbury and Washington met twice, four years apart. Asbury and his cofounder of North American Methodism, Thomas Coke, requested the first meeting, in June 1785, when they visited Washington at Mount Vernon. Asbury recorded the meeting in his journal. Asbury's journal and letters amount to almost 2,100 printed pages of both the

---

43. Russell Richey, *Early American Methodism*, ch. 3; L. C. Rudolph, *Francis Asbury* (Nashville, TN, 1966); Charles Ferguson, *Organizing to Beat the Devil: Methodists and the Making of America* (New York, 1971), p. 62. On Asbury as a "Sinbad on land," see Sprague, *Annals of the American Pulpit*, vol. VII, p. 141; Asbury counted his sixtieth time over the Alleghenies in March 1814, two years before his death, see *JLFA*, vol. II, p. 753. Also in 1814, he wrote that he had traveled "annually a circuit of 3000 miles, for forty-two years and four months," ibid., vol. III, p. 499. The figure of 300,000 miles comes from Methodist historians cited above.

44. *JLFA*, vol. II, p. 152. Italics in original.

45. Porter, p. 192.

46. On Asbury's will, see Henry Boehm's reminiscence, reprinted in William B. Sprague, *Annals of the American Pulpit* (New York, 1859), vol. VII, p. 25; J. Manning Potts, "Francis

inveterate diarist's recording of daily life—meals, weather, meetings, sermons—and the organizing missionary's serial observations on human and divine character. *The Journal and Letters of Francis Asbury* describes hundreds of locales and thousands of people. The entry concerning his first meeting with Washington reads, in its entirety: "Thursday, 26. We waited on General Washington, who received us very politely, and gave us his opinion on slavery." In fact, Asbury and Coke had initiated the meeting in order to request Washington's signature on an anti-slavery petition. Citing his position in the Virginia politics, Washington demurred; then assured Asbury and Coke that he personally hated slavery.[47]

In the spring of 1789, following Washington's first inauguration, Asbury met Washington for the second time. The Methodists had been on the wrong side of the Revolution. John Wesley's bitter attacks, still fresh in memory, had combined high principles with low tactics. For different reasons, a Methodist benediction at Washington's inauguration appealed to both groups. At the end of May 1789, a month after the actual inaugural, Asbury and Bishop Thomas Coke visited Washington in New York and recited their address. The event created a small stir among the New York newspapers. They celebrated the reconstruction of the Methodists, characterizing the "Address" as "respectful and affectionate," proof that the Methodists were "warmly attached to the Constitution and the United States."[48]

Written by Asbury and Coke, "The Address of the Bishops of the Methodist-Episcopal Church" promised the Methodists' prayers on behalf of Washington, his presidency, and the United States. It also reminded Washington that sovereignty belonged to God alone, that freedom was the gift of God, and gently challenged the president to "prove a faithful and impartial patron of genuine, vital religion," a euphemism for revealed religion popular on the frontier. In fact, Asbury and Coke's "Address" offered a more qualified endorsement than a 1784 prayer for "the supreme rulers of the United States" that John Wesley had composed and sent to American

---

Asbury: 'The Prophet of the Long Road,'" *William and Mary Quarterly*, vol. 22, no. 1 (January 1942), pp. 39–44; William Larkin Durhem, *Francis Asbury: Founder of American Methodism and Unofficial Minister of State* (New York, 1928).

47. *JLFA*, vol. I, p. 489, n39.

48. On Wesley's bitter attacks on the American Revolution and Americans, see Kingswood Brooks, *Politics in the Order of Salvation: Transforming Wesleyan Political Ethics* (Nashville, TN, 2001), pp. 111–154; Ferguson, *Organizing to Beat the Devil*, attributes to Asbury the idea that the Methodists offer Washington a benediction. Though possible, Ferguson provides

Methodists.[49] Wesley's oddly named prayer was an attempt by a man who bitterly opposed American independence to allay suspicions over his booming Church. It was an effort that he could not make in earnest. The awkward prayer lacked an actual blessing, or any mention of God, offering only a gratuitous acknowledgment of US sovereignty.

> The congress, the general assemblies, the governors, and the councils of state, as delegates of the people, are rulers of the United States of America, according to the division of power made to them by the general Act of Confederation, and by the Constitutions of their respective states. And the said states ought not to be subject to any foreign jurisdiction.

For years, the Church reprinted a close approximation of Wesley's prayer in its annual *Discipline*, rather than the more coherent and elegant "Address" that Asbury and Coke had composed. Asbury recorded nothing about any of these events in his journal. Covering the relevant Conference meeting, he wrote only: "Our work opens in New York State. New England *stretcheth out the hand* to our ministry, and I trust thousands will shortly feel its influence. My soul shall praise the Lord."[50] Less surprisingly, Washington did not record the meeting with Asbury and Coke in his diary either. From the perspective of the development of American nationalism and the relation of the nation-builders to the peoples of the interior, these silences are of interest. Asbury probably knew more people than any other man in North America. In Washington, he encountered a counterpart from the world of nation-states, a living legend and one of the most widely known men in the Western world. The chasm of consciousness that separated the two men was also the problem that faced the American nation-builders.

Asbury's journal and letters, though they cover the years 1771–1816, spent ceaselessly traveling throughout the eastern half of the continent, are striking in their indifference to the Revolutionary War and the United States of America. In nearly half a century of almost daily journal entries,

---

no citation, and Asbury's journals and letters offer no evidence for the claim, p.16; cf. *JLFA*, vol. I, p. 598, n40.

49. On Asbury as a leader and in the pulpit, see Sprague, *Annals of the American Pulpit*, vol. 7, pp. 18, 20, 21, 25, 27–28; Wesley's prayer reprinted in Emory, p. 108.

50. The "Address" is reprinted in *JLFA*, vol. III, pp. 70–71; the journal entries surrounding the day of its recitation in ibid., vol. I, p. 598.

he mentions George Washington a total of seven times, never with any real interest. One of the more detailed references was in response to the sermon of a Presbyterian minister that Asbury heard in Elizabethtown, New Jersey. The sermon linked the American nation with the second coming of Christ. "The 22d chapter of the Revelation of Jesus Christ to St. John," explained the minister, "the time and place of the coming and kingdom of Christ; General Washington being Zerubabel, and himself Joshua the high priest." The linking of the patriot cause to the advent of a Christian millennium was fairly common in American politics, but it struck a strange note to Asbury. "All this appeared to me," he wrote, "like wildness on the brain."[51] In 1799, upon learning of Washington's death, Asbury eulogized him as "disinterested father, first father, and temporal saviour of *his* country." Even during the middle of revolutionary war, Asbury objected to the mixing of American issues with religion. In 1779, he attended a Presbyterian meeting, where he heard a sermon that, he complained, was "so full of politics" that it "turned all religion out of doors."[52]

Asbury conceived of the American national project with a good-natured disinterestedness that resists easy reconciliation with the way historians have organized modern history around the nation-state. In June 1776, Asbury was arrested in Baltimore for publicizing his refusal to serve as a juror. His refusal had aggravated popular suspicions that Methodists were agents of the Crown. But Asbury's refusal to serve was not a protest against the American government but against involvement in civic affairs. He paid his five-pound fine and was released. Two years later, the Patriots' suspicion of Methodists had increased enough that Asbury, in March 1778, took his only non-illness related break from itinerancy. Fear for his personal safety compelled him to hide for 10 months in home of a friend, Judge Thomas White of the Courts of Delaware.[53]

At White's house, in October 1792, Asbury read Thomas Jefferson's *Notes on the State of Virginia*. The book, which angered many acute Christians, bemused Asbury. He wrote, I "read in haste the most essential parts of 'Jefferson's Notes.' I have thought, it may be I am safer to be occasionally among the people of the world, than wholly confined to the

---

51. *JLFA*, vol. II, p. 94.

52. Ibid., p. 221. Emphasis added; *JLFA*, vol. I, p. 322.

53. On Asbury's 1776 arrest and self-imposed internal exile of 1778, see William B. Sprague, *Annals of the American Pulpit*, vol. VII, p. 15.

indulgent people of God." Interestingly, Asbury and the other Methodists did not typically share the driving anger at Enlightenment figures that animated many Reformed Protestants. In their 1789 "Plan for Education" at Cokesbury College, for example, the Methodists praised Rousseau's educational theories. They noted in passing that although Rousseau was "essentially mistaken in his religious system," his "wisdom in other respects, and extensive genius, are indisputably acknowledged." Asbury's judgment of Jefferson's *Notes*—"He who sometimes suffers from a famine will the better know how to relish a feast"—was also equanimous.[54]

With its own members, especially its itinerants, the Methodists were not known for equanimity. They did not aspire to be democratic but to be pious and holy. The Church required "the public worship of God." It prescribed 16 rules concerning "proper" singing. "Speaking evil of. . . itinerants" was forbidden. The ban on traveling preachers publishing books or pamphlets was supplemented by forbidding ministers or members from singing "hymns of your own composing." Neglect of any duties, as well as any "imprudent conduct" or any "disobedience to the order and discipline of the church" was to be met with "proper humiliation." If the member did not show "real humiliation, the member must be cut off." The Church provided formal procedures for members' trials and appeals. In order to make sure that they held no debts and could serve as impartial judges, Asbury required itinerants to submit to public examinations. Though not incompatible with republicanism, this anti-liberal requirement owed more to an ideal of "competency" and independence than to Atlantic world political theory.[55]

Not all the codes were negative. The *Discipline* favored "employing them [fellow Methodists] to others, buying one of another, helping each other in business." The world, they explained, "will love its own and them *only*."[56] Clear consequences attended violations. Society members were charged with the responsibility to "watch over" those who "observe them not." *The Discipline* formalized the means for "bringing to Trial,

---

54. For Asbury's comments on Jefferson's *Notes*, see *JLFA*, vol. I, p. 732; "The Plan of Education" for Cokesbury College reprinted in Emory, quote from p. 165.

55. *The Discipline* (1813), pp. 80–82, 89, 101–102; *The Discipline* (1801), pp. 62, 55. On the enforcement of the requirement that itinerants be debt-free, see Heyrman, *Southern Cross*, p. 289 n36. For Asbury and Coke on the necessity of excluding the laity from Church governance, see Heyrman, p. 100; Daniel Vickers, "Competency and Competition: Economic Culture in Early America," *William and Mary Quarterly*, vol. 47 (1990), pp. 3–29.

56. *The Discipline* (1801), p. 54. Italics in the original.

finding Guilty, and reproving, suspending, or excluding" members and ministers. The Church chose "agriculture and architecture" as the "recreation" allowed its seminary students. The curriculum for their Cokesbury College celebrated "Peter, the Russian emperor" as "the greatest statesman that perhaps ever shone" because Peter "disdained not to stoop to the employment of a ship carpenter." This was artisanal biblicism, not artisanal republicanism, which would not have celebrated a czar.[57]

The early Church's requirement that its ministers be debtless did not apply to the Church itself. In 1820, for example, the New England circuit fell $11,062 short of $16,487, the funds spent in support of their itinerants. One historian put it well, writing that Methodist itinerants and officials lived in "ostentatious poverty." Itinerants' 1800 and 1816 salaries, $80 and $100, respectively, were about one-fifth those of Congregationalist ministers and, in many places, less than an unskilled laborer could earn. Asbury, who (like James Monroe) signaled his belonging to a disappearing world by wearing already antiquated knee breeches, lost a battle to accept only single itinerants who took a vow of celibacy. Methodist asceticism bore no relation to Poor Richard's asceticism of accumulation. Church officials were fond of quoting Matthew, advising against earthly "treasures" which "moth and rust doth corrupt" and that thieves may "break through and steal." Think only of heaven, they advised, where there is "neither moth nor rust" and "thieves do not break through." The itinerants' "brotherhood of poverty" meant, in particular, cash poverty.[58] Baynard Rush Hall, the first professor at Indiana Seminary, told of his encounter with an itinerant in the early 1820s. The itinerant had returned from a trip of a thousand miles, through "woods and prairies," wrote Hall, with the "identical *pecunia* carried with him for expenses—viz. Fifty Cents! That, on leaving home, he had supposed would be enough;—it proved too much!"[59]

The itinerant Jacob Young told of how in Marietta, Ohio, in 1805, an illness had left him with a $27 doctor bill, but he had no cash. Another Methodist preacher, a man whom Young "had never seen of or heard

---

57. The "Plan of Education" for Cokesbury College was reprinted in *The Discipline* from 1789 to 1796; reprinted in Emory, quote from p. 162.

58. David Hempton, "A Tale of Preachers and Beggars: Methodism and Money in the Great Age of Transatlantic Perspective, 1780–1830," in Mark A. Noll, ed., *God and Mammon*, pp. 132–133; *The Discipline* (1813), p. 104; Charles W. Ferguson, *Organizing to Beat the Devil: Methodists and the Making of Modern America* (New York, 1971), p. 96.

59. Robert Carlton, *The New Purchase* (Princeton, NJ, 1916), p. 59.

of before," paid the doctor's bill with a canoe full of "corn, wheat, rye, oats, and potatoes." The generous act redoubled Young's commitment to the Methodists.[60] The doctor's request for cash payment, then acceptance of a canoe full of food for barter, captures the liberal civil society and economy taking over the frontier, nipping at the Methodists' heels. Though often portrayed as liberalizers, Methodist society was ambivalent about capitalism. On the one hand, its maxims of thrift and individual moral responsibility were a nursery of petty bourgeois virtues. At the same time, it harbored a suspicion of civil society, paper money, the market system, and consumerism. *The Discipline*, for example, prohibited "the use of many words in buying and selling." We "conceive it scarcely possible," explained the Church, "to use many words in buying and selling, without being frequently guilty of lying."[61]

Rather than to any doctrinal distinction or theological innovation, the Methodists owed their astounding growth to their ability to fill a social role. One frontier itinerant rightly described their special gift as upholding "the cords of brotherly love" in this "new. . . state of society." Amid all the different "phases of social life," Methodists "bore each other's burdens" and served as "the insurer of the other's reputation." Methodists "inquired after" one another with "as much care and solicitude" as one might expect from "some member of a family." Such "mutual interest in the spiritual welfare of each member of the Church," he wrote, "constituted the true secret of the early character of Methodism." After compiling the autobiographies and recollections of dozens of the earliest itinerants, James Finley concluded that the "great success" of the early Church in America must be attributed more to "this wholesome, social regulation" rather "than to any other peculiarity of doctrine." With the itinerants as an avant-garde, the Methodist system of social regulation preceded American presence in frontier regions acquired by both the 1783 Peace of Paris and the 1803 Louisiana Purchase. It prescribed guidelines in matters ranging from money lending and borrowing to proper attire. Lillian Smith remembered Methodist ministers in the South quoting *The Discipline* against the wearing of jewelry ("sinful baubles") or makeup ("painting of the face") into the twentieth century. That which the nationalists strove to do, to bring

---

60. Young's account excerpted in Baker, *History of Ohio Methodism*, p. 186.

61. Thomas Coke and Francis Asbury, *The Doctrines and Disciple of the Methodist Episcopal Church* (Philadelphia, 1798), p. 140.

governance to the periphery, the Methodists achieved earlier, and, at least in the beginning, for their own reasons.[62]

In 1800, in order to govern the West, the Methodists organized the Western Conference. The Western Conference divided the frontier, from the Appalachians to west of the Mississippi, into districts. Following a combined logic of geography and patterns of settlement, the Methodist organization of North America, between the Appalachians and the Mississippi River, differed significantly from US political geography. The Holston District comprised only a small portion of western Tennessee; the Cumberland District wound from the western corner of Virginia, across central Kentucky, and then dipped into central Tennessee. The Miami District was made from a swatch of what would become western Ohio and eastern Indiana, while the Illinois district snaked down through south-central Illinois across the Mississippi, well into what would become Missouri. The Wabash District encompassed what would become south-central Indiana and then extended west, including a good portion of southern Illinois. In a long, gentle curve flanking the riverbanks, the Mississippi District simply followed the river southward all the way from what would become Missouri to New Orleans. Not until 1828 did the Methodists get around to at least partially resolving some confusion by changing the "Kentucky Conference [to] include the state of Kentucky."[63]

The Western Conference also straddled free and slave areas, and counted members in Canada. At the 1802 Annual Conference, the Philadelphia secretary complained that it was "morally impossible to ascertain the numbers in the respective states." The Westerners, however, continued to count membership by circuits drawn independently of US political geography.[64] Methodists who took positions in national

---

62. James B. Finley *Sketches of Western Methodism: Biographical, Historical, Miscellaneous* (Cincinnati, 1857), p. 109; Smith, *Killers of the Dream*, p. 206; On the tendency of modern nationalist programs to co-opt the means of at least initially independent Protestant missionary efforts, see Gellner, *Nationalism*, pp. 75–76.

63. Western Conference circuit maps in "Being the Journal of the Western Conference, 1800–1811," reprinted in William Warren Sweet, ed., *The Rise of Methodism in the West* (New York, 1920), p. 34; Emory, p. 235.

64. *Minutes Taken at the Several Annual Conferences of the Methodist-Episcopal Church in America, for the Year 1801* (Philadelphia, 1801), p. 13 (hereafter cited as *MMEC*). For the Secretary's complaint, see *MMEC* (Philadelphia, 1802), p. 13; it continued: "in sundry instances, the circuits take in a part of the two states; part of the numbers in one, and part in the other." Twentieth-century denominational historians have devised formulas to retroactively reallocate membership by state. See, for example, John H. Wigger, *Taking Heaven by Storm*, pp. 197–200.

politics tended to be Jeffersonians, particularly approving of Jefferson's close association with disestablishment.[65] The definitive moments in the political history of the early republic, however—events that were propelling many of the migrants who swelled the ranks of the Methodist Church in the interior of the continent—remained outside the consciousness of the organized Church. During the first decade of the nineteenth century, the Western conference issued periodic letters on "the Temporal and Spiritual State of the Western Conference." We "live in an age," they wrote, "in which there is a great need to cry aloud." They did not, however, "cry aloud" about any of the definitive moments of the history of the early republic. For the years 1800 to 1811, for example, the minutes of the annual conference meetings record no discussion of Thomas Jefferson's election in 1800, the Louisiana Purchase of 1803, the recession created by the 1807 Embargo Act, or James Madison's 1808 election.[66]

The authority of the American nation and the institutions of American society made only sideways appearances in the annals of the Western Conference, usually in matters related to slavery. The Western Conference claimed broad authority over slavery, approving official interventions against Church members known to be slave owners. In 1806, for example, the Conference sent a letter to "Benjamin Wofford, on the business of his two Negroes in South Carolina." The Methodists advised Wofford "to measures that may secure their emancipation." Four years later, the Conference heard an appeal from Jacob Addams, a Kentucky Methodist who had been expelled from the Church by the Lexington District "for Purchasing a Negro woman and child with Speculative motives." The Conference turned down Addams's appeal, upholding his expulsion.[67]

---

65. Gary B. Nash, "The American Clergy and the French Revolution," *William and Mary Quarterly*, vol. 22 (1965), pp. 392–412. On the Jeffersonian tendency of Eastern Methodists, see Andrews, pp. 188–196.

66. "Being the Journal of the Western Conference, 1800–1811," pp. 101–102; Gordon S. Wood lists these as the "great headline events. . . big political and diplomatic happenings" of the early republic that coincide with the period of the minutes of the annual meetings of the Western Conference examined here. Wood argues that an interest in political history fell out of currency with the post–World War II dismantling of the Progressive interpretation, which, not coincidentally, was rooted in the early republic, see Wood, "The Significance of the Early Republic," *Journal of the Early Republic*, vol. 8 (Spring 1988), pp. 1–20, quotes from pp. 1, 4.

67. "Being the Journals of the Western Conference, 1800–1811," pp. 117, 184. I have corrected several misspellings from the conference minutes.

Despite the prohibition of slavery in the Northwest Ordinance, the 1820 census reported 190 slaves in Indiana, part of the Methodist Western Conference. The Conference also included a substantial amount of territory where slavery was not prohibited, and the straddling of free and slave areas made for a troublesome issue for Church governance. At the 1811 annual meeting, for example, the Conference held a hearing over the fact that Samuel Sellars, a Methodist elder in the Western Conference, owned a 14-year-old boy. The Methodist committee decided "that the Black boy shall serve him until he be 22 years of age," then freed, a decision to which Sellars apparently acquiesced. The Western Methodists also assumed a more aggressive anti-slavery authority than their fellow Methodists in the original states. Judging from the phrasing of their resolution against Benjamin Wofford, Wofford himself was not in South Carolina, but the Western Methodists still ordered him "to emancipate his two Negroes in South Carolina." No state or federal official in the West would have dared to claim the authority to order a frontier settler to emancipate his slaves in South Carolina.[68]

Methodists' participation in a 1796 slave auction in North Carolina distressed Francis Asbury. "My spirit was grieved," wrote Asbury. Asbury feared that owners or overseers' would "cut, skin, and starve" those being sold, and he thought Methodists selling their slaves responsible. "I think such members ought to be dealt with," he wrote, "on the side of the oppressors there are law and power, but where are justice and mercy to the poor slaves?" His powerlessness to effect any Church actions led him to fall back upon the tactics of moral suasion: "I will try if words can be like drawn swords to pierce the hearts of their owners."[69] Virginia's plantation society caused Asbury particular anguish. While traveling through the state, in 1798, he lamented, "O! to be dependent on slaveholders is in part to be a slave, and I was free born." He concluded that slavery will exist in Virginia "for ages" because Virginia had "neither sufficient sense of religion nor of liberty to destroy it." He predicted a depopulation of the state: "poor men and free men will not live among slaveholders, but will go to new lands." Only slaveholders

---

68. On the figure of 190 slaves in Indiana in 1820, see Jacob Piatt Dunn, *Indiana and Indianans: A History of Aboriginal and Territorial Indiana and the Century of Statehood* (Chicago, 1919), p. 306. Piatt Dunn also reports that a local 1830 census of Vincennes, Indiana, showed 30 slaves in that locale; Sweet, ed., "Being the Journals of the Western Conference," p. 203.

69. *JLFA*, vol. II, p. 109.

and those "dependent on them will stay in old Virginia."[70] In 1812, near Bryant, Virginia, Asbury found himself faced with civil charges for ordaining a "colored" man alleged to be legally enslaved. Acknowledging civil authority, he produced state papers to prove the man's freedom: "A charge had been brought against me for ordaining a slave; but. . . I was ready with my certificates to prove his freedom." With the disdain and powerlessness of sarcasm, he conceded the imperative of the master class: "the subject of contention was nearly white, and his *respectable* father would neither own nor manumit him."[71]

The larger and more powerful it became, the more the Church compromised early, forthrightly anti-slavery principles. In 1808, for example, when the General Conference turned over authority on the issue of slavery to the smaller Annual Conferences, the South Carolina Conference quickly issued a new edition of *The Discipline*, from which they expunged any mention of slavery. The same year, the Western Conference reaffirmed their anti-slavery rule, prescribing expulsion for any Methodist who bought or sold a slave, for any reason other than manumission.[72] This new, federalist-style principle allowed the Methodists to preserve membership, keep dues forthcoming, and maintain influence by accommodating local interests. Evangelical Protestantism could and did accommodate and sanction slavery. There was a good reason that the Bible was the only book that the master class permitted among the enslaved. As Eugene Genovese has written, Methodist anti-slavery sentiments have been done too much honor. Nonetheless, the planters' suspicions of the Methodists had some basis in reality. It was, for example, Francis Asbury who, in 1799, ordained Richard Allen, the founder of the African Methodist Episcopal Church, thereby becoming one of the godfathers of Afro-American religion. Asbury and Allen enjoyed an enduring friendship, and Asbury himself was one of African-Americans' most reliable allies in the early republic. More important, planters found it safer to support established churches, which were dependent on the planters' political and financial support. The then famous Rev. Charles Colcock Jones, a

---

70. Ibid., p. 151.

71. Ibid., p. 694. Italics in original.

72. Walter Brownlow Posey, "The Influence of Slavery upon the Methodist Church in the Early South and Southwest," *The Mississippi Valley Historical Review*, vol. 17 (1931), pp. 534–535; "Journals of the Western Conference," p. 148; Donald G. Mathews, *Slavery and Methodism: A Chapter in American Morality, 1780–1845* (Princeton, NJ, 1965).

noted, popular revivalist in plantation society, worked for the planters and was dependably pro-slavery. Enthusiastic revivalism stirred by itinerant frontier ministers was unlikely to win planter support.[73]

The North American Methodists' indifference to the War of 1812 was also indicative of their distance from the American national mission. Religiously inspired opposition to the war was not necessarily a sign of distance from the national project. Some anti-war New England newspapers reprinted James Madison's first wartime religious proclamation to help turn religious Americans against "Mr. Madison's War." They rightly anticipated that Madison's tepid proclamation would only incite their acutely Protestant readers. One such Anglo-Protestant nationalist, the Rev. Benjamin Bell, preached to his congregation that Great Britain was spreading "the Gospel throughout the world," and that to make war on her "was to fight against God; and I say it still." In order to gin up their fellow Anglo-Protestant nationalists, American Bible societies and New England newspapers published accounts of British missionary work in India, reminding readers that Britain and America were not enemies but allies, united in Christ to enlighten the heathens of Asia. During the war, *Christian Researches in Asia*, the evangelical Anglican Claudius Buchanan's account of his 12 years as a British missionary in India, became an unlikely national bestseller. New Englanders in particular celebrated Buchanan as a heroic foot soldier in the Anglo-Protestant mission to the darker races.[74]

The frontier Methodists, who were in fact one of the most dynamic Anglo-Protestant movements since the Reformation, took no position. In their indifference to the war, the Methodists differed from New England Christians and Western nationalists. Believing that it would extend American sovereignty farther into the continent and strengthen Western congressional interests, Western congressmen were among the lead agitators for the war. Once again stoking suspicions of loyalty to Britain, the Methodists refused to take sides, and the Church forbade its men to fight. Most itinerants in upstate New York, Vermont, and Canada suspended their rounds. After traveling through a soldier recruitment drive in Uniontown, Pennsylvania, Asbury acknowledged little stake in

73. Richard S. Newman, *Freedom's Prophet: Bishop Richard Allen, the AME Church, and the Black Founding Fathers* (New York, 2009); quoted in Posey, "The Influence of Slavery upon the Methodist Church in the Early South and Southwest," p. 530.

74. Gribbin, *The Churches Militant*, pp. 20–24, 42–46.

the war. "We have serious times," he wrote, "it becomes us to be silent, and let God judge the nations, and correct the guilty." Asbury did offer to bless the soldiers, but as individual men, not as an American fighting force.[75]

To the Ohio Conference, the most noteworthy aspect of the War was that it began "immediately following the formation of the Ohio Conference." They reported the chief "effect of the War" as the resulting "high prices for provisions," particularly flour, which shot up to "sixteen dollars a barrel." They complained that the prices "continued throughout the second winter of the war."[76] Mostly, they worried about the impact of the war on Church membership, as "war spirit was. . . harmful to their work." They saw the most notable results of the war as an increase in "loud and long" cursing, rampant extortion on subsistence commodities, and the greater market for the sinful "selling [of] liquid fire." In his autobiography, the itinerant Jacob Young lamented that the people were "so much taken up with politics and war that they lost their zeal in the cause of God." Even Peter Cartwright, whose nationalism was an anomaly among early circuit-riders, understood the war primarily as threat to an independent Church mission. "This year [1812–1813]," wrote Cartwright, "there was a considerable decrease in membership in the Methodist Episcopal Church, owing chiefly to the war with England." Officials of Virginia Methodism, which was concentrated in the western part of the state, saw falling Church membership, not the war itself, as the evidence of declension. The Virginia Methodists' denunciations of "war fever" led, again, to charges that the Methodists were Loyalists, Tories, and traitors.[77]

---

75. On the causes of the War of 1812, see George Dangerfield, *The Era of Good Feelings*, (New York, 1952), pp. 90–91, 105–121. For an argument that focuses on American imperial ambitions for Canada, see J. C. A. Stagg, "James Madison and the Coercion of Great Britain: Canada, the West Indies, and the War of 1812," *William and Mary Quarterly*, vol. 38, no. 1 (January 1981), pp. 3–34. On the Eastern churches and the war, see Gribbin, *Churches Militant: The War of 1812 and American Religion* (New York, 1973). On the Methodists' position of neutrality in the War of 1812, see Heyrman, *Southern Cross*, p. 229, and Adamson, p. 435. For Asbury's proclamation of neutrality, see *JLFA*, vol. II, p. 708.

76. Journals of the Ohio Conference reprinted in William Warren Sweet, ed., *Circuit-Rider Days along the Ohio: Being the Journals of the Ohio Conference from Its Organization in 1812 to 1826* (New York, NY, 1923), pp. 30–33.

77. Ibid.; Jacob Young, *Autobiography of a Pioneer* (Cincinnati, OH, 1858), p. 309; William Warren Sweet, ed., *Virginia Methodism: A History* (Richmond, VA, 1955), pp. 170–171; Cartwright quoted in Sweet, *Circuit-Rider Days along the Ohio*, p. 30, n6; Ernest Tuveson, *Redeemer Nation: The Idea of America's Millennial Role* (Chicago, 1968), pp. 52–63.

Unfortunately for Methodist itinerants in Canada, American accusations of their "Toryism" and "loyalism" failed to impress actual Tories or Loyalists. In 1786, Loyalist settlers in Upper Canada attacked Major George Neal, the first Methodist itinerant in Upper Canada, stoning him in the streets of Queenston, Ontario. In 1805, residents in Kingston, Ontario, attacked William Case and Henry Ryan, two Methodist itinerants, again for unauthorized public preaching. In 1810, the Ontario House Assembly, dominated by Anglican Loyalists, expelled two Methodist lay preachers who had won election to the House. In Canada, Methodists' anti-elitism, lack of education, emotional preaching style, and popularity in the United Sates sowed suspicions that they were agents of Yankee imperialism. As early as 1791, John Graves Simcoe, the first lieutenant-governor of Upper Canada, justified the need for a state church on the grounds of the protection it would offer from the "fanatic" Methodists who were winning a "superstitious hold of the multitude."[78]

Whether they were in Canada or the United States, the War of 1812 brought trouble for North American Methodists. Fostering the misimpression that the War of 1812 precipitated a joint rise in nationalism and Church growth, a contemporary Methodist historian and preacher reported that Methodism in the West and South made "considerable" progress during the war.[79] Though in some cases in the South, such as the Mississippi Baptists, the upheaval of war expanded membership in popular Protestantism, the war actually slowed the growth of Methodism on the frontier. Progress "was most considerable" in the sense that membership declined less than in the other conferences. Not until 1815 did the Western Methodists recover from the attrition of 1812–1813. Although Church membership actually increased in one Indiana circuit, a contemporary observer attributed that exception to a series of earthquakes in the winter of 1811 and 1812, sometimes called the New Madrid quake, not the war.[80] The earthquakes brought the "most vile and hardened sinners" rushing

---

78. On Methodist opposition to Fourth of July celebrations, see Heyrman, *Southern Cross*, p. 316, n36. On the Anglican, Loyalist opposition to Methodists in Canada, see Christopher Adamson, "God's Continent Divided: Politics and Religion in Upper Canada and the Northern and Western United States, 1775–1841, pp. 434–437; Elizabeth Cooper, "Religion, Politics, and Money: The Methodist Union of 1832–33," *Ontario History*, vol. 81 (June 1989), pp. 89–108.

79. A. G. Meacham, *A Compendious History of the Rise and Progress of the Methodist Church, Both in Britain and America*. . . (Hallowell, UK, 1832), p. 416.

80. On the growth of Baptism in Mississippi during the War of 1812, see Adam Rothman, *Slave Country: American Expansion and the Origins of the Deep South* (Cambridge, MA,

to the churches, "to tremble and quake. . . and weep and pray." A contemporary newspaper reported that after the earthquakes, every preacher, both traveling and local, "began to hold meetings with more earnestness than ever" and it seemed as if "almost everybody would become religious that winter and spring."[81] A Tennessee merchant told of how before the earthquakes, he sold "ten packs of cards where he sold one bible, now he sold ten bibles where he sold one pack of cards." A Missouri itinerant remembered that the earthquakes, not the War, brought people into the Church. Such fears, which were as prevalent on the frontier as social regulation was lacking, also helped early North American Methodism grow.[82]

Francis Asbury wrote almost nothing for publication, excepting his annual edition of hymns, the *Pocket Hymn-Book*. Many sing of sickness or despair:

> *Come, ye sinners, poor and needy,*
> *Weak and wounded, sick and sore,*
> *Jesus ready stands to save you,*
> *Full of pity, love and pow'r*
>
> *Come, ye weary, heavy-laden'd,*
> *Brusi'd and mangled by the fall,*
> *If you tarry till you're better,*
> *You'll never come at all. . . [83]*

The hymns spoke of the world as a place of suffering, but a fleeting place, versus eternity of the afterlife:

> *Pain endless misery!*
> . . .
> *Thee we adore, Eternal Name,*
> *And humbly own to thee,*

2007), ch. 1; William Warren Sweet, *Circuit-Rider Days along the Ohio* (New York, 1923), pp. 41–42.

81. From the *Western Christian Advocate*, January 9, 1846, quoted in Sweet, *The Rise of Methodism in the West*, p. 29.

82. Samuel J. Mills, *Communications Relative to the Progress of the Bible Societies in the United States* (Philadelphia, 1813), p. 11; William Stevenson on the New Madrid earthquake and how it brought people to the Church, see Walter N. Vernon, *William Stevenson: Riding Preacher*, p. 35.

83. Thomas Coke and Francis Asbury, *Pocket Hymn-Book* (Philadelphia, 1800), pp. 5–6.

How feeble is our mortal frame,
What dying worms we be!
. . .
So shall I spend my life's short day,
Obedient to thy will.[84]
Our wasting lives grow shorter still,
As days and months increase.
And ev'ry beating pulse we tell,
Leaves but the number less.[85]

Such misery marks the world that one must bear in mind the moment
of judgment day, to be prepared to greet doom with joy:
Wak'd by the trumpet's sound,
I from my grace must rise,. . .
How shall I leave my tomb!
With triumph or regret?
A fearful or a joyful doom.

The saved knew the pains and the pleasures of the world were transient:
No room for mirth or trifling here,
For worldly hope or worldly fear,
. . .
No matter which my thoughts employ
A moment's misery or joy.[86]

The hymns exemplify themes common in Christianity of the poor: the world is a cold and alien place, bearable because it is transient, and the merit of one's conduct will find recognition in the afterlife. "Nothing," went one of Asbury's hymns, "is worth a thought beneath" how to "make election sure." Believers and good Methodists could expect that "when I fail on earth, secure / A mansion in the skies."[87] The music of Methodism was not just about otherworldy revenge or delayed justice. Methodist hymns recognized free will, the power of individual discipline, and the possibility that change lay within reach. There was no fate, no predestination. If one could change one's place in regard to God's grace, worldly change was a comparably small

---

84. Ibid., pp., 14, 11.

85. Ibid., p. 12.

86. Ibid., p. 15.

87. Ibid.

thing. In an important departure from Calvinism, Methodist hymns celebrate that through Christ, God offered salvation to everyone. First in *A Pocket Hymn-Book* was always Charles Wesley's "O for a Thousand Tongues to Sing." Its message is evangelical, asking for divine help to "spread through all the earth abroad" God's word. Evangelicalism is meaningful because, through Jesus, God has offered salvation to all humanity: the sacrifice of Jesus offers everyone hope: "His soul was once an off'ring made / For every soul of man." The name of Jesus "charms our fears" and "bids our sorrows cease." Even to the sinner, Jesus's death promises "life, and healthy, and peace." Sin and sinners, explains the hymn, cannot constrain Jesus:

> *He breaks the power of cancell'd sin,*
> *He sets the pris'ner free;*
> *His blood can make the foulest clean;*
> *His blood avail'd for me.*

The focus on Jesus (as opposed to God), the evangelical obligation, the possibility of grace for everyone, and the implicit (but to Reformed Protestant thinkers clear and objectionable) recognition of human agency, even possible human holiness, were neither Methodist innovations nor unique to Methodism, but no one carried these ideas to more people in nineteenth-century America than the Methodists.[88]

Republican ideas or ambitions were not part of the Methodist mission. In 1792, in the name of republicanism and American principles, the Chesapeake Methodist James O'Kelly mounted an internal challenge, against Asbury and the Methodist Church, to grant itinerants' rights in the placement of their itinerancy. O'Kelly's main grievance was that Bishops Asbury and Coke (the Methodists, typically off-note when it came to nationalist politics, changed their titles from superintendent to bishop in 1787) possessed despotic powers over circuit appointments. O'Kelly wanted a democratic process. Calling himself "a son of America," he denounced the hierarchical structure of the Church as indicative of the "British yoke" and shameful "lordship" that the Revolution had discredited. In the hyperbolic rhetoric of the American Revolution, O'Kelly alleged the Church had slipped into "POPERY," and accused it of conspiring "through a species of tyranny" to make its own

---

88. Robert Spence, Thomas Coke, Francis Asbury, *A Pocket Hymn-Book: Designed as a Constant Companion for the Pious* (Philadelphia, 1790), pp. 5–6.

ministers "slaves." The Church rejected O'Kelly's democratization campaign. He left to form the Republican Methodist Church and, eventually, a universalist Christian organization. The schism led to renewed
accusations that the Methodists were, in the words of another veteran of
the Revolution, "Enemies to the Constitution of the States." To patriots
caught up with the American cause, Methodist indifference could look
like enmity.[89] O'Kelly lost his campaign to republicanize the Methodists
because most itinerants backed Asbury: any sacrifice of individual
rights as construed by American principles was less important than
their effectiveness in the grand work before them: "the salvation of
souls."[90] In the weeks preceding the second national elections in 1792,
the same year that O'Kelly brought his democratization campaign to the
Methodist General Conference, Asbury complained of democracy as a
distraction from the kingdom of God. Preaching in Delaware, Asbury
noted that the "minds of the people were so occupied by the approaching of the election. . . that I fear there was little room for things of more
importance." Asbury and the early Methodists were not democratizers
but popularizers. Their mission was to bring God to as many people as
possible. They did so by serving the poor, especially the poor migrants
in the interior of the continent.[91]

In his 1813 "Farewell Address," in the middle of the War of 1812, Asbury
reiterated to the leaders of the Methodist Church their independence
from the United States and its civil society. He invoked a continental
dominion, writing: "Our continent is three thousand miles in length. . .
all of which, with very few exceptions, we have visited." He emphasized
their pastoral and social role, "we have planted and watered. . . and we
do water still." In contrast to the Methodists concerns, the United States
belonged to the profane world. "We neither have, nor wish to have,"
he reminded Methodists, "anything to do with the government of the
States, nor, as I conceive, do the states fear us. Our kingdom is not of this

---

89. On the change from superintendent to bishop, see Emory, p. 82. Internal resentments
against the great power Asbury wielded over the Methodist Church were a consistent
feature of early Church politics; see Dee. E. Andrews, *The Methodists and Revolutionary
America, 1760–1800*, pp. 218–221. At their height, the Republican Methodists counted
10,000 members, mainly in eastern Virginia; see Mark Noll, *America's God: From Jonathan
Edwards to Abraham Lincoln* (New York, 2002), pp. 168, 339–340. See also Gaustad and
Barlow, eds., *The New Historical Atlas*, p. 221. On the schism leading to renewed charges
against the Methodists, see Heyrman, *Southern Cross*, p. 230.

90. Mark A. Noll, *America's God*, pp. 335, 339–340.

91. *JLFA*, vol. I, p. 696.

world."[92] Well into at least the second decade of the nineteenth century, the Church emphasized "the absolute necessity" of union, not among Americans but among Methodists. Early American Methodism, in the words of one historian, "lacked a concept of the nation"; it "simply looked right through the nation." It was marked by what another historian called "apolitical pietism," a feature of Methodism that could appear consistent with American secularism. The Methodists, however, had come to separate religion and politics for their own reasons, and independently of influence from properly secular principles. The Methodists did not belong to the Jeffersonian tradition of secularism, which aimed to protect the nation from religious passions, but to the Roger Williams tradition of separating politics from religion in order to protect the integrity of religion.[93]

At times, the Church separated the Methodists from the authority of civil law, as when it forbade "brother *going to law* with brother" in civil suits. The Church had its own set of procedures for complaints against members for non-payment of debt. It forbade members borrowing money "without a probability of paying," and it forbade "usury." If "one of the parties be dissatisfied with the judgment given," it outlined an appeals process through two higher levels of Church governance, followed by two more committees of arbitration, and then recourse to punishments. Any Methodist who bypassed Church governance and chose to "enter into a [civil] law-suit, in cases of debt or other disputes. . . shall be expelled."[94] Interestingly, though the Church claimed jurisdiction over matters of money and morals, it recognized that marriage fell under the civil law.[95] For its first 20 years as a separate Church, North American Methodism claimed the right "to purge our society" of members who married those lacking "godliness." In 1804, however, the Church softened their position, promising to merely "discourage" such marriages.[96] A bourgeois civil law and its culture of professional lawyers would not begin to permeate the

---

92. *JLFA*, vol. III, p. 480.

93. *The Discipline*, pp. iii, 33, 39; Russell E. Richey, *Early American Methodism*, p. 33; Edmund S. Morgan, *Roger Williams: The Church and the State* (New York, 1967), pp. 28–56, 86–120.

94. Quote taken from Charles G. Sellers, *The Market Revolution* (New York, 1994), p. 160; *The Doctrines and Disciplines of the Methodist Episcopal Church in America* (Philadelphia, 1801), pp. 23, 26–27.

95. Ibid., pp. 53, 60. Italics in original; The 1812 *Discipline* is excerpted in Emory, p. 150.

96. Emory, p. 188.

Middle West, the area of the Western Conference north of the Ohio River, for over two decades, and then it also implemented a circuit system of itinerants. Asbury and the Methodists did not invent the circuit system, which had been practiced in places since the Middle Ages. But by the time a culture of professional legal practice reached the Middle West, the Methodists had already accustomed the settlers of the Old Northwest to the exercise of law and justice through itinerancy and a circuit-system.[97]

With the Northwest Ordinance, American statesmen had tried to define "the rules of everyday conduct on both the private and public levels" in the Old Northwest. The Ordinance was good at providing macro guidelines of colonization, but it could not establish rules of everyday conduct.[98] The Methodists did. Asbury saw the two systems, the government of the Church and "the government of the states," as inherently incompatible. For him they were. In 1806, he wrote to a Western elder, "The glory of the Kingdom of Christ, the organization of the primitive Church of God, these are all my objects; was it possible to set a glass to my heart, you should see them engraven there by the word & spirit of the living God." Asbury loved "Americans" because he was able to fill the "primitive Church of God" with them, to thereby add to "the Kingdom of Christ." Neither he nor early American Methodism held any notion of a mythical or sacred American nation. With its effective pastoral system and heart-oriented evangelicalism, Methodism probably gave more to early nineteenth-century American society than it took. In particular, Methodism is helpful to any understanding of the distinctive combination of anti-elitism and social conservatism that permeates middle-class life in the American South and Midwest.[99]

Another consequence of the early Methodists' independence from the American national project was, at least on the frontier, an integrated church. In 1816, when the nation-state builders chose Columbus as the seat of Ohio government, they turned to George McCormick, a local Methodist lay-minister and carpenter, to build the first statehouse. McCormick's band included Moses Freeman, a black man, who assisted

---

97. On the development of the civil law and a bourgeois culture of professional lawyers in the Midwest, see Timothy R. Mahoney, *Provincial Lives: Middle-Class Experience in the Antebellum Middle West* (New York, 1999), pp. 168–212. Mahoney does not explicitly compare the itinerant ministers and the itinerant lawyers and judges and their respective circuit-systems, but the similarities are evident.

98. Andrew R. L. Clayton and Peter S. Onuf, *The Midwest and the Nation: Rethinking the History of an American Region* (Bloomington, IN, 1990), p. 3.

99. *JLFA*, vol. III, p. 566.

McCormick in the organization of first Methodist society of Columbus. Life for people of African descent in Ohio, however, was easier before the consolidation of American nationalism, and its peculiar racial ideology, on the frontier. Despite having probably helped McCormick in the construction of the first Ohio statehouse, Freeman chose not to remain where he and many other Methodists had helped to prepare the way for American "manifest destiny." Instead, Freeman opted to continue his work as a Methodist missionary in Liberia.[100]

From the perspective of American nationalists, Methodist itinerants were a wild card in the deck of governance. They came and went freely. Their itinerancy gave them a perspective on social relations that might be obscured by neighborly bonds and obligations. They maintained that God spoke to common people. They told people to believe in their own ability to think about the scriptures, and people who believe they know the word of God are less likely to be cowed by the authority of man. During the 1800 "Gabriel Conspiracy" in Richmond, a rumor circulated that the conspirators intended to incite the slaves to rise and kill all white men, excepting Frenchmen, Quakers, and Methodists. Methodist denunciations of Fourth of July celebrations as licentious, un-Christian rites contributed further grounds for questioning their political loyalty. On shifting grounds of alleged secret "Tory" commitments, or accusations of revolutionary opposition to slaveholding republicanism, South Carolina mobs continued, well into the nineteenth century, to periodically attack Methodist itinerants. As late as 1855, with *The Great Iron Wheel; or, Republicanism Backwards and Christianity Reversed,* James Robinson Graces, a prominent Tennessee Baptist minister, debater, and editor, published a 600-page attack on the Methodist Church as a crypto-Catholic and anti-American internal threat.[101]

No sensible ruling class would have welcomed the rise of Methodism. Elite Northeastern Reformed Protestants and Southern planters found different, sometimes conflicting, reasons to oppose Methodists. Both

---

100. On McCormick and Freeman, see John Marshall Barker, *History of Ohio Methodism: A Study in Social Science* (Cincinnati, OH, 1898), p. 356.

101. On the rumors surrounding the "Gabriel Conspiracy," see Robin Blackburn, *The Overthrow of Colonial Slavery, 1776–1858* (New York, 1988), p. 279. On the tendency of the planter class to implicate evangelical Protestantism as a cause of early nineteenth-century slave insurrections, both real and imagined, see John Scott Strickland, "The Great Revival and Insurrectionary Fears in North Carolina: An Examination of Antebellum Southern Society and Slave Revolt Panics," in Orville Vernon Burton and Robert C. McMath, Jr.,

sometimes brought up John Wesley's opposition to American independence, and Wesley's Tory sympathies. At the same time, Canada's Tory, Anglican gentry denounced Canadian Methodists as republican revolutionaries. In the 1820s, John Strachan, a prominent Ontario politician, attacked Methodists as enemies of the Crown. Strachan emphasized their "zeal without knowledge" and "disdain" for learning. He warned that their "knowledge. . . and sentiments" came "from the Republican States of America." He told Canadians that the Methodists "were hostile to our institutions, both civil and religious." Strachan's campaign contributed to the harassment, as disloyal agitators, of several either loyal or apolitical Canadian circuit-riders. In order to counter the alleged republican, American component of Methodism, Strachan and John Colborne, the lieutenant-governor of Upper Canada, helped convince officials in Britain and Canada to invite British Methodists to return their missionaries to Canada. Strachan was an Anglican archdeacon, and Upper Canada leaders represented an Anglican establishment. Had he been alive, John Wesley would likely have relished the fact that Anglicans, enjoying the protection of state establishment, sought assistance from Methodist missionaries. In fact, the British Methodists received a warmer welcome from Tory Anglicans in Canada than from North American (Episcopal) Methodists. "It may sound very well as a flourish of Speech that Methodists are the same all over the World," Strachan told the British Methodists in 1831, "but I cannot hardly conceive two Christian denominations who differ more widely in practice than the Methodists in England and Those of the United States." The "rancour" of the North Americans against the state church and "all Colonial institutions and all persons in authority," explained Strachan, was "notorious." On the other hand, Strachan found the more refined British Wesleyans to his liking.[102]

Though in sound agreement on Christian doctrine, social differences between the British and the North American Methodists produced tension and animosity. The British Wesleyan Methodists found the North Americans overly rigid in their Sabbath observance and avoidance of both alcohol and profanity. To the British Methodists, the North Americans' manners and

---

eds., *Class, Conflict, and Consensus: Antebellum Southern Community Studies* (Westport, CT, 1982), pp. 57–96. On Methodist itinerants in the South and slavery, see also Christine Leigh Heyrman, *Southern Cross: The Beginnings of the Bible Belt* (New York, 1997), pp. 227–232. On Graves, see Mark A. Noll, *America's God*, pp. 244–246.

102. Elizabeth Cooper, "Religion, Politics, and Money: The Methodist Union of 1832–33," pp. 89–91, 101.

education also seemed deficient. In turn, the North American Methodists complained about the British Wesleyans' conservative politics and thought them so mannered as to be "servile" and unmanly and so "secularized" as to be un-Christian. These difficulties did not stop the North American Methodists in Canada from seeing that they had little choice but to accept union with British Wesleyans. The North Americans' hopes that the well-financed Wesleyans would bring prosperity, and that union would put an end to their harassment as disloyal republicans, proved well founded. So did their concern over new strictures. For the Canadians, the 1832 union of Canadian and British Methodism meant direct rule by London. The British instituted and enforced a "no politics" rule among ministers: expressing radical or reforming political views met with either transfer or expulsion. The Methodist Union of 1832 marks a key moment in the history of religion in North America, a point at which Protestantism in Canada took a different, more establishment course than it would in the United States.[103]

The Union of 1832 was another step toward comparative stability in Canada. Officials had instituted an at least equally effective measure to support Britishness in Canada in 1815, when the Crown had authorized the governor of Quebec to refuse land grants to Americans. Over the opposition of commercial interests, the governor exercised the power. In 1825, he was still maintaining that the "speedy settlement of the Colony however desirable is a secondary object compared to its settlement in such a manner as shall best secure its attachment to British Laws and Government." Despite interest from Americans, Upper Canada was peopled by Irish, English, and Scottish immigrants who arrived as the return cargo in ships that had carried Quebec timber to Britain. Immigration to America was more diverse. Land titles on the American frontier were also less secure, especially south of the Ohio River. American conditions differed: freedom of religion, richer agricultural lands, greater insecurity of land ownership, and more religious diversity contributed to the unusually vibrant and disorderly birth of popular religion in the United States.[104]

Finally, there is almost no chance whatsoever, to my mind, that the absence of national consciousness among the Methodist leadership was either confined to the Church leadership or, in popular frontier religion, unique to Methodism. John Strachan and the Canadian Methodists, for example, both discovered that in politics, culture, and manners, British

---

103. Ibid., pp. 89, 99, 104.

104. D. W. Meinig, *The Shaping of America*, vol. 2, pp. 50–51.

Methodists had more in common with Canadian Anglicans than they did with North American Methodists. Despite their denominational difference and geographic distance, British Methodists and Canadian Anglicans both identified with, broadly speaking, middle-class society. Before launching the schismatic Republican Methodist Church, James O'Kelly had tried and failed to Americanize the Methodist Church, but O'Kelly was from the Virginia Tidewater, one of the nurseries of American nationalism. O'Kelly won some supporters, but the westward-looking Methodist Church rejected his call for Americanization. Some Baptists served as leaders in the American Tract Society, American Bible Society, and other nationalist missionary organizations, but they were elite, New England Baptists. The preponderance of Baptist growth came from economically insecure people on the frontier.[105]

Frontier and rural Baptists took particular exception to the large missionary associations, in which Northern business interests and American nationalism played formative roles. Among rural, poor peoples, several different sectarian Baptist groups took shape out of direct opposition to the missions movement. Reacting against the well-apportioned Northern missionary agencies, the primitive Baptists, the "Hard-Shell" Baptists, "anti-effort" preachers, and other anti-mission Baptists objected to what they saw as the unscriptural contrivances of the missionary movement. As instruments of Christian evangelizing, anti-mission Baptists found no scriptural justification, and therefore no legitimacy, for steam-powered presses, the postal service, railway lines, any association larger than the simple church, or for that matter Sunday schools, music, or even seminaries. Seminaries, a Kentucky Baptist remarked, were an expensive way to turn graceless and lazy young men into bad preachers. Anti-mission Baptists alleged that the Northeastern missionaries' regard for mathematics, philosophy, and law elevated these "human sciences" to a false equality with divine revelation. They asked why missionaries preferred their "little tracts of four pages" to the Bible. Even the Baptists' own tract society received most of its support from the Northeast. In 1831, for example, the 40,000 Baptists of Kentucky contributed a total of one dollar to the Philadelphia-based Baptist Tract Society. When asked to give money to a missionary society, a prominent Baptist in Kentucky replied that he had no counterfeit money, and he would not waste good money on such a cause. Antipathy for the missionaries was not confined

---

105. Bertram Wyatt-Brown, "The Antimission Movement in the Jacksonian South: A Study in Regional Folk Culture," *The Journal of Southern History* (November 1970), pp. 501–505, 507; Walter Brownlow Posey, *Religious Strife on the Southern Frontier* (Baton Rouge, LA, 1965), pp. 66–79.

to the South. In 1830, the Apple Creek Baptist Association in Illinois issued a declaration of their "unfellowship with foreign and domestic missionary societies." As a rule, missionary societies were rich, and frontier Baptists poor. Yet the Apple Creek Baptist Association advised their members not to give to "such beggarly institutions" as the missions. The characterization captured the pride of independent freeholders and their low view of the missionaries' fund-raising methods. The center of anti-mission activity was Tennessee, where, by the mid-1820s, Baptist churches began issuing resolutions rescinding any association with missionary organizations. Some refused to admit anyone who belonged to a missionary, bible, or tract society. A Richland, Tennessee, Baptist group referred to the missionary organizations as "unscriptural and disorganizing societies." A Green River, Kentucky, Baptist group called them the "missionary unscriptural societies" and asked why a Christian ought to look to the local nabobs who ran the missionary societies rather than to Peter, John, and other "inspired" witnesses to Christ, whose words were in the Bible.[106]

Frontier Baptists and Methodists in the early republic often disliked each other. The enmity was more prevalent among the ministers than the laity, in part because they competed for the same potential church members. Despite their rivalry with the Baptists, and real differences between the two groups, Methodists, too, often found the missionary association phenomenon an alien and alienating affair, one that raised more questions than it answered. James B. Finley, a Methodist itinerant who was converted at the historic Cane Ridge revival meeting, in 1801, wondered if the associations' proliferation of books and tracts did not succeed mainly in "diverting the mind from the Bible." Finley suspected that the "multiplicity of benevolent associations has a tendency to divert the mind from the Church." Beginning in the late 1820s, William G. "Parson" Brownlow, a prominent Methodist itinerant from East Tennessee, published a series of polemical attacks on his rivals, including the American Bible Society and American Home Missionary Society. After riding circuit for a decade, Brownlow established himself in Tennessee politics, where he became a fierce critic of Andrew Johnson and, eventually, during Reconstruction, the military governor of Tennessee. During the 1820s and 1830s, however, Brownlow's preferred opponent was the missionary movement. He

---

106. Wyatt-Brown, "The Antimission Movement in the Jacksonian South," pp. 502, 511–513; Walter Brownlow Posey, *The Baptist Church in the Lower Mississippi River Valley* (Lexington, KY, 1957), pp. 69–70, 72, 76–77.

charged that the missionaries were driven by "mercenary motives to enrich themselves on the spoils of simple natives." He thought them more sectarian than Christian, in particular that they were fronts for elite Northern Congregationalists and Presbyterians.[107] Finally, for a time, Barton W. Stone's Stoneites and Alexander Campbell's Disciples of Christ, both of which flourished on the frontier, especially in Kentucky and Ohio, also opposed the missions movement. The grounds for their objections should be by now familiar: they found no scriptural justification for missionary and benevolent associations, while perceiving the organizations as greedy, mendacious sectarian projects hiding behind a mask of Christian piety.[108]

In conclusion, much of the scholarly apparatus on the history of American religion—monographs, archives, anthologies—is organized by denomination. When it comes to understanding the appearance and development of nationalism in American religion, the denominational model can be misleading. In trying to establish order and stability, the Canadian Anglican establishment reached out to British Methodists, with whom they found a class affinity, to help subdue North American Methodists. While some prominent New England Baptists served in high positions in missionary associations, a variety of anti-mission Baptist groups took shape on the frontier and in rural areas, especially in the South. These examples suggest that social and geographic factors can be as important as denominational affiliation in understanding the appearance and development of nationalism in popular American religion. With the Methodists, the fastest-growing church in the early republic despite its lack of general lack of patriotism, a Republican Methodist insurgency, an attempt to Americanize the Church, did rise. But it rose, and fell, on the Virginia Tidewater, where American nationalism was very strong, while the Church as a whole, flourishing on the periphery, remained indifferent to the American national project, well into the early republic. The Methodists, with their organizational discipline and continental reach, provide broad perspective understanding of what drove the popularization of American Protestantism, as well as what was not necessary to its popularity. In the following chapter, Richard McNemar, a schismatic Presbyterian turned Shaker, and fully a product of the agrarian periphery, allows a finer-grained look at the world of frontier revivalism and its political possibilities.

---

107. Ibid., 68; Idem, *Religious Strife on the Southern Frontier* (Baton Rouge, LA 1965), pp. 18–19, 21.

108. Posey, *The Baptist Church in the Lower Mississippi River Valley*, pp. 72, 76.

4

Sovereignty and Salvation on the Frontier of the Early Republic

Awaking from this rapture, salvation was my theme,
The multitude supposing I only had a dream;
But some at length believed the living truth of God,
And flaming with the spirit, they spread it all abroad.
Soon as the fountain open'd for the souls to be baptiz'd,
The land was in commotion; the people all surprised:
In thousands they resorted to this living pool,
And as they felt its virtue, each acted like a fool.
—RICHARD MCNEMAR, "John the Baptist," a hymn composed
in commemoration of the camp meeting at Cane Ridge,
Kentucky, 1801

IN DEMOCRACY IN *America*, Alexis de Tocqueville claimed that a uniform democratic and republican ethos suffused American religion, vitally stabilizing the young republic"s political society. "No religious doctrine" in the United States, he wrote, "displays the slightest hostility to democratic and republican institutions. The clergy of all different sects hold the same language, their opinions are consonant with the laws, and the human intellect flows onward in one sole current." Tocqueville's 1835 claim was an early and eloquent statement about the alleged formative influence of American nationalism on American religion, but it was wrong. Nonetheless, scholars have continued to find national ideals and ideologies—republicanism, individualism, democratization—defining popular religion in the early American republic. In fact, even into the nineteenth century, some important and popular religious movements on the frontier flourished independently of nationalist ideals and influences. In some ways, the weakness of American nationality in the interior of the American continent during the nineteenth century should not be a surprise. The newly independent United States, a precarious experiment in republican government, embarked on a massive and unprecedented colonizing project without a state church—indeed, without much of a state at all—and also without extending the kind of exclusive land grants and labor market monopolies that had guided seventeenth- and eighteenth-century colonization. At the outset of the US turn to westward colonization, on which the federal government relied for revenue from land sales, dozens of Native American tribes, as well as Britain, France, and Spain, claimed sovereignty over large parts of the continent. Internal migration was disorderly; settlers had been pouring into the interior of the continent since before the American Revolution. The removal of British imperial restraints unleashed many more.[1] Amid these extraordinary conditions, settlers invented new forms of authority, including popular American Protestantism. It offered alternative forms of sovereignty. One of these forms was frontier revivalism, which was a kind of leveling theocracy, embracing men and women of all colors and stations, though perhaps not the planter elite, and based on the authority of divine revelation.

One of the great figures in frontier revivalism, Richard McNemar, is today less well known than his protege, Barton W. Stone. Stone would gain fame for, in 1832, cofounding the Disciples of Christ, which remains one of the largest Protestant denominations in the United States. McNemar was the driving spirit behind a series of revival meetings in central and southern Kentucky that began in the late 1790s and culminated, in August 1801, at Cane Ridge, Kentucky. Like Francis Asbury, the founder of North American Methodism, and many of the early Western Methodists, McNemar understood the world in terms greater and simpler than one constituted by nation-states. Neither ever indicated that class, nationality, or color prescribed any religious obligation to subservience or rule, obedience or command. For them, Christianity was a greater and more radical force than the revolutionary republicanism of secular intellectuals. Even Tom Paine, perhaps most internationalist among the American revolutionary republicans, dreamed of nation-states. Paine predicted that the United States would be an "asylum for liberty." For the

---

1. Alexis de Tocqueville, *Democracy in America* (Stilwell, KS, 2007), p. 219. On the republican spirit of popular religion in the early American republic, see Gordon Wood, *Empire of Liberty: A History of the Early Republic, 1789–1815* (New York, 2009). On the effects of American independence on westward colonization and migration, see Fred Anderson, *Crucible of War: The Seven Years' War and the Fate of Empire in British North America* (New York, 2001).

revivalists, the frontier, which McNemar called "an asylum. . . for those who were cast out," was the refuge from this society, built on the principles of Anglo-American libertarianism.[2]

Cane Ridge was a kind of Christian Woodstock of the early republic. A loosely planned festival that began on the banks of the Red and Gasper Rivers, it attracted a massive number of people, many of whom spent days in the woods pursuing all manner of agony and ecstasy. The prevalence of physical as well as spiritual ecstasy led to a contemporary saw about how camp meetings produced more souls than they saved. A Dominican missionary who had fled Belgium and French Jacobinism found Kentucky's frontier religion a scandal; its dancing, twitching, and baying, amounted to a "sad commentary on the Protestant rule of faith." In Protestant countries, he concluded, the "weakness of the human mind, when left to itself," led to these excesses.[3] Encouraged by the "holy" results of Cane Ridge, Richard McNemar and other frontier revivalists turned to establish friendly relations with a group of American Indians camped nearby.[4] These particular Indians would soon distinguish themselves in ways that would lead some to view the white ministers and their religion as treasonous. Over the course of 1810 and 1811, Colonel James Smith, a powerful local settler, mounted a spirited assault, first by pamphlet, then by mob, on McNemar and his followers. The contest between McNemar and Smith, a war hero and famous author, captured the essence of the conflict between frontier revivalism and the intensely Protestant patriotism, the

---

2. Stone and McNemar began a series of revivals in Kentucky in 1798. Along with McNemar and Stone, William Elsey Connelley and E. M. Coulter, *History of Kentucky*, vol. I (Chicago, 1922) single out the brothers John and William McGee (the former a Methodist, the latter a Presbyterian minister) at Cane Ridge, p. 538; italics in the original. Gordon Wood termed McNemar a representative of "republican religion" who wanted to bring about "the working out of the Revolution in religion"; see Wood, *The Rising Glory of America, 1760–1820* (Boston, 1990), p. 80. Nathan Hatch, *The Democratization of American Christianity* (New Haven, CT, 1989), is the fullest exponent of this "Second Great Awakening" argument, made earlier by Perry Miller and William McLoughlin, *Modern Revivalism* (Chicago, 1968), and which sees the frontier revivalists as the inheritors of the more democratic and egalitarian impulses of the Revolution. Donald G. Matthews, "The Second Great Awakening as an Organizing Process, 1780–1830: An Hypothesis," *American Quarterly*, vol. 21 (1969), made a more subtle argument for the Second Great Awakening as an "organizing process."

3. M. J. Spalding, *Sketches of the Early Catholic Missions of Kentucky; From Their Commencement in 1787 to the Jubilee of 1826–7* (New York, 1972). Originally published in 1844.

4. Richard McNemar, *The Kentucky Revival; Or, A Short History of the Late Extraordinary Outpouring of the Spirit of God in the Western States of America. . .* (New York, 1848), pp. 43–44. Originally published in Cincinnati, 1807.

nationalist evangelism, which, riding high from victory in the Revolution, had turned to the mission of continental colonization. It was a fight about many things—about what were and were not legitimate sources of religious knowledge, about law and land, and about how the heavens and earth were linked—but it was in essence a fight about sovereignty and salvation. That each side was evangelical Protestant did little to dispel the conflict. Waged in the name of God, country, and family, James Smith's attacks, and Richard McNemar's countercharges, provide an important coda to the Cane Ridge revival, an illuminating moment in the fight within Protestantism that was reshaping American nationalism.

"A Continual State of Agitation"

In 1800, the population of Kentucky was under 221,000. Just 18 years earlier, in 1782, it had been under 3,000. The locale of Daniel Boone was also the setting where, just six years before the 1792 admission of Kentucky into the Union, an Indian had killed Abraham Lincoln's grandfather in a dispute over a land claim. The first permanent statehouse, an unimpressive, three-story brick building that resembled a New England schoolhouse, had been completed only in 1794—two years after Kentucky became a state. The authority of central government in Kentucky was very weak. Some of the early settlers had outpaced the state-builders and had arrived in Kentucky before the start of the Revolution. Though the recently arrived planters tended to see such settlers as degenerate squatters, they enjoyed established local prerogatives and considerable numbers. Almost daily, they were joined by poor migrants who arrived to assert, either by tenuous land claims or simply by axes, their right of settlement.[5]

Problems stemming from land speculation and disputed land claims afflicted most states and every territory on the American frontier. The situation in Kentucky, however, was particularly chaotic. Most Kentucky residents, legally, owned no land, while non-resident speculators claimed vast tracts. Some residents arrived as grandees. In 1783, for example, Thomas Marshall left a 2,000-acre plantation, with 22 slaves, in Faquier County,

---

5. On the earliest Kentucky settlers, see William Burke, "Autobiography of Reverend William Burke," in James B. Finley, ed., *Sketches of Western Methodism* (Cincinnati, OH, 1854), pp. 22–23. On the character of early Kentucky society, Ellen Eslinger, *Citizens of Zion: The Social Origins of Camp Meeting Revivalism* (Knoxville, TN, 1999); George Lee Willis, Sr., *Kentucky Democracy: A History of the Party and Its Representative Members—Past and Present* (Louisville, KY, 1935), vol. I, pp. 48, 59, 34.

Virginia, for 8,054 acres in Kentucky. Marshall also assumed a position as a land surveyor, by which he soon acquired thousands more Kentucky acres. As his deputy, he appointed his nephew Humphrey Marshall, who, upon his arrival in Kentucky, at age 23, acquired 4,000 acres. In 1812, Humphrey Marshall published *The History of Kentucky*, the first general history of the state.[6]

In the Northwest Ordinance, Congress had stipulated the Ohio River, which separates Ohio and Kentucky, as the southern boundary of the Ordinance. The Ordinance was perhaps the most successful colonizing measure in US history. It surveyed the land into six-mile-square townships, with each township subdivided into 640-acre sections, and each section again subdivided into half, quarter, and smaller acreages. The Ordinance provided a kind of algorithm for land purchases, migration, and settlement. To preserve the balance of power between free states and slave states, however, the Ordinance, which forbade slavery, did not apply in Kentucky, or anywhere south of the Ohio River. North of the Ohio River, the Ordinance bequeathed land surveyed into plots marked for schools. South of the Ohio River, the process of conquest, colonization, and settlement unfolded with more disorder and violence. In 1776, for example, the Revolutionary convention in Williamsburg, Virginia, responded to pleas from their Kentucky brethren by donating 500 pounds of gunpowder.[7]

Because large portions of Kentucky were not suited to plantation agriculture, small farmers and artisans also emigrated. They were as likely to come from Pennsylvania, New York, or New England as from Virginia or South Carolina. Regardless of whether they came from North or South, they tended to be proud and independent, sometimes desperate, people who had at best an uneasy relationship with land speculators and planters. European immigrants, unfamiliar with the land or the language or both, were arriving from England, Germany, Switzerland, Scotland, Belgium, and France. West Indians, Africans, and American-born blacks

---

6. On disparity between the resident landless and the non-resident speculators, see Thomas Perkins Abernathy, *Western Lands and the American Revolution* (New York, 1959), pp. 326–327. On the Marshalls, see Norman K. Risjord, *Chesapeake Politics, 1781–1800* (New York, 1978), p. 235; Humphrey Marshall, *The History of Kentucky*, vol. 1 (Frankfort, KY, 1812).

7. On the Northwest Ordinance, see Charles Beard, *A Basic History of the United States* (New York, 1944), pp. 180–181, and Peter Onuf, *Statehood and Union: A History of the Northwest Ordinance* (Bloomington, IN, 1992). On Virginia's donation of 500 pounds of gunpowder, see Willard Rouse Jillson, *Tales of the Dark and Bloody Ground: A Group of Fifteen Original Papers on the Early History of Kentucky* (Louisville, KY, 1930), p. 61.

came as slaves. Various Native American peoples, primarily Cherokee and Shawnee, reeling from violence, aggressive settlement, disease, and alcoholism, were also present, contesting land claims, raiding farms, stealing horses, and engaging in deadly skirmishes with settlers. This convergence of peoples took place amid isolation difficult to imagine. Communications with Richmond, Virginia, took eight weeks, round trip. It took 30 to 35 days to get to New Orleans, the closest port city. Returning from New Orleans required 40 to 45 days of dangerous travel. Many found it easier to return from New Orleans to Lexington via New York, embarking at New Orleans for New York and Philadelphia, then traveling from Philadelphia to Pittsburgh, and finally heading down the Ohio River to Kentucky.[8]

In the late 1780s, Kentucky frontiersmen turned to Congress for help, pelting Congress with petitions calling for action against the "nabobs" who claimed ownership of the farms that pioneers had settled, planted, and often defended from attack. In the 1790s, a writer to a Maryland newspaper cautioned speculators and migrants alike that some tracts were beset by "8 or 10" overlapping claims, warning that one did not purchase land in Kentucky; one purchased a lawsuit.[9] Visiting Kentucky in 1802, the French botanist François André Michaux wrote that "of all the states in the union" the "difficulty of proving the right of property" was greatest in Kentucky. Every man whose home he visited, reported Michaux, "was persuaded of the validity of his own right but. . . seemed dubious of his neighbor's." The situation, he observed, led to an "inexhaustible source of tedious and expensive law-suits." Indeed, "the difficulty of land titles in Kentucky," recalled Abraham Lincoln (born in Kentucky, in 1809) was the chief reason his father moved the family, in 1816, to Indiana, where the Northwest Ordinance applied.[10] In the words of a Kentucky circuit-rider, the convergence of these circumstances "kept the country in a continual

---

8. Risjord, *Chesapeake Politics*, pp. 234–237; François André Michaux, "Travels West of the Allegheny Mountains, 1802," in Reuben Gold Thwaites, ed., *Early Western Travels*, vol. 3 (Cleveland, OH, 1904), p. 239.

9. On the petitions to Congress, see Frederick Jackson Turner, "Social Forces in American History," in Turner, *The Frontier in American History* (Tucson, AZ, 1986), p. 325; letter to Maryland newspaper quoted in Peter Onuf, *Statehood and Union: A History of the Northwest Ordinance* (Bloomington, IN, 1987), pp. 29–30.

10. Michaux, *Travels West of the Allegheny Mountains, 1802*, in Thwaites, ed., *Early Western Travels*, vol. 3, pp. 227–228; Abraham Lincoln, "Autobiography Written for Campaign," in Gore Vidal, ed., *Lincoln: Selected Speeches and Writings* (New York, 1992), p. 265.

state of agitation." Another itinerant minister described Logan County in the 1790s as filled with "refugees, from all parts of the Union, fled to escape justice or punishment." There "was law," he recalled, "yet it could not be executed." The effect, wrote the historian Frederick Jackson Turner, rendered Kentucky a "military training school." The most important religious revival meeting in American history grew out of this disorder. Historically, Cane Ridge marked the beginning of the end of European Protestantism in the United States.[11]

Popular American Protestantism began with a boom. One observer counted 1,143 wagons at Cane Ridge, and several observers estimated attendance at between 20,000 and 25,000 people. By way of context, the show of force marshaled to crush Shays' Rebellion in 1787 amounted to a hastily organized militia force of 4,400. By contemporary standards, Cane Ridge was a massive gathering: 10 percent of the entire population of Kentucky.[12] By all accounts, many experienced Cane Ridge as a kind of holy ignition. The Methodist William Burke recalled that 10 words into his sermon at Cane Ridge, "hundreds fell prostrate to the ground." He saw no less than "five hundred. . . lying on the ground in the deepest distresses of agony." People had come from Tennessee, Ohio, and Indiana, as well as all over Kentucky. Every "few minutes" Burke saw worshippers falling to the ground, where they would groan and writhe, and then, "rising in shouts of triumph," begin the process again. After four days of ecstatic mass worship, wrote Burke, the people dispersed and the "tidings of Cane Ridge meeting were carried to almost every corner of the country, and the holy fire spread in all directions." More certainly, Cane Ridge helped popularize the camp meeting in the early American republic. By 1811, Francis

---

11. On Kentucky in the 1790s as in "a continual state of agitation," see "Autobiography of William Burke," in Finley, ed., *Sketches of Western Methodism*, p. 42. On the absence of a clearly sovereign law in early Kentucky, see Cartwright, *Autobiography*, p. 24. On "the bulk" of the Western populace as "either outside the [national] market or peripheral to it," until the advent of upriver steam navigation in 1816, see Douglas C. North, *The Economic Growth of the United States, 1790–1860* (New York, 1966), pp. 64, 68. See also Stephen Aron, *How the West Was Lost: The Transformation of Kentucky from Daniel Boone to Henry Clay* (Baltimore, MD, 1999).

12. For McKendree on the frontier origins of the camp meeting, see Sprague, *Annals of the American Pulpit*, vol. VII, p. 164. On attendance at Cane Ridge, see Meacham, p. 399. The figures of 20,000–25,000 attendance and 1,143 wagons at Cane Ridge are reported in Connelley and Coulter, eds., *History of Kentucky*, vol. I, p. 539. On Shays' Rebellion, see Robert A. Gross, ed., *In Debt to Shays: The Bicentennial of an Agrarian Rebellion* (Charlottesville, VA, 1993) and Leonard Richards, *Shays' Rebellion: The American Revolution's Final Battle* (Philadelphia, 2002).

Asbury estimated that over three million Americans attended camp meetings annually.[13]

"Dangerous to the Souls of Men"

Born in 1770, in western Pennsylvania, McNemar was the son of farmers. Like the Mormon prophet Joseph Smith, he worked as an itinerant farm laborer before he labored as an itinerant minister. In 1791, with the prospect of furthering his education, he followed Princeton-graduate-turned-frontier-minister Robert Finley to Kentucky. Finley's knowledge of classical languages, his alcoholism, and his wanderlust, as well his ability to build architecturally sound log cabin churches, earned him a reputation on the frontier. By the time Finley ordained McNemar, in 1798, the latter had been the minister of the Presbyterian Church in Cabin Creek, Kentucky, for two years. Like Finley, against whom he would later bring charges of drunkenness, McNemar provoked controversy. He enjoyed a reputation as a "hot" preacher. His sermons were renowned for provoking choruses of children to spontaneous, howling exhortations of repentance and grace. He displayed eccentric habits, for example a yen for arranging the bodies of fallen worshippers into geometric patterns. Even by the generous standards of frontier religion, such sights and sounds captured attention.[14]

McNemar's work began with destruction. Reporting on his Kentucky revivals, he wrote, the revivalists had been "united in breaking down, and burning that which was old and rotten." Destruction, he wrote, must precede "building up that which is sound and permanent." Ideally, the revivalist preachers, he wrote, "struck-down, and held under the power of death for a time, then raised up in a new world of light and vision." By an immodest analogy, he warned listeners that, initially, their salvation would earn them enemies who spoke the truth. The "disciples of

---

13. Latourette, vol. 4, see ch. 3, esp. p. 194; Burke excerpted in Barker, *History of Ohio Methodism*, pp. 180–181.

14. On Joseph Smith as an itinerant farm laborer and preacher, see Richard L. Bushman, *Joseph Smith and the Beginnings of Mormonism* (Champaign, IL, 1987). McNemar's biographical details are from John A. Garraty and Mark C. Carnes, eds., *American National Biography* (New York, 1999), vol. 15, p. 175. On McNemar's preaching and his relationship with Finley, see McNemar, pp. 24, 21, 26, as well as Paul K. Conkin, *Cane Ridge: America's Pentecost* (Madison, WI, 1990), pp. 70, 71, 80, 124–128, 102.

Jesus," he wrote, "were much more mistaken at first than his avowed enemies." Jesus's enemies had foreseen that "he would be the occasion of taking away their place and nation," whereas Jesus's disciples had naively "imagined. . . that his whole place was to build them up." In addition to alcohol, cursing, slavery, and all forms of profligacy (save religious enthusiasm), McNemar slated distinction by class, sex, and color as sins that must all be destroyed.[15]

As the offspring of Virginia, Kentucky was created for slavery. The state's Constitution called it the "right of property." The founders of Kentucky were American nationalists. They named Paris, Kentucky, in gratitude for French support in the American Revolution. They named Lexington, Kentucky, for the Massachusetts town "from whence the first shot of freedom had reverberated." They were also planters, however, and they did not welcome leveling attacks that claimed divine authority to dispossess them of their property. In contrast to Virginia, however, planter hegemony in Kentucky was a work-in-progress. In attempting to secure their "right of property," the planter-dominated state constitutional convention had prohibited the election of any minister to the legislature. The second state constitutional convention, in 1799, extended the exclusion to the governorship. The anticlericalism of Kentucky's state-builders stemmed from some Christian settlers' opposition to slavery. One, the Rev. David Rice, had raised some planters' ire when, at the 1792 state constitutional convention, he delivered a speech called "Slavery Inconsistent with Justice and Good Policy."[16] McNemar and his fellow revivalists took a more radical approach. Rice had signaled his deference to the civil law by using the state's constitutional convention to criticize slavery. The revivalists gave no indication that they thought much of such formalities. The French botanist François Michaux, traveling through Kentucky at the time, noted that local elites did not "share the opinion with the multitude with regard to this state of ecstasy." The Rev. George Baxter, president of Washington Academy in Lexington, Kentucky, denounced Cane Ridge as the natural outgrowth of Kentucky's "remarkable. . . vice and dissipation," calling participants "infidels." The popularity of "the infidels," however, was growing. In the two years following Cane Ridge, Kentucky's

---

15. McNemar, pp. 37, 62, 41; Eslinger, *Citizens of Zion*, concludes that the historical significance of revivalism was "the temporary creation of an ideal republican society," p. 241.

16. On the naming of Lexington, see Jillson, *Tales of the Dark and Bloody Ground*, p. 59; Willis, pp. 56–57; Niels H. Sonne, *Liberal Kentucky: 1780–1828* (New York, 1939), pp. 6–10.

anti-slavery Baptist and Methodist Churches swelled with 16,250 new members.[17]

The revivalists' success put the Presbytery in the difficult situation of trying to retain but tame their young and controversial star. Three elders from McNemar's own Cabin Creek, Kentucky, congregation pushed the problem to the fore. In the autumn of 1801, just two months after Cane Ridge, they filed a complaint against McNemar with the Presbytery. The complaint charged, among other points, that McNemar had repeatedly declared, "Christ has purchased salvation for all the human race without distinction." In other words, McNemar was advocating Arminianism, a theology by which good works could win one salvation. To Presbyterians, this was crypto-Catholicism. Six months later, in March 1802, the Cincinnati Presbytery negotiated a truce in which McNemar and the complainants agreed to "pass over all past altercations" and take communion together, while also relocating McNemar from Cabin Creek to the Turtle Creek Church near Lebanon, Ohio, just over the Ohio–Kentucky border. The move was both a promotion and probation. McNemar's new appointment to Turtle Creek was only part-time; yet, save for Cincinnati, Turtle Creek was the most important Presbyterian congregation in the Miami River Valley. Within weeks of McNemar's Turtle Creek appointment, he was preaching to crowds of 2,000.[18] Just as quickly, one of the Turtle Creek Church elders denounced McNemar on matters of doctrine to the Presbytery. Breaking its rule requiring a written allegation (none had been provided), the Presbytery called McNemar for what it called an "examination on the fundamental doctrines of Scripture." It was perhaps the first heresy trial in the Northwest Territory.[19]

The strange outcome revealed both the high stakes of the contest for the souls of frontier settlers and the power of popularity in the new republic. By a small majority, the Presbytery found McNemar guilty of preaching "Armenian [*sic*]" doctrines dangerous to the soul and "hostile to the interests of all true religion." In light of the guilty finding, the Presbytery took an extraordinary course. After judging him guilty of heresy, they

17. Connelley and Coulter, *History of Kentucky*, vol. I, attribute the "vigorous opposition" that arose among Kentuckians to slavery and liquor at this time to the influence of frontier revivalism, p. 540.

18. MacLean, *Sketch of the Life and Labors of Richard McNemar* (Franklin County, OH, 1905), reprints the petition of Joseph Darlington, Robert Robb, and Robert Robinson, p. 9.

19. Ibid., pp. 9–12.

reaffirmed his Turtle Creek appointment and directed him to preach two Sundays at the Orangedale, Kentucky, church; two Sundays at the Clear Creek, Ohio, church; two Sundays at the Beulah, Ohio, church; and one Sunday at Mad River (now Dayton), Ohio. They also encouraged him to preach at other Presbyterian churches "at discretion." McNemar, however, felt his doctrine sound, and the heresy ruling stung him.[20] Six months later, in April 1803, 60 members of the Turtle Creek Church petitioned the Presbytery to appoint McNemar to their church on a full-time position. The Synod refused the request, and formally restated their ruling that McNemar was a heretic, whose teachings were "dangerous to the souls of men and hostile to the interests of all true religion." This time McNemar struck back. Drawing on the lexicon of Presbyterian reform movements, he and Barton W. Stone, calling themselves the "New Lights," withdrew from the Synod to pursue a "pure" Presbyterianism. By the invitation of the Turtle Creek Church members, McNemar moved into a cabin next to the church. He served as the minister to the now schismatic Turtle Creek Church until March 1805, when three Shaker missionaries from New Lebanon, New York, knocked on his door. When the missionaries convinced him to join, Shakerism won one of its most notable converts. Within a month, almost the entire Turtle Creek Church followed McNemar to the Shakers. Presbyterianism in the Miami River Valley never recovered.[21]

"He Can Dream of God"

In 1807, Richard McNemar published a collection of writings that included his history of the Kentucky revival, along with original hymns, letters, and an account of his conversion to Shakerism. Its long title concluded by placing his experience in history as *A Memorial of the Wilderness Journey*. His single reference to United States of America was not friendly. The proponent of destruction who had heard the word of God leveled a sarcastic attack on the Age of Revolution as the Age of Reason:

> For many ages the Christian religion, so called, had been incorporated with civil government, and they had mutually supported one another; consequently when that revolution in politics began,

20. Ibid., pp. 17–18.

21. Ibid., p. 18.

which aimed at the overthrow of a monarchy, and the establishment of a republic, *that religion* was particularly involved. Kings. . . had claimed the Bible as "the only rule to direct them" in their unnatural wars, dire oppressions. . . and unparalleled cruelties. . . consequently, when the eye of reason began to open upon the *rights of man*, the tyrant's *Canon* must appear in very pernicious colors—no book in the universe so mischievous and hateful. And under this view, the Bible was attacked by the political reformers of the last century, and the dictates of a lawless nature cried up, in opposition to its sacred requirements.[22]

McNemar staked his opposition to the Revolution on a simpler and broader base than the Loyalists' commitment to constitutional monarchy. He rejected the whole notion of a beneficent natural law, the foundation of Enlightenment political culture. Instead of a political science derived from discourses of an ordered natural history, as Thomas Jefferson propounded in *Notes on the State of Virginia*, for example, McNemar found a powerful view of history, as well as a language of order and justice, in the Bible. Sovereignty must reside with the Church, he announced, because "no man can serve two masters." Christianity, he had made clear, began with destruction only so that it could proceed to creation. The act of creation led to the right to rule: "he who *creates*, has a right to *govern*." These were not American ambitions.[23]

McNemar held that Church sovereignty extended to any matter that related to the Holy Scriptures, "the only standard of doctrine and discipline." He maintained that any moral matter must be subject to the "government and discipline" of the entire Church of believers, gathered publicly. In brief, McNemar was a theocrat, a disposition that he attempted to balance with a leveling spirit and a commitment to a community-enforced egalitarianism.[24] He was sure that once people understood the error of Calvinism, that Christ's death and resurrection had destroyed sin and brought grace within reach, that they would be governable. "No form of doctrine or discipline," he wrote, would be needed.[25]

---

22. McNemar, *The Kentucky Revival*, p. 10. Italics in original.

23. Ibid., pp. 6, 140. Italics in original.

24. Ibid., p. 45.

25. Ibid., pp. 47–48; Conkin, *Cane Ridge*, ch. 2.

To McNemar, the universality of Christ's offer of salvation meant that "Christians were united, all of one heart and one soul." It followed, he thought, that true Christians must live amid equality, without distinction. Cane Ridge had shown that this was possible; there, "all distinction" of "name. . . age, sex, color" was laid aside. Everything of a "temporary nature," the distinctions between "old and young, male and female, black and white" had given way to "equal privilege." To the revivalists, the distinct "doctrine and manner of worship" of the camp meetings made this simple Christian truth evident, even to skeptics. At the revival meetings, he wrote, Christ made men and women's hearts "glow with love."[26] There, they had seen local grandees "turn pale and tremble at the reproof of a woman, a little boy, or a mean African." Bloodshed and slaughter, he wrote, could not "overcome beings so fierce," yet their Christianity had. Driven by their leveling creed, distinguished by their mode of worship, and exalted by their success, the revivalists extended the challenge to planter authority.[27]

Ministers at Cane Ridge, including McNemar, had offered public prayers for "the poor Indians," but the Indians had rebuffed missionaries sent to them. In 1805, four years after Cane Ridge, a great number of Native Americans, from across North America, began to gather at the Ohio–Kentucky border. This time as one of a group of Shaker missionaries, McNemar approached the Indians. The missionaries saw a makeshift village of "50 or 60 smoking cottages" surrounding a large central house. They did not know it, but this small encampment would give rise to a historic Indian resistance movement. The Shakers asked the Indians if they were friendly:

A. O yes we are all brothers.
Q. Where are your chiefs—we wish to have a talk with them?
A. They are about four miles off making sugar.
Q. What are their names?
A. Lal-lu-e-tsee-ka and Te-kum-tha.
Q. Can any of them talk English?
A. No: but there is a good interpreter here, George Blue-jacket. He has gone to school and he can read and talk well.

---

26. McNemar, *The Kentucky Revival*, p. 31.

27. Ibid., pp. 35–36.

Q. What is that big house for?

A. To worship the Great Spirit.

Q. How do you worship?

A. Mostly in speaking.

Q. Who is your chief speaker?

A. Our prophet, Lal-lu-e-tsee-ka. He converses with the Good spirit, and he tells us how to be good.

Q. Do all that live here, believe in him?

A. Yes, we all believe—he can dream of God.[28]

The Indians then dispatched a guide, "a pilot" as McNemar referred to him, along with the interpreter George Blue-Jacket, to take the white ministers to the prophet. Arriving at the sugar camp, the prophet rejected the Shakers, telling them he would "not talk to us," McNemar recalled, because "the white people" thought his beliefs "foolish." The ministers protested that they were "not that kind of minister." Speaking through the interpreter, the prophet asked them, "Do you believe a person can have true knowledge of the Great Spirit, in the heart, without going to school and learning to read?" The prophet could hardly have asked a question better designed to galvanize the missionaries' support. Yes, they assured him that they thought divine revelation the "best kind of knowledge"—a human revelation that won the Shakers an invitation into the prophet's tent.[29]

The prophet spoke for half an hour to the other Indians (no one translated) before turning to the Shaker missionaries and sharing his revelation. In a "time of general sickness," the "Great Spirit" came and took him down a long forked road, explaining that *"eternity"* was a choice that men and women could make. The right-hand way "led to happiness and the left to misery." Alcohol, the Spirit continued, lined the path of the left-hand way, which was the way of the drunkard, the popular way, peopled by "vast crowds. . . great multitudes," but these people were also miserable. The Spirit mocked the prophet's past, pressing liquor "resembling molten lead" upon him, urging him to drink: "you used to love whiskey." The prophet explained that he came to the sugar camp to heed the Great Spirit's direction to the right way, a new way of sobriety that would bring

28. Ibid., pp. 123–125.

29. Ibid., pp. 126–127.

together Native Americans from many tribes. Soon other Indians flocked "from different tribes" to hear and judge Lal-lu-e-tsee-ka's vision for themselves, and this vision, he explained, had polarized his people.[30] The Shakers questioned the prophet about his theological beliefs:

Q. Do you believe that all mankind are gone away from the Good Spirit by wicked works?

A. Yes; that is what we believe: And the prophet feels great pity for all.

Q. Do you believe that the Good Spirit was once himself known to the world, by a man that was called Christ?

A. Yes, we believe it, and the good Spirit has shown. . . that what has been in many generations and he says he wants to talk with some white people about these things.

Q. What sins does your prophet speak most against?

A. Witchcraft, poisoning people, fighting, murdering, drinking whisky, and beating their wives because they will not have children. All such as will not leave off these, go to Eternity—he knows all bad people that commit fornication, and can tell it from seven years old.[31]

Notably, the Indians' belief in a controversial Catholic idea (Vatican doctrine establishes seven as the "age of reason") did not trouble the Shakers, who were more interested in the Indians' apparent belief in the divinity of Christ and the efficacy of good works. When the Indians found out that the Shakers, too, were teetotalers, they invited them back to their village for dinner, and then to stay the night.[32]

Witnessing the Indians' morning prayer (the Indians believed that the Great Spirit was most within reach at dawn and dusk) impressed the Shakers. One of the Indians mounted a log in the corner of the camp and began an hour-long service, "with a loud voice, in thanksgiving to the Great Spirit." The solemn scene that followed could not have differed more from the euphoric bustle of Cane Ridge. The Indian villagers remained "in their tents. . . yet they could all distinctly hear, and gave a solemn and loud assent. . . from tent to tent, at every pause." At this point, the white ministers experienced an epiphany. Casting the Indians into sacred history,

---

30. Ibid., pp. 127–128.

31. Ibid., pp. 128–129.

32. Ibid., pp. 129–130.

McNemar described them much as he no doubt saw himself and his fellow frontier revivalists, as "the tribes of Israel" on the "vast open prairie." Their piety was simple, unaffected, and marked by "ardent desires for the salvation of their unbelieving kindred." Neither "hunger, fatigue, hard labor" nor other "sufferings" would slow their efforts. The shabbiness of the Indians' encampment added to the impression. Overcome with emotion, the ministers cited Jacob: "*'How dreadful is this place! Surely the Lord is in this place!* And the world know it not." They concluded, "God, in very deed, was mightily at work among them."[33] McNemar and his party were not ecumenicists. For theologically minded men to conclude that "God, in very deed, was mightily at work among them" was unusual, evidence of a deeply felt affinity. Before departing, the missionaries left "ten dollars for the purpose of buying corn" and invited the Indians to visit Turtle Creek. Three months later, the Indians made good on the invitation, departing Turtle Creek with "27 horses. . . loaded back with provision." In the controversy that would soon descend upon the Shakers, these two acts of charity would prove important details.[34]

Lal-lu-e-tsee-ka and Te-kum-tha, better known to the world as Tenskwatawa and Tecumseh, were not just any Indians. The seemingly fanciful directive that the Great Spirit had delivered to Tenskwatawa to "instruct all from the different tribes that were willing to be good" had not yet made its mark on the world. But in a few years, the power of Tenskwatawa's prophecy, combined with Tecumseh's diplomatic and military leadership, would draw followers from as far west as the Great Plains, northeast from New York State, south into the Florida panhandle, and deep into Canada, where Tecumseh is still honored as a hero who saved British Canada from American conquest during the War of 1812. Together, the Shawnee brothers would lead the most impressive and unified Indian opposition to American imperialism in the history of the United States.[35] The Indians' anti-colonial ambitions did not matter much, if at all, to the Shakers. The ministers were so moved by the

---

33. Ibid., p. 130. Italics in original.

34. Ibid.

35. According to one historian, it was after the meeting with the Shakers, while in the chiefly Delaware towns on the White River in Indiana, that the Prophet changed his name from "Lal-lu-e-tsee-ka" (the Loud Voice) to "Tenskwatawa" (He who keeps the Door Open). See Jacob Piatt Dunn, *Indiana and Indianans: A History of Aboriginal and Territorial Indiana and the Century of Statehood* (Chicago, 1919), p. 265; John Sugden, *Tecumseh: A Life* (New York, 1997), pp. 3–10; Anthony F. C. Wallace, *The Long, Bitter Trail*, p. 18.

prophet Tenskwatawa, they failed to record anything about Tecumseh, the resistance movement's political and military force. In fact, not only was Tecumseh present throughout their visit, he was also the "pilot" who took the ministers to Tenskwatawa. At one point, Tecumseh even showed the ministers letters of friendship from American military officials, including the governor of Ohio—then, as now, an unusual dossier for a Native American to be carrying around the Miami River Valley. The Shakers did not find the incident worthy of recording. Like William Wells, the US Indian agent at Fort Wayne, who held the prophet, not Tecumseh, in isolation, the missionaries were more interested in Tenskwatawa than his now more famous brother.[36]

Tenskwatawa's meeting with the white ministers revealed the social and political possibilities, as well as the limitations, of frontier revivalism in the early American republic. Despite the schism that led McNemar to leave the Presbytery, he shared more of their theology than he did that of Tenskwatawa. It was Tenskwatawa's revelations, however, that he and the others accepted as the word of God. The Shakers thought that the Indians, "in real light, as well as behavior. . . shame the Christian world."[37] They thought little of delivering a caravan of supplies to the Indian encampment. Others saw them as treasonously provisioning an Indian resistance movement that the US military considered a foe of the first rank. Their alliance was not a fixed idea of frontier revivalism, but it lay within its potential, and in this case the potential gave way to the actual. Tenskwatawa's movement and Shakerism did share some unusual traits. Both emerged from social disorder, claiming the authority of divine law. Both called for the destruction of old loyalties to create a new society. Both aggressively pursued and attracted converts and accepted women as religious visionaries.[38] Both forswore alcohol, venerated the land, and led an ascetic way of life that required the rigid regulation of sensual appetites and the rejection of luxuries. For their authority, both rested upon the claims of charismatic leaders to knowledge revealed directly by a supreme being. The integral role of revelation, over which the white ministers and Tenskwatawa initially bonded, left both movements vulnerable to fracture

---

36. Sugden, pp. 138–142, 6.

37. McNemar, p. 132.

38. Carroll Smith-Rosenberg, "Women and Religious Revivals: Anti-Ritualism, Liminality, and the Emergence of the American Bourgeoisie," in Leonard I. Sweet, ed., *The Evangelical Tradition in America* (Macon, GA, 1984), see esp. pp. 201–204.

by contradictory revealed truths. Both movements rested on an irrevocable division between the saved and the damned that could swing between a violent apocalypticism and a millennialism that was itself a form of violence. In political terms, both combined radical elements with a reactionary foundation and a nostalgic vision. Profound differences between the two movements existed, too, beginning with Tenskwatawa's nativism and the Shakers' mystical enchantment with pre-industrial craft production. Nonetheless, the differences faded in the light of common traits, an ambition that arced across frontier society, an ear to the heavens, an aggrieved sense of justice, and, perhaps most important, what David Hume described as the characteristic traits of the religious enthusiast: "hope, pride, presumption, a warm imagination, together with ignorance."[39]

"The Soul of General Washington Confessed his Sins"

On the frontier of the early American republic, friendly relations between a pan-Indian resistance movement and a popular white mystic were bound to draw attention. One local grandee, Colonel James Smith, took it upon himself to destroy the threat. Like McNemar, Smith was born to a western Pennsylvania farm family. In 1755, while working in the western Pennsylvania wilderness to clear a road from Fort Loudon to Bedford, an Indian war party returning from a victory over General Braddock took the eighteen-year-old Smith captive. After four years of captivity, Smith escaped. Over three decades McNemar's senior, Smith was a veteran of both the Seven Years' War and the Revolutionary War. In both wars, he distinguished himself as an Indian fighter, from 1763 to 1769 as a leader of the "black boys," a group of frontier vigilantes who imposed and protected white settlers' claims on contested frontier lands. For his leadership of the "black boys" (so called because they concealed their identities by painting their faces), Smith won a position as a regularly commissioned lieutenant in the Ohio Country.[40]

A patriot, Smith volunteered for the Revolutionary Army, where he attained the rank of colonel by again fighting Indians on the western frontier. In 1785, he moved to Kentucky, where he adjusted land claims, and

39. David Hume, "Of Superstition and Enthusiasm," in Richard Wollheim, ed., *Hume on Religion* (Cleveland, OH, 1964), p. 247.

40. On Smith's biography, see Paul David Nelson, "Smith, James," in Garraty and Carnes, eds., *American National Biography*, vol. 20, pp. 211–212.

was elected a delegate to the 1792 Danville convention (which endorsed the separation of Kentucky from Virginia). For several years he represented Bourbon County in the Kentucky state legislature. In 1799, he published *An Account of the Remarkable Occurrences in the Life and Travels of Col. James Smith, during his Captivity with the Indians.* The account garnered Smith international fame, and in 1812 he followed it with *A Treatise on the Mode and Manner of Indian War, Their Tactics, Discipline and Encampments.* Figuratively speaking, after his escape at 22 from four years of Indian captivity, Smith dedicated a long and energetic life to the resumption of building the westward road upon which Indians had captured him.[41]

Smith and McNemar shared more than a migration from boyhoods on western Pennsylvania farms to frontier activism. Both were of Scottish lineage, people whom Pennsylvania Quakers considered hard and rough and therefore had encouraged to settle as neighbors to Indians on the Pennsylvania frontier.[42] McNemar and Smith had also crossed paths in the Transylvania Presbytery. Barton W. Stone, one of McNemar's earlier followers, had been Smith's minister. When McNemar left the Presbyterian Church to join the Shakers, Stone left to start the "Christians," a sect that also endeavored to create a universal Christianity. Though he soon returned to the Presbyterians, James Smith had initially followed Stone to this short-lived sect. Smith then went to work as a Presbyterian missionary to Ohio and Tennessee Indians. It is not a coincidence that both McNemar and Smith, with their strong resolves to govern the frontier, turned to missionary work. For his missionary work, however, Smith obtained a license from the Presbyterian Church, an acknowledgment of civil law that indicated a different sensibility from that of frontier revivalists. In brief, Smith was exactly the kind of missionary from whom McNemar and the other frontier ministers had distanced themselves (we are not "that kind of minister") in order to gain an audience with Tenskwatawa.[43]

In 1810, in Paris, Kentucky, Smith published a pamphlet denouncing, in strong terms, Shakerism and McNemar. In what has been called the genre of counter-subversion, Smith attacked McNemar with a series of

41. James Smith, *A Treatise on the Mode and Manner of Indian War* (Paris, KY, 1812); Paul David Nelson, in Garraty and Carnes, eds., *American National Biography*, vol. 9, pp. 211–212.

42. J. H. Elliott, *Empires of the Atlantic World: Britain and Spain in America 1492–1830* (New York, 2006), p. 276.

43. Ibid.

accusations that exemplified nationalist discourses directed against popular frontier religion, and camp meetings in particular. The nature and logic of opposition to popular religion on the frontier came in many registers—bemusement, indignation, mockery, paternalism—and Smith's attack mined many of the central themes, themes that represented the fundamental tensions within Kentucky society. Growing out of the fears, hopes, and desires of Smith and others who were committed to imposing the institutions of American society onto the frontier, he sought to unify a disorderly and fragmented frontier society by galvanizing patriotic opposition to an alleged anti-American conspiracy in their midst.[44]

Many people, Smith insisted, shared his view that the Shakers were anti-American. He was merely a spokesman, he wrote, and his pamphlets were meant to inform, not incite. In fact, Smith's actions amounted to the mobilization of the forms and symbols of American nationalism against the Shakers. Smith meant to prove "that the shakers are fundamentally & practically opposers of the United States' government." His key piece of evidence was the charitable provisioning of Tenskwatawa and Tecumseh's encampment. Though McNemar had published his own account that clearly described provisioning the Indians, Smith asserted that the Shakers suffered from a lack of credibility so total that even their confessions must be independently verified. Smith therefore collected and published a deposition from John Davis, John Wilson, and Robert Wilson, three Ohioans who swore before the Lebanon County, Ohio, justice of the peace, that the Shawnees told the Ohioans that, "some time in March 1807," the ministers "gave them ten dollars." Two of the Ohioans also swore that the Shawnees had revealed to them that, over the next five months, the Shakers provided them with over 75 horse loads of supplies and "twenty-five dollars to buy ammunition in Lebanon."[45]

Interestingly, Smith's main accusation was not that the Shakers had provisioned the Indians. His main charge was that the Shakers' religion was built on a belief that God engaged in divine revelation—to the Shaker leaders. As a result, Smith alleged, Shakers believed in their elders' "infallibility." To Smith, infallibility was not just a theological abstraction. Comparing it to Satan's guise in the creation story of Genesis, Smith called

---

44. David Brion Davis, "Some Themes of Counter-Subversion: An Analysis of Anti-Masonic, Anti-Catholic, and Anti-Mormon Literature," *Mississippi Valley Historical Review*, vol. 47 (1960), pp. 205–244.

45. Smith, *Shakerism Detected*, pp. 15–17.

infallibility "the *snake* in the grass that will. . . produce despotic bondage." McNemar hatched his most ominous threat, Smith maintained, during the meeting with Tenskwatawa, another proponent of divine revelation. "For three years past," Smith claimed, the Shakers have "been using art-ful measures to excite the Indians to fall upon the defenceless frontiers, belonging to the United States." Invoking fears about the need for open-ness and accountability in a virtuous republic, he assailed Shakerism as a "system. . . founded on falsehood and supported by secrecy and deceit." As a patriot, Smith insisted that it "was contrary to the laws of our coun-try to oppose, interrupt, or disturb any people in their way of worship." He also insisted that the Shakers' "erroneous faith & mode of worship" resulted in (here he began addressing McNemar directly), "your beloved toryism. . . your treasonous proceedings with the Indians." To Smith, the Shakers' support for Tenkswatawa and Tecumseh was reminiscent of revolutionary-era British alliances with Native Americans, against the American patriots. Their sympathies, it seemed to him, must therefore be related to "toryism." Still, Smith's main accusation was that the Shakers believed in their elders' infallibility, and he insisted that McNemar was lying about this key matter: "Why did you deny infallibility? Because you well knew that was the *snake* in the grass. . . [the] distructive [*sic*] serpent that is gnawing at the root of the tree of liberty." Several times, Smith repeated the connection between the Shakers' alleged adherence to the infallibility of their elders, via direct revelation from God, and his charge of treason: "We have sufficient, positive proof that the shakers hold infalli-bility and implicit faith and obedience." All of their "treacherous dealings with the Indians" springs from "this fatal root, *infallibility* and *implicit faith* and *obedience*."[46] To Smith it was clear, as it had been to Alexander Hamilton and James Madison: if the civil law was ideally no respecter of persons, revealed religion could lead to an imperative of divine law that was no respecter of civil law.[47]

Smith claimed it was "well known" that Tenskwatawa and Tecumseh did not begin "stirring up the different tribes to fall upon the frontiers" until after conferring with the Shakers. This seems unlikely, but there is no direct evidence concerning what influence, if any, the Shakers had in the Shawnee brothers' resistance movement. Nonetheless, Smith pressed this point: "We have now both positive and strong presumptive

---

46. Ibid., pp. 3–5, 6, 15.

47. Ibid., pp. 39–40. On Madison, see ch. 1.

proof," he wrote, "of the shakers treasonous designs." Smith offered to produce Indian witnesses to this treason, but the problem, he acknowledged, "is that the Indians are not legal witnesses."[48] Feeling constrained by the boundaries of the civil society that he sought to defend, that is, the Indians' inadmissibility as legal witnesses, Smith attempted to surmount it by producing more evidence. As further proof of the Shakers' "artful designs," Smith extracted a piece from "A Lover of Peace and Justice" that had appeared in the *Western Star* newspaper. The writer (probably Smith himself) charged the Shakers with treason and called for the immediate mobilization of the militia. In an attempt to convince by simple assertion that the use of the militia "for dispersing or expelling the shakers" would not violate the freedom of religion clause in the Constitution, he assured readers "the cause will be found to originate in the civil department." In a statement that says more about the artfulness of more famous treason charges than the validity of his own, Smith added: "There was more evidence against the shakers. . . than what was against Aaron Burr." Smith sarcastically speculated that if Burr had only pretended to be a Shaker and "sheltered all his doings under the pretence of worshipping God," Thomas Jefferson could not have had Burr tried for treason.[49]

To Smith and his allies, the problem was clear: the Shakers' pretense of religious freedom masked an ambition to govern the frontier. This was true. Once subjected to the threatening scrutiny that followed Smith's initial accusations, various Shakers offered conflicting versions of their relationship with the Shawnee-led resistance movement. Upon further provocation, a piece appeared in the *Western Star*, signed by 17 Shakers, affirming their loyalty to the US government. Initially, however, they had openly expressed their support for Tenskwatawa and Tecumseh's movement. Smith called attention to these discrepancies as further proof of the Shakers' deceitfulness, their unfitness for citizenship. He compared them unfavorably to "Mahometans, Pagans or Roman Catholics," insisting that "shakerism far exceeds popish bondage." How, he asked, could they be entrusted with an oath, a contract, or as a member of a jury, as they "have nothing to do with our civil law." Their elders' "mandates is their law," he wrote, and it is a complete system of "rewards and punishments" carrying "absolute" authority. Only the intervention of our "civil law," Smith wrote, could avert a frontier "civil war." In fact, Smith was

---

48. Smith, p. 40.

49. Ibid., pp. 40–41.

in the midst of marshaling the civil law in his counter-subversion campaign against the Shakers. Though over 70 years old, Smith had ridden through Ohio and Kentucky to convince 10 people to give sworn depositions, before four different civil authorities, in three separate jurisdictions. He published the depositions, imprinted with the seal of the clerk of the District of Kentucky, which established his right to ownership over "claims as author" and, complying with federal law, deposited them in the state office. When a Shaker threatened to sue him, he taunted them to enter the jurisdiction of the civil law: "I hear that a Shaker has positively. . . asserted that he will sue me at the civil law. . . he dare not do it. Shakerism. . . cannot bear the light." The Shakers, in other words, were too profane to undertake the sacred rites of the state.[50]

The moment for such allegations to stir Kentucky was ripe. State authority was not firmly established. Tecumseh and Tenskwatawa were attracting a surprising number of followers, and the practitioners of McNemar's type of frontier religion were flourishing across the western periphery of the United States as never before. Smith and the deponents of his allegations also told a story of the consequences of the Shakers' purported belief in "infallibility and implicit faith, and obedience." It was a story of a family torn apart by the conversion of one of its members. The family was Smith's own. The Shakers had first attracted his serious attention upon the conversion of his son, also named James Smith. The public staging of this well-known family's disintegration must have generated considerable interest. A detailed narrative of the Smith family's story is beyond the scope of this work, but a couple of key themes and details will make clear what Smith's campaign of counter-subversion aimed to defend. His story portrayed a cunning enemy already at work upon two vulnerable fronts, one within and one without. The Shakers' alliance with the Indians, Smith claimed, incited danger from what he time and again described as our "defenceless frontiers." The Shakers, Smith wrote, were also subverting from within the family. Under the pretense of true religion, the Shakers "disturbs the peace of families; separates husbands and wives; robs women of their offspring; destroys natural affection; dissolves the marriage covenant, which is the main pillar of any state or kingdom."[51]

---

50. Ibid., pp. 40, 42–43, 44; James Smith, *Remarkable Occurrences, Lately Discovered among the People called Shakers; of a Treasonous and Barbarous Nature, or Shakerism Developed* (Paris, KY, 1810), pp. 23–24.

51. Smith, p. 35.

The contrast between Smith and McNemar's different choices, from a shared background as Scottish settlers on the Pennsylvania frontier, may bring to mind the American legend of individualism, but their substantive exchanges repeatedly returned to the family as the central institution of society. To dramatize charges that the Shakers were anti-family, Smith told terrible anecdotes of the Shakers referring to marriage as "whoring," snatching sugar out of the hands of crying children, of a small boy (probably Smith's grandson) "held. . . forcibly" from his mother until both cried, and other distressing details of an alleged Shaker assault on the most cherished and intimate bonds.[52]

A somewhat odd story moved Smith to particular outrage, as he told it in multiple pamphlets attacking the Shakers and also asked some of his deponents to attest to its veracity. It was a story, in Smith's words, about "a little boy," living with the Shakers, who took a piece of cake. The Shakers, Smith reported, punished the "little boy for taking a piece of cake without leave," by making "a circle on the floor about a foot in diameter, and compelled the boy to stand within the circle with his face upwards," apparently toward God, from noon until dark. The boy may have been Smith's grandson. Moreover, the story hit the same note, one of pathetic vulnerability: vulnerable frontiers, nascent laws, fragile families, susceptible women, and helpless children, all under assault by malevolent Shakers. He even claimed that the Shaker program "perhaps murders infants. . . (but this I cannot yet prove.)"[53]

In addition to attacking the Shakers, Smith also attempted to defend himself, primarily by situating himself in a sacred, national history. By 1810, sacred national histories were rather common, but Smith's is unusual. In an earlier exchange, McNemar had asked if, in fact, Smith did not owe his prominence to having "burned and destroyed. . . peacable" frontier settlements. In fact, in 1765, Smith led the "black boys" in the burning of a storage settlement owned by George Croghan, a notable frontier power-broker and trader. Croghan and Smith were deeply invested in rival land speculation companies.[54] Invoking his status as a veteran ("I suffered much in procuring the happy liberty that we now

---

52. Ibid., pp. 35–36.

53. Smith, *Remarkable Occurrences*, p. 7; idem, *Shakerism Detected*, pp. 10, 35.

54. On Smith's burning of Croghan's settlement, see Abernathy, *Western Lands and the American Revolution*, p. 81. On Croghan as trader, speculator, and power-broker, see Alan Taylor, *William Cooper's Town: Power and Persuasion on the Frontier of the Early American Republic* (New York, 1996).

possess"), Smith countered McNemar's allegations of terrorism with a political mysticism characteristic of nationalist discourse. Smith characterized his wartime killings as service on behalf of America, specifically Western Americans. He then again switched to addressing McNemar by name: "Richard," he wrote, "you have stated this patriotic. . . expedition, in a false light." He promised to provide a "true statement" of "said expeditions."[55] In the lengthy narrative that followed, for which Smith collected another six depositions attesting to events by then over 40 years in the past, Smith made a remarkable claim about the Seven Years' War. British General Braddock's ineptitude, he wrote, which brought "all the nations of the Indians against the white people," Smith recalled, placed him, as the head of the frontier irregulars the "black boys," in a difficult position. Following the Stamp Act in 1765, their position grew only more difficult—"America almost unanimously opposed it," Smith recalled. "The country was then in an awful dilemma. . . between two fires," he wrote. According to Smith, the "two fires" that had been bearing down on the "black boys" were the British and the Indians, not the British and the French, nor the French and the Indians. Given that Americans were British subjects, fighting with the British Army against the French and the Indians, Smith's claim to have been pursuing, during the Seven Years' War, a distinctly American agenda is notable. The rest of his narrative depicts a series of bold vigilante actions in which the "black boys"—by threat, arson, siege, and direct attack—prevented the British provisioning of Indian allies. We could not bear, he wrote, "to see those warlike stores going to supply our savage enemies." This American nationalist commitment led the "black boys," in Smith's account, to open defiance of the British, including the taking of British prisoners at Fort Loudon.[56]

The veracity of Smith's account is difficult to ascertain, but the point is that his way of responding to McNemar's allegations captured a mode

---

55. Smith, *Shakerism Detected*, pp. 18–19.

56. Ibid., 18–21. Fred Anderson, *The Crucible of War: The Seven Years War and the Fate of Empire in British North America, 1754–1765* (New York, 2000). Anderson does not mention Smith or the "black boys," but Smith's account of General Braddock's disastrous dealings with the Indians is confirmed by Anderson. By Anderson's chronology, Smith's claims to have been fighting a war for the prerogatives of American imperialism from 1763 onward would be the earliest example of such a program that I have seen. Francis Parkman called Smith's captivity narrative, *Account of Remarkable Occurrences in the Life of Colonel James Smith*, "perhaps the best of all the numerous narratives of captives among the Indians," but Parkman does not use the later source or mention the "black boys." See Parkman, *Montcalm and Wolfe* (New York, 1984), p. 123.

of nationalist discourse with mystical dimensions. Representing himself as an American nationalist from 1765 (a very early date), and as a heroic defender of the American land interests on the frontier, Smith did not deny McNemar's allegations that he had attacked and killed innocent people during the war. Instead, he countered that these actions were part of his difficult and dangerous service to the nation. In other words, he did not seek exoneration from McNemar's specific charges, but atonement, to cleanse the stain of his own bloody past in the sacred fountain of national origins.[57] An important flourish, the reprinting of popular patriot songs, followed Smith's narrative of his military service. The verses, he wrote, would "give the reader some additional ideas of the Stamp Act and the Sideling-hill expedition." The first, "On Liberty," began, "Freedom and liberty they are very good / They ought to be praised like to our daily food / But bondage and slav'ry Americans abhor / Whilst, freedom and liberty they ever adore." Some verses of the second, unnamed, song were more pertinent to the substantive conflict with the Shakers: "Let those Indian traders claim; / Their just reward, in-glorious fame." Generally, however, the verses had nothing to do the specific charges of war crimes leveled against Smith. Rather, they provided the symbolic completion of a proposed sociological substitution. Smith was not just opposing the Shakers' provisioning of the Indians. In place of the Shakers' invidious doctrines, hollow symbols, and despotic bondage, he offered the alternative of the nation, the rites of its just civil law, the savage Indian and cherished family as its antithetical symbols, and, in the patriot ditties, its inspiring litany.

In the nearly stateless early republic, especially on the frontier, the governing purview of frontier sects and churches extended farther than it did in post-revolutionary New England, the metropolitan centers of the East, or the planter-dominated Low Country. Nonetheless, McNemar chafed at the already loose boundaries of sectarian authority on the frontier. To create a more righteous society, he sought to extend religious authority even further. On the other hand, Smith could imagine that the frontier revivalists had already achieved a measure of force and momentum that threatened the viability of the American experiment.[58] The passion and bitterness of the conflict between Smith and McNemar derived, in part, from their common goals. They both sought not just to govern, but, as one

57. Carolyn Marvin and David W. Ingle, *Blood Sacrifice and the Nation: Totem Rituals and the American Flag* (New York, 1999).

58. Graham-Voelker, p. 176.

of the prerogatives of governance, control over the production of the means of salvation. In a remarkable moment, the "upperworldly" dimension of the contest crystallized in a fight over the fate of a sacred, national symbol. Producing another deposition, Smith charged "that the shakers say that the *soul of General Washington came to them after his decease and confessed his sins; and also the ancient prophets and apostles!!!*"[59] When it came to matters of justice, Smith, like the Shakers, used the language of Protestant morality; for example, Washington did not plead guilty to crimes, but had confessed his "sins." Another of Smith's deponents reported that the Indians had told him that "Richard M'Nemar told us that the white people had cheated us out of our land," but that "it was not the book's fault, for no good man who adhered to that book would wrong them or do them any injury." McNemar allegedly told the Indians, " 'the word of God. . . is good. . . bad men. . . made it bad.' " In brief, McNemar and Smith each saw himself as the defender of the scriptures. They drew contradictory meanings from those scriptures, however, and both, but especially McNemar, believed that theology authorized particular social and political changes.[60]

In contrast to New York and Boston and other metropolitan centers, the frontier of the early American republic was filling with settlers from more diverse backgrounds than one would find anywhere in the original states. Unlike immigrants to cities, migrants and immigrants to the frontier encountered few if any established institutions. Nor was the frontiersman of nationalist mythology inclined toward conventional political participation. Davy Crockett's path from frontiersman to congressman concluded with his rejection of Congress and was in any event highly atypical. Across the frontier, it was the ministers who offered governance, a language for speaking and thinking about order and morality and bonds of mutual obligation.[61]

In conclusion, three points merit emphasis. First, McNemar and the Shakers' alliance with Tenskwatawa and Tecumseh's resistance movement

---

59. "Upperworldly" is Peter Brown's characterization of the Christian saints, in particular their concern and involvement in mundane matters while acting as liaisons to the Heavens. See his *The Cult of the Saints: Its Rise and Function in Latin Christianity* (Chicago, 1981); Smith, *Shakerism Detected*, p. 32. Italics in the original.

60. Ibid., 30.

61. Malcolm J. Rohrbough, "Diversity and Unity in the Old Northwest, 1790–1850: Several Peoples Fashion a Single Region," in Ralph D. Gray, ed., *Pathways to the Old Northwest* (Indianapolis, 1988); Andrew R. L. Clayton, "The Origin of Politics in the Old Northwest," ibid., p. 63. On Davy Crockett, see Marquis James, *The Raven: A Biography of Sam Houston*

did not represent any inherent tendency of frontier revivalism. Like most frontier settlers, frontier revivalists tended to see the Native Americans as savages. Yet the alliance did happen. To Smith and the mob, it was not necessary to imagine the subversion of civil authority that might result from imperatives of divine law. The frontier revivalists made the actual, an alliance with a pan-Indian resistance movement, emerge from the potential, and the threat was plain. Second, the shared forms of authority, ritual, and rhetoric of evangelical Protestantism could just as easily embitter as ameliorate conflict. Smith and McNemar fought with such acrimony, in part, because they invoked common authority in attempts to consolidate incompatible social orders. Notably, they did not fight over issues that had for centuries divided European Christians: the language of the liturgy, the number of sacraments, ecclesiastical hierarchy, or the canon of the scripture. They could not have been more at odds, however, over what the word of God meant for those living in the Miami River Valley at the beginning of the nineteenth century. The impasse between Smith and McNemar, each of whom was an evangelical and a Protestant, shows that care must be taken when presuming how much meaningful commonality evangelical Protestantism alone establishes.

Finally, the alliance between the frontier ministers and the Native American resistance movement raises questions about the role of religion in the development of American racial ideology and the formation of American nationality. For the politically ambitious, the frontier was a place to gain a reputation as an "Indian fighter." In fact, between 1820 and 1852, six of the 11 major candidates for US president would climb onto the national political stage either as generals in wars with Indians or as secretaries of war whose primary responsibility was warring with Native American tribes. Yet some notable frontier religious movements were anti-racist. For generations, scholars have interpreted egalitarian components of popular religion in the early national period as deriving from republican and democratic discourses. Under several different sectarian banners (Presbyterian, New Light, "Christian," Shaker), Richard McNemar, and his brethren led movements that found the authority for

---

(Indianapolis, 1929), p. 17. Alan Kulikoff wrote, "By examining local communities, analysts of the transition to capitalism have underplayed the significance of the nation-state and nationalizing processes in the creation of commercial and capitalist economic relations and the perpetuation of non-market relations of production," see his essay "The Transition to Capitalism in Rural America," *William and Mary Quarterly*, vol. 46 (January 1989), pp. 135–136.

their anti-elitism in scripture, divine revelation, and social experience, rather than democratic or republican institutions, much less the legacy of the American Revolution. Together, these facts suggest that the nationalization of frontier religion occurred later than scholars have maintained. They also suggest that the popularization of racial ideology, as well the role of Protestantism in forming American nationality, are questions for which the answers must be found in the nineteenth century.[62]

---

62. Gellner, *Nationalism*, pp. 15–16; Frederick Jackson Turner, "Western State-Making in the Revolutionary Era," *American Historical Review*, vol. 1 (October 1895), pp. 86–87, and "Western State-Making in the Revolutionary Era II," *American Historical Review*, vol. 1 (January 1896). On the invention of denominationalism to nationalize frontier religion, see Haselby, *The Origins of American Religious Nationalism*, ch. 6; Garry Wills, *"Negro President": Jefferson and the Slave Power* (New York, 2005), p. 61. On the growing anti-Indian racism in the early American republic, see Anthony F. C. Wallace, *The Long, Bitter Trail: Andrew Jackson and the Indians* (New York, 1993); Frederick Jackson Turner, *The Frontier in American History* (Tucson, AZ, 1986), pp. 250–257; Michael Paul Rogin, *Ronald Reagan, the Movie: And Other Episodes in Political Demonology* (Berkeley, CA, 1987), p. 136; Freeman Cleaves, *Old Tippecanoe: William Henry Harrison and His Time* (New York, 1939). On the bad faith that characterized American dealings with Native Americans, see Alan Taylor, *The Divided Ground: Indians, Settlers, and the Northern Borderland of the American Revolution* (New York, 2006), and Stuart Banner, *How the Indians Lost Their Land: Law and Power on the Frontier* (Cambridge, MA, 2005). McNemar's alliance with the Shawnee brothers receives no attention in Stephen J. Stein, *The Shaker Experience in America: A History of the United Society of Believers* (New Haven, CT, 1992). The still dominant interpretation of frontier revivalism is that of Nathan Hatch, *The Democratization of American Christianity* (New Haven, CT, 1989).

5

"The Love of Order and Righteous Laws"

EARLY NATIONAL LIBERALS AND THE MISSIONS
MOVEMENT

SECULARISM WAS THE means by which a class of American nationalists, some of whom were associated with Enlightenment deism, helped
to advance democratic revolution. Frontier revivalism developed out of
the disorder attending the American colonization of the continent. The
Northeastern (meaning New England and Middle States) Protestant
establishment was a pioneering nationalist class, with strong imperial ambitions, but they did not welcome either secularism or popular
Protestantism, experiencing both as threats. They answered these challenges with ecumenism and missionary outreach. Ecumenism and
missionary outreach were born of a marriage between New England
Protestant literary intellectuals and the Northeastern bourgeoisie; the former brought their peculiar cultural strengths and the latter their money.
Ecumenism and missionary outreach were substitutes for power in party
politics as well as a strategy, launched by the sons of the founding fathers,
to continue or surpass the work of the American Revolution.

Nearly all Protestants from the Northeastern establishment accepted
the political theology of nationalism and pursued extraordinary means to
amalgamate and organize into Protestant associations. Protestant intellectuals emphasized the newness of inter-sectarian cooperation, and its
millennial possibilities. By misrepresenting the history of religion in
America, especially New England, as one devoted to missionary work,
they also masked the theological implications of their acceptance of the

nation as the true community of salvation. To be sure, notable differences existed between liberal and conservative New England Protestant intellectuals. They also, however, shared deep and powerful commitments that distinguished them from popular religion on the frontier. In their embrace of ecumenism and missions, their nationalization of a selective version of the New England past, their literary prowess, their partnership with the American bourgeoisie, and most of all their nationalism, liberal Protestant intellectuals joined in a common enterprise with Timothy Dwight and the conservatives. It was a remarkable movement of national evangelism. The liberal wing of national evangelism was more diffuse and eccentric than the conservative branch, for which the Connecticut Wits and Yale served as crucibles. Nonetheless, William Ellery Channing at Harvard and the Philadelphia-born lawyer and evangelical Elias Boudinot are important figures. Channing shaped Unitarianism, nurtured a generation of American writers, and embodied the turn from theology to nationalism and institution-building. Boudinot was the most influential Christian layman in America. He was a successful lawyer, politician, and businessman who wanted to be a writer and intellectual. He served as a bridge between Protestant intellectuals and the Northeastern bourgeoisie.

Historians have pointed to the 1805 election of the Unitarian Henry Ware to the Hollis Chair at Harvard as the beginning of American liberal Protestantism. It is true that in the colonial era it would have been impossible for a minister with Unitarian theology to hold the renowned Hollis Chair. It is also true, however, that Protestant theology is a more important part of seventeenth- and eighteenth-century New England history than it is of the history of the nineteenth-century United States. Puritanism, for example, was a theological movement with political dimensions, whereas, though both had a theology, Transcendentalism was an intellectual movement and abolitionism a political one. A better indication of the new age than the theology of the holder of the Hollis Chair is William Ellery Channing's 1813 turn from teaching theology to endeavors that he saw as suited to reach the mass of men—to institution-building and missionary work.

Channing was the godfather of both Transcendentalism and abolitionism. Ralph Waldo Emerson called him "our bishop." In 1813, Channing resigned from the Divinity School at Cambridge, after only one year, to take seat on the Board of the Harvard Corporation, where he would serve for 13 years. Channing left the Divinity School because he no longer wanted to teach theology, he explained; he wanted to be a missionary.

Theology schools, he wrote, could not escape their "monkish, gloomy. . . superstitious air." Missionary work was "practical" and might reach "the *mass of men*." To that end, missionary work must leave behind abstruse theology, focusing instead on "character." For early republic reformers, character assumed the place that "virtue" had occupied for the revolutionary generation. Classical virtue seemed to require an adversary, even a great contest. Character, its Protestant successor as a person or society's moral inclinations, might be practiced in peace. Channing's move from theology to missionary work captured this budding spirit of the second decade of the nineteenth century. It had been developing slowly. Channing recalled that, a decade earlier, in 1800 and 1801, he had attended a monthly prayer and religious revival meeting in Cambridge, Massachusetts, at which solicitations for missionary work were made. "As most of us were very poor," he wrote, "our contributions did not greatly exceed the widow's mite." By 1809, when Jedidiah Morse, on behalf of the Society for Propagating the Gospel Among the Indians and Others in North America, pleaded with Harvard College to support a mission to Native Americans, the Corporation of Harvard responded with a donation of just $100. The same year, several individuals in Cambridge gave as much as, or more than, the College.[1]

In 1810, three years before he left teaching to devote himself to social reform and outreach, Channing began to help build the Bible Society of Massachusetts. He would serve as chairman of the Bible Society of Massachusetts for eight years, from 1812 to 1820. In 1813, the same year that Dwight sermonized to the American Board of Commissioners of Foreign Missions on the holy and regenerative force of missions, Channing, too, wrote that there could be no doubt that a "sincere Christian" was "bound to contribute to the diffusion of Christianity through the world" by supporting missions. Missionary work, he wrote, was the "sublime and merciful work of God." Like his conservative Protestant opponents, Channing welcomed the rise of inter-sectarian missionary and evangelical institutions. He told the Massachusetts Bible Society that the joining together of

---

1. Emerson quoted in Perry Miller, ed., *The American Transcendentalists* (New York, 1957), p. 4; Channing's private papers reprinted in William Henry Channing, *The Life of William Ellery Channing, D.D.* (Boston, 1899), pp. 291–293, 295. Channing's account of the fruitless solicitations for missionary work at the 1800 Cambridge meetings, in William Henry Channing, ed., *Memoir of William Ellery Channing* (Boston, 1851), vol. 1, p. 138; Joseph Badger, "Letter from the Rev. Joseph Badger," *Panoplist and Missionary Magazine United* (June 1809), p. 428.

so many Christians of "different denominations" served as a bright light of hope to challenge the darkening crises afflicting the world. He wrote that God had prescribed that men with means ought to be "Christian philanthropists." He characterized the ecumenical imperative as a willingness to recognize as Christians many with whom one would not want to share a home.[2] As secularists, and their Dissenting supporters, advocated a separation of religion from government, the ecumenists responded with an impressive and entirely new campaign to unify and coordinate Protestantism. In 1815, Channing reported to Massachusetts Bible Society members that the world had not seen such a movement toward Christian unification since the history of early Church. The identification with the early Christians was a favorite conceit of bourgeois Protestants in the early republic, one that says more about the burden they felt as the sons of the founding fathers than it does about the late antique world. In 1816, Channing told Bible Society members that they were participating in a unique endeavor: "Human history," he wrote, "affords no example of such extensive co-operation." The profusion of Protestant associations, "founded by the most illustrious men, patronized by sovereigns, endowed by opulence," had no precedent. This was true. Like many of his contemporaries, Channing interpreted the historic advent of ecumenism and Protestant cooperation as a "glorious manifestation of the power of Christianity," whereby "all flesh shall see the salvation of God." This grand work of "Christian nations," he wrote, signaled an imminent millennium, a popular Christian enthusiasm of the time, at least among Channing's class.[3]

The early Christians found support among soldiers and traders in port cities, and, especially, among the poorest and the slaves of the Roman Empire. For their missions, Channing and the Unitarians, like Dwight and the Congregationalists and Presbyterians, looked to the middling sorts and the bourgeoisie. In a June 1819 letter to Henry Ware, Jr., Channing cautioned Ware to remember that while Christians bore a special obligation to the poor ("Christ preached to the poor," and "no system bears the stamp of his religion, or can prevail" that does not reach out to them),

2. Reports of the Bible Society of Massachusetts excerpted in Channing, pp. 289–291; William Ellery Channing, Memoir of William Ellery Channing (London, 1850), vol. II, p. 259.

3. Ibid. On the fractious and diverse world of early Christianity, see Elaine Pagels, The Gnostic Gospels (New York, 1989); Peter Brown and Geoffrey Barraclough, The World of Late Antiquity (New York, 1989); Keith Hopkins, A World Full of Gods: The Strange Triumph of Christianity (New York, 2001), esp. ch. 4.

Unitarianism would rise on the backs of "middling sorts." Channing advised Ware, who was in the midst of organizing a Unitarian society in New York, to look for "friends and adherents. . . in the middling classes." They would give the most "hearty" and "earnest" support. If the middling sorts were to fill Unitarian churches, Channing knew, the elite—or to use his term, the "opulent" classes—must lead the way. In social reform, he wrote, the "more opulent and improved class" must devote itself to the "greater good." To encourage the rich to give, he advised the publishers of religious tracts to emphasize, above all, that the highest manifestation of the religious principle was to exhibit "brotherly love." It was, he advised, a message that would be welcome among the poor while not offending the elite.[4]

The turn of New England's Protestant intellectuals from theology to launching ecumenical missionary and social reform organizations was new. They, however, claimed that their missionary and ecumenical organizations marked continuity with a great missionary past. The official history of the American Board of Commissioners for Foreign Missions, for example, begins: "The first settlement of New England was a missionary enterprise."[5] This was simply not true. The Calvinist Protestantism of which New Englanders were heirs and standard-bearers required an educated laity, and they undertook the obligation with seriousness. In comparison to Spanish Catholics, Anglo-American Protestants, especially Dissenters, were also poor. For both of these reasons, they had no ecclesiastical orders: no Jesuits, Dominicans, or Franciscans. For the first two centuries of its settlement, the imperative to scrutinize its own flock, so that they could transform the wilderness into the garden, and their relative lack of resources, had helped keep New England education exclusive and inward-looking. There was, for example, no North American, much less New England, counterpart to the College of Santa Cruz in Tlatelolco. Founded in 1536 to teach Latin, Spanish, and Greek to young Aztecs, the college drew on support from the Spanish government to produce a hispanicized native elite. Compared to the Franciscan College of Santa Cruz, the Puritans' Indian College at Harvard and the Virginia Anglicans'

---

4. Channing's letter to Ware reprinted in John Ware, ed., *Memoir of the Life of Henry Ware, Jr.* (Boston, 1846), pp. 117–119; Channing, ed., *Memoir of William Ellery Channing*, vol. II, pp. 193, 197.

5. Tracy, *History of the American Board of Commissioners for Foreign Missions*, p. 11. Hereafter cited as *HABCFM*.

Henrico College (1619), both founded to educate Indians, were shabby and short-lived enterprises.[6]

During the colonial era, Harvard had remained a theologically oriented and parochial institution, focused on producing good Puritans. The theologian and historian George Huntston Williams described the college's character in the colonial era as "essentially medieval." It is remarkable, Williams noted, that despite their rejection of things Anglican and Catholic, the Puritans embraced an unaltered Anglican and Catholic form of the college. Its founders saw Harvard in exactly the same manner that Pope Gregory IX had seen the University of Paris, as a "provisional paradise or garden" dedicated to the "monastic-scholastic tradition of the licit pursuit of the knowledge of good and evil under the tutelage of Christ, the Second Adam." Within this role, however, Cotton Mather noted with approval, Harvard College differed from the Catholic "Seminaries of Canada and Mexico." It was not intended to proselytize to pagans but to maintain the purity of Puritans. In what Williams called an early chapter in the history of academic freedom, Increase Mather, president of Harvard, battled to keep the college curriculum beyond the influence of taxpayers in good standing with the Massachusetts Bay Colony who happened to also be Anglicans, or Congregationalists of too broad sympathies, or the Spiritualist successors of Anne Hutchinson. Harvard was to be a college, wrote Cotton Mather, fit for a "protestant and puritan country."

Keeping skepticism at bay could bring forth extraordinary efforts. In order to incorporate Cartesian logic into the curriculum, for example, William Brattle (1662–1717), an influential Harvard tutor and devout Puritan minister, produced an amended edition of Descartes while also brokering a Puritan theological concession that allowed for the recognition of free will in certain philosophical pursuits while still privileging theology. The resulting textbook, Brattle's *Compendium of Logick*, enabled Harvard, well into the eighteenth century, to teach a version of Cartesianism that supported the intellectual hegemony of Puritanism in New England. Likewise, the original mottos of the college, *In Christi Gloriam* ("For the Glory of Christ"), adopted in 1650, and *Christo et ecclesiae* ("Christ, the Church"), used since 1682, give a more accurate indication of the role of religion in the first half of the College's history than "Veritas."

---

6. J. H. Elliott, pp. 73–77.

Harvard did not adopt the latter as a motto until the mid-nineteenth century.[7]

At the beginning of the nineteenth century, with a new sense of themselves as stewards of a nation and an empire, New England's elite colleges began to transform. Yale emerged as the imperial force of American tertiary education and missions, but other colleges and universities also played roles. Amherst, Princeton, and Columbia, as well as Andover Theological Seminary and Williams College, contributed men, ideas, and money to the missions movement. From Harvard, William Ellery Channing shone as the leading light of liberal American Protestantism. Channing helped to nurture a generation of liberal Protestant intellectuals, including Henry Ware, Jr., Ralph Waldo Emerson, and others. By numbers, the Unitarians counted a small minority, but their literary talents, their appeal to an elite, and their willingness to nurture a broad range of reformers and eccentrics gave them a disproportionate influence.[8]

In contrast to the Connecticut Federalists, and though they may not have voted for him, the Unitarians admired Thomas Jefferson's faith in man's natural moral abilities. Deism and Unitarianism shared an optimistic spirit, and the latter rose as the former was expiring. In some sense, Unitarianism may be regarded as the nineteenth-century successor to deism. Unitarians considered Trinitarianism needlessly mystical, thought humanity had outgrown the Calvinist doctrine of man's total depravity, and emphasized Jesus's expansive love and divine mercy, as opposed to God's watchful retribution and divine justice. Among liberals, criticism from more orthodox Protestants led to a certain amount of self-pity, exemplified by Henry Ware, Jr.'s characterization of the Unitarians as "the intolerable class [of] the present age," and victims of widespread "persecution."[9] To be sure, some Unitarians did suffer

---

7. George Hunston Williams, "Transaltio Studii: The Puritans' Conception of Their First University in New England, 1636," *Archiv für Reformations geschichte* (1966), p. 152, 175; Rick Kennedy, "The Alliance Between Puritanism and Cartesian Logic at Harvard, 1687–1735," *Journal of the History of Ideas* (October–December 1990), pp. 558, 570–571; Bernard Bailyn, "Foundations," in *Glimpses of the Harvard Past* (Cambridge, MA, 1986), p. 6.

8. Six graduates of Yale, and one of Harvard, founded the College of New Jersey, later Princeton, and Yale gave Princeton its first three presidents. See Francis L. Broderick, "Pulpit, Physics, and Politics: The Curriculum of the College of New Jersey, 1746–1794, *William and Mary Quarterly* (January 1949), vol. 6, p. 46.

9. Adams, *History of the United States during the Administrations of Jefferson and Madison*, p. 115. Christopher Clark, "Culture, Ideology and Social Change in America, 1700–1860," *The Historical Journal*, vol. 36 (Sept. 1993), p. 740. The most important deist periodical,

discrimination. When his young son Henry died, for example, the English chemist, and Unitarian, Joseph Priestley discovered that no cemetery in Pennsylvania's Susquehanna Valley would permit a Unitarian to be buried on its grounds. It took the intervention of a neighboring Quaker family to secure young Henry Priestley's interment.[10]

Early nineteenth-century American Protestants, whether Unitarian, Congregationalist, Presbyterian, or Transcendentalist, were literate, philosophically minded, and took theology more seriously than have subsequent generations of Americans. As historians have detailed, these characteristics led to squabbling. New England Protestants' propensity for disputation, including with one another, should not obscure the foundational political theology they shared. Viewed in the context of nation and empire, college-educated American ministers of the Northeast, liberal and conservative, shared some dogmas of nationalist political theology that distinguished them from the frontier revivalists.[11]

Like Congregationalists and Presbyterians, Unitarians and Transcendentalists thought patriotism a moral and religious duty. They believed that the United States of America had been chosen to play a sacred, Christian role in history. Unlike the state constitutions, virtually all of which were explicitly Christian, the godlessness of the US Constitution may have made Protestant nationalists especially eager to sacralize it. Without question, disestablishment at the federal level led Reformed Protestants of the Northeastern establishment to conclude that religion was more, not less, important to society than ever. They shared a conviction that American missionary and moral improvement associations, acting as instruments of a spiritual regeneration, would remake the world. Northeastern Unitarians, Transcendentalists, Presbyterians, and Congregationalists accepted without question that nations were the fundamental building blocks of history. God was now, in Theodore Parker's

---

the *Theophilanthropist*, closed in 1811; see Herbert M. Morais, *Deism in Eighteenth Century America* (New York, 1960), p. 177. In 1815, Channing wrote, "would Trinitarians tell us what they mean, their system would generally be found little else than a mystical form of the Unitarian doctrine"; see Channing, p. 214.

10. See Henry Ware, Jr., D.D., *The Miscellaneous Writings of Henry Ware Jr., D.D.* (Boston, 1846), p. 103 (hereafter cited as *The Miscellaneous Writings*); Caroline Robbins, "Honest Heretic: Joseph Priestley in America," *Proceedings of the American Philosophical Society*, vol. 106 (February 1962), pp. 60–61.

11. Charles Capper and Conrad Edick Wright, *Transient and Permanent: The Transcendentalist Movement and Its Contexts* (Boston, 1999).

words, "the Divine Father of the nations." Among this class of Protestants, the cult of the nation was not new. The King James Bible, translated almost two centuries earlier (1611), used "nation" as a translation for four different Hebrew words. It translated Jeremiah 10:7, for example, as "Who would not fear thee, O King of Nations?" The fourteenth-century Wycliffe Bible had referred to God as "A! thou King of folks," and the Syriac version of the Bible reads "O King of all worlds." Among the middle classes, however, at the beginning of the nineteenth century, the power of nationalism to transform religion and politics had never been greater. Following the demise of the Federalist Party, the second decade of the century came to be known as "the Era of Good Feelings." Really it was the era of one-party rule, and, deprived of their party, many former Federalists threw their energies into missionary and moral improvement associations.[12]

Liberal Protestants did not produce any work resembling the grandiosity of Dwight's *Conquest of Canäan*, or Joel Barlow's *Columbiad*, but their theology and politics also were evident in their literary work, which was much more influential. Channing, for example, based the Unitarian method of reading the Bible on US Supreme Court Chief Justice John Marshall's opinion in *McCulloch v. Maryland*. *McCulloch* originated over an attempt by the state of Maryland to effectively tax the Baltimore branch of the Bank of the United States out of existence. In finding Maryland's tax on the Bank unconstitutional, the Marshall Court delivered the most sweeping nationalist ruling of the nineteenth century before the Civil War and Reconstruction years. In April 1819, a month and a half after the Court delivered its decision in *McCulloch*, Channing was in Baltimore for the ordination of his protégé Jared Sparks, who was assuming the pulpit in one of the first Unitarian churches outside New England.[13] Channing

---

12. Daniel Walker Howe, *The Unitarian Conscience: Harvard Moral Philosophy, 1805–1861* (Cambridge, MA, 1970); Andrew Delbanco, *William Ellery Channing: An Essay on the Liberal Spirit in America* (Cambridge, MA, 1981); Ware believed the Unitarians were persecuted because they were the true inheritors of the mantle of the Reformation, via seventeenth-century English Puritanism. On the King James Bible, see Diarmaid MacCulloch, "How Good Is It?" *London Review of Books* (February 3, 2011), p. 21. On the Era of Good Feelings, see George Dangerfield, *The Awakening of American Nationalism, 1815–1828* (Long Grove, IL, 1994).

13. Davis, *Challenging the Boundaries of Slavery*, p. 50. Twenty years before *McCulloch*, after graduating from Harvard, Channing had worked as a tutor in Richmond, Virginia, where he met Marshall. "Marshall is a great character," he wrote, "He bids fair to be the first character in the Union"; see Channing's letter in William Henry Channing, *The Life of William Ellery Channing* (Boston, 1899), p. 51.

told the packed church that Unitarians read the Bible just as the Marshall Court had read the US Constitution:

> We reason about the Bible precisely as civilians do about the constitution under which we live; who, as you know, are accustomed to limit one provision of that venerable instrument by others, and to fix the precise import of its parts by inquiring into its general spirit, into the intentions of its authors, and into the prevalent feelings, impressions, and circumstances of the time when it was framed. Without these principles of interpretation, we frankly acknowledge that we cannot defend the divine authority of the Scriptures. Deny us this latitude, and we must abandon this book to its enemies.[14]

That James Madison soon disavowed the Marshall Court's "broad and pliant" reading of federal power in the Constitution as "anticipated. . . by few, if any" of the framers made no more difference to Channing than it did to the Marshall Court. Jared Sparks, whose ordination provided the occasion for Channing's address, went on to continue his mentor's work. Sparks became one of Alexis de Tocqueville's hosts and primary informants, president of Harvard (1849 to 1853), and the editor of the George Washington papers (12 volumes, 1834–1837). In the latter capacity, he removed colloquialisms and edited the letters so as to Christianize Washington's views. From 1817 to 1818 and again from 1824 to 1830, Sparks edited *The North American Review*, which for nearly half a century was the most important intellectual periodical in the United States.[15]

When the logic of Protestantism empowered seemingly wild-eyed frontier ministers, the liberal establishment found the consequences less salutary. Henry Ware, Jr., for example, could not decide if there was a method or just madness driving the popular revivalist Charles Grandison Finney, but he was sure that Finney's followers were "impudent" and "threatening." Finney's example, wrote Ware, had liberated "all the subalterns. . .

14. Channing, "Unitarian Christianity," p. 4.

15. Madison quoted in Dangerfield, *The Era of Good Feelings*, p. 173. The literary scholar Sacvan Bercotvitch has written that whereas the "Puritans had discovered America in the Bible" the "Jacksonians discovered the Bible in the Declaration of Independence and the Constitution." In fact, Channing and other New England divines sacralized America's founding texts before the rise of Jacksonian nationalism. Though opponents of Jacksonianism, the shared nationalism would help limit Jackson's opponents to less radical measures than those of Lincoln; see Bercovitch, *Rites of Assent*, p. 11.

who are let loose" in the countryside, traveling "in bands, assailing passengers in the street, and prying into families." Ware found Finney's preaching "violent, loud," his prayers "unscriptural," and he suspected the popular minster was a con artist, "acting a cold, calculating part." Ware found Finney's physical comportment, his "affected groanings" and his "writhing of the body as if in agony," evidence of poor character and incapacity for ethical public conduct.[16]

Historians have debated whether Charles Grandison Finney and the upstate New York revival in which he played a prominent role was a conservative or progressive force. In a large republic without a state church, with a vast and porous frontier, a free market in scriptural interpretation and divine revelation struck many establishment Protestants as a map to mayhem. Without question, by the early nineteenth century, revelation was a reactionary mode of establishing authority. Some historians have argued that the ability of Protestantism to recast problems of social and political structure in terms of individual ethics worked to the advantage of the bourgeoisie, or the status quo. At the same time, popular revivalism helped fortify men and women from the lower orders—"the subalterns," Ware called them—to social and political action. Overall, popular Protestantism simply lacked a clear, coherent social theory of the kind inherent in the artisanal republicanism of urban journeymen. It was too ambiguous and too unstable to serve exclusively, or even chiefly, as either a means of bourgeois domination or a tool of working-class resistance. Popular religion did, however, offer the poor and uneducated a venue for establishing social authority and even advancement. To middling sorts, the storms stirred by popular lay preachers usually appeared as they did to Henry Ware—disorderly and threatening.[17]

Popular revivalism posed a more serious challenge to Unitarians and liberal Protestants than it did to conservatives, who accepted hierarchy, and their position near the top, as natural and necessary. Conservatives simply saw the lay ministers as out of order, as impudent and deluded. The Unitarians' more optimistic view of human nature distinguished them

---

16. Ware's letter reprinted in John Ware, M.D., *Memoir of the Life of Henry Ware, Jr.*, pp. 203–204.

17. Ibid. On evangelical Protestantism in the early republic as a source of working-class resistance and tool of bourgeois domination, respectively, see Teresa Anne Murphy, *Ten Hours Labor: Religion, Reform, and Gender in Early New England* (Ithaca, NY, 1992) and Paul E. Johnson, *The Shopkeeper's Millennium: Society and Revivals in Rochester, New York, 1815–1837* (New York, 1978); Sean Wilentz, *Chants Democratic*, passim.

from their Calvinistic brethren. They were proud of their Christocentric emphasis on the nurturing dimensions of Christianity. It was in part what made them who they were, which was self-consciously modern and progressive. In the Baltimore sermon that he gave at Jared Sparks's ordination, considered the foundational statement of Unitarianism, Channing said: "I am a leveler, but I would accomplish my object by elevating the low, by raising from a degrading indigence and brutal ignorance the laboring multitude." Channing imagined a new kind of preaching, one that would neither admonish nor frighten to piety but rather "raise" listeners "to an intensity of intellectual and moral action of which they were incapable before." Of course, the act of raising, as in Jesus raising from the dead, occupies a special place in Christianity. It is what demonstrates that Jesus was Christ. Bringing about a social version of the essential Christian act became a central concern of liberal American Protestants. "Christianity," wrote Channing, "teaches us to raise others. Christianity calls us to narrow the space between ourselves and our inferiors." How was this to be done? "By communicating to them. . . what is most valuable in our own minds." For Channing and other liberal Protestants, missionary work and social raising involved a complex process of introspection and careful communication.[18]

Samuel Gilman, a Harvard-educated Unitarian minister from a prosperous Gloucester, Massachusetts, merchant family, wrote a representative dramatization of the challenge inherent in the Unitarians' twin commitments to elevating and cultivating. Upon his graduation from Harvard in 1811, Gilman became a banker and a regular contributor to the *North American Review*. In 1817, at age 26, answering a call to the Unitarian ministry, he returned to Harvard. Two years later, Gilman began his mission, accepting a position at the Archdale Street Unitarian Church in Charleston, South Carolina. In Charleston, Gilman and his wife Caroline, along with their five children, founded a local "New England Society," whose quixotic mission was to spread enlightened Yankeeism to the South Carolina plantation society.[19]

In Charleston, Gilman wrote *Memoirs of a New England Village Choir*, in which he parodied the tensions of the early republic social structure. *Memoirs of a New England Village Choir* dramatizes the problem of

---

18. Channing, ed. *Memoir of William Ellery Channing*, vol. II, pp. 26, 175.

19. Daniel Walker Howe, entry for "Samuel Foster Gilman," *American National Biography*, vol. 9, pp. 63–64.

governance in the new nation through the story of the tribulations of a single New England church choir. The story is set in the fictional town of Waterfield during the "ten years, bordering upon the last and present centuries." It offers an opportunity to view what the Unitarians meant when they said, as Channing did, that religious organizations should steward American society in the manner of "our views of God in one word. . . Parental."[20] The story begins when Waterfield's long-time choir director, Mr. Pitchtone, departs to settle on the frontier. Charles Williams, a young shoemaker's apprentice in the village, demonstrates exceptional musical gifts, but choir director is deemed too elevated a position for a shoemaker's apprentice. Gilman accepted that a young cobbler's apprentice was unfit for choir director of a respectable church, but he was also troubled by it. Young Williams could not be called "*ignoble*, nor any other term of disparagement or contempt," wrote Gilman, because America is "neither a nation of noblemen nor plebeians." No American, Gilman wrote, could properly be called noble or ignoble, lord or peasant, because those "very political relations" were what Americans had repudiated. Instead, Gilman describes the social implications of American doctrines of freedom and equality as unclear, and unsettling.[21]

In the absence of ascribed social status, a fearfully maintained and ambiguous set of subtle class distinctions reigned. "No American lady," he explained, would ever refuse a social invitation on the grounds that it came from a woman of lower social class, yet any such invitation would be met with a refusal "as prompt and decided as any lady's in England." Americans, Gilman wrote, were still obsessed with social rank, they were just not sure how to determine it. In Gilman's experience, a combination of ancestry, profession, money, education, and distance from manual labor determined one's social standing. It was not mere pedigree, but pedigree "is one of its elements." Money and education "have something to with it" but "different vocations in life have much more." In a pinch, as good a guess as any could be made based on "the degrees of the softness and whiteness of the hands." Whether the criteria of class distinction would change, and how, remained to be seen: "This whole subject is extremely unsettled. The mass is fermenting, and how the process will

---

20. Samuel Gilman, *Memoirs of a New England Village Choir* (New York, 1984), p. 1. Originally published in 1829. Channing, "Unitarian Christianity," p. 14.

21. Gilman, p. 59.

result eventually, time only can decide." Who would be elevated, men with talent to rouse a mob, or men with gifts to govern?[22]

Gilman allegorized this question into the problem of who would lead the choir. With a series of imperfect choices for the position of Waterfield's choir director, Gilman confronts the problem of social advancement in the early republic. The village doctor's apprentice seems a socially appropriate choice, but his tin ear drives people away from the church. After the doctor's discordant tenure, the village turns back to an older, more confident Williams. His musical gifts and hard work re-fortify the church, but Williams's success precipitates a new problem. Waterfield's leading citizens decide that their admired choir director ought not be a cobbler. So the village takes up a collection and sends Williams to Dartmouth College. While Williams is at Dartmouth, trouble filling the position continues, until the town turns to Mary Wentworth, a young woman with exceptional musical aptitude. Though she works as a domestic servant for one of Waterfield's "richer families," no one calls her a servant. She is instead known, wrote Gilman, "under the denomination *help*." Americans consider *servant* objectionable, Gilman wrote, because it suggests a feudal order and "seems to stamp an irretrievable character on the person who bears the appellation." In contrast, *help* "seems to admit into the mind. . . a hope of rising in the world." The dilemma that liberal Protestants and other uplifters faced was that, more often than not, the hope was misplaced.[23]

A century before the American Revolution, when Samuel Danforth gave the sermon describing the "errand into the wilderness," 5 percent of the Puritan settlers owned 25 percent of the community wealth. Just before the Revolution, when the Connecticut Wits, Benjamin Franklin, and dozens of others were praising the egalitarianism of the American colonies, 3 percent of the colonists owned 33 percent of the wealth. By the 1830s, when Alexis de Tocqueville became the most influential reporter of America's egalitarian democracy, one percent of Americans owned almost half the wealth in the nation. At the same time, the increase in aggregate wealth, from 1670 to 1830, meant that even as the rich grew into a richer, and relatively smaller, class, social advance did happen.[24] "Unavoidable

---

22. Ibid., pp. 60–61.

23. Gilman, pp. 16, 22, 18–19.

24. Statistics on wealth in Sacvan Bercovitch, *The Rites of Assent: Transformations in the Symbolic Construction of America* (New York, 1993), pp. 46–47.

inequalities of fortune," wrote Gilman, mean that the "young heirs of poverty and dependence" must "solace themselves with the substantial comfort of assuming a title, which places them, in imagination at least, on a level with their employers, and soothes the sting" of subordination. Like Williams, Mary Wentworth's musical gifts produce "astonishing" and "enchanting" choral music, but the town cannot send a young a woman to college. The challenge that her elevated talents and low social rank present to the citizens of Waterfield brings about the one crisis in the story for which Gilman cannot present a solution. The women of the choir simply refuse to be led in choir by a servant. They would, he wrote, not "endure that a girl at service should aspire to an equality with themselves," so the Waterfield choir goes silent. Social mobility could be unsociable.[25]

Samuel Gilman's *Memoirs of a New England Village Choir* captures the dilemma of liberal Protestantism in the early republic. In contrast to their colonial predecessors, liberal Protestants felt "elevating the low," as Channing put it, as a strong Christian obligation. At the same time, they were insecure about their own social positions and, more so, felt misgivings about the consequences of raising the unrefined to influential positions. Gilman thought that there were two ways of rising: capitalism or college, either by going to work for "some wholesale or retail merchant in Boston, and the other, to pass through college." The town of Waterfield sent Williams to Dartmouth, while another son of the village, Mr. Forehead, chose Boston commerce. Forehead is the villain of the story, and his character dramatized the threat that rising without education and refinement posed to the community.[26] A Waterfield native, Forehead clashed with other locals and left the village for Boston, where he became a rich lawyer. His vulgar, aggressive return to the village takes place in middle of Sunday service, announced "by the loud crack of a whip." The cracking whip interrupts prayers, bringing the choir rushing to the window, where they see a "gig and a tandem" of horses carrying "a pair of gaily dressed gentlemen," and Forehead abusing his horses. Gilman

---

25. Channing, p. 258; Gilman, pp. 63–64, 67, 124–125.

26. Bercovitch, *The Rites of Assent: Transformations in the Symbolic Construction of America* (New York, 1993), p. 47. Gilman left no doubt that he intended the story as an allegory for the nation. "Time," he wrote, "which effects such mighty revolutions in the affairs of empires, condescends also to work the most important changes in the aspect of humble villages, and still humbler choirs." In his "memoirs of a single collection of singers [lay] several features common to all others [communities]." All communities, he explained, however small, "are a kind of arena for the exhibition" of what he called "human infirmities"; see pp. 136–137.

describes an almost diabolical entrance: "The confident and conscious footsteps of their creaking yellow-top boots" brings the church service to a standstill. Forehead's haughty nod humiliates Williams, who, though choral director, feels he ought to "bow" in return. Forehead and his associate join the choir, but "instead of lending us their voices," they jump in with a dissonant "singular stridor, emitted through nearly closed lips." Their mocking, discordant participation leaves the church "frightened" and "shocked," and the choir again falls silent. The realization that the unrefined rich presented as great a danger to the community as did the thwarting of the talented poor amounted to a strong incentive to liberal reform.[27]

Gilman's *Memoirs of a New England Village Choir* presents a United States of America pregnant with potential but also full of imperfect choices. The rich Forehead and his associate were presented as parasitic and almost foreign figures. The series of socially respectable fill-ins for choir director came with the cost of betraying the church music. This, too, was a serious problem. The sacred music was not only a beautiful experience, it cultivated "taste" and character. Character was necessary to stave off the degradation of institutions and societies. The attempts of the low to rise receive the most sympathetic attention, but also raise real concerns. Gilman worried that Williams was motivated by "mere ambition," that the cobbler harbored no "holier aspiration than. . . to acquaint himself with applause," to be, in Gilman's derisive characterization, a "performer." Likewise, an "effervescence of republican feeling," rather than a formal duty to the sacred music, seemed to be driving Mary Wentworth's full-throated display of the "whole blazing extent of her musical powers." Talent brought a responsibility for humility, so should not a talented servant especially be required, asks Gilman, to retain a "prudent humility?" Did the subalterns have the character to be "true leaders"? Gilman wondered. He meant the novella to be an endorsement of social uplift without illusions, a hardheaded affirmation of the liberal Protestant creed. The Connecticut Wits were committed to reproducing their social order; liberal Protestants were not as convinced about the natural rightness of New England town hierarchy. They were committed to activism and uplift, fighting in the trenches of "taste" and "character" on behalf of America.[28]

---

27. Ibid., pp. 136–138.

28. Ibid., pp. 51, 54, 55, 130.

The conclusion of *Memoirs of a New England Village Choir*, the "solution" Gilman offers for this crisis of religion and republicanism, is the revered Revolution. At the end of the novella, amid another crisis in maintaining a harmonious choir, four elderly veterans of the Revolutionary War, "the very oldest members of the congregation," emerge to restore social and musical harmony. The veterans had answered "the necessities of their country and the voice of Heaven." They are "laurelled old men" and "saviours of your country." They are "authors of unimaginable blessing for your posterity." They can sing. Their deus ex machina appearance, saving the day, dramatizing fidelity to revolutionary principles, is a classic ritual of American nationalism, one that the Protestant logic of sacralizing foundings helps make sensible. But it is not just the deep workings of Protestantism behind the appeal of this "solution." Elites' insecurity about their own position in American society, explains Gilman, gives the revolutionary veterans another important role. Just as Williams and Wentworth could not, properly, be called plebeians, "it is equally a solecism to regard ourselves, even metaphorically, as noblemen." In a country without a historical nobility, a sacred pantheon of revolutionaries allowed Americans to see themselves as descendants of manly virtue and courage, a kind of republican nobility.[29]

Gilman meant his New England church choir as a metaphor for the nation. America, like his choir, was caught in a crisis: the coalescing of a new nation was reconstituting social morality. As with being in a church choir, serving in Congress presented challenges, and possibilities, that newspapers could not effectively convey to readers. "Our National Congress," Gilman wrote, "elicits from its component members certain specific virtues and vices... certain modifications of feeling, passion, and talent, denied to us mere readers of newspapers at home." In other words, the experience of participating in government changed people, and this coalescence would change the nation. Where, asked Gilman, "but on the floor of the American Capitol, would the peculiarities of a certain member's sarcasm, and of another member's sublime statesmanship be generated and developed?" As "in a church choir, there somehow arise certain shades of freaks, certain starts of passion, certain species of whim, certain modes of folly, and let me humbly suggest, also, certain descriptions of virtue, to be found exactly in no other specimens throughout the moral

---

29. Gilman, pp. 59, 114–115, 116.

kingdom of man." Congress, like a church choir, was a whole greater than the sum of its parts, a site of sacred possibilities.[30]

The moral of *Memoir of a New England Village Choir* was twofold. First, obviously, if Congress was the choir, the nation was the church, the new sacred community. Second, for the new type of man, the American, formed by and forming an experimental republic, religion was more important than ever. It was all evident in the history of New England, he wrote, which proved the indispensability of Christian institutions. Only religion could check a human tendency to selfishness, Gilman wrote. Only religion, he believed, could teach men that social duty was not rote obligation but rather man's best imitation of divinity. *Memoirs of a New England Village Choir* engages issues that animated a distinctive and influential class of Protestant intellectuals in the early republic. The focus on social morality as the terrain for which religion has uniquely valuable contributions also suggests how these Protestant intellectuals could conceive of missionary work and nation-building as almost one and the same.[31]

The final lesson derives from the fact that Gilman chose literature, a novella, to make his statement. *Memoirs of a New Village Choir* will never be read for its literary qualities, but Samuel Gilman was a full-time minister and part-time missionary, and the novella is a respectable effort. With the partial exception of Joseph Smith's unique Book of Mormon, the upstart frontier revivalists did not produce readable literary work. They lacked the leisure time and the education. Deists and freethinkers had the education and the time to produce sophisticated literary representations of the American nation, to write American history, but it is an interesting fact that the deists and freethinkers did not do so. One might imagine Tom Paine, for example, writing history, but instead he wrote *The Age of Reason* and then left the United States, carrying designs for an iron bridge he hoped to build in Europe. Thomas Jefferson and James Madison recognized the special skills the New England clerisy brought to nationalist historiography when they asked Joel Barlow, the apostate member of the Connecticut Wits, to write the history of the American republic. Jefferson and Madison promised Barlow free access to their private papers, if he would write a history of the revolutionary era and the early republic. Barlow agreed in principle to Jefferson and Madison's offer, but he never got around to doing it. Like Paine, he instead devoted his time to more

30. Ibid., pp. 93–94.

31. Gilman, pp. 47–48, 24.

overt political writing, *Advice to the Privileged Orders* (1792), and scientific technology, in his case as patron of Robert Fulton's designs for the submarine and the steam engine.

The deists' overlooking of history writing and other literary pursuits grew, in part, out of their optimism about the consequences of scientific and technological advances. Nationalist history also brought difficult technical challenges. How does one write the history of a people as a modern nation? The affinities between the actual political community and the nation have to be emphasized, often to the point of distortion, yet not beyond popular credibility. Common things have to be rendered sacred. New things have to be made to appear old. Glory has to be distributed, but without provoking grievances. Members of the nation have to be shown to share a substantial, profound affinity, what the scholar of nationalism Benedict Anderson called a "deep, horizontal fraternity," but the potential social and political implications of this affinity must be delimited. Shared suffering and defeats have to be retold, but without calling into question the basic nationalist enterprise. It all has to be put into narrative. Clerics were accustomed to thinking about the movement of a group of people through time. Widespread literacy and strong educational institutions were Protestant obligations that New Englanders took with particular seriousness. Dissenters, especially Congregationalists, had cultivated a sharp consciousness of the political body as maligned from without but equitable within. Exceptions emerged, especially as writers of popular history, in particular Parson Weems. With his *The Life of Washington* (1800), Weems, a backwoods preacher and traveling Chesapeake book agent, became the most widely read writer of history in nineteenth-century America. As a class, however, perhaps no group in the Western world, at the beginning of the nineteenth century, was better positioned than New England's Protestant literary intellectuals to undertake the unusual challenges of nationalist historiography.[32]

To see how Puritan literary conventions could give even second- or third-rate Protestant nationalist literature, such as Gilman's, a structure, a coherent style, and certain familiar themes, one need only look to the work of Elias Boudinot. Boudinot was an important figure in the formation of the American missions movement, serving as a bridge between

---

32. Karen Ordahl Kupperman, "The Founding Years of Virginia: And the United States," *The Virginia Magazine of History and Biography* (Winter 1996), pp. 103–112; Phillips quoted in Peter Novick, *That Noble Dream: The "Objectivity Question" and the American Historical Profession* (New York, 1988), p. 73; Roger Friedland, "Religious Nationalism

the ministers and early, local Bible societies, and the Northeastern monied elite. Boudinot was not a descendent of Puritans, however, but like John Jay, who would serve as president of the American Bible Society, Boudinot was of French-Huguenot ancestry. With *Age of Revelation* (1801) and *A Star in the West* (1816), he, too, tried to reshape American political culture through literature, before turning to institution-building. Boudinot was a successful lawyer, president of the Continental Congress (1782–1783), and a New Jersey congressman (1789–1795). He was an anti-slavery activist and a proponent for civil rights for American Indians. George Washington appointed him director of the US Mint, where he served for a decade (1795–1805). In addition to a successful practice in mercantile and real estate law, he made money speculating in Western lands. Benjamin Rush, to whom he was related by marriage, described his "canine appetite for wealth." His childhood baptism by the Calvinist Methodist George Whitefield, of whom his father was a follower, began a lifelong relationship with American popular religion. In the last years of the eighteenth century and the beginning of the nineteenth, he was probably the most distinguished Christian layman in America.[33]

In Congress, Boudinot served as an early and strong advocate for Western land companies and the broad authority of the federal government. As a Federalist, he believed that the government had a responsibility to the "well ordering of the whole Civil Society." For Boudinot, "the whole Civil Society" included the periphery of the republic, and he understood that bringing the institutions of bourgeois society to the frontier was essential to national development. Since the earliest days of Massachusetts and Virginia colonies, westward settlement had involved challenges. Most observers agreed that the great test of the American experiment would be the establishment of US sovereignty over the frontier; in fact, the area between the Appalachians and the Mississippi was sometimes seen as a foreign and

---

and the Problem of Collective Representation," *Annual Review of Sociology* (2001), pp. 125–152; Sydney G. Fischer, "The Legendary and Myth-Making Processes in Histories of the American Revolution," *Proceedings of the American Philosophical Society* (April–June 1912), pp. 53–75. It is worth noting that the exceptional Parson Weems, the most popular writer of American history in the early republic, had no relation to New England literary culture. A Southerner, Weems was part American Virgil, part backwoods preacher, and part patriot propagandist.

33. H. James Henderson, *American National Biography*, pp. 243–244; Richard L. Bushman, *Joseph Smith and the Beginnings of Mormonism* (Chicago, 1984), p. 137. On Boudinot's baptism, see John Jay, "John Jay and Benjamin Franklin Reminisce," in Richard B. Morris, ed. *John Jay: The Winning of the Peace: Unpublished Papers 1780–1784* (New York, 1980), p. 716.

potentially hostile land. The revolutionaries were acutely conscious of the fact that the Revolution had occurred on the Eastern seaboard. In the years following the end of the war, Shays' Rebellion, the Whiskey Rebellion, the Regulators, the Franklin movement, and other events had demonstrated that peoples on the periphery were willing to rebel against faraway government.[34]

Benjamin Franklin's 1755 "A Plan for Settling Two Western Colonies" had warned of the "the great country back of the Appalachian mountains." It was, wrote Franklin, distinct from "our people, confined to the country between the sea and the mountains." Franklin proposed organizing civilian militias as a colonial avant-garde and marching them "under the conduct of the government to be established over them," into the interior. Franklin saw "many thousands. . . that are ready to swarm" into "the Ohio country" and, seeing no reason to presume their continued allegiance to "our people," worried about the loyalty of the most likely migrants. It was reasonable to expect that "our debtors, loose English people, our German servants, and slaves," wrote Franklin, may not want to be Americans.[35] Other political elites shared Franklin's sense of distinctness from the people of the interior and his fear that Western settlers would develop their own nationalisms, or turn for support to Spain, France, or even back to Britain. In the spring of 1786, James Monroe, chairman of the congressional committee charged with turning Jefferson's 1784 Land Ordinance into the 1787 Northwest Ordinance, wrote to James Madison about his worries that a misstep would "separate these people" west of the Appalachian Mountains "from the federal government & perhaps throw them into the hands. . . of a foreign power."[36] The next year, Jefferson wrote to Madison, expressing the same fears, asking what to do if Westerners "declare themselves a separate people," adding that "we are incapable of a single effort to retain them."[37] John Jay, too, thought such a crisis likely. "I fear that

---

34. Onuf, *Statehood and Union*, p. 1.

35. Benjamin Franklin, *Papers of Benjamin Franklin*, ed. Leonard W. Labree (New Haven, CT, 1962), vol. V, pp. 457, 462, 458. The Labree edition has substituted, in brackets, "charge" for "conduct," but provides a footnote indicating that the manuscript copy read "conduct." In addition to being Franklin's choice, "conduct" conveys a broader meaning than the substitute "charge." It also makes evident the process as a problem of governance in the terms used throughout this work. I have also modernized Franklin's spelling.

36. Monroe quote in Harry Ammon, *James Monroe: The Quest for National Identity* (New York, 1971), pp. 55–56.

37. Michael Allen, "The Mississippi River Debate, 1785–1787," *Tennessee Historical Quarterly*, vol. 36 (Winter 1977), pp. 447–467; Jefferson to Madison, January 30, 1787, in Julian O. Boyd, ed., *Papers of Thomas Jefferson* (Princeton, NJ, 1955), vol. 11, p. 93.

Western Country will one day give us trouble," wrote Jay in 1787. "To govern them will not be easy, and whether after two or three generations they will be fit to govern themselves is a question that merits consideration." Three months after Jay's letter to Jefferson, in July 1787, Congress responded with the Compromise of 1787, the Northwest Ordinance. Even as the Northwest Ordinance adopted means directly from the British example, such as the extension of the sovereignty of the common law, its choice of the word "territory" signaled an original, homegrown discourse of empire.[38]

History offered no clear model for establishing a large, imperial republic, much less one abutted by a vast, porous, and isolated frontier boundary. Even many optimistic spirits found the state of frontier settler life reason for worry. The distance of the settlers from the institutions of civil society, it was thought, would lead to moral degeneration. Among European intellectuals, this basic idea was known as creolean degeneracy theory. The theory held that the farther one went from the European centers of civilization, the smaller and more primitive flora and fauna, including men, became. Jefferson wrote *Notes on the State of Virginia* to repudiate the Comte de Buffon's use of the theory against America and Americans. This impetus of Jefferson's only published book partially accounts for the author's meticulous attention to the weights of Virginia's beavers and boars.[39] More quixotically, in 1788, George Washington expressed his hope that Joel Barlow's poetry would be "sufficient to refute (by incontestable facts) the doctrines of those who have asserted that every thing degenerates in America."[40]

In 1787, John Jay warned about the degenerative effect of the frontier on settlers. The unregulated settlement of the frontier, he wrote, presented

38. Jay to Jefferson, April 24, 1787, ibid., pp. 313–314. I have modernized Jay's spelling and capitalization for clarity. Anders Stephanson, "A Most Interesting Empire," an unpublished essay, shows the historical novelty of the American method of continental imperialism and surveys major transformations in types of empire over the course of US history. Cited with permission of author. As with the Constitution, the actual meanings of the provisions of the Northwest Ordinance immediately became a matter of dispute. Most of the dispute revolved around the precise manner in which the Ordinance balanced and prioritized federal, state, and territorial powers. When this delicate arrangement was confronted with the problem of slavery, the whole system would collapse. The initial act to incorporate the frontier into civil society, however, required a clear assertion of federal sovereignty.

39. Jefferson, *Notes on the State of Virginia*, pp. 43–58.

40. Richard M. Gamble, " 'The Last and Brightest Empire of Time: Timothy Dwight and America as Voegelin's 'Authoritative Present,' 1771–1787," *Humanitas*, vol. 20, no. 1–2, p. 13, n2.

peril: "Shall we not fill the wilderness with white savages?—and will they not become more formidable to us than the tawny ones which now inhabit it?" Would it not be self-destructive, wrote Jay, "[t]o pitch our tents through the wilderness in a great variety of places, far distant from. . . education, civilization, law and government which compact settlements and neighborhoods afford?" Distinguishing the vanguard of settlers from farmers, Timothy Dwight called them "foresters," those "who begin the cultivation of the wilderness." The foresters thought they "can not live in regular society" and Dwight thought them right: they are "too idle; too talkative; too passionate; too prodigal; too shiftless; to acquire either property or character." They could not abide "law, religion, and morality," preferring a "half-cultivated" state. "We have many troubles even now," he concluded, "but we should have many more if this body of foresters had remained at home."[41] In 1800, in his *Ten Letters to Dr. Priestley*, Noah Webster wrote, "The human race do not degenerate in the western world. Opportunity, means, patronage alone are wanting to raise the character of this country to an eminent rank among nations." Priestley had not even mentioned degeneracy theory, but American nationalists could feel its sting, especially from European intellectuals, even when the accusation passed unsaid. The insecurity contributed to a worrisome eye fixed on the Western settlers. The rise of popular Protestantism on the frontier did nothing to quell these concerns.[42]

Elias Boudinot wanted to civilize the frontier. Not content with high office and fortune, Boudinot also wanted to be a writer, and his subject was the United States and its role in Christian history. His millennial nationalism was evident in a July 4, 1793, oration he delivered at Elizabethtown, New Jersey, where he eulogized Revolutionary War veterans as men of peerless integrity and unparalleled bravery who embodied the virtues of patriotism. Independence Day, he said, was not to talk about the living, but to commune with the dead, those who gave "the invaluable price of their blood" and who "fought and bled" for present happiness. Boudinot called the casualties of the war "martyrs to liberty," instruments of a "divine-over-ruling hand." They had won the opening round in a war for "political salvation." Their sacrifice had brought the world the possibility

---

41. Jay quoted in Allen, "Mississippi River Debate," p. 461; Timothy Dwight, *Travels in New-England and New-York* (New Haven, CT, 1821), vol. II, pp. 459, 462.

42. Noah Webster, *Ten Letters to Dr. Priestley*, excerpted in Homer D. Babbidge, Jr., ed., *On Being American: Selected Writings, 1783, 1828* (New York, 1967), pp. 114–115.

of global change, paid for by "the blood. . . of our brethren" by those "who have mingled our blood together. . . in one rich stream." The casualties of the war had forged "a union cemented by blood" that made Americans "more than brethren." We are, he repeated, "a band of brethren," united by "interest, gratitude, and love." The emphasis on blood grew out of uncertainty if American nationality could persevere, if it could really serve as the bonds of a viable political community.[43]

Boudinot hoped to see the achievements of the American Revolution brought to the world. "The eyes of the nations of the earth are fast opening," said Boudinot, and "To you, ye citizens of America! Do the inhabitants of the earth, look." He spoke of how the American nation would "console the earth." His expectations reached millennial proportions. He thought "the happy period, when all the nations of the earth shall join in the triumph of this day" approaching. He expected to live to hear "one universal anthem of praise. . . arise to the general creator, in return for the general joy." The United States, he told his audience, "for which we have fought and bled," stood poised to "become a theatre of greater events than yet have been known to mankind." The scale was geopolitical, even theological and cosmic. With the exceptions of the hallowed Revolutionary War veterans and George Washington, he did not mention people. Throughout the address, the agents were nations, not people. He did, however, specify the universality of the message: "All men," he said, "however different with regard to nation or colour" were potential brothers. His allusion to others' color prejudice put this picture into a particular place in American politics.[44]

For Boudinot, America's providential role in the world depended on its fulfilling its own promise, which meant going the Federalist way. He thought the martyred patriots had bled and died for a Federalist American nation. He described "*life, liberty,* and *property,*" and "*the rational equality and rights of men*" as their cause. God had made it clear that "there should be distinctions among members of the same society" and that "order is heaven's first law." Christians and true patriots must not follow those who would see the aims of the revolution "perverted to oppression or licentiousness." He warned that Americans must be "religiously careful in our choice of public officers." Boudinot stressed that all began "in the family,"

---

43. Elias Boudinot, *An Oration Delivered at Elizabeth-Town* (Elizabeth-Town, NJ, 1793), pp. 8–12, 16.

44. Ibid., pp. 22, 9, 13–15.

where "political character" took shape. Interestingly, despite the global, even cosmic, scope of the vision, Boudinot did not plan for much social change. He imagined the future as merely the static, spatial expansion of late eighteenth-century commercial and agrarian society. "Look forward a few years," he said, "behold our extended forests. . . converted into fruitful fields and busy towns." America's "immense lakes" would be "united to the Atlantic States, by a thousand winding canals." Transporting the produce of interior farms, coastal cities would flourish. He described beautiful cities "crowded with innumerable, peaceful fleets, transporting the rich produce from one coast to another." In this Federalist millennium, no one too poor, no one was excessively rich, and there were neither plantations nor factories.[45]

In 1801, while still the director of the US Mint, Boudinot published *The Age of Revelation: Or the Age of Reason Shown to Be An Age of Infidelity*, a defense of the validity of knowledge revealed directly from God. Essentially, Boudinot argued that revelation was both affirmed by reason and above reason; and that while valid, revelation required proper interpretation to ascertain its true meaning.[46] Boudinot's writings were not just contributions to debates; they were literary efforts. In length and scope, *Age of Revelation* far exceeds the requirements of its argument. Over 300 pages, it is highly stylized and combines attacks on Tom Paine with scriptural exegesis, Federalist political commentary, providential American nationalism, and historical interpretation. Like the Wits, Boudinot saw women's roles as powerful shorthand for the different types of societies, and *Age of Revelation* presents an involved defense of feminine virtue and modesty. By the standards of millennial literature, Boudinot's writings are calm and scholarly, but his measured tone dissolved when it came to Paine. Indignation at Paine's lack of deference to his social superiors crackles throughout the work: Paine is guilty of "wicked and perverse temper of mind. . . a degree of forward and indecorous pertinacity" and "ignorant declaration and ridicule" and "idiotism" and "indecent boldness of manner and disrespect." As did Timothy Dwight with his "The Duty of Americans at the Present Crisis," Boudinot also borrows phrases from *Common Sense* and tries to put them to opposite purposes of encouraging

---

45. Ibid., pp. 19, 25–26.

46. Elias Boudinot, *The Age of Revelation: Or the Age of Reason Shown to Be an Age of Infidelity* (Philadelphia, 1801). Hereafter cited as *Age of Revelation*. Boudinot used the spelling "Shewn."

social deference. Boudinot's authorial stance as the popularizer and judicious explicator of learned knowledge is also clearly modeled after Paine's technique.[47]

In 1816, Elias Boudinot published *A Star in the West*, in which he claimed that the American Indians were the lost tribes of Israel. Boudinot saw the relationship between American Protestants and Native Americans as integral to the advent of the millennium. Rational calculations, he wrote, indicated that "these are the latter times" and that "the *last times* of the scriptures" were approaching "with rapid strides." He also argued that in order to make good with God, the Native Americans must returned "to their own land and the ancient city. . . the city of Zion," or Jerusalem. He speculated that God's mysterious ways may have brought the patriots their unlikely victory against the British Empire simply for the "very purpose" of moving the American Indians to Palestine.[48] Boudinot maintained that European crimes against Native Americans had obligated them to "repatriate" the natives to Jerusalem. They have "perished in our wars and by our means," he wrote. We have "been the original cause of their sufferings" and we are "in possession of their lands." He asked readers, "Have we not been enriched by their labors? Have they not fought our battles, and spilt their blood for us, as well as against us?" From its beginnings, the matter of justice for Native Americans, and their place in political society, animated the American missions movement.[49]

Boudinot intended *A Star in the West* to initiate the American-led millennium. As soon as the implications of the fact that the Native Americans were the lost tribes of Israel became clear, Americans would mobilize to return them "their own land" of Palestine. Then "all the nations of the earth" would come "to the acknowledgement of the true God, even our Lord Jesus the Christ." Among peoples colonized by Europeans, Native Americans had proven almost uniquely uninterested in Christianity. The fact that two hundred years of Christian proselytizing had accomplished little in the way of Christianization, especially to Protestantism, was well known. Boudinot's expectation that Indians from across the Americas would soon convert to Protestantism and move to Palestine seems a kind

---

47. Boudinot, *Age of Revelation*, pp. 28, 29, 323.

48. Elias Boudinot, *A Star in the West: Or, A Humble Attempt to Discover the Long Lost Tribes of Israel, Preparatory to Their Return to Their Beloved City, Jerusalem* (Trenton, NJ, 1816), pp. 79, 279.

49. Ibid., p. 300.

of folly, but it speaks to the degree to which American independence had, for some American Protestants, stoked a sense of infinite, irrational possibility. It is notable, however, that *A Star in the West* also carried an ambition that brought comparably meager results. Like his *Age of Revelation*, his *A Star in the West* was meant to mark Boudinot a star—a literary star.[50]

Boudinot approached the path to literary stardom the way a practical man might: he emulated successful models. As his *Age of Revelation* was patterned after Paine's *Age of Reason*, *A Star in the West* was a knockoff of Claudius Buchanan's 1809 bestseller *A Star in the East*. Buchanan was a Scottish minister of the Church of England and a missionary in India. *A Star in the East* was originally given as sermon at the Parish Church of St. James, Bristol, England, in February 1809. In the sermon, Buchanan claimed to have discovered "200,000 Christians. . . in the sequestered region of Hindoostan." Kerala, in southwestern India, was not as sequestered as Buchanan imagined. He had "discovered" the Malankara Christians (sometimes also called the St. Thomas Christians) whose claims to conversion by Jesus's apostle Thomas would have made them Christians since a time when the English, much less the Scottish, were worshipping stones and grottoes. India's Malankara Christians had their long period of relative isolation from European Christians interrupted in the seventeenth century, when, in an effort to resist Portuguese control, they had established alliances with Rome and the Syriac Orthodox Church in Antioch. Buchanan's *A Star in the East* was, however, built around his misapprehension that the Malankara Christians had existed in complete isolation, "in the very midst of India, like the bush of Moses, burning and not consumed." The representation of non-European peoples as members of static, unchanging cultures, rather than active societies with complex histories, is a hallmark of modern colonial discourse. Protestantism, dependent for its own authority on historical claims about Jesus's life, gave a particular twist to this colonial discourse. Buchanan's *A Star in the East*, for example, told readers that the Indian Christians were today "speaking in their churches that same language which our Saviour himself spake in the streets of Jerusalem." For certain Christians, especially devout Protestants, such concrete survivals from the era of Jesus affirmed the truth of Christianity.[51]

---

50. Ibid., pp. 23–24, 25, 28, 27.

51. Eric Wolf, *Europe and the People Without History* (Berkeley, CA, 2010); Johannes Fabian, *Time and the Other: How Anthropology Makes Its Object* (New York, 2002).

For Protestants, the dominion of Rome had rendered the first millennia and a half of Christian history corrupt. Following Luther's example, they turned instead to the founding moment, including its texts, as uniquely authoritative. In this manner, too, Boudinot's *A Star in the West* mimicked Buchanan's *A Star in the East*. The Native Americans, like the Malankara Christians, had to be the lost tribes of Israel, had to have their role in salvation history, even their existence, accounted for in the scriptures. Boudinot's claim that the American Indians' repatriation would catalyze the Christian millennium was just a resetting to the Western Hemisphere of Buchanan's claim that the Malankara Christians would be a "special instrument for the conversion of the surrounding heathen." While in India, Buchanan also obtained a Bible from antiquity, written in Estrangelo Syriac, and ancient documents from Indian Jews, known as the Malabar Geniza, all of which are now part of the Oriental Manuscripts collection at the University of Cambridge. He claimed that these "ancient writings of India" vindicated the "*history* of Christ" and proved "the *general truth* of the Christian Religion." [52]

Buchanan's *A Star in the East* became one of the unlikeliest of bestsellers in American history. A Hartford, Connecticut, printer published the sermon in 1809 and, in less than a year, an Albany, New York, printer went through at least nine editions. Before the end of 1809, the New York City printer J. Seymour went through at least eight editions, and printers in Pittsburgh and Philadelphia published it. In 1810, a Chilicothe, Ohio, printer went through at least ten editions. A few upstate New York printers found the work saleable. At least two printers in New Hampshire and in Massachusetts, as well as others in Connecticut and Pennsylvania also published the sermon. By July 1810, a Danbury, Connecticut, firm published a commentary on *A Star in the East*, without including the whole of the original, because, they explained, it was already so widely available. Buchanan's *A Star in the East* moved Adoniram Judson to abandon his own literary ambitions and dedicate his life to God. Judson spent 38 years (1812–1850) in Burma. The American Board of Commissioners for Foreign Missions (ABCFM) credited *A Star in the East* as the inspiration for its founding.[53]

---

52. Claudius Buchanan, *A Star in the East* (New York, 1809), pp. 10–11, 6.

53. For an edition with supplemental materials, see Claudius Buchanan, *Star in the East: Selections* (Hartford, CT, 1810). On the decisive influence of Buchanan's sermon on Judson and his peers, see Francis Wayland, *A Memoir of the Life and Labors of the Rev.*

In the War of Independence, it was implacable New England Protestants who had led America to rebel against Britain. A generation later, New England Protestants embraced as natural and even holy joint Anglo-American missionary enterprises. Two changes account for the difference. First, independence meant that the New Englanders could participate in joint missionary activities as Americans, rather than as colonial subjects. Second, the momentum of Jeffersonian democracy had pushed New England Protestants back toward their British brethren. Interruptions that the War of 1812 brought to the Anglo-American mission contributed to New Englanders' disaffection over that war. New England ministers even preached that the war was undermining God's plan to bring Christianity to the masses, and that President James Madison was to blame. In 1813, this climate helped to give Claudius Buchanan, with his *Christian Researches in Asia*, another American bestseller. Buchanan's work emphasized a joint Anglo-American Protestant identity, set against the darker, heathen races. The idea was not entirely new. With his 1794 *Letters on Missions*, written from Sierra Leone and addressed to British Protestants, the Anglican Melville Horne had called for a unified British Protestantism devoted to missions. Horne's *Letters on Missions* led to the 1795 founding of the London Missionary Society, as well as the Missionary Society of New York (1785), the Northern Missionary Society in the State of New York, the Missionary Society of Connecticut (1798), and several other American organizations.[54]

By the time Buchanan's *Christian Researches in Asia* appeared, it provided a rationale for changes already underway in American religion, at least among Anglicans, Presbyterians, and Congregationalists. At an opportune moment for opponents of the War of 1812, Buchanan provided a way for Anglo-American Protestants to embrace colonialism as part of the Protestant cause, even when it brought developments that ran counter to centuries of Protestant doctrine. Instead of decrying the addition of great numbers of Catholics, Hindus, Muslims, and others to the British Empire, for example, Buchanan maintained that these gains amounted to turning the soil for the "true Gospel." Asking non-Protestants to support

---

Adoniram Judson, D.D. (Boston, 1854), p. 29. On Buchanan's sermon as the inspiration for the ABCFM, see Tracy, *HABCFM*, p. 30.

54. William Gribbin, *The Churches Militant: The War of 1812 and American Religion* (New Haven, CT, 1973); Charles L. Chaney, *The Birth of Missions in America* (South Pasadena, CA, 1976), pp. 158–174.

the Empire also made maintaining hierarchical distinctions among Protestants at home less tenable. Conditions in the field of colonial missionary work, Buchanan explained, showed that differences between various Protestants were not so important. Melville Horne and Claudius Buchanan's calls for Protestant unification were also a response to the derision of potential Indian and African converts, who noted that different Christian missionaries seemed to disagree with one another. "We have no contentions in India, like those in Britain, between Protestants of different names," wrote Buchanan: "They are all friends." Anglo colonialism was beginning to create a new, ecumenical ideal of religious community at home, too, at least among elite and middling types. "Even the term 'Protestant,'" wrote Buchanan, was "in a certain degree exclusive or sectarian." It is very difficult to imagine such a sentiment finding either a popular audience or clerical approval in either seventeenth- or eighteenth-century New England. Yet the idea became an organizing principle of nineteenth-century Anglo-American Protestantism.[55]

Only a generation earlier, Anglo-American Protestants had a different response to imperial religious toleration. Britain's recognition of Catholicism in neighboring Quebec angered and terrified New England Protestants. The First Continental Congress denounced Quebec as an alien and hostile society. "So total a dissimilarity of religion, law and government," declared Congress, deserved no protection from Britain. Congress charged Britain's 1774 Quebec Act with "erecting a tyranny" that presented a "great danger" to the colonies. A generation later, the Louisiana Purchase promised not mere recognition of a neighboring Catholic society, but the addition of a significant Catholic population into the actual American political community. The leaders of New England Protestantism responded differently to the Louisiana Purchase. Quebec was contiguous with New England, and it was a society built on small farms and towns. It was much more similar to New England than the plantation society of the Deep South. Yet the New England Protestants who had found the Quebec Act a horrible aggression rejoiced over the Louisiana Purchase. Again, it was not hypocrisy that accounted for the change, so much as the fact that American Protestants now had their own imperial nation. Nations were the building blocks of history, the powers of the earth, and the agents of redemption, and the riches of Louisiana promised to strengthen the capacity of the American nation to bring the light of true religion to the heathen, at home and abroad. "Including Louisiana," wrote an approving Timothy Dwight, the United States was now "a larger empire than any, which the world has ever seen, excluding the Russian and the Chinese." Indeed, within five years of Buchanan's *A Star in the East*, the value of exports from the port of New Orleans totaled over $5 million. That total amounted to just under a third of the federal government's income. Soon only the port of New York would generate more federal revenue than that of New Orleans.[56]

Unlike Claudius Buchanan's *A Star in the East*, Boudinot's *Age of Revelation* and *A Star in the West* failed to win popular appreciation or critical acclaim. Nor could Boudinot, in his turn to institution-building, rival the theological and genealogical authority that Dwight brought to the missions movement. But Elias Boudinot did help deliver something that was at least as definitive of the American missions movement: money. Boudinot did not just give money to the movement; he brought together members of a nascent American bourgeoisie in an enterprise that would help them define themselves. In appealing to these Christian elites, Boudinot made an analogy that would become central to the missions movement. He described the capital of the leaders of the American missionary movement as the modern version of the labor of the original evangelists. Boudinot was not the only American Protestant trying to describe the rise of capital and enlist it in Christian missions. In an 1805 sermon to the Massachusetts Missionary Society, the Rev. Paul Litchfield put forth the basic elements. Litchfield sermonized about how holy works "demand a liberal contribution of property." The scriptures told that the building of temples "required *labor*," Litchfield said, and "incurred *expense*." He spoke of how money could do more than ever, and the original apostles were the ones willing "to *spend and be spent*." There was nothing new about asking members of a religious organization to give money. The anxious reassurances that giving money was the modern replacement of labor, and that

---

56. First Continental Congress resolution responding to Britain's Quebec Act reprinted in Hezekiah Niles, ed., *Weekly Register* (September 1811–March 1812), vol. 1, p. 14; Timothy Dwight, *Travels in New England and New York* (London, 1823), vol. IV, p. 499. Within two decades, in the years of boom cotton crops, the value of exports from the port of New Orleans would surpass those of New York; see Robert Greenhalgh Albion, *The Rise of New York Port* (Boston, 1967), pp. 104–105, 390, 400. On the general economic significance of Louisiana and New Orleans in particular, see Edward Channing, *The Jeffersonian System, 1801–1811* (New York, 1906), pp. 29, 50, 53, 56–57, 63.

the givers of money were the modern apostles, were new. Others spoke of these general elements, of labor and of capital, about how the sons of the founders of the United States were akin to the apostles of Jesus, about how prophesy linked the age of the apostles, the Reformation, and the founding of the United States in sacred time.[57]

Elias Boudinot was among the most effective early missionary organizers, in part because of his strong relationships with members of the Northeastern merchant and political class. In addition, his organizational appeals offer his best writing, with simple and evocative descriptions of the problems facing the missions movement, and of the solutions generally adopted. As an organizer, he is a different writer from the one who, when he tried to write for popular acclaim, ricocheted between florid hyperbole and petty vendetta. In organizing first the New Jersey Bible Society, in 1811, Boudinot turned to the jeremiad, a public exhortation for spiritual renewal, but with an important adaptation. He warned of backsliding citizens and a degenerating national spirit, and he also warned the New Jersey members that they might be "excluded from a share in the divine reward." The British were making "manly exertions" and "the harvest may be past," he wrote. Throughout Boudinot's appeal, the perils of salvation as a people lay in the competitive arena of the souls and destinies of nations. The assumption of the nation into the role of the salvation community marks a break from the early modern to the modern form of the jeremiad.[58]

In 1815, as president of the New Jersey Bible Society, Boudinot circulated to other local societies a proposal for a national association. Four years earlier, in 1811, when Congress had refused to re-charter the Bank of the United States, one of the effective arguments against re-charter had been the view that Congress lacked the right of incorporation. Henry Clay, for example, an opponent of the Bank, said: "Is it to be imagined that a power so vast would have been left by the wisdom of the constitution to doubtful inference?" Boudinot was a former director of the Bank of the United States, and since he was in effect proposing exactly the creation of a

---

57. Paul Litchfield, *A Sermon Preached before the Massachusetts Missionary Society* (Salem, MA, 1805), pp. 4–6, 9, 18. Italics in original. See, too, John H. Livingston, *A Sermon Delivered before the New York Missionary Society, at their Annual Meeting, April 3, 1804* (Worcester, 1807), passim, but esp. pp. 4–8; Edward D. Griffin, *The Kingdom of Christ: A Missionary Sermon* (Philadelphia, 1805).

58. Elias Boudinot, *An Address Delivered before the New-Jersey Bible Society* (Allinson, NJ, 1811), p. 8. Hereafter cited as *New-Jersey Bible Society*.

national Bible society, the Philadelphians' use of the word "national" made him nervous. Instead, he proposed naming it *"The General Association of the Bible Societies in the United States."* The Philadelphians had found the proposed name unwieldy and, in their reply, referred simply to "a National Institution." In reply, Boudinot wrote, "I have not taken notice of your saying 'a National Institution,' as I presume it was a slip of the pen." He argued that a voluntary association could not by definition be a national association: "You would hardly call any voluntary association, however enlarged their plan, a National Institution, without being constituted by the government by Charter, in which case all terms of it must be legal." Regardless of Boudinot's parsing, the Philadelphians' use of the word "national" was if anything too modest, as the ABS would quickly become a transnational institution.[59]

The skeptical Philadelphia Bible Society also replied to Boudinot's proposal that local associations were best able to do local missionary work. The president of the Philadelphia society, Jackson Kemper, asked why, with "between sixty and seventy Bible Societies in the Union"—in fact, there were already over one hundred—another was needed? Kempner asked why "touch the wheel that moves well?" Any attempt at conglomeration would produce more "unkind feelings" and "jealousies" than "cooperation" between rival sects. The Philadelphians predicted that a national society would run roughshod over local customs, and they objected to the homogenization of local organizations, of different religious sects, and of community prerogatives. Among American Bible societies, Philadelphia was first among equals, the oldest and the best funded. Recently, they had made a capital-intensive investment in innovative and expensive stereotype print technology. Any authoritative conglomeration would require their participation, so Boudinot did not accept their demurral.[60]

---

59. Ibid., p. 10. Approximately two-thirds of acts of incorporation passed by the Massachusetts General Court during the 1780s, and half passed during the 1790s, were for units of local government. "By far the greater part" of the rest of the 1780s charters went to "religious associations, educational institutions, and groups formed for charitable or other non-profit purposes such as the Massachusetts Historical Society." This began to change in the 1790s, when businesses, mostly internal improvement companies, were granted approximately one-quarter of corporate charters granted by Massachusetts. See Pauline Maier, "The Revolutionary Origins of the American Corporation," pp. 53–54; Clay quoted in Babcock, *The Rise of American Nationality*, pp. 9–10.

60. Elias Boudinot, *An Answer to the Objections of the Managers of the Philadelphia Bible Society* (Burlington, NJ, 1815), pp. 2–6 (hereafter cited as *An Answer to the Objections. . .*).

The Philadelphians' investment in sophisticated printing technology may have put them a step ahead of the crowd, but their reservations about conglomeration were behind the times. Homogenization was the point, and Boudinot tried to explain its advantages. Consolidation could bring a higher rate of growth in Christian piety than they had imagined and would make possible new levels of organizational efficiency. Existing Bible societies could each assume control of a type of activity or region of the country and the authority of the national society could be limited. He offered a perhaps disingenuous concession: cooperation could be limited to fundraising.[61] He noted that the British and Foreign Bible Society (BFBS), a benefactor of both the New Jersey and Philadelphia societies, had already endorsed "our plan to be enlarged" into a national association. The BFBS had pledged a donation for a general American society, which, wrote Boudinot, would allow Americans to join the examples in "zeal, activity, and expenditures" of the BFBS, as well as Bible societies in Finland, Poland, and Russia. Even Leipzig, he wrote, "the centre of destruction" from the Napoleonic wars, had an active Bible society. In essence, Boudinot was telling the Philadelphians that their patron had already backed the venture and that they were jeopardizing America's standing in the race of nations. Given the tendency of centralized financial management to lead to a consolidation of institutional authority, it is also unlikely that the Philadelphians found reassurances in the suggestion that consolidation would be limited to finances.[62]

In an important variation on the form of the jeremiad, Bouidnot's *An Answer to the Objections of the Managers of the Philadelphia Society* returned time and again to the realities and dangers presented by the new, national political community. He warned that many in America's "large towns," including her "soldiers and sailors. . . have no Bibles" and that social unrest loomed. The cities were a place of potential danger, but the state of the frontier presented an even greater threat. A sister Bible society in Salem, Massachusetts, he wrote, had prepared a report on the dire state of religion and morals on the American frontier. Their investigation ought

---

Kempner's letter is reprinted in Boudinot's published reply. The number of "over 100" functioning local Bible societies in 1816 comes from Nord, "Financing Evangelical Book Publishing," p. 154; David Paul Nord, "Benevolent Capital: Financing Evangelical Book Publishing in Early Nineteenth-Century America," in Noll, ed., *God and Mammon*, p. 154.

61. Boudinot, *An Answer to the Objections. . .*, pp. 4, 7.

62. Ibid., pp. 5–6.

to remind Americans that the need for charity in the "newly settled parts of the country" was acute. Religious and civic obligations tied them to the frontier settlers, Boudinot wrote: "Surely the Soul of a man on the Missouri is as precious to him, as it is to any Citizen of the States." The fact that Boudinot's plea moved from the soul, a mystical entity, to citizenship, a civic status, speaks to the knotted nature of religion and nationalism within the elite of Anglo-American Reformed Protestantism. At the same time, the challenge he posed, of enlarging one's moral community, was key to the missions movement and central to Christianity. To the Philadelphians' concern about aggravating sectarian rivalries, Boudinot answered with scorn. A public meeting, he wrote, of "respectable and pious" Protestants, gathering for the purpose of "publishing the benefits of redeeming Love to those who sit in darkness. . . should prove injurious—injurious to whom!" They were, in other words, obligated to think larger than their sect.[63]

Nationalism was a driving force behind the American Bible Society. The means of the process were, in the technical sense, bourgeois. Elias Boudinot told potential benefactors that their money could do that for which the original evangelists had to labor, or even give their lives. "Money will now produce," wrote Boudinot, "what it cost the primitive Believers, not only labour, sorrow and trouble, but even life itself, to publish to mankind." Money would be the modern substitute for the life-threatening labor of the original apostles. This idea—that capital would replace labor—is the essence of capitalism. Boudinot's 1811 letter was an early statement, with a pithy characterization, of one of the defining changes in modern history, the rise of capitalism. Capital came from God, Boudinot argued, who gave it with obligations: "God, in his wise providence, has so united the means and the end, that we have no right to expect the last without using the first." In the context of Boudinot's analogy with the original apostles, the message was a celebration of modernity: unlike the original apostles, who gave their labor and their lives, patrons of the missions movement only had to give their money. For the audience, it was an especially apt analogy, appealing to their religious consciousness, and to the quandary facing the sons of the founding fathers.[64]

---

63. On those supporters of the missionary and moral improvement societies who had doubts about the providential role of the United States, see Mark Y. Hanley, *Beyond a Christian Commonwealth: The Protestant Quarrel with the American Republic, 1830–1860* (Chapel Hill, NC, 1994); Boudinot, *An Answer to the Objections. . .*, pp. 5–6, 8.

64. Boudinot, *New-Jersey Bible Society*, p. 60.

For help organizing the American Bible Society, Boudinot turned to Samuel J. Mills, considered the best-known fundraiser of the time. Mills came from the milieu of Connecticut Congregationalism; his father was a minister in Torringford, Connecticut, and the editor of the *Connecticut Evangelical Magazine*. Mills was a New Divinity man, and after studying at Williams College, he went to Yale, in 1810, to study theology under Timothy Dwight. Upon graduation, in 1812, he attained his license as a Congregationalist minister. Mills gained prominence in the missions movement as a field agent arguing for the conglomeration of Bible societies into a national organization. He had helped organize the ABCFM, the United Foreign Society, and the Presbyterian Missionary Society. Mills was the driving force behind the American Colonization Society, which was his dearest project. The ACS appealed to slaveholders for its prospect of removing free people of color from the United States. Mills and other missionaries believed that the removal of people of African descent from the United States was key to the Christianization of both America and Africa. In 1813, the Philadelphia, Connecticut, and New York Bible Societies sent Mills and John J. Schermerhorn on a reconnaissance tour of the frontier. From Nashville, along with 1,500 Tennessee volunteers on their way to Natchez, Mississippi, and war with Britain, Mills and Schermerhorn descended the Mississippi River on General Andrew Jackson's steamer. A biographer captured some of the contemporary feeling when he wrote: "The Protestant invasion and occupation of the Louisiana Purchase" had begun.[65]

Mills and Schermerhorn found the Mississippi Valley a dire scene. Ohio and Indiana showed little progress. Kentucky and Tennessee were riddled with "party spirit or sectarian zeal," the Christians there "could not unite," and were in "great want of the scriptures." In Mississippi, despite weeks of advertising in the newspapers, they could not get "more than five persons" to attend a Bible society meeting. Mississippi Territory governor David Holmes, a Jefferson appointee, volunteered to form the committee of the Mississippi Bible Society, as well as draft its constitution. Holmes promised he would fill out the Bible society committee with state officials. The offer of state support led Mills and Schermerhorn to report that only a little "perseverance and energy" were "necessary for securing. . .

---

65. Mills graduated from Williams, but went to Yale during Dwight's term as president to do graduate work in theology; see Thomas C. Richards, *Samuel J. Mills: Missionary Pathfinder, Pioneer and Promoter* (Boston, 1906), pp. 40, 49, 51; P. J. Staudenraus, *The African Colonization Movement, 1816–1865* (New York, 1961), pp. 18–19, 37–47; Gellner, *Nationalism*, pp. 15–16; Richards, *Samuel J. Mills*, p. 158.

the prosperity of Zion. . . [and] the happiness of the human family" in Mississippi. In contrast to the early Christian movement, which suffered centuries of Roman opposition, state support for the American missions movement came early and easy.[66] Mills and Schermerhorn ended their report with a suggestion to nationalize, to form a "general bond of union," they wrote, to benefit "our brethren in the West." The managers of the Bible societies that sponsored the trip attached an appendix further substantiating, and lamenting, the "'famine of the word'" in the West. It was an astonishing claim, as the American frontier was in the midst of one of the largest and most dynamic instances of growth in the history of religion.[67]

Mills's next report, *Missionary Tour through that part of the United States which lies West of the Allegheny Mountains,* co-authored with Daniel Smith, reached the level of literature. Organized as a series of dispatches, and addressed to American Protestants, *Missionary Tour* is thoughtful and literary and insistent on the crisis of the frontier. Paraphrasing Isaiah 55, Mills and Smith wrote that they wished to "make our frontier country blossom as a rose."[68] The form of Mills and Smith's *Missionary Tour,* that of the covenant corrupted by betrayal, only to finally achieve restoration through heroic efforts, is that of the jeremiad. Unlike seventeenth-century Puritan literature, however, or contemporaneous frontier revivalists' memoirs and journals, it had little to say about actual people. It was more interested in the criteria and mechanism of salvation, how souls were "awakened" or brought to grace, than the individuals themselves. It took as its subject the West and its settlers, as an unspecific and degenerate group, and it claimed authority by travel into the interior of the continent. It also differed from travelers' accounts, a very popular genre, which weighed

---

66. On Mills and Schermerhorn as guests of Andrew Jackson, see Henry Otis Dwight, *The Centennial History of the American Bible Society* (New York, 1916), p. 11; Samuel J. Mills, *Communications Relative to the Progress of the Bible Societies in the United States* (Philadelphia, 1813), pp. 3–4, 6–7, 11, 13. On Anglo-American anti-Catholicism, see John Wolffe, "Anti-Catholicism and Evangelical Identity in Britain and the United States, 1830–1860," in Mark A. Noll, et al., eds. *Evangelicalism: Comparative Studies in Popular Protestantism in North America, the British Isles, and Beyond, 1700–1900,* pp. 179–197.

67. Ibid., p. 17; Hatch, *The Democratization of American Christianity,* passim, makes clear that the force of the revival came from the rural West. On Asbury counting over 400 Methodist camp meetings in 1811, see Dickson D. Bruce, Jr. *And They All Sang Hallelujah,* p. 52.

68. Samuel J. Mills and Daniel Smith, *Missionary Tour through that part of the United States which lies West of the Allegheny Mountains. . .* (Andover, 1815), p. 11; Boudinot, *New-Jersey Bible Society,* p. 12.

the virtues and vices of American democracy, often for an international audience.[69]

In contrast, Mills and Smith's report, and Boudinot's circular letters, are examples of national evangelism, a new type of literature addressed to compatriots, in this case especially the elite, calling for a nationalization of the wilderness as a way to spiritual renewal and a step to geopolitical power. National evangelism differed from the jeremiad in that the Revolution had given it a new sacred political community, one that disallowed some of the defining elements of Puritanism: the covenant of grace, the ideal theocracy, and the community of saints. National evangelism was essentially an optimistic genre, promising a simple and grand vision of belonging to a nation engaged in a regeneration of the world. In this way, in the literal sense of evangelist ("the bearer of the good news"), it brought the "good news" of the American nation to the frontier, and abroad. One influential sermon, John H. Livingston's 1804 *Sermon Before the New-York Missionary Society*, compared American missionaries not to the apostles or the original evangelists, but to angels. Since the word "angel," wrote Livingston, expressed "not so much" the nature of a "celestial being" as, in essence, a messenger, whose job was to call people to God, Livingston maintained, missionaries were angels. American missionary organizations often cited Livingston's sermon comparing missionaries to angels, and, more frequently, Boudinot's analogy comparing the work of missionaries to that of the apostles and the original evangelists. As national evangelists, Boudinot and Livingston shared a focus on the national political community, the historic opportunity of the American missionary, and the frontier as the place of crisis and opportunity.[70]

For a generation, historians have focused on the frontier as a zone of imperial violence, as a liminal and contested space, a middle ground poised between effective control by empires, first European then American, and

69. Sacvan Bercovitch, *The American Jeremiad* (Madison, 1978); see also, idem, *The Rites of Assent: Transformations in the Symbolic Construction of America* (New York, 1993), especially chs. 3 and 4. See also Daniel Shea, *Spiritual Autobiography in Early America* (Madison, 1988), p. xxvii; Thomas D. Clark, "The Great Visitation to American Democracy," *Mississippi Valley Historical Review*, vol. 44 (June 1957), pp. 3–28.

70. Bercovitch has many critics, but the one who has most influenced my understanding of the problem is David W. Noble, *The End of American History: Democracy, Capitalism, and the Metaphor of Two Worlds in Anglo-American Historical Writing, 1880–1980* (Minneapolis, 1985), pp. 3–15. Noble, too, emphasizes the continuity of the jeremiad, but primarily its rejuvenation, after the pessimistic conclusions of Turner's "Frontier Thesis," through the Progressives' embrace of new naturalizing and universalizing laws of economic development, i.e., deliverance through an American-led globalization of capitalism, whereas the

American Indians. Americans in the early republic too often saw the frontier as a historic battleground, the place where the American experiment would either falter or prove itself. The missionaries saw this battle in global, and theological terms, a fight between forces of darkness and those of light. The first native-born New Englander to see what would be the frontier of the early republic, however, saw things very differently. For, Joseph Kellogg, who had been abducted from Deerfield, Massachusetts, and traveled down the Mississippi River Valley in 1710, with six French traders, it was more like Cockaigne, a land of almost mythical plenty. Kellogg traveled from Montreal through the Great Lakes and down the Mississippi and its tributaries. He wrote of the "prodigious bigness" of trout, several "more than fifty pound weight." The water of the Great Lakes was "clear, sweet and fresh" and he caught "Sturgeon of ten foot long." The movement of his party down rivers raised "an infinite number of wild fowl, such as Cranes, Geese, Duck; and Swans in great abundance." The fowl, wrote Kellogg, feed on wild oats that grow along the riverbanks. These oats were "a very good grain," he noted, and they swell from "one quart to ten or twelve" when boiled. A "man may fill a Canoo with the grain in a few hours," wrote Kellogg. He saw "wild Apple Trees and Plumb trees" and an abundance of a "fruit much like Cucumber that grow upon small Trees or Shrubs." Heading south, a traveler to the "River Mississippi," Kellogg wrote, "found himself in a new world. . . everything gay and pleasant" with an "abundance of fine fruit Trees" and riverbanks full of "stocks of small Parrots." On the Missouri River, Kellogg passed a French village, likely that of St. Louis, where "they raise excellent Wheat, very good Indian Corn, have a windmill, and have a stock of Cattle." They even "make a very good sort of wine." Traveling through the Missouri and Ohio River Valleys, Kellogg noted the "land produces excellent Melons, good Beans, turneps and all sorts of Garden herbs." Walnuts were also plentiful. So were "vast numbers of wild Cattle." In the Old Northwest, Kellogg had come face to face with natural luxury on a wondrous scale. He called it a "noble country."[71]

One hundred years later, New Englanders looked with different eyes on the same country. Mills and Smith wrote of the "wretched

---

emphasis here is on the changes to the content of the jeremiad precipitated by nationalist continental expansion and economic development.

71. Timothy Hopkins, *The Kelloggs in the Old World and the New* (San Francisco, 1903), vol. I, pp. 60–62.

condition" of the settlers and their "earnest cries for aid." It was not "strangers and foreigners" suffering, but "members of the same civil community with us." The task of civilization was the challenge to fulfill America's providential role in world history. They called for "more efficient means" to bring the light to this "benighted portion of our country." They found the frontier "desolate." Without missions and tracts and Bibles from New Englanders, the frontier would remain in "deplorable state." The "whole country, from Lake Erie to the Gulf of Mexico," which Joseph Kellogg had found munificent, the national evangelists reported was "the valley of the shadow of death." Despite the effusion of popular religions and the material wealth that drew settlers from across the Appalachians and across the Atlantic, Mills and Smith saw the defining characteristic of the frontier as "darkness." Its condition "is a foul blot on our national character. Christian America must arise and wipe it away." The only chance to surmount the peril and redeem the promise of America, they wrote, lay in "union" and "co-operation."[72]

From this early reconnaissance moment of the missions movement, its substantial financial resources were evident. For their nine-month tour, the Massachusetts Missionary Society, Philadelphia Bible Society, and Philadelphia Missionary Society provided Mills and Schermerhorn with $1,300. In contrast, for all of 1815, the Methodist Ohio (formerly Western) Conference, which comprised the entire Western frontier, from New Orleans into Canada, spent $994.19 to support 73 circuit-riders and two bishops. The 23 itinerants with children divided an additional $188.25. The Methodist Church had paid 75 frontier ministers, on average, $15.77 per year. For a tour of less than a year, the American bourgeoisie gave Mills and Schermerhorn $650 each. In the contest between national evangelism and frontier revivalism for governance of the frontier, the difference in material resources would play an important role.[73]

Smith and Mills's *Missionary Tour* galvanized Northeastern Protestants. The American Bible Society called Mills one of history's "inconspicuous workhorses. . . who made the dreams of great men come true." Lyman Beecher credited him with having "prepared the way for a

---

72. Mills and Smith, *Missionary Tour*, pp. 21, 39, 20; 47.

73. *Journal of the Ohio Conference*, pp. 135–136; Boudinot, *New-Jersey Bible Society*, p. 60; Mills and Smith, *Missionary Tour*, p. 21; Boudinot, *New-Jersey Bible Society*, pp. 60, 11.

harmonious concurrence" of the national organization of the ABS. The American Board of Commissioners for Foreign Missions paid tribute to Mills as one of the "first to understand, and cause others to understand" the need for their "great and effectual movement in human society." Mills's work, with the *Missionary Tour* as his outstanding contribution, led directly to the creation of several national and transnational missions organizations, dozens of local and state Bible societies, and even to the state of Liberia.[74]

---

74. Beecher quote in Foster, *Errand of Mercy*, pp. 95, 110; Dwight, *Centennial History of the American Bible Society*, pp. 11–15; *HABCFM*, ed. Kwiat, p. 28; Richards, *Samuel J. Mills*, pp. 152, 157–159, 163. On Mills and the creation of Liberia, see also Lamin O. Sanneh, *Abolitionists Abroad: American Blacks and the Making of Modern West Africa* (Cambridge, 1999).

6

"A Complete Chain of Communication"

RELIGIOUS LITERATURE AND PROTESTANT NATION-BUILDING

I have no reason to hope that I am a Christian, and should feel I was assuming, to pretend to aid this object as a Christian, but I think it commends itself to the patriot as well as to the Christian, and as a patriot I will cheerfully give.

—Anonymous donor to the American Home Missionary Society, quoted in the Society's *Seventh Annual Report* (1833)

THE GREAT PROTESTANT missionary and moral improvement organizations that appeared and flourished in the early American republic coincided with the beginning of systematic Protestant missionary activity in the West. They played an important role in the development of American religious nationalism. Because they produced influential, often spurious, accounts of their own past and that of the nation, they can be difficult to appreciate in historical perspective. One must understand that they were crucibles of nationalism and capitalism, that they excelled at organization and made historic efforts, especially through publishing, to bring the "good news" of the nation to the world, especially the American frontier.

In essence, nation-building aims to homogenize. Nation-building institutions and programs work to diminish the differences between sects, to in effect turn sects into denominations. Timothy Dwight wrote his best work, *Travels in New-England and New-York* (1821–1822), in part, to answer what he called "the great question" facing the republic: whether her different sects might "live together harmoniously under a government which confers on them equal privileges." Equal privileges for religious groups involved the leveling of religious diversity, a project that America's large missionary organizations undertook. The American Board of Commissioners for Foreign Missions, for example, described itself as committed to ensuring "the same Gospel which is preached in the Middle and Southern and Western States, is also preached in the Eastern States." Religious literature was a means of fostering American nationality, of making people more the same. The greatest efforts to homogenize Americans, in the early republic, came from Protestant missionary and moral improvement societies. Their impetus and goal was to stabilize and strengthen American society and its political institutions. There are a dozen ways, from contributions to corporate practice to class consolidation, in which the great Protestant missionary organizations engaged in American nation-building. Because it epitomized a major development in nineteenth-century history, the focus here is on their work to reduce religious distinctions, at least among Protestants, while introducing racial distinctions. The latter also distinguished the missionary organizations from the anti-racism of the Connecticut Wits.[1]

Protestantism gave their nation-building programs a certain focus and a distinct character, and the large, national American missionary societies were bourgeois as well as Protestant. Bourgeois Protestants felt a calling (the concept of a calling itself is a Protestant notion) to bring their society and its values to others, in North America and abroad, in a way that deists, for example, did not, and with means, voluntary associations run by laymen, that would have been inconceivable to Catholics. Of course, upstart and frontier Protestants also sought converts far and wide, but it took them some time to develop a national consciousness, much less nationalist political strategies. As late as 1830, the annual report of the Methodist Missionary Society mentioned the nation just once, when it reported that the "missions in Upper Canada are now no longer" counted with those in the United States. The Methodists concluded their annual report with a plea to remember the unregenerate, but of the world, not the nation. Of the "eight hundred millions of human beings which. . . dwell on the face of the whole earth. . . only about one fifth are nominally Christian," they wrote. The Methodists also lacked the political and economic resources

---

1. In his 1813 *A Sermon. . .. before the American Board of Commissioners for Foreign Missions, at their Fourth Annual Meeting* (Boston, 1813), Dwight spoke not of sects but of "Christians of different classes," see pp. 26–27; idem, *Travels*, vol. I, p. xiii; Tracy, *HABCFM*, p. 125.

to build institutions that might compete with the American Tract Society (ATS), or the American Bible Society (ABS), or the American Board of Commissioners for Foreign Missions (ABCFM). The noise and numbers of the frontier revivalists always remained the many actions of a multitude; whereas the historically novel cooperation of the missionary, tract, and Bible societies, with their simplified dogma, accumulation of all kinds of capital, and easy cooperation, amounted to the one action of many men. Their Protestantism was evident in their entrepreneurial corporatism, their dynamic and extraordinary print campaigns, and the character of their engagement with the problem of inequality.[2]

The advent of serious Protestant missionary activity also brought a turn away from serious theology and toward Protestantism as ethics and maxims. This turn occurred because it helped gather diverse Protestants into the new church of the nation. Rousseau, a generation earlier, had described it as the appearance of the dogmas of civil religion. These dogmas, he observed, "must be simple and few in number, expressed precisely and without commentaries." He listed five positive dogmas: "The existence of an omnipotent, intelligent, benevolent divinity that foresees and provides; the life to come; the happiness of the just; the punishment of sinners; the sanctity of the social contract and the law." He might also have listed "tolerance." In the age of nationalism, providing the religious group observes the positive dogmas of civil religion, especially the sovereignty of the civil law, they merit "toleration." If the religious group does not respect the sanctity of the civil law, they remove themselves from the protections of civil religion, becoming instead "sectarian."

The matter can be glimpsed in changes in the vocabulary of "sect" and "denomination." "Sect," in essence, became a pejorative word for a religious group that could not be counted on to acquiesce before the civil law. In 1785, for example, the word "sectarian" appeared in print 750,000 times. In English-language books and periodicals published in 1840, "sectarian" appeared 150 million times. "Denomination" was used rarely in the eighteenth century, most often to refer to a school of philosophy. By the end of the 1850s, however, the adjective "denominational" was being used 40 million times a year, and was rising fast. As the authority of

---

2. Methodist Church, *Eleventh Annual Report of the Missionary Society of the Methodist Episcopal Church* (New York, 1830), pp. 10, 14–15; Michel Foucault, "Governmentality," in Graham Burchell, Colin Gordon, and Peter Miller, eds., *The Foucault Effect: Studies in Governmentality* (Chicago, 1991), pp. 87–104; Benedict Anderson, *Imagined Communities: Reflections on the Origins and Spread of Nationalism* (London, 1983), chs. 1–2.

the nation-state became naturalized, "sectarian" and "denominational" grew commonplace, and stabilized in meaning, as shorthand to indicate the relation of the religious group to the national, or imperial, project. Hence, in 1817, when the New England Congregationalist Hannah Adams published a new edition of her 1784 *Alphabetical Compendium of the Various Sects*, she renamed it *A Dictionary of All Religions and Religious Denominations.*[3]

In its inaugural *Address to the People of the United States* (1816), the American Bible Society offered citizenship as the solution to fractious logic of sectarianism. The *Address*, written by John Mitchell Mason, a Presbyterian minister and the provost of Columbia University, echoed the plea against factions in George Washington's "Farewell Address." Opening with the suggestion that the nation was the new family, Mason explained the American Bible Society's principle of inter-sectarian cooperation as consistent with the classical republican opposition to faction or party. "Fathers, brothers, fellow-citizens, the American Bible Society has been formed," he said. "Local feelings, party prejudices, sectarian jealousies are excluded by its very nature," wrote Mason. Its move to consolidate various religious groups was based on "every hallowed. . . principle." In their "dignified, kind, venerable, true" endeavor, "sectarian littleness and rivalries can find no avenue of admission." In important ways, the organizations marked a rupture with both revolutionary republicanism and the history of Protestantism. James Madison recognized the anti-republican aspects of the large Protestant missionary and benevolent enterprises, which are best understood as national evangelist associations: sophisticated institutions committed, in a manner religious and almost professional, to bringing the "good news" of the American nation to the frontier, and to the world. For their concentration of power, Madison called them "evil lurking under plausible disguises." Not finding anything republican about these "ecclesiastical corporations," he warned of "the danger of silent accumulations & encroachments by Ecclesiastical Bodies." Their "accumulation of property" and "holding it in perpetuity" by the rights of incorporation, he wrote, was "an evil which ought to guarded [against]." He thought that legislatures should only grant corporate charters to "Religious corporations" on the condition that the legislature also "limit

---

3. Figures from Google Ngram Viewer; Leigh E. Schmidt, "A History of All Religions," *Journal of the Early Republic*, vol. 24 (Summer 2004), pp. 327–334.

the duration of the charters. . . & the amount of property acquirable by them."[4]

Madison's disapproval owed as much to the eighteenth century as to classical republicanism. Even Adam Smith, generally regarded as the father of liberalism, had judged banking, canal, aqueduct, and insurance companies as the only ventures that deserved corporate status. Awarding the privileges of corporations to other enterprises, Smith warned, would "scarce ever fail to do more harm than good." The nineteenth century may have made Madison and Smith's suspicion of corporations seem part of a distant past, but in the early republic many Americans shared their distrust. In 1784, the State of New York had established the Regents of the University of the State of New York in order to regulate philanthropic, educational, and religious organizations. In 1792, the Commonwealth of Virginia had repealed colonial laws allowing charitable trusts, while also confiscating, in the name of the public good, endowments managed by the Anglican Church. Skepticism of private corporations contributed to Virginia's 1818 founding of University of Virginia as the nation's first public university.[5]

New Englanders were less suspicions of incorporation. Like literacy and voluntary associations, incorporation was something of a New England specialty. By 1800, Massachusetts and Connecticut had granted more corporate charters than all other states combined. Between 1787 and 1827, New Englanders alone established 933 different Protestant missionary or moral improvement associations. In terms of power, these religious associations compensated for the simultaneous process of the disestablishment of state churches in the early republic, and they are a big reason that disestablishment is a misleading index of the vitality of establishment Protestantism in the early national period. Indeed, the proliferation of the Protestant moral and missionary associations, which were often accompanied by conglomerations and mergers, transformed

---

4. John Mitchell Mason, "Address to the People of the United States," reprinted in *Constitution of the American Bible Society* (New York, 1816), pp. 15–16. Mitchell is identified as the author in Dwight, *Centennial History*, p. 27; Elizabeth Fleet, ed., "Madison's 'Detached Memoranda,'" pp. 557, 558; "Madison's 'Detached Memoranda,'" pp. 554, 556.

5. Madison to the Rev. Jasper Adams, 1832, reprinted in *Religion and Politics in the Early Republic: Jasper Adams and the Church-State Debate*, ed. Daniel L. Dreisbach (Lexington, KY, 1996), p. 120; Adam Smith, *Wealth of Nations*, vol. II, see pp. 733–758, quotation from p. 758; Peter Dobkin Hall, "Historical Perspectives on Nonprofit Organizations in the United States," in Robert D. Herman, ed., *The Jossey-Bass Handbook of Nonprofit Leadership and Management* (San Francisco, 1994), pp. 7–12.

American Protestantism. The establishment Protestantism that emerged was stronger and more dynamic, imbued with clearer lines of authority and simplified doctrine, than colonial American Protestantism. The charter statement of the American Bible Society captured the spirit of the age. Explaining the efficacy of the ABS, why their object was "best attained" by a "national society" of "undisputed magnitude," their secretary, John Mitchell Mason, defended the conglomeration's unusual concentration of power. He spoke of how their mission to unite "national feeling" required "accumulated intelligence."

In a statement that captures much of how capitalism and religion supported the rise of American nationalism, Mason explained that "[c]oncentrated action is powerful action. The same such powers, when applied by a common direction, will produce results impossible to their divided and partial exercise." The concentration sought was a concentration of capital, technology, administration, and theology. The result sought, he explained, was nationalism, which would in turn enable the accumulation of more resources and the expenditure of greater energies: "A national object unites national feeling and concurrence. Unity of a great system combines energy of effect with economy of means. Accumulated intelligence interests and animates the public mind."[6] Mason predicted that the work of the ABS, conducted with its "economy of means," would give America "a place in the moral convention of the world." It was a nationalist ambition, much as Jefferson, in the Declaration of Independence, described the goal of American independence to be "among the powers of the earth." Then, wrote Mason, invoking a classic Jeffersonian term, America might "act directly upon the universal plans of happiness which are now pervading nations." Much separated Thomas Jefferson and the American Bible Society, but they also shared an absolute value—nationalism—that united them, apart from the upstart Protestants of the early republic.[7]

The creation of large national organizations both required and furthered the consolidation and concentration that Mason described. In 1825,

6. Mason, "Address to the People of the United States," pp. 16–17.

7. On the count of 933 Protestant missionary and moral improvement associations, see David Paul Nord, "Financing Evangelical Book Publishing," in Noll, ed., *God and Mammon*, pp. 149–150; Tocqueville, *Democracy in America*, vol. II, pp. 106–107; C. A. Bayly, *The Birth of the Modern World, 1780–1914* (Malden, MA, 2004), pp. 330–345; Michael Zakim, *Ready-Made Democracy: A History of Men's Dress in the Early Republic, 1760–1860* (Chicago 2003), pp. 1–10.

when the property of the New York, Northern, and Western Missionary Societies, recently united as the United Foreign Missionary Society, was placed under the purview of American Board of Commissioners for Foreign Missions, the latter issued a report outlining the terms of union. Nowhere did the report mention God or any theological concern or claim. Three separate articles affirmed that the ABCFM "is a National Institution," that the Presbyterian concerns of the United Foreign Missionary Society would recognize the ABCFM as a "National institution," and resolved that following the merger the ABCFM "will endeavor to merit the high character of a truly National institution."[8] In 1826, the American Home Missionary Society, the product of another conglomeration, stated in its Constitution: "the promotion of 'Home Missions' is. . . indispensable to the moral advancement and political stability of the United States." They explained: "we are doing a work of patriotism, no less than that of Christianity." Thus streamlined and more dynamic, Reformed American Protestantism launched itself across North America and onto the world stage. The unrepublican aspects of this enterprise probably contributed to the missions movement paying frequent tribute to republican ideals.[9]

The move away from colonial and revolutionary-era conceptions of incorporation suggests the extent to which the national evangelist organizations belonged to the nineteenth century. As corporations operating nationally (even transnationally), the legal status of the national evangelist organizations was a delicate subject. Elias Boudinot had been concerned enough about political and legal opposition that he had asked the officers of the Philadelphia Bible Society not to even use the word "national." A "national institution," he reminded them, would require a congressional charter. As it happened, the ABS functioned as a national corporation for years before the Marshall Court's *Dartmouth College v. Woodward* (1819) made it legal to do so. The opposition Boudinot had feared never materialized. It is a good example of how, as Madison pointed out, disestablishment and American discourses of religious freedom tended to draw attention to the intellectual and theological dimensions of religious endeavors, and away from the institutional and economic. The same

8. American Tract Society, *A Brief History of the American Tract Society* (Boston, 1857), p. 9; Tracy, *HABCFM*, pp. 27, 137–152.

9. American Home Missionary Society, *Constitution of the American Home Missionary Society* (New York, 1826), pp. 4, 47.

tendency allowed churches to become the first social institutions wholly controlled by Afro-Americans.

Other political elites shared Madison's distrust of the American missions movement. Privately, Thomas Jefferson and John Adams mocked John Jay's assumption of the presidency of the American Bible Society. Adams joked that if John Quincy's letters to his sons on religion ever became public, the necessary terms of "peace" might oblige John Quincy "to retire like a Jay to study Prophecies to the End of his Life." Adams responded to the 1816 founding of what he called the "National Bible Society" (American Bible Society) with "physician heal thyself" dismay, lamenting that American Christians were asking the faithful for money to "propagate" their "Corruptions" the world over. The creation of "our bible societies" also struck Jefferson as dismal news. "These Incendiaries," he wrote to Adams, "finding the days of fire and faggot are over in the Atlantic hemisphere, are now preparing to put the torch" to the rest of the world. Jefferson compared the American missionaries to "colonies of Jesuit priests with cargoes of their Missal and translations of their Vulgate, to be put gratis into the hands of everyone who would accept them." He derided the national evangelists' publications as "satellites of religious inquisition."[10]

Despite the aversion of Jefferson, Madison, and Adams to the missions movement, few members of the American political elite doubted the need for nation-building programs. In 1784, for example, George Washington had proposed a series of canals that would connect the Eastern seaboard to the Ohio River and link the Ohio River with Lake Erie. By bringing the "produce of western settlers to our ports," Washington predicted, Americans would be "binding these people [in the interior of the continent] to us by a chain which can never be broken." The same year, the *Virginia Gazette* called a proposed canal on the Potomac "one of the grandest chains for preserving the Federal Union." In 1787, Madison had warned Thomas Jefferson that the Constitution "will neither effectually answer its *national object*, nor prevent the local mischiefs which everywhere excite disgust against the State Governments." In other words, the Constitution did not allow the kind of nationalist programs the country needed. In the early republic, John C. Calhoun, Henry Clay, John Quincy Adams, and

---

10. Lester J. Cappon, ed., *The Adams-Jefferson Letters* (Chapel Hill, NC, 1959), pp. 360, 493–494, 496; See also Ralph Ketcham, *James Madison: A Biography* (Charlottesville, VA, 1971), pp. 651–652.

other American elites had advocated for an "American System," a series of mostly material improvements designed to help foster American nationality by facilitating commerce and communication. Like Jefferson's plans for secular, republican schools and libraries in Virginia, fears of centralized power, local jealousies, and lack of resources kept the "American System" a subject of congressional debate. In the US Congress, nationalist sentiment was simply not strong enough to pass the "American System," or any other purposeful system of internal improvements.[11]

Joel Barlow, the former Connecticut Wit turned freethinking radical, proposed that the federal government launch a more culturally oriented nation-building institution. In *Prospectus of a National Institution* (1806), Barlow argued for a nation-building organization that would combine the role of the Royal Society of London and the National Institute of France. He called it a "truly national" program to foster the arts and sciences, and Barlow outlined an imaginative and far-reaching endeavor, a kind of National Science Foundation, National Endowment for the Humanities, National Institute of Health, and national university rolled into one. Barlow's National Institution would "civilize" Indians and educate students and teachers in mineralogy and botany, chemistry, mathematics, medicine, and the mechanical sciences. It would sponsor a national medical school, mining school, engineering school, and natural history museum, as well as promote "drawing, painting, statuary, engraving, music, poetry, ornamental architecture, and ornamental gardening." The curriculum Barlow described would raise "researches in literature," which hitherto had been "so vague in their nature, and so little methodised," to one of the proper sciences. He specified that "moral and political research" would be core to the purpose of the National Institution. In France and Britain, he wrote, the state had already undertaken the work of educating its citizens; he wanted the United States to do so, too. With its "democratical system" and the "vast regions of our continent" in need of "improvement," the need for nationalizing institutions in the United States was greater.[12]

---

11. Madison complained to Jefferson that the Constitution did not allow the government to take effective nation-building measures; see Dangerfield, *The Awakening of American Nationalism*, p. 5; on various nation-building programs, see idem, pp. 14–35. See John Lauritz Larson, "'Bind the Republic Together': The National Union and the Struggle for a System of Internal Improvements," *Journal of American History*, vol. 74, no. 2 (September 1987), pp. 363–387.

12. Joel Barlow, *Prospectus of a National Institution to be Established in the United States* (Washington, DC, 1806), pp. 4, 7–10, 13, 19–25.

Instead of Barlow's national arts and sciences institution, the contemporary federal institution that did the greatest nationalizing work was probably the postal system. The postal system merely delivered the mail, however; they did not, as did the missionary societies, write the literature and give it away, nor did the postal service run schools or auxiliary "postal societies." In contrast to the system of canals and roads that formed the heart of the American System, or the ambitious national institution of arts and sciences that Barlow described, the missionary societies faced surmountable political and legal obstacles. The Northeastern bourgeoisie could endow them with resources beyond either the means or authority of Congress.[13] If the question of their legality as national corporations, and the sincerity of their republican commitments, led to dissembling, no one hesitated to describe their nationalizing purpose. In May 1816, for example, when leading members of the Northeastern business and political classes met with some of the nation's foremost Protestant clergy, they said that God's ways in nation-building had brought them together, in lower Manhattan, for the inaugural meeting of the American Bible Society. Meeting in the Consistory Room of the Dutch Reformed Church on Garden (now Exchange), they began with a recitation from Isaiah 55: "Behold, thou shalt call a nation thou knowest not, and nations that knew not thee shall run unto thee." A century later, the ABS's official historian, Henry Otis Dwight, a descendant of Timothy Dwight, commemorated the inaugural assembly of the American Bible Society as "a meeting of clergy and laymen interested in the question of whether the new West could be led to learn God's ways in nation-building."[14] The American Tract Society explained its 1823 renaming, from the New England to the American Tract Society, in the same manner. The name change was necessary, they wrote, because the name "American" was "nothing more or less than to simply indicate what it is designed to *be* and to *do.*"[15] The tens of millions of pages of tracts that they sent into the Mississippi River Valley aimed to promote freedom, the rule of law, the right of property, and Christian values. They hoped

---

13. Richard R. John, *Spreading the News: The American Postal System from Franklin to Morse* (Cambridge, MA, 1998).

14. American Bible Society, *First Annual Report* (New York, 1817), p. v; Henry Otis Dwight, *The Centennial History of the American Bible Society* (New York, 1916), p. 21.

15. Seth Bliss, *Letters to the Members, Patrons and Friends of the Branch of the American Tract Society in Boston* (Boston, 1858), also wrote that that "the nationality of its name was meant to express the comprehensiveness and nationality of its operation and object," see pp. 35–36, italics in original. The American Home Missionary Society defended their lack of international activities by their devotion to nationalization. We had to become "an

that the millions of pamphlets would "prove like so many 'leaves' from the tree of life 'for the healing of nations.' "[16]

The American missions movement's homogenizing efforts began with theological differences. In 1817, the Westchester County Auxiliary of the American Bible Society passed a resolution forbidding prayer, preaching, or discussions of religious worship at meetings. The Board of Managers reported that the organization had been "strengthened" by the move to disallow "the exercise of prayer and preaching at their meetings." The ban was consistent with their general principle "to avoid all interference with the various opinions of its members respecting the forms of religious worship." Several years later, the American Bible Society also resolved, excepting the reading of a piece of Scripture to open proceedings, to forbid any form of "religious exercise" during their board meetings. In 1825, when the American Bible Society reported that a decade of society business had been conducted "in a spirit of brotherly kindness and love," it was true. The same year, Episcopalians, Presbyterians, Congregationalists, as well as others, gathered from all over the United States, in New York, for the consolidation of the American Tract Society. Their meeting, they reported, consisting of "a respectable number of religious denominations" under the guidance of "gentleman of high consideration," agreed upon a constitution "with a most delightful unanimity." On most theological matters, the British writer C. S. Lewis's remark about the Reformation captures the general spirit of the missions movement. "The theological questions really at issue," wrote Lewis, "have no significance except on a certain level, a high level, of the spiritual life." The missions movement enjoyed a general consensus to contain theology, so it would not become a source of dissent. No such consensus existed among frontier revivalists.[17]

The turn away from the deeply theological Protestantism of colonial New England was a defining quality of the missions movement. There is perhaps no better illustration of the tertiary role of theology to national

---

AMERICAN and a HOME Society" because America was not yet "Christianized" and its "widely dispersed" population, they wrote, suffered from "the very freedom of its institutions." It was "patriotism" that kept their efforts focused on North America, they wrote. See American Home Missionary Society, *The Eighth Report of the American Home Missionary Society* (New York, 1834), pp. 10–12.

16. American Tract Society, *Fourth Annual Report*, pp. 21, 23.

17. Lewis quoted in W. H. Auden, "The Protestant Mystics," in Edward Mendelson, ed., *Forewords and Afterwords* (New York, 1989), p. 53; American Bible Society, *Eighth Annual Report* (New York, 1824), p. 2; American Tract Society, *Address of the Executive Committee of the American Tract Society to the Christian Public* (New York, 1825), p. 3.

evangelism than the Syrian Protestant College, later the American University of Beirut (AUB). Arguably the greatest achievement of the American missions movement, the American University of Beirut, which evolved from a school founded by American missionaries in the city in 1824, has never taught theology, nor had a seminary, nor even a religious studies department, and was from the beginning in fact not a mission, but a college. It grew out of a "society for scientific purposes" (renamed in 1842 the Society of Arts and Sciences), cofounded by Americans and Syrians. The two leading Americans were Eli Smith, a graduate of Yale (1821), who designed an Arabic letterpress and founded a publishing house, and Cornelius Van Dyck, a Philadelphia physician who published three medical textbooks, three mathematics textbooks, two books on astronomy, one on geography, and five books on chemistry, all in Arabic, which he learned in Beirut. In addition to science, the other pillar of the curriculum was literature. The missionaries called it the Hellenistic approach to conversion. Moreover, the American Board of Commissioners for Foreign Missions, which founded AUB, was the most committed of the American missionary associations to Congregationalism and the New England way. Such was the modern, liberal, and non-theological ethos that nationalism required and that suffused the missions movement.[18]

The sacred status of the nation led the bourgeoisie to look to national political institutions as models for the missionary organizations. Elias Boudinot, for example, explained that the institutional structure of the Bank of the United States served as the model for the American Bible Society. Attempting to convince the reluctant Philadelphians that his plans for a national institution were practical and fair, he wrote, "Let me remind you of a civil institution as a model. . . the late Bank of the United States respected the whole Union." He wrote of how the structure of the Bank accommodated national participation and would work for the ABS as well: "The stockholders belonged to every state in the United States," he wrote. "They chose Managers, or rather Directors, in every part of the States. . . they did not fail to have a quorum ever ready to transact

---

18. Dwight, *Centennial History*, p. 62; George Sabra, "A.U.B. and Religion: Never the Twain Shall Meet. . . Again?" lecture delivered in the General Lecture Series of the Anis Makdissi Program in Literature at the American University of Beirut, April 6, 2005, and available at the Anis Makdissi Program website: http://www.aub.edu.lb/fas/ampl/Pages/lectures. aspx; A. L. Tibawi, *American Interests in Syria 1800–1901, A Study of Educational, Literary and Religious Work* (Oxford, UK 1961), pp. 160–170; John M. Munro, *A Mutual Concern: The Story of the American University of Beirut* (Delmar, NY, 1977), pp. 10–14.

the necessary business."[19] Similarly, the American Tract Society referred to its Publishing Committee as "the Supreme Court of the Society." Its Publishing Committee held final authority within the organization, and the ATS compared the authority of the Publishing Committee to that of the US Supreme Court exercising judicial review. The Committee, they wrote, was "as much obligated to decide, either to accept, or to reject it, as is the Supreme Court of the United States to decide any case lawfully before it." Their bylaws stated that, as with the Supreme Court, "there is no appeal" from the decisions of the Publishing Committee.[20]

Alexis de Tocqueville found the tight weave of patriotism and Protestantism in the cloth of American political culture remarkable. He marveled how it combined with Americans' geographic mobility, in particular at the willingness of New England missionaries to migrate to the frontier in the cause of religion and patriotism. "I met with wealthy New Englanders who abandoned the country in which they were born in order to lay the foundations of Christianity and of freedom on the banks of the Missouri, or in the prairies of Illinois," wrote Tocqueville. New Englanders sometimes experienced the same migration with less sanguinity. Perhaps the best-known New England missionary to the West, Timothy Flint, alleged that false dreams of ease and wealth in the West lured the sons of New England over the mountains. In an 1815 address, Flint warned, "Our dwellings, our school-houses and churches. . . will have mouldered to ruins; our graveyards will be overrun with shrub oaks." New England would be left to "but here and there a wretched hermit, true to his paternal soil, to tell the tale of other times." In Flint's view, New England's migrants to the frontier were due for disappointment. They would not find in the West anything resembling "that glorious emblem of the law, justice and order, of industry and temperance. . . the village church."[21]

Timothy Dwight took an even dimmer view of New Englanders who went West, and their prospects. Those who migrated were the ones who "cannot live in regular society." They were, alleged Dwight, "too idle; too talkative; too passionate; too prodigal, and too shiftless to acquire

---

19. Boudinot, *An Answer to the Objections of the Managers of the Philadelphia Bible Society*, p. 10.

20. Seth Bliss, *Letters to the Members, Patrons and Friends of the Branch American Tract Society in Boston* (Boston, 1858), p. 21.

21. Alexis de Tocqueville, *Democracy in America* (Stilwell, KS, 2007), trans. Henry Reeve, p. 222; Flint quoted in John Ervin Kirkpatrick, *Timothy Flint: Pioneer, Missionary, Author, Editor 1780–1840* (Cleveland, 1911), pp. 52–53.

either property to character." Dwight saw them leaving New England not because, in Tocqueville's telling, they were embarking on a happy project of civilization, but because they could not abide the "restraints of law, religion, or morality." They wanted to exercise their false conviction that they understood "medical science, politics, and religion better than those who have studied them through life." Though their own lives were examples of incompetence and dissolution, wrote Dwight, they "feel perfectly satisfied that they could manage. . . the nation." Migrants, Dwight insisted, were not the best sons of New England; rather they fled from "a kitchen fire, [from] every blacksmith shop, [from] every corner of the streets." Facing poverty, public contempt, and jail at home, they "leave their native places, and betake themselves to their wilderness." On the other hand, at least concerning their own motives, Dwight and Flint would have found some agreement with Tocqueville's characterization that, in the United States, "religious zeal is perpetually stimulated. . . by the duties of patriotism." In contrast to French Catholic priests, Tocqueville found the American missionaries worldly and pragmatic. Conversing with them, he noted that they spoke little of "eternity" and quite a bit more about "the goods of this world." In America, he noted, you "meet with a politician where you expected to find a priest." In fact, the American missionaries were often more effective than American politicians.[22]

While Congress could not manage the commissioning of a canal, the missions movement launched Anglo-American Protestantism onto the world stage. By 1830, the American Home Missionary Society (AHMS), a Presbyterian organization, had established 801 missionary districts. In 1832, they received $68,627 to run 770 Sabbath schools instructing 31,140 pupils, and 378 Bible classes instructing 11,195 pupils. It was $17,000 more in income than that of Harvard University for 1830. From 1825 to 1832, their 606 missionaries had performed a total of 1,774 years and nine months of missionary labor for the Society. The AHMS estimated that between 1826 and 1831, they alone had reached "probably more than one half the annual increase in adults in the United States." Noting that they "laboured not alone" but in coordination with "other organizations," such endeavors constituted grounds for great expectations. Since "God works by means," they foresaw that "the work of salvation will advance in a geometrical ratio." By 1840, the ABCFM alone was supporting missionary

22. Dwight, *Travels in New-England and New-York*, vol. II (New Haven, CT, 1821), p. 459; Tocqueville, *Democracy in America*, p. 222.

endeavors in India, Ceylon (Sri Lanka), China, Burma, Singapore, Siam (Thailand), the Sandwich Islands (Hawaii), Athens, Beirut, Persia, Cyprus, Syria, Liberia, Sierra Leone, among the Zulus in Southern Africa, and across the North American frontier. By 1829, the American Bible Society had built a network of 645 local auxiliary societies. By the same year, the American Tract Society had coordinated 713 "auxiliaries and branches, immediately connected with the National Society" in 27 American states and territories. By any measure, the scale of the national evangelist front, encompassing thousands of auxiliary societies, schools, and committees, was impressive. It is not difficult to imagine why their accomplishments, and the historic cooperation between sects, led (in "less than half a century," predicted the Presbyterians, " 'violence shall no more be heard in thy land' ") to millennial expectations. Nor is it difficult to understand why their critics, often frontier revivalists or cosmopolitan freethinkers, saw them as a menacing phalanx.[23]

Ironically, Tom Paine had been an early advocate for new inter-sectarian cooperation under nationalist auspices. "I look on the various denominations among us," he had written in 1776, "to be like children of the same family, differing only, in what is called their Christian names." However, like Jefferson and Madison, looking at the national evangelist organizations, Paine would have seen fear and ambition, rather than love and salvation. Nonetheless, his vision that the sects would be like siblings to the parent of the nation was coming to pass, though with a principle aim of undoing the perceived influence of deism and religious freedom.[24]

The American Tract Society, the American Home Missionary Society, and the American Bible Society in effect organized a process of national social communication, especially between the Northeastern elite and the frontier.[25] The churches, missionary districts, Sabbath schools, auxiliary

23. ATS, *A Brief History of the American Tract Society* (Boston, 1857), p. 47; David Paul Nord, "The Evangelical Origins of Mass Media in America, 1815–1835," *Journalism Monographs* (May 1984), p. 14; American Home Missionary Society, *The Seventh Report of the American Home Missionary Society* (New York, 1833), pp. 49–50; American Home Missionary Society, *The Sixth Report of the American Home Missionary Society* (New York, 1832), pp. 58–59.

24. Foot and Kramnick, eds. *The Thomas Paine Reader*, p. 100; In *The Age of Reason*, Paine wrote, "All national institutions of churches—whether Jewish, Christian, or Turkish, appear to me no other than human inventions, set up to terrify and enslave mankind and monopolize power and profit." See also Mead, p. 47.

25. My description bears only a superficial resemblance to Donald G. Mathews's characterization of the "Second Great Awakening" as an "organizing process." Mathews argued that the Second Great Awakening "helped give meaning and direction" to the lives of

societies, and the distribution of millions of publications required institutions and bureaucracies. Institutions and bureaucracies were also required to implement their nationally standardized pricing plans, national distribution networks, and national business plans, all of which were firsts; so too were their national marketing campaigns and national scales of operation. Together, Protestantism and bureaucratization form a strong nationalizing tandem. Bureaucratization means communication with a center, similar training, standardization of rules and norms, and even a prescribed idiom of communication. "If the bureaucracy lasts and is effective," wrote the social anthropologist Ernest Gellner, "its idiom is liable to become the language of the entire society, either right down to the intimacy of family life, or at least the level of public business." The national evangelists advanced an ambitious idiom for American national life, with some successes, and some equally significant failures. An important effect of the organizing process, however, was to diminish distinctiveness among Reformed Protestants in America. The incorporation and growth of the missionary associations tended to encourage their own homogenization, too, in structure, practical operations, and political interests, an organizational phenomenon that sociologists call "structural isomorphism." The general agreement in the missions movement to cooperate and focus on common goals further discouraged debate over divisive issues, including theology.[26]

In 1824, the American Bible Society marveled at the auxiliary societies and Sabbath schools it had established on the banks of the Wabash River in Indiana and Illinois. We have done the same, wrote an ABS agent, in "almost every settlement" and our "evangelical labors. . . may be regarded as wielding the destinies of unborn millions." The same year, the American Board of Commissioners for Foreign Missions boasted that they had created a network of social communication between all classes of Americans. They claimed, between their print media and their thousands of local auxiliary societies, that they had created "a complete

---

frontier settlers and in this sense organized rural settlers. See Donald G. Mathews, "The Second Great Awakening as an Organizing Process, 1780–1830," *American Quarterly*, vol. 21 (1969), pp. 22–43.

26. Ben Primer, *Protestants and American Business Methods* (Ann Arbor, MI, 1979), ch. 1; Mark A. Noll, *God and Mammon*; Eric Hobsbawm, *The Age of Revolution* (New York, 1996), p. 223; Kathleen D. McCarthy, *American Creed: Philanthropy and the Rise of Civil Society, 1700–1865* (Chicago, 2003), p. 58; Robin Klay and John Lunn, "Protestants and the American Economy in the Postcolonial Period: An Overview," in Noll, ed., *God and Mammon*, pp. 31, 39; Gellner, *Nationalism* (London, 1997), p. 76.

chain of communication" throughout the nation. The national evangelists also continued the well-established practice of the ministerial home
visit. Methodist circuit-riders brought the practice to the frontier, but the
national religious societies followed, resolving, as they would with the
philosophes' print media, to learn from and outdo their enemies. The
busiest missionaries reported in the neighborhood of "200 family visits"
annually.[27] A prospective ATS missionary wrote that he had resolved to
"devote my whole heart to the Tract service" and "to risk my life amongst
the fevers of the West" when he learned of the ambition of their plans to
visit every settlement and leave tracts in each home. "If I understand the
design," he wrote, "it is nothing less than that your Agents shall *visit every
settlement west of the mountains, and shall leave no one till they are sure your
publications have reached. . . every house.* I am ready to offer my services. . .
till the plan is carried through." The ATS acknowledged that a population
of 12 million people was "a great many." But with their steam-powered
presses and papermaking technology and stereotype plates, "twelve millions of tracts can be printed in one year." The goal, the historian David
Paul Nord has noted, was to put in the home of every American the same
tracts, to have every American reading the same thing. It was not popular
literature because there was no popular demand; rather it was the first
instance of American mass media: media produced with the strategic
goal of mass distribution.[28]

A generation later, in 1852, Frederick Douglass would say that if "the
great ecclesiastical, missionary, Bible and tract associations of the land
array their immense powers against slavery and slave-holding. . . the
whole system of crime and blood would be scattered to the winds." How
actually powerful were they? It is difficult to say, but two things are certain. First, the extent of the national evangelist presence across North
America, not only in print but also in a variety of types of affiliated, local
voluntary societies and schools, had no rival. A century ago, the historian

---

27. Tracy, *HABCFM*, p. 125; *Seventh Report of the American Bible Society* (New York, 1823),
p. 28; *Tenth Report of the American Bible Society* (New York, 1826), p. 59. These figures
compiled from the Annual Reports summarized in American Tract Society, *Tenth Annual
Report* (New York, 1835), p. 2. For a typical account of home visits to frontier settlers by
Eastern missionaries, see *An Address of the Congregational Missionary Society in the
Counties of Berkshire, Columbia, and Their Vicinities, Also, A Report of the Trustees of the
Congregational Missionary Society* (Stockbridge, MA, 1805), pp. 9–11.

28. Letter reprinted in ATS, *Fourth Annual Report* (New York, 1829), p. 24. Italics in
the original. ATS report on plans to put tracts into every home quoted in Nord, "The
Evangelical Origins of Mass Media in America," pp. 12, 20.

Martha L. Edwards wrote that these Protestant groups "exercised both civic and social functions, caring for the poor and sick, educating the children, providing intellectual diversion and social relaxation, taking the leadership in business and political affairs." They were unusual and busy organizations. Second, the missions movement combined traits of the New England clerical and the Northeastern commercial classes, whose cooperation brought the movement into existence.[29]

The New England clerics and the Northeastern bourgeoisie made an at times awkward alliance. Despite the New England clerics' critical role in authorizing the missions, and their visionary nationalism, they did not run the national evangelist associations. Nor did they want to. At an organizational meeting for the American Bible Society, the decision to entrust the institution to the direction of laymen made Lyman Beecher cry tears of joy. The managers of the great American missionary and moral improvement associations came from the Northeastern bourgeoisie. The New England clerics, who as a class were on the way down, found in the Northeastern business elite a partner on its way up. A shared providential nationalism made the partnership possible: Who are God's chosen people? This is the primary apocalyptic question, and both were sure that the chosen people would not be a sect. It would be a nation. It could be America, both were certain; it could be them. A certain coincidence of more worldly interests also existed between the two classes. Both stood for a commercial society that fundamentally differed from the plantation South that dominated the political life of the United States. Both valued social order over equality, though the bourgeoisie did not share the New England clerics' suspicions about luxury or their conviction that inequality must be limited. The bourgeoisie also lacked the tendency for anti-racism, and the strong anti-slavery stance, that Timothy Dwight, Elias Boudinot, William Ellery Channing, and many New England Federalists, especially in the ministerial class, advocated. On the other hand, they brought all of the attributes that made them one of the most dynamic classes of entrepreneurs in history. The capitalist class of the Northeastern United States in the early republic possessed an ethic of hard work, ascetic tendencies, and an optimistic outlook, as well as significant and burgeoning economic resources. They also were able to cooperate and organize. When the leaders of the American Bible Society contemplated their large network of

---

29. Martha L. Edwards, "Religious Forces in the United States," *The Mississippi Valley Historical Review*, vol. 5 (March 1919), p. 448.

local branches and auxiliaries, in 1829, they noted its "systematic organi-zation" and its potential for "judicious and systematic division of labor." The same year, to put its tracts into every one of New York City's homes (as well as its wharfs, markets, hospitals, and other public institutions), the American Tract Society devised a sophisticated plan involving wards, committees, canvassing and distribution instructions, and procedures for recording and reporting progress. Even Arthur and Lewis Tappan, who had designed the system, went door to door.[30]

The simplest indication of the rise of the profile of the bourgeoisie in the missions movement was the shift of the center of gravity of the American missions movement from New England to New York. The New England Tract Society renamed itself the American Tract Society and moved to Nassau Street, in lower Manhattan. Announcing the consolida-tion, the American Tract Society explained that the capital requirements of investment in stereotype print technology were "a powerful argument in favor of union." Tracts were "now exceedingly cheap," admitted the ATS, but they were sure "the formation of the American Tract Society [would] render them cheaper."[31] Notably, the American Board of Commissions for Foreign Missions held out, continuing to hold annual meetings in Hartford, Salem, New Haven, and other New England towns. Well into the early republic, the ABCFM remained an organization of New England Reformed Protestants, excluding Baptists and Methodists and Quakers. It was not until 1826, 17 years after its founding, that non–New Englanders constituted a majority on its Board, and they resisted going to New York to raise money. The New England merchant class still had means, and the ABCFM pushed hard on the middling sorts for money, too. By 1830, the ABCFM was spending $100,000 a year, almost twice Harvard University's 1830 total annual income, to support a missionary force of 224 ordained ministers, 600 native teachers, and 50,000 students. The industrialization of New England played an important role. In 1829, Amos H. Hubbard, a paper mill owner in Norwich, Connecticut, bought the first steam-powered papermaking machine in the United States. Over the course of the first half of the nineteenth century, steam-powered paper-making machines greatly increased production, while cutting the price of

---

30. On the "primary apocalyptic question," see Elaine Pagels, *The Origin of Satan* (New York, 1996), p. 51; David Paul Nord, "The Evangelical Origins of Mass Media in America, 1815–1835," pp. 18–21.

31. Ibid., p. 9.

paper by about 60 percent. "I find that Papermakers generally do not feel very cordial to me," wrote Hubbard in 1830, "because I sell paper so cheap. One man remarked that it would oblige him to stop his Mill."[32]

In general, however, the American missions movement alliance with American capitalism was made in New York. The partnership between the clerical and bourgeois classes coincided with the rise of New York and the relative decline of Boston. It was New Yorkers, not New Englanders, who, in 1817, established the first trans-Atlantic packet service. It was New Yorkers, not New Englanders, who, also in 1817, began construction on the Erie Canal, an important initiative in the economic history of the Atlantic World. New England had the colleges and universities, but the officers of the American Bible Society, the American Tract Society, and the other large national evangelist associations were the American political and economic elite, not the intellectual or clerical elite. They included Secretary of State John Jay, Associate Justice of the Supreme Court (and nephew of the first president) Bushrod Washington, New York governor DeWitt Clinton, Vice President and New York governor Daniel D. Tompkins, New York City mayor Richard Varick, Connecticut governor John Cotton Smith, and the president of the Bank of New York, Matthew Clarkson. Contemporary mores did not preclude current holders of high political office from serving on the boards of Christian philanthropic associations, and a dozen additional members of the national political elite served as officers of the national evangelist associations. Supporting the missionary associations required neither belief in prophecies and miracles, as Thomas Jefferson and John Adams had joked, nor missionary impulses. Even John Quincy Adams, a Unitarian of at best tepid Christian commitment, served as a vice president of the American Bible Society.[33]

Whereas the officers of the organizations came from the political class, the mangers of the big missions organizations came from the economic elite. The managers were drawn from the rising urban gentry, arrivistes mainly from Philadelphia and New York, together with representatives of the old landowning colonial elite. ABS managers, for example, included William Havemeyer, a German immigrant and successful sugar

32. *Report of the American Board of Commissioners for Foreign Missions* (Boston, 1830), pp. 103–104; Seymour E. Harris, *Economics of Harvard* (New York, 1970), p. 210; Nord, "The Evangelical Origins of Mass Media in America," pp. 9, 11–12.

33. *Fifth Report of the American Bible Society* (New York, 1821), n.p.

merchant, whose son, also William, would become mayor of New York. The younger Havemeyer followed in the nationalist footsteps of his father and, during the Civil War, became a prominent Union Democrat. John Pintard, an entrepreneur in the China trade and insurance business, and a founder of the New York Historical Society, was an ABS manager. So was William Colgate, an English immigrant who came to America as a young man, and who went from an apprenticeship as a soap-maker to make himself, with what would become Colgate-Palmolive, one of the richest men in New York City. Robert Ralston, another ABS manager, was a Philadelphia merchant whose East India trade business made him rich. Counted as a percentage of the gross domestic product, the fortune of Stephen Van Rensselaer, another ABS manager, makes him the tenth richest American of all time. Like Van Rensselaer, Leonard Bleecker, an original signatory to the 1792 Buttonwood Agreement creating the New York Stock & Exchange Board, was a representative of the Knickerbocker colonial elite. Theodore Dwight, original member of the Connecticut Wits, a US congressman, secretary of the Hartford Convention and brother of Timothy, was also an ABS manager. John Aspinwall, the founder of what was becoming one of the great mercantile fortunes of nineteenth-century New York, found serving as ABS manager congenial. So did Thomas Eddy, a Philadelphia-born Quaker, the son of Irish immigrants, who went from an apprentice tanner in Burlington, New Jersey, to make (and lose) a couple of fortunes in insurance, banking, and trans-Atlantic shipping. Like the aristocratic Van Rensselaer, the arriviste Eddy was an early advocate for the Erie Canal. By in effect joining the Midwest, and its wheat flour, to the Atlantic, via New York City, the Erie Canal transformed a patchwork of local or regional economies into a national one. It helped make New York City the capital of capital, and it raised the city's commercial elite to new riches. By way of contrast, in 1828, when an agent for the American Sunday School Union secured appointments with James Monroe and James Madison, he suspected that the former presidents would not be able to afford the price of a lifetime membership in the American Sunday School Union.[34]

In New York, the national evangelist associations served a purpose as a venue of class consolidation that simply was not necessary in Boston.

---

34. Ibid.; Daniel Walker Howe, *What Hath God Wrought*, pp. 117–120; American Sunday School Union agent anecdote in Bertram Wyatt-Brown, "The Antimission Movement in the Jacksonian South," p. 522.

Despite the greater stability of Boston's upper class, New York's old colonial elite emerged from the American Revolution in better shape, with relatively minor losses. New York's old colonial elite, the Van Rensselaers and Bleeckers and Stuyvesants, remained rich families in the early national period, whereas among Boston's colonial rich only Thomas L. Winthrop remained. At the same time, the New York–Philadelphia corridor in the early republic produced some exceptional newly rich, self-made men. New York's new rich of the early national period tended to be overseas traders and manufacturers, whereas Boston's rich were likely merchant capitalists and textile manufacturers. Jefferson's 1807 Embargo Act had compelled some of Boston's prosperous trans-Atlantic shippers, Jacob Lawrence of Lawrence Mills, for example, to turn from the sea to the mills, a choice that sometimes made them richer, but also changed their horizons, contributing to Boston's transformation into a regional, rather than a national or international, city. One of the unusual traits of New York's upper class in the early republic, however, was its "lost generation." Early national New York had more old rich than Boston, as well as more and richer new rich, and little in between. In 1828, only 3 percent of New Yorkers assessed at least $100,000 were second-generation or "middle-aged" money. In Boston the number was 14 percent. The difference was significant. The more dynamic New York economy, and the city's more mutable society, made the absence of second-generation rich felt more keenly than it would have been in Boston. When looked at from the perspective of literary and cultural history, the unusual shape of New York's upper class in the early republic, compared to that of Boston, is more familiar. It is, in a sense, the difference between Washington Irving and Henry Adams. By the beginning of the nineteenth century, it was clear to Washington Irving, whose family the War of 1812 ruined, that the ascendancy of the old style Federalist rich was already over. Not until the end of the nineteenth century, with Henry Adams and Oliver Wendell Holmes, did a self-conscious awareness of the end of the patriciate overtake the Boston elite.[35]

For some of the same reasons that made New York's upper class so dynamic and mutable, the city became the preferred home of the national

---

35. Richard W. Pointer, "Philadelphia Presbyterians, Capitalism, and the Morality of Economic Success," in Mark A. Noll, ed., *God and Mammon*; Wallace, *Rockdale*, pp. 297–350; Frederic Cople Jaher, "Nineteenth-Century Elites in Boston and New York," *Journal of Social History*, vol. 6 (Autumn 1972), pp. 32–77.

evangelist organizations. In 1825, the same year that the New England Tract Society relocated from Boston to New York and renamed itself the American Tract Society, New York's Erie Canal opened, along with 500 new mercantile businesses in New York City. In 1826, Arthur and Lewis Tappan, the great merchant capitalists and patrons of Protestant reform in the early American republic, relocated from Boston to New York. The Tappans were moved by New Jersey Senator Theodore Frelinghuysen's warning that "floods of wickedness will by and by come over us [from the frontier], that will sweep away the last vestiges of hope and freedom." They gave generously to the American Bible Society, the American Sunday School Union, the American Tract Society, and the American Home Missionary Society.[36]

Many of the national evangelist organizations became venues of class consolidation. The American Bible Society, for example, became a place where the Van Rensselaers and Bleeckers, representatives of the old colonial elite, could meet the Aspinwalls and Phelpses and other parvenus. For the old families, mixing with the new promised marriages and investment opportunities to replenish accounts. For the new rich, it brought social opportunities. For both, it was doing well by doing good. Otherworldly motives also played a role. As a report prepared for the Executive Committee of American Tract Society put it, "And shall not rich men *try* to go to heaven? And shall you not *try* to get this money?"[37] In 1825, speaking of the "famine. . . which kills the soul—a famine deeply affecting the first elements of society in all the Western states and Territories," the American Bible Society wondered how to find the means to reach out to the settlers. The Board resolved that they must "look for an answer to the increasing exertions of the friends of God," what they called "the growing liberality of the rich" and the "praiseworthy economy of the poor."[38]

The founders, directors, board members, and managers of large and pioneering missionary organizations, including the American Board of Commissioners for Foreign Missions, the American Bible Society, and the American Tract Society, were leading members of the business

---

36. Bertram Wyatt-Brown, *Lewis Tappan and the Evangelical War Against Slavery* (Cleveland, OH, 1969), pp. 49–50, 45.

37. Ibid., pp. 37–41; Rev. Plumer's report for the Executive Committee of the ATS, reprinted in American Tract Society, *Eleventh Annual Report* (New York, 1836), quotes from pp. 42–43.

38. ABS, *Ninth Annual Report* (1825), pp. 21–22.

and political classes. They were merchants and manufacturers, college presidents, senators, congressmen, and federal and state judges. They used the state to secure privileges, as well as to promote reform. Living primarily in the Northeastern cities of Boston, New York, Philadelphia, and their environs, they enjoyed an acute sense of posterity, planned for the distant future, and thought of themselves, accurately, in elitist and nationalist terms, as the leading Americans. They are properly understood as a bourgeoisie, distinct from a middle class or "middling sorts." Reaching out to and enjoining the support of regional and local middling sorts was something the missions movement did very well, but the bourgeoisie was the force behind the movement.[39] A commissioned biographer of the ABCFM missionaries, Francis Wayland, the president of Brown University, described the movers of the missionary organizations as "the mountain tops" of American society. He compared the advent of American missionary organizations to the rays of a rising sun falling first on the highest elevations. "The beams of the sun had only fallen on the tops of the mountains," wrote Wayland, "they had not yet rested upon the hillsides; much less had they penetrated into the valleys. But the mountain tops testified that the sun had risen."[40] Wayland was an influential economist, an early proponent of capitalism and free trade. His *Elements of Political Economy* (1837), a popular nineteenth-century textbook, argued strongly on behalf of a laissez-faire economy, against the granting of monopolies, compulsory labor laws, sumptuary laws, and restrictions on industry. Wayland opposed poor laws because of their presumption that the rich had an obligation to the poor. As long as education and a real opportunity to advance through one's own labor existed, Wayland maintained that the market was the best provider. He even opposed public funding for schools, arguing that "voluntary contributions from

---

39. Mary Ryan, *The Cradle of the Middle Class: The Family in Oneida County New York, 1790–1865* (New York, 1981, has described as the middle class as "occupants of intermediate, middle-level social ranks located somewhere in the vast undifferentiated status category Americans call the middle class" and as those "struggling to find a comfortable place for themselves within a changing social and economic structure," p. 13, 14; Burton J. Bledstein, "Introduction: Storytellers to the Middle Class," in Bledstein and Robert D. Johnston, eds., *The Middling Sorts: Explorations in the History of the American Middle Class* (New York, 2001), has described the "middling sorts" as who those "could not count on the privileges and patronage conferred by the State" and those who experienced a "shaky independence in the precarious marketplace," p. 5.

40. Wayland, *A Memoir of the Life and Labors of Rev. Adoniram Judson, D. D.* (Boston, 1854), vol. I, p. 471.

philanthropic individuals" was "the preferable method." Wayland suspected that though the radically laissez-faire approach was optimal, it would only work in a Protestant society. Catholicism shrouded the masses in ignorance, monopolized learning in a class of useless hierophants, and discouraged labor. He thought that the ability of Protestant mechanics and artisans to emigrate from the Continent to Britain and Holland during the religious wars of the Reformation was the "principal cause of the rapid improvement of those nations." Most important, Protestantism diffused learning and "sanctified industry and made it respectable." Timothy Dwight and the Connecticut Wits would have approved of Wayland's Protestant exceptionalism, but his faith in the market and his disavowal of social regulation to limit poverty and inequality were departures from the New England way.[41]

The reshaping of the missions movement by these bourgeois views is important to understanding the role it played in the formation of American nationality. In the first place, the resources of the bourgeoisie made possible its extraordinary material accomplishments. The thousands of schools and auxiliary societies, the pioneering national corporations with sophisticated business practices, the missions from the Mississippi to Mount Lebanon, and the invention of American mass media all required resources beyond the means of New England literary intellectuals. Second, when the nationalizing program of the missions movement generated strong antipathy on the American frontier, it did so as bourgeois movement, especially for its association with the Northeastern financial and commercial elite. Finally, and perhaps most interesting, though pared down from the theological richness of Puritanism, the national evangelist programs still amounted to the first systematic, self-conscious Protestant influence on American nationality. In *Britons: Forging the Nation 1707–1837*, her study of how increasing numbers of Welsh and English and Scots came to think of themselves as British, the historian Linda Colley argued that "Protestantism was the foundation that made the invention of Great Britain possible." The role of Protestantism cannot be as simple as Colley's statement makes it appear. Both Britain and the colonies knew too long and bloody a history of strife between Anglicans and Dissenters for Protestantism to be the foundation of either British or American nationality. Within the fractious community of Dissenting

---

41. Francis Wayland, *The Elements of Political Economy* (London, 1857), pp. 256, 260, 262.

Protestants, a bitter history of mutual enmity also existed. The contest between James Smith and Richard McNemar, who came to know one another as fellow Presbyterians, is just one example of intra-sectarian discord escalating to violence. On the other hand, Protestantism could also foster bonds transcending national political communities. By the late eighteenth century, the Quaker movement founded by George Fox had grown into a sophisticated, international group of brethren whose members could engage in complex, long-distance commercial relationships that they would not risk with mere compatriots. Protestant fears that Catholicism would supersede national loyalties persisted until the 1960s. Moreover, if Protestantism were the foundation of American and British nationality, the War of Independence would be even more difficult to explain. Protestantism was not the basis of American nationality, but it provided grounds on which elite, Northeastern Reformed Protestants, disillusioned with American democracy and threatened by popular religion, came together to form an influential missions and moral improvement movement.[42]

Importantly, the national evangelist movement coincided with a revolution in communications technology. In the second and third decade of the nineteenth century, stereotype plates, machine-made paper, and steam-powered printing presses generated almost as much enthusiasm as have, in more recent times, the congruence of electricity, phone lines, wireless signals, and personal computers into the Internet. "This is the age of ingenuity," explained the New England Tract Society. The pioneering use of print is one of the important, and distinctively Protestant, characteristics of the Anglo-American missions movement. The scale, from Upper Canada to the Southern Andes, of early modern Catholic missionary work, and its ambition, exemplified by *reducciones*, the massive, forced resettlements of Peruvian and Mexican Indians, rivaled or exceeded Protestant plans. Yet the Catholic Church did not promote widespread literacy, much less mass religious literature. In fact, the Anglo-American

---

42. Linda Colley, *Britons: Forging the Nation, 1707–1837* (New Haven, CT, 1992), p. 54. For an insightful review of Colley's *Britons*, see Gerald Newman, "National Revisited," *The Journal of British Studies*, vol. 35 (January 1996), pp. 118–127. On the potential for identification with like-minded Protestant brethren, rather than countrymen, see the introduction by Tony Claydon and Ian McBridge, eds., *Protestantism and National Identity: Britain and Ireland, c. 1650–c.1850* (Cambridge, UK, 1998). On the Quaker International, see for example Toby L. Ditz, "Shipwrecked: Or, Masculinity Imperiled: Mercantile Representations of Failure and the Gendered Self in Eighteenth-Century Philadelphia," *Journal of American History*, vol. 35 (June 1994), pp. 51–80.

Protestant translation and dissemination of the scriptures compelled Pope Leo XII to issue the *Ubi Primum* of May 1824, condemning the British and Foreign Bible Society for "endeavoring to translate, or rather pervert, the Scripture into the vernacular of all nations." Leo XII's papal bull warned that translation would pollute the sacred scriptures, even perhaps delivering it to the devil: "by false interpretation, the Gospel of Christ will become the Gospel of men, or still worse, the gospel of the devil." It would be over a century before the Vatican accepted the legitimacy of the vernacular scriptures and religious mass media, while Islam remains committed to Arabic as its truth-language, a commitment that, in the modern history of Islam, has limited the role of vernacular languages and mass media.[43]

Understanding the particularity of the Protestant enthusiasm for vernacular languages, print, and mass media helps clarify why the Anglo-American missionaries saw themselves as revolutionaries. In the first millennia of Christian history, the Bible had been translated into all of ten languages. The Reformation catalyzed the translation of the Bible into 22 European languages, but this process took 300 years, until the beginning of the nineteenth century. In contrast, in just the first part of the nineteenth century, Anglo-American Protestants published Bibles in 160 different languages or dialects, producing, in a single generation, Bibles in sevenfold the number of languages as had the previous 19 centuries of Christians. By 1825, the American Bible Society itself was distributing Bibles in 140 languages. These numbers suggest one basis for the national evangelists' self-perception that they were worthy successors to the original evangelists. They were, in fact, making the word of God available, for the first time, to most of humankind.[44]

These massive campaigns of translating and printing separated the national evangelists from their own Protestant forebearers while coinciding with the rise of nationalism. The printing of religious literature

43. *The Publications of the American Tract Society* (Boston, 1824), vol. 1, p. 9; David Lawton, *Faith, Text, and History: The Bible in English* (Charlottesville, VA, 1990), p. 57; American Tract Society, *Eighth Annual Report* (New York, 1833), p. 40; E. C. Tracy, *Memoir of the Life of Jeremiah Evarts* (Boston, 1846), pp. 250–251; Leo XII's *Ubi Primum* discussed in Tibawi, *American Interests in Syria*, p. 28. On Islam and vernacular languages, see Michael Cook, *The Koran: A Very Short Introduction* (Oxford, UK, 2000), pp. 26–27.

44. Greek, Syriac, Coptic, Latin, Ethiopic, Armenian, Gothic, Slavonic, Arabic, and, perhaps, Anglo-Saxon. See R. S. Sugirtharajah, ed., *The Bible in the Third World: Precolonial, Colonial, Postcolonial Encounters* (Cambridge, UK, 2001), p. 56; *Ninth Report of the American Bible Society* (New York, 1824), pp. 40–41.

and Bibles had been rare in colonial America. The first King James Bible printed in America, for example, was not produced until 1782. It was not until 1790 that Matthew Carey published the first Catholic Bible in America. It was Charles Thomson, secretary of Congress and originator of the eagle as the American national symbol, whose 1808 version was the first English translation of the Bible done in the United States. The monopolies held by the university presses at Oxford and Cambridge only partly account for the rarity of Bible printing. The appearance of the first American Bibles following national independence was prologue to the explosion of religious pamphlets and periodicals. It may also have been indicative of some reason that US nationality took hold in a way that it did not in Gran Colombia, in South America.[45]

America's establishment Protestants shared a broad consensus that print was a way to God, and reaching out to the masses was holy work. They saw contemporary technological advances, such as stereotype printing technology and steam-powered presses, as divine handiwork. "God will use THE PRESS," proclaimed the American Tract Society, "as an important auxiliary to missions, in their illumination and conversion." William Ellery Channing called the press "the mightiest engine ever set in motion by man." To fulfill its potential, wrote Channing, the press must produce "a freer intercourse, a more intimate connection" and a more "rapid communication of thoughts and feelings than was every known before. . . between different classes of society." In 1824, the ABCFM boasted that with their efforts in print media and the creation of thousands of local auxiliary societies, that they had created "a complete chain of communication" throughout the nation.[46] To a Vatican official, or Catholic missionary, such views about the power of the press and mass religious literacy were likely to seem naïve, if not heretical. Anglo-American Protestant missionaries held that mass printing technology possessed a unique power to foster bonds between different classes. It would, wrote Channing, start, "a freer intercourse, a more intimate connection, a more rapid communication of thoughts and feelings than was ever known before." Channing thought that mass religious media would fortify the all-important "moral and religious sentiments" of the national community. It would be these moral and

---

45. Reinhard Wittmann, "Was There a Reading Revolution at the End of the Eighteenth Century?" in Guglielmo Cavallo and Roger Chartier, eds., *A History of Reading in the West* (London, 1999), p. 291; J. H. Elliott, *Empires of the Atlantic World*, pp. 215–216.

46. Channing, pp. 261, 478; Tracy, *HABCFM*, p. 125.

religious sentiments, not the "outward power of government," that would determine the future of the young republic. Like most of the missions movement, Channing imbued contemporary mass religious literature with patriotic and Protestant hopes that could not be fully separated.[47]

Driven by these patriotic and religious passions to make a nation, the national evangelists created American mass media. Their pamphlets and periodicals were the first media conceived of and produced for the general American population. In quantitative terms, their output dwarfed earlier publishing ventures. Tom Paine's *Common Sense*, for example, the most influential and widely circulated English-language political pamphlet of the late eighteenth century, sold 500,000 copies in 1776. In contrast, from 1814 to 1824, the New England Tract Society alone published and distributed 4,217,500 pamphlets (whereas in 1800–1824, the London Tract Society published and distributed 61,500,000 pamphlets). In the first decade of its existence (1816–1826), the American Bible Society published and distributed 528,502 copies of the scriptures. The ABS fretted over reports that, by 1826, they had supplied only half of Indiana's 40,000 families with a copy of the scriptures. Such availability of the scriptures was unprecedented. The American Tract Society, with its hundreds of morality and civility tracts, was the pacesetter. In the first decade of its existence (1825–1835), the ATS printed a staggering 531,954,014 pages of 754 different pamphlets, distributing 480,990,418 of these printed pages. The numbers alone suggest an important role for these Protestant pamphlets in American political culture. In addition to the outpouring of pamphlets, the national evangelists published dozens of different periodicals for mass distribution. In terms of quality, secular publications may have won the day in the early republic, but in quantitative terms religious publications easily predominated. In 1823, *The Methodist Magazine* remarked that it was not "many years" ago that "a religious newspaper would have been a phenomenon... but now the groaning press throws them out in almost every direction." In 1824, the *Hopkinsian* counted 22 weekly religious newspapers. By 1828, they counted 73. Congregational, Presbyterian, and Unitarian efforts led the way. Again, the frontier and Western missions were favorite subjects. The description of frontier revivalism as a "'a torrent of infidelity'" appears frequently.[48] The Anglo-American Protestant faith in print could

---

47. Channing, pp. 261, 478.

48. On Paine's *Common Sense*, see Gordon Wood, *The American Revolution: A History*, p. 55; On the New England Tract Society figures, see *Proceedings of the First Ten Years of*

seem more peculiar abroad. In nineteenth-century Syria, for example, officials of the French and Ottoman Empires, and the Maronite Patriarch, referred to ABCFM missionaries as *"les Biblistes."* In Uganda, converts to Protestantism were known as *abasomi,* meaning "readers."[49]

The emphasis on literacy and print was consistent with the New England origins of the missions movement. The New England clerics and the Northeastern bourgeoisie also united in their intention to vanquish the influence of deism and the errors of the Enlightenment. Hopes for progress, for a moral society, for the opportunities God held out before them, depended on beating back what they saw as irreligion and the excesses of political democracy. The deists and philosophes were never more than a small group, but to appreciate how profoundly they set the tone of the era, one need only read the national evangelist literature. In *The Panpolist,* or *The Missionary Herald,* as well as in the annual reports, periodicals, and pamphlets of the national evangelist associations, Paine and Diderot and Voltaire and "false philosophy" often appear to stand astride the world. From their charter statements, the Anglo-American missionary organizations announced themselves as the real victors of a war, a war that in some senses they had already lost. Soon the world would see, they wrote, that the French Revolution was just an "outward" happening, "only events," a "surface-tide" on the sea of history. It was, they wrote, the Anglo-American missions movement that had expressed the historic depths of the moment and gave to the era its "true significance." Future generations, they wrote, would learn not the names of Paine or Danton or Robespierre, but of Jedediah Bushnell. Now an obscure figure, Bushnell, in 1799, had been sent by the Connecticut Missionary Society to western New York, making him the first domestic missionary in the United States.[50]

The counter-Enlightenment agenda was foundational. In its charter statement, the American Bible Society dismissed confidence in man's

---

the *American Tract Society* (Boston, 1824), p. 178, and for the London Tract Society figures, idem, p. 184; Frank Luther Mott, *A History of American Magazines, 1714–1850* (Cambridge, MA, 1966), pp. 369, 136, 132; David Paul Nord, "The Evangelical Origins of Mass Media in America, 1815–1835."

49. A. L. Tibawi, *American Interests in Syria, 1800–1901* (Oxford, UK, 1966), pp. 43, 45; R. S. Sugirtharajah, ed., *The Bible and the Third World,* p. 69.

50. Williams College, *Proceedings of the Missionary Jubilee Held at Williams College* (Boston, 1856), pp. 26–27; see, for example, *The Missionary Herald at Home and Abroad* (Boston, 1807), June, pp. 264–265 and *The Panoplist* (Boston, 1813), June, p. 281.

moral capacity as dangerous vanity. "The sublimest speculations of Philosophy are incapable of restraining his [man's] turbulent passions," they wrote. The whole of human history, they wrote, "serves but to demonstrate the feebleness of the light of nature, however improved by science." Without worship of God and recognition of the light of Jesus, man could expect, as they put it, ignorance, vice, and ruin. In one of its charter statements, the New England Tract Society warned that they lived in an age when "the mechanic, the manufacturer, the artist, and the philosopher" were all making great strides in "their peculiar art or science." It would be a "humiliating disgrace" if the "professed disciples of Jesus" did not with "vigor" also pursue "every [new] way of access for truth into the human heart." One issue of *The Panoplist* (in 1821 renamed *The Missionary Herald*, the premiere publication of the American Board of Commissioners for Foreign Missions) devoted its first 16 pages to analyzing the death, 30 years earlier, of David Hume, describing Hume as "one of the most flagitiously immoral men that ever lived." By labored overinterpretation, *The Panoplist* "proved" that the details of Hume's death betrayed the moral impoverishment of deism and irreligion. The moralizing account includes an attack on Adam Smith's description of his friend's passing. Samuel Finley, president of the College of New Jersey from 1761 to 1766, had alleged a dark bond between Smith and Hume to undermine Christianity, accusing Smith of masking the extent of his friend's depravity.[51]

The purported deathbed contrition of deists and philosophes was a subgenre of national evangelist literature. An issue of *The Panoplist* alleged that Diderot, on his deathbed, conspired with a faithful servant to bring a priest to deliver last rites. Refusing to allow the priest to enter, Diderot's irreligious friends foiled the philosopher's wish to die a Christian, according to *The Panoplist*. The pathetic death of Tom Paine, as told by *The Panoplist*, was "an argument of great weight in favor of Christianity." In his sickness, they reported, Paine, "repeatedly and constantly cried out 'O, Lord, help me! God, help me! Jesus Christ, help me!'" *The Panoplist* reported that Paine's "brethren in infidelity" discouraged Paine from his purported desire to see a minister. They descended on his deathbed, *The Panplolist* alleged, in order to "to strengthen him in his

---

51. *The Publications of the American Tract Society* (Boston, 1824), pp. 8–9; ABS, *Tenth Annual Report* (New York, 1826), p. 34; see, for example, *The Panoplist* (Boston, 1813) December 31, vol. IX, p. 34, where Voltaire's conspiracy to "destroy the Christian religion" is described;

rejection of the truth." Formulaic stories about the regrets of dying deists, the poor company they kept, and their immoral lives, appear and reappear in *The Panoplist* and *The Missionary Herald*. The annual reports of the major missionary societies published similar stories, and the American Tract society published *The Repentance and Happy Death of the Earl of Rochester, Universalism Exposed*, and other exposes on repentant libertines and deists. Indeed, in the literature of the American missions movement, Voltaire and Paine appear as colossal, indispensable figures. One wonders how many people heard of them, for the first time, in *The Missionary Herald* or *The Panoplist*.[52]

The missions movement conceded that the success that deists and philosophes had enjoyed with the pamphlet form encouraged emulation. "The splendid talents of Voltaire," wrote the New England Tract Society in 1814, "were never employed against Christianity with so much effect, as when they were devoted to the writing of small Tracts." Laying responsibility for the French Revolution and the Napoleonic Wars at the feet of the deist pamphleteers, the New England Tract Society blamed the scurrilous tracts of men they saw as blasphemers peddlers of false erudition. It was these "efforts of a few infidels," they wrote, that were responsible for "producing those terrible convulsions, which have since shaken the civilized world."[53] The American Tract Society described its publications as continuing the battle waged by the English writer Hannah More, a prominent figure in the British counter-Jacobin movement. More was a prolific writer of religious literature and, to the national evangelists, a powerful foil to the philosophes: "Mrs. Hannah More. . . has done more for the preservation of England, by her Cheap Repository Tracts, than did the celebrated Nelson, as a naval commander, by all his splendid achievements." Following in Hannah More's footsteps, the Americans dedicated themselves, through the dissemination of free religious tracts, "to counteract the delusive and irreligious spirit of the French revolution." As

---

The Panoplist (Boston, 1806) June, vol. I, assails Voltaire's skill as a reader; *The Panoplist* (Boston, 1818), vol. XIV, describes Voltaire and David Hume as the heroes of the "champions of infidelity," pp. 159–160. *The Panoplist* (Boston, 1809), June, vol. 1, includes the section on Hume and Adam Smith, also describing Hume as the "the head of those enemies of revelation who attempt to *reason*; as Voltaire stands without a rival among those who only *scoff*"; see pp. 241–257. Dozens of other examples are easily found.

52. For the Diderot anecdote, see *The Panoplist* (Boston, 1809) June, pp. 213–214. On Paine's death, see *The Panoplist* (Boston, 1810) June, vol. II, pp. 400–404.

53. *The Panoplist* (Boston, 1814) May, vol. X, p. 157.

the historian David Paul Nord has emphasized, their motives were not market-oriented, but religious and political.[54]

A contrast with their near-contemporaries in French nation-building reveals how the United States and France approached this inescapable problem, of religion and nationalism, from opposite directions. Revolutionary French nationalists had based their state educational system, one of the primary nation-building institutions, on the Church. Jean-Paul Rabaut, the architect of the French state education system, explained that the Church had mastered the heretofore unique authority to plant itself in the intimacies of life, and how to do so over the span of a human life. In 1791, standing before the National Convention in Paris, he had told members that the way to nationalize people was to use the means of the Church to deliver a different message: The revolutionaries must, he said, find a "means of transmitting. . . to all the French at once, the same uniform ideas." The Church knew how, Rabaut explained. "The secret was well known to the priests," he said, "They took hold of man at birth, grasped him again in childhood, adolescence and adulthood, when he married and had children, in his moments of grief and remorse, in the sanctum of his conscience. . . in sickness and in death." Calling on the National Convention to co-opt the methods of the Church, Rabuat asked them to "do in the name of truth and freedom" what the Church had done so "often did in the name of error and slavery?" Published in 1792, as *Project of National Education*, Rabaut's proposals became French state policy. Perhaps it took a Protestant such as Rabaut, who was a Calvinist minister as well as a Girondist, to imagine reclaiming the methods of Rome for revolution. Reading alone was not enough, Rabaut said, calling attention to the art and song and ritual of the Church. Nationalists, he said, must also learn from the Church's "catechisms, their processions. . . their ceremonies, sermons, hymns, missions, pilgrimages, patron saints, paintings." The goal was not to impose values or ideas from the outside, but by various means applied over the course of life, to build citizens from the inside out.[55]

---

54. On the model of Hannah More, see *Proceedings of the First Ten Years of the American Tract Society*, p. 60. On the religious literature of the early republic as the birth of American mass media, see David Paul Nord, *Faith in Reading: Religious Publishing and the Birth of Mass Media* (New York, 2007).

55. David A. Bell, *The Cult of the Nation in France: Inventing Nationalism, 1680–1800* (Cambridge, MA, 2003), Rabaut quoted on pp. 2–3, 216.

In order to make people French, particularly in the countryside, the French revolutionaries devised an ambitious educational system based on the methods of the Church and run by the secular state. On the other hand, in order to nationalize the peoples on the frontier, America's national evangelists self-consciously co-opted the pamphlet media of deistic French Enlightenment writers. Tocqueville captured part of this contrast when he noted, "Wherever at the head of some new undertaking you see the government in France, or a man of rank in England, in the United States you will be sure to find an association." Tocqueville, however, mistook popular religion in the early republic for a nationalist movement, and, in Perry Miller's words, never "comprehended the sociological import of these associations."[56] Of the many contemporary commentators on religion in the United States, English traveler Frederick Marryat came closest to understanding the role of the national evangelist associations. In his *Diary in America*, written after touring the United States in the 1830s, Marryat wrote, "In America religion severs the community," wrote Marryat, "but these societies are the bonds to which a certain degree reunite it." In fact, the national evangelist associations were trying to unite America, not reunite it. To the extent they did so, among frontier people, it was in part in opposition to their religious and political agenda.[57]

Though telling of a general political orientation, in the scope of national evangelist literature, abusing deists and philosophes was something of a sop for the New England clerics. Bourgeois control of the missions movement also brought important changes to the social philosophy from which the missions movement originated, as described by the Connecticut Wits. They had described the ideal society as a modestly prosperous New England township, with republican commitments, and dominated by an elite steeped in neoclassicism and Reformed Protestantism. Under bourgeois guidance, that missions movement turned to a more stark and capacious form of liberalism, one that emphasized economic growth and political rights. The change most telling of the bourgeois guidance of the missions movement was the new and distinctive approach to the problem of inequality. Frontier revivalism formed a large and diverse movement, but the early Methodists under Asbury, the followers of the mystic McNemar, and others, were of "the last shall be first, and the first last"

---

56. Miller, *Life of the Mind*, p. 48.

57. Marryat, *Diary in America*, vol. II, p. 165.

branch of Christianity. For them, inequality was an affront for which Christianity was the redress. For the Connecticut Wits and their brand of Protestant Federalism, inequality was an organic and inevitable feature of all societies, one that a godly community, led by righteous men, would manage and limit. In their New England tradition, a community allowing great gaps between its rich and its poor had lost its way.

The missions movement advanced a more complex response to inequality. Their literature accepted inequality, and without apparent limit, while conferring upon the subordinated or subjugated a kind of spiritual superiority. It was a kind of "the first shall be first, and the last remain last, but glowing" hybrid of liberalism and Protestantism. The splitting of religious and spiritual authority was a new and awkward project. It departed from the colonial New England past, as well as Anglican and Catholic traditions, which all seek, in different ways, a closer alignment between religious, spiritual, and political authority. It grew out of a combination of nationalism and liberalism. The nationalism of the bourgeoisie encouraged, in the missions literature, some kind of recognition for the laborers and slaves, servants and maids, of American society, a role short of admission to the political community. At the same time, their liberalism could neither countenance an endorsement of simple inferiority, as the Southern planters would do, nor encourage the more egalitarian or leveling possibilities of Christianity. The result led the missions movement, in their literature, to sanction various kinds of inequality, including slavery, for their own, nationalist reasons, well before Southern planters developed a systematic and self-conscious proslavery argument.[58]

In a large republic based on claims of the ability of common men to govern, the persistence and even growth of a gap between the poor and the rich in the early republic presented a more important problem than deism. The New England tradition observed some distinctions between civil and religious government, but it found religious, spiritual, and political authority in society's elite. The national evangelist literature engaged with social and political inequality by conferring on the subordinate and subjugated—maids, poor laborers, and slaves—a kind of spiritual superiority. *The Happy Negro*, for example, an American Tract Society pamphlet originally published in 1814, stands out for this kind of racism, a racism that differed from that of the planters. *The Happy Negro* tells of a

---

58. On the development of proslavery thought in the antebellum South, see Drew Gilpin Faust, *Southern Stories: Slaveholders in Peace and War* (Columbia, MO, 1992), p. 78.

conversation between "an English gentleman" and a middle-aged Negro slave. The perambulating gentleman encounters the slave as he is tilling the ground of a large New York plantation. Without hesitation, the traveler asks the slave if he would like to be free, if "his state of slavery was not disagreeable to him, and whether he would not gladly exchange it for his liberty." The slave does not give a direct answer but instead remarks on the poverty of his soul contrasted with the material comfort his master has provided. "'Massah,' he replies, 'I have a wife and children; my Massah takes care of them, and I have no care to provide any thing; I have a good Massah, who teach me to read; and I read good book, that makes me happy.'" In the context of the national evangelist movement, the slave's literacy, and the fact that he owned a Bible, were important details.[59]

The Bible, the slave explains, brings him happiness and comfort. He calls it "God's own book." The skeptical gentleman asks the slave if he can understand as well as read the Bible, and the slave's answer, providing a "full account" of his "convictions of sin," compels further questions. Following a conversation about reading and theology and the nature of conversion, in which the slave tells of his "very bad heart," his "vile and naughty" and "wicked" heart, he describes how he read and reread the Bible until he "felt a pain in my heart." Suspicious that the slave is reciting missionary propaganda, the gentleman asks how he learned to talk this way. The slave answers that "Christ bade me come into him." Properly speaking, no missionary, school, or book converts anyone; conversion is always the work of God. The slave's apparent grasp of this important detail impresses the gentleman, who marvels "what great things God had done." The emphases on original sin, literacy and reading the Bible, and conversion by Christ are all consistent with the broad traditions of Protestant evangelicalism that shaped the missions movement.[60]

The real subject of *The Happy Negro* is not "the happy Negro," but the gentleman traveler, or more precisely, the unusual transaction between the gentleman traveler and the slave. *The Happy Negro* tells the story of how the slave's happiness and spirituality facilitate the experience of grace for the gentleman. The slave's spirituality begins to work its power on the gentleman when the latter is drawn in by the slave's "artless" answers. Moved, the gentleman pushes the conversation to matters of faith: the merit of works, the power of grace,

---

59. New England Tract Society, *The Happy Negro* (Andover, MA, 1815), p. 1.

60. Ibid.

justifications of sinners. For hours, according to the pamphlet, the two converse on theology and religion, a conversation in which the gentleman finds "tenderness and expression far beyond the reaches of art." It brings him "joyful tears" and recognition of his own saving grace. Representing a slave as happy and possessing a spirituality that raises the white gentleman to a higher religious consciousness signaled a new combination of inequality and superiority. The "happy Negro" is not only happy, but enslaved and spiritually powerful. He shows a "tenderness" and an authenticity that provides a "richness of grace," a spiritual experience, for the gentleman. The gentleman, on the other hand, is less spiritual than aesthetic. His account is artful, an aestheticizing experience enabled by the artlessness of the slave, whom he describes as "beyond the reaches of art."[61]

The gentleman also describes the experience of conversing with the slave as a "communion of the saints," a phrase that an early modern Puritan would recognize as the earthly approximation of salvation. In *The Happy Negro*, however, instead of a righteous church congregation, it is the strong impression that the slave's authenticity makes on the refined gentleman that brings forth the communion of saints: "We looked upon each other," the gentleman says, "and talked with that inexpressible glow of Christian affection, that made me more than ever believe, what I have often too thoughtlessly professed to believe, *the communion of saints.*" To the gentleman's eye, the experience of grace is reciprocal: "I shall never forget, how that poor excellent creature seemed to hang upon my lips, and to eat my very words." The gentleman apprehends the slave not in scriptural terms but art historical: "His eager, delighted, animated air and manner, would have been a masterpiece for a Reynolds."[62] The pamphlet ends with an affirmation that the world is just. "Neither the colour of his body, nor the condition of his present life," states *The Happy Negro*, "could prevent him from being my dear brother in our dear Saviour." Soon they would have "another joyful meeting in our Father's house, where we should live together, and love one another, for eternity." The slave concurs: " 'Amen, Amen, my dear Massah; God bless you, and poor me too forever and ever.' " A coda to pamphlet asks readers to "subdue animosities" and remember that they are all *"brethren."* The Christian

---

61. Ibid., p. 2.

62. Ibid., pp. 2–3. Italics in original.

consanguinity brings assurances of a happy reunion in the afterlife, not emancipation.[63]

The same unequal exchange of social position for spiritual authority occurs in *The Pious Laborer*, another widely distributed ATS tract. *The Pious Laborer* begins with a "gentleman of very considerable fortune" on a "solitary walk through part of his grounds." The gentleman's walk brings him to "a mean hut, where a poor man lived, with a numerous family, who earned their bread by daily labour." Hearing loud voices coming from within the poor laborer's home, the gentleman stops to eavesdrop.[64] To his astonishment, he hears the family praying, "giving thanks, with great affection, to God." The father is leading the family in thankful prayer to God "for the goodness of [their] providence" for "supplying them with what was necessary. . . in the present life." The contrast between his good fortune and irreligion, and the poor laborer's poverty and piety, fills the gentleman with "astonishment and confusion." Marveling that "this poor man" who knows only "the meanest fare" and that "purchased by severe labour" gives thanks to God, while he enjoys "ease and honour" while maintaining a cavalier indifference to the author of the universe, compels him to God. He resolves to change his life, shaping it to give "acknowledgement to my Maker and Presever!" A coda summarizes *The Pious Laborer*: "It pleased God, that this providential occurrence proved the means of bringing him to a real and lasting sense of religion." *The Pious Laborer* told the same story as *The Happy Negro*, again featuring a wandering gentleman whose life of ease and refinement had alienated him from simple religious truth.[65]

The Negro Servant, another New England Tract Society publication, represented American slavery as God's way of bringing Africans to salvation. *The Negro Servant* features a minister interviewing a slave named William, who attributes his enslavement to God. God and the slave-traders, William explains, brought him from Africa, the "land of darkness," to the West Indies, the "land of providence," and then to salvation in America, the "land of light." In the following excerpt, the minister questions William about the state of his soul:

---

63. Ibid., pp. 3–4.

64. New England Tract Society, *The Pious Laborer* (Andover, MA, n.d.), p. 6.

65. Ibid., p. 7.

"What was your state by nature?"

"Me wicked sinner, me know nothing but sin, me do nothing but sin, my
soul more black than my body."

"Has any change taken place in you since then?"

"Me hope so, Massa, but me sometimes afraid no."

"If you are changed, who changed you?"

"God the good Father; Jesus his dear Son; and God the Holy Spirit."

"How was the change brought about in you?"

"God make me a slave, when me was a little boy."

"How William, would you say, God made you a slave?"

"No, Massa, no: me mean God let me be made a slave by white men, to
do me good."

"How to do you good?"

"He take me from the land of darkness, and bring me to land of light."

"Which do you call the land of light; the West India islands?"

"No, Massa, they be the land of providence, but America be the land of
light to me; for there me first heard good minister preach. And now
this place, where I am now, is the land of more light: for here you teach
me more and more how good Jesus is to sinners."

". . . Who sent the good minister in America to awaken your soul by his
preaching?"

"God, very certainly."[66]

Christian apologism for slavery was not new. Though the acute
Christianity of the abolitionist movement can lead to the misapprehension that American religion opposed slavery, Frederick Douglass spoke
the truth when he observed that American churches stood as a "bulwark
of American slavery." In brief, though the abolitionists were Christians,
American Christians were not abolitionists. *The Negro Servant* and *The
Happy Negro* tracts deepen Douglass's point, showing that the missions
movement devised a unique pro-slavery argument, for their own, nationalist reasons, at least a decade before Southern writers began to assemble
a systematic pro-slavery case.[67]

The Connecticut Wits gave the beginnings of the missions movement in the anti-slavery soil of New England Federalism, but carrying

---

66. New England Tract Society, *The Negro Servant* (Andover, MA, 1815), p. 37.

67. On the abolitionists, see James B. Stewart, *Holy Warriors: The Abolitionists and
American Slavery* (New York, 1996); Douglass quote in William McFeely, *Frederick*

the principle into large nation-building organizations would have meant undermining one of the foundations of American national power and prosperity. For most supporters of the missions movement—even, for example, John Jay and other sincere anti-slavery advocates—national union and strength were simply more important. As a result, the voice of the missions movement on the issue of slavery is neither abolitionist nor anti-slavery, but a more complex aestheticization of the suffering of the subordinate or subjugated. In fact, both *The Happy Negro* and *The Negro Servant* conclude with the conversion of white people. The minister's interrogation of the slave William had occurred in the presence of several onlookers, who listened with "affectionate anxiety to all that passed." At the end of the dialogue between the minister and William, one of listeners interjects, "'I see, Sir, that though some men are white, and some are black, true Christianity is all of one colour. My own heart has gone with this good man every word he has spoken.'" The watchful audience of white Christians provides a chorus: "'And so has mine,' gently re-echoed from every part of the room." The men improvise a hymn, honoring the slave's role in proving Christ's offer of salvation:

> *See, a stranger comes to view;*
> *Though he's black, he's comely too;*
> *Comes to join the choirs above,*
> *Singing of redeeming love.*
>
> *Welcome, Negro, welcome here,*
> *Banish doubt and banish fear,*
> *You, who Christ's salvation prove,*
> *Praise and bless redeeming love.*[68]

In the context of the settlement of the Western Hemisphere, the experience of slaves as forced migrants was unique, and nineteenth-century American slavery was an exceptional institution. For these reasons, the kind of asymmetrical exchange, exemplified by *The Happy Negro* and *The*

Douglass (New York, 1991), p. 81. On the Tappan brothers' acrimonious falling out with the American Tract Society over its pro-slavery nationalism, see Bertram Wyatt-Brown, *Lewis Tappan and the Evangelical War Against Slavery*, pp. 114, 314–316; see also Alan Gallay, "Planters and Slaves in the Great Awakening," in John B. Boles, ed., *Masters and Slaves in the House of the Lord: Race and Religion in the American South* (Lexington, KY, 1988).

68. *The Negro Servant*, p. 38.

Negro Servant, contributed in distinctive ways to the growing color prejudice in the United States.

In form, however, national evangelist literature had the same response to
the general problem of inequality. *The Dairyman's Daughter*, another widely
distributed ATS tract, announced that though it was "happy" when grace
coincided with "the allurements of luxury. . . in general if we want to see religion in its purest character, we must look for it among the poor of this world,
who are rich in faith." According to *The Dairyman's Daughter*, the "most
striking demonstrations of the wisdom, power, and goodness of God" were
to be found "in the poor man's cottage, the palace of God." Christianity can
offer a strong affirmation of the dignity of the downtrodden, but this focus
on the spiritual authority of slaves, servants, laborers, the afflicted, and their
relationships with the elite departed from Puritan and Anglican, as well as
Catholic, tradition, which all tried, in different ways, to combine religious
and spiritual authority and realize them in worldly institutions. Second, the
consistent irreligion of the rich and the piety of the poor described in the
national evangelist literature might, just as logically, lead one to forswear
religion. National evangelist literature makes the opposite case. This convention of the literature, in which the elite envies and resolves to emulate the
poor and marginal member of his community, is what makes the national
evangelist literature a new kind of conservative genre.[69]

The ATS published hundreds of titles. More than a few, *To a Person Engaged
in a Lawsuit*, for example, were dedicated to the worldliest of concerns. Tom
Paine's old friend Benjamin Rush contributed *Defence of the Use of Bible in
Schools*. Other ATS tracts address conventionally religious matters. *The Bible
of Divine Origin* and *Importance of Salvation* and *More Than One Hundred
Incontrovertible Arguments for the Divinity of Christ* are just a few examples.
It is fair to say, however, that the tracts displayed a preoccupation with the
role of individuals from the subordinate classes, or the weak and afflicted, in
the problem of grace. Among elite American Christians, with the nation as
the new sacred political community, the role of those excluded from, or marginal to, the national political community, the problem of grace caused real
consternation. In many ATS tracts—including *The Poor Villager; Parley the
Porter; Poor Sarah, the Indian Woman; Blind Ellen; The African Servant; The
Happy Waterman; The Cottager's Wife; The Praying Negro; Poor Joseph*; as well
as others—it is possible to see bourgeois and middling American Protestants

---

69. Leigh Richmond, *The Dairyman's Daughter* (Andover, MA, 1819), p. 1; American Bible
Society, *Ninth Annual Report* (New York, 1825), pp. 21–22.

struggling with this problem. Their solution was to represent laborers, servants, maids, poor farm women, and slaves with a heightened spirituality and piety that reacquaint the refined with simple religious truths, bringing the enfranchised closer to Christ. This strange accommodation was not a self-conscious program. It is important, however, because, along with the control by the Northeastern merchant classes, it represents in short form a bourgeois and liberal ethos for which contemporaries came to resent the missions movement. It also contributed to the way in which Protestantism lent itself to inequality, an accommodation that struck Tocqueville. Coming from Catholic France, Tocqueville found that social inequality made itself more easily at home in Protestant America. "If Catholicism predisposes the faithful to obedience," he wrote, "it certainly does not prepare them for inequality; but the contrary may be said of Protestantism, which generally tends to make men independent, more than to render them equal."[70]

Daniel Smith, whose 1814 *Missionary Tour through that part of the United States which lies West of the Allegheny Mountains* helped consolidate the core organizations of the American missions movement, distributed copies of *The Negro Servant* during an 1816 trip to Natchez, Mississippi. Smith reported that a Natchez, Mississippi, slave had made it "[h]is business every Sabbath day to read" *The Negro Servant* "to wicked Negroes." Another slave in Natchez called the same tract a "gift of heaven," assuring the missionaries that he carried the pamphlet everywhere he went "in his bosom" pocket. Calling the tracts "winged messengers of salvation," Smith wrote that he distributed "many of the Tracts. . . with my own hands; but by far the greater part, I sent for distribution. . . in the southern and western states." Over the course of his travels from 1814 to 1816, Smith distributed 23,000 pamphlets. By the standards of either the influential pamphlets of the Revolutionary War or the contemporary literary marketplace, it was a huge number. In the waves of national evangelist literature, it was a trickle. Thanking New England Tract Society officials for their parcels of pamphlets, a Mississippi minister wrote, in 1816, "Our worthy New England friends are doing a great work." The New England missionaries thought so, too.[71] The few surviving responses from slaves or colored people to the tracts show more ambiguity than was apparent to the missionaries. One such "endorsement" came from a "colored man"

---

70. Tocqueville, *Democracy in America*, vol. 1, trans. Henry Reeve, p. 212.

71. October 11, 1816, letter from Daniel Smith reprinted in *Proceedings of the First Ten Years of the American Tract Society* (Boston, 1824), pp. 44–46.

in an Ohio village. A local minister wrote to the American Tract Society, relaying, in dialect, what he took as an endorsement of the ATS tracts:

> O, massa, it do me soul good, I neber knew before why da call 'em *Tracks*. But when I read dat little book, it *track* me dis way and it *track* me dat way; it *track* me all day, and it *track* me all night when I go out in da barn, it *track* me dare; when I go out in da woods, it *track* me dare; when I come in de house, it *track* me dare; it *track* me ebdry where I go. Den I know why da call 'em *Tracks*.

Missionaries are not ironists, and the ATS reprinted the colored man's at best ambiguous words as an endorsement of the potency of their publications.[72]

Perhaps the most familiar product of the national evangelist literary movement is Noah Webster's *Dictionary*. Long before the collapse of the Federalist Party, at which point Webster turned to education, founding Amherst College, he had undertaken, at Timothy Dwight's suggestion, what he called the "vast labor" of his dictionary. In 1828, he released the first complete dictionary of American English. Hundreds, perhaps thousands, of Webster's definitions, either through the definitions themselves or the quotes he chose to illustrate them, celebrate quiet, Christian obedience and deference to authority. In his dictionary entry for "reason," for example, Webster offered the illustrative sentence: "God brings good out of evil, and therefore it were but *reason* we should trust God to govern his own world." To illustrate the verb form of *love*, which Webster defined as "a sense to be pleased with," he wrote: "The Christian *loves* his Bible. . . if our hearts are right, we *love* God above all things." To illustrate the need for an American dictionary, Webster called attention to the "new sense" that Americans had given to the word "association." The word now meant, he wrote, groups of ministers organizing into political entities. In the eighteenth century, organized ministers were called by sectarian names: a synod, a congregation, or a presbytery, for example. There was no at-hand word for ministers allied in inter-sectarian organizations, no word to properly denote the national evangelist organizations, and so Americans began to call the organized ministers an "association."[73]

---

72. ATS, *Fifth Annual Report* (New York, 1830), p. 62. Italics in original.

73. Noah Webster, "Introduction" to *A Compendious Dictionary of the English Language*, excerpted in Webster, *On Being American*, ed. Babbidge (New York, 1967), p. 133, originally

In historical perspective, the national evangelist movement abounds with newness. The bourgeoisie was new, and so was its alliance with a New England–trained clergy. Together, they invented new organizations and new print campaigns that described a new way to salvation—through the nation. They embraced capitalism and nationalism in ways that transformed Protestantism. Yet, like the American revolutionaries, they saw themselves in some ways as conservatives, emphasizing a view that their movement was a restoration. Time and again, they invoked as their goal the restoration of an imagined past Christian unity, one that they in particular associated with the history of early Christianity. The 1832 assessment of the American Home Missionary Society was typical: "Never. . . since the days of the Apostles, has the cause of salvation, in any country, made so great an advancement, in so short a period." In fact, though they did not know it, America's elite and middling Protestants were far more unified than had been the early Christians.[74]

The force of national evangelists' religious passions and worldly interests came to bear on the American frontier. The Domestic and Foreign Missionary Society, an Episcopal body, reminded Americans that frontier settlers were "our fellow members of the same communion." Patriots were obligated to bring to them the "sound of the Gospel." The missionaries' strong association of Christianity with liberalism and nationalism led them to see the West as devoid of religion. They liked to invoke the Twenty-third Psalm, referring to the frontier as "the valley of the shadow of death." The ATS warned that only if Christianity came to the frontier could "free institutions and privileges" be sustained. One need only look to the "convulsed. . . civil revolutions" afflicting South America, they wrote, where the "confiscation of property" was rampant, to see the "instructive and dear-bought lesson" that Protestantism and civilization were partners. The Prussian traveler Francis Grund thought that in sum the national evangelist societies might be spending more money than the Church of England.

published in 1806; Richard M. Rollins, "Words as Social Control: "Noah Webster and the Creation of the American Dictionary," *American Quarterly*, vol. 28, no. 4 (Autumn 1976), pp. 427–428, 430; V. P. Bynack, "Noah Webster's Linguistic Thought and the Idea of an American National Culture," *Journal of the History of Ideas*, vol. 45, no. 1 (January–March 1984), pp. 99–114; Noah Webster, *A Compendious Dictionary of the English Language* (New Haven, CT, 1806), pp. 81, 270.

74. American Home Missionary Society, *The Sixth Report of the American Home Missionary Society* (New York, 1832), p. 2. On the diversity of early Christianity, see Elaine Pagels, *The Gnostic Gospels* (New York, 1989).

"The actual stock in any one of those firms," he wrote, "is, of course, less than the immense capital of the Church of England; but the aggregate amount of business transacted by them jointly, may, nevertheless be greater in the United States."[75]

For the national evangelists, the course of future happiness, greatness, and—the essentially religious quality that distinguished national evangelism from simple nationalism—salvation lay in the advance of liberal political democracy over the continent. In 1832, the American Home Missionary Society proclaimed that they had "been chosen of God, as the instrument of salvation to many souls."[76] In *Motives for Increased Exertion: Much Land Remains to be Possessed,* an ATS report, the organization reminded members that it was their "duty to convey. . . the way of salvation" to those "who inhabit the moral wastes of our country." Their work, they wrote, would save frontier settlers' "souls from death" while adding "new stars in our Savior's crown of glory." The "growing importance" of the Mississippi Valley, predicted the ATS, assured that it would "within twenty years" be home to "the majority of our whole population." Their tracts, what they called *"the instrumentality of these publications,"* performed holy work, as God had filled them with *"the special influences of the Holy Spirit."* God had made them *"evident means of salvation to multitudes."* In 1828, the ATS reported that they distributed 15,216,000 pages of tracts, and that they had brought the cost down to one cent for almost 12 pages of tract. The next year, the ATS sent 24,099,800 pages of tracts "into the country West and South of the Alleghenies," aimed at frontier settlers.[77] In the first decade of their existence, the American Tract Society produced a staggering 531,954,014 pages of 754 different tracts, circulating 480,990,418 of these printed pages. For 1830, in a country of under 13 million people (12,866,000), 480 million pages amounted to 37.5 pages of pamphlet for every man, woman, and child in the United States.[78]

---

75. Grund, *The Americans*, p. 45.

76. American Home Missionary Society, *The Sixth Report of the American Home Missionary Society* (New York, 1832), p. 2.

77. ATS, *Third Annual Report*, pp. 20–27; American Tract Society, *Fourth Annual Report*, (New York, 1829), pp. 8–10, 16–21, 40; American Tract Society, *Fifth Annual Report* (New York, 1830), pp. 7, 37–39; American Tract Society, *Eighth Annual Report* (New York, 1833), p. 40.

78. Figures compiled from American Tract Society, *Tenth Annual Report* (New York, 1835), p. 2.

Frontier revivalists lacked the means to produce such quantities of literature, and they also lacked the consciousness that would express itself in terms of statistical forecasts of national population. In their religion, the nation was not a factor in the mechanics of salvation. Upon founding their Book Concern in 1802, the Methodists stated simply that "our principal design, in this business, is to promote the Spiritual interest of our fellow creatures." They hoped, they said, that they could thereby help in making people "wiser and better. . . in the love of God."[79] The national evangelists pioneered what Benedict Anderson called "print capital," and they did so from a privileged position, as a kind of auxiliary state. The Chief Justice of the State of New York, for example, presided over the official launch of the American Bible Society, which took place at New York's City Hall. The mayor of the City of New York, then the governors of the New York hospital, and finally the New York Historical Society provided free meeting accommodations for the American Bible Society. With their leadership drawn from the country's political and economic elite, they did not have to succeed in a competitive marketplace. New York printers, eager to win the favor of powerful business and political leaders, donated their services to print, free of charge, "any communications which the Board may deem necessary to make to the public."[80] A report prepared for the ATS Board of Managers captured the special place in American society that the missionary societies occupied, combining advantages of private corporations with privileges of the government. Recommending that the ATS utilize its special advantages, the report urged the managers to publish even more: "Even if private capitalists should furnish the books for the market, it would be at such *prices* as the poor can ill afford to pay." You, the writer

79. Methodist Church, *Minutes Taken at the Several Annual Conferences of the Methodist Episcopal Church of America* (Philadelphia, 1802), p. 23.

80. On the ACS meeting in the US House of Representatives, see American Colonization Society, *Sixteenth Annual Report of the American Colonization Society* (Washington, DC, 1833), p. iii. On the public launch of the ABS at City Hall, see Foster, *An Errand of Mercy*, p. 115. On the state and the business classes' donations of free accommodations and printing, see ABS, *The First Annual Report of the Board of Managers of the American Bible Society* (New York, 1817), p. 19, and Dwight, *Centennial History*, pp. 33–34. Touring America in the early 1830s, the Prussian traveler Francis J. Grund observed the vital support that the American Tract Society enjoyed from political leaders. "Americans," he concluded, "are capable of a strong religious excitement," he noted. They consider "morality. . . a national cause; and. . . their political leaders, convinced of the importance of moral and religious institutions, are willing to aid in securing and promoting their influence." See Francis J. Grund, *The Americans in Their Moral, Social, and Political Relations* (New York, 1968), p. 189. Originally published in 1837.

told the managers of the ATS, have "the means of doing the work cheaply. You also have a reputation for economy and efficiency."[81]

The frontier revivalists paid their own way. The Methodists complained that government support of the national evangelists' print campaigns made it impossible to compete. In 1832, reflecting on the four years since its previous meeting, the Methodist General Conference reported that "the American Bible, Sunday School, and Tract Societies" were "patronized and aided by the public munificence," allowing them "to supply the demand for their respective publications almost at cost." It "was soon found," the Methodists noted, "that we could not compete with them in the market." Even modest printing jobs were often beyond the means of the upstarts. The fact that Joseph Smith's follower Martin Harris was willing to mortgage his farm to pay the costs of printing of *Book of Mormon* was one of the exceptional aspects of Mormon beginnings that helped it, among the many new religious ventures in the early republic, gain traction. Trying to obtain their own means of publishing, the Shakers sent Richard McNemar to Cincinnati to negotiate for the purchase of a printing press, but he failed to find a satisfactory price.[82]

To many Christians from the Northeastern elite, the improbable patriot triumph in the Revolution had, it seemed, brought them to the precipice of possibilities of which Protestants had dreamt since the Reformation. A prevalent, post-revolutionary feeling was one of dizzying opportunity, as well as responsibility. All that was wanting, it seemed, was to collect the ideas reborn in the Reformation, which men had been refining for three hundred years, and, in the words of Orestes Brownson, to "mold them into one harmonious, complete, and living system." To make that system "the principle and law of the new moral and religious organization" was a project worthy of the sons of the founding fathers, meriting comparison with the original evangelists. To this end, bourgeois Northeastern Protestants embarked on what the American Tract Society called a "great plan of National Evangelical Union."[83]

---

81. American Bible Society, *Third Annual Report* (New York, 1819), n.p; Tracy, *HABCFM*, p. 182; Rev. Plumer's report reprinted in American Tract Society, *Eleventh Annual Report* (New York, 1836), quotes from pp. 43, 42.

82. Nathan Bangs, D.D., *A History of the Methodist Episcopal Church* (New York, 1839), vol. IV, ch. 10; Marvin S. Hill, "The Rise of Mormonism in the Burned Over District: Another View," *New York History* vol. 61 (October 1980), pp. 411–430.

83. Clifford S. Griffin, *Their Brothers' Keepers: Moral Stewardship in the United States, 1800–1865* (New Brunswick, NJ, 1960); Charles I. Foster, *An Errand of Mercy: The Evangelical*

"Union" was the key word. Historians talk of "the nation" or "the republic," but the great contemporary term was "union." More than the flag, more than the national anthem, by the late 1820s, "union" stood as the high object of general loyalty. The connotative meanings are suggestive of the spiritual role that the nation played in their lives. "Union" represented an ideal of collectivity, an antidote to the social and geographic mobility, and libertarian individualism, which characterized Northern capitalism. Orestes Brownson thought the leaders of the missions movement were "sick at heart with what they had," and saw them as "demanding in their interior souls a religious institution of some sort." All living religions offer a combination of mystical, intellectual, and institutional elements. The national evangelists built their new missionary and moral improvement institutions to evangelize a new way to salvation, through the nation. In their vital drive and aptitude to organize and evangelize, if not in their ideal community or theology, they were at least the equals of the early Christians who served as their role models. Their plans to Christianize and civilize the frontier brought mixed results. They wanted to be role models to the frontier settlers, to move the inhabitants of the frontier to emulate bourgeois social mores. To members of the aspiring provincial middle class, membership in the auxiliary Bible and missionary societies was useful and appealing, an active association with members of the Northeastern elite. Many frontier revivalists, however, found the missionary movement an affront and the missionaries imperious, and un-Christian, agents of Yankee capitalism. By making enemies, as much as emulators, the national evangelists helped draw frontier settlers into a fight, one that found an outlet in national politics.[84]

United Front, 1790–1837 (Chapel Hill, NC, 1960); see also reviews by Frank Thistlethwaite, *Mississippi Valley Historical Review*, vol. 47 (March 1961), pp. 687–689, and Sidney E. Mead, *William and Mary Quarterly*, vol. 18 (July 1961), pp. 439–442.

84. On the "great plan of National Evangelical Union," see ATS, *A Brief History of the American Tract Society* (Boston, 1847), p. 46. On the importance of "union," see Richard P. McCormick, "The Jacksonian Strategy," *Journal of the Early Republic*, vol. 10 (Spring 1990), p. 5. Characterization of the spiritual motives of national evangelism taken largely from Orestes Brownson. On Brownson, see Oliver Wendell Holmes, "The Pulpit and the Pew," p. 420, and Brownson's autobiography, *The Convert; or, Leaves from My Experiences*, originally published in 1857, excerpted in Perry Miller, ed., *The American Transcendentalists*, quotes from pp. 41–42. On the necessity of any "living" religion offering a combination of mystical, intellectual, and institutional elements, see Friederich von Hügel, *The Mystical Element of Religion* (London, 1923). On the early Christians' aptitude for organizing, see Keith Hopkins, *A World Full of Gods: The Strange Triumph of Christianity* (New York, 2001).

7

A *Monster and the Wandering Savage*

THE RESOLUTION OF FRONTIER REVIVALISM AND
NATIONAL EVANGELISM

ANDREW JACKSON REPRESENTED important features of both the nationalist missionary movement and frontier revivalism. Jackson's championing of independent producers, as well as his rustic manners and spare formal education, made him a distinctly frontier figure, but he also possessed a predatory nationalist conviction. At least from the 1820s, tensions inherent in the development of American capitalism and the democratization of American politics were evident in the competition between the missionary movement and frontier revivalism. A spirited critique of Northeastern capitalism, for example, resembling in both spirit and letter the opposition to the Second Bank of the United States, came from frontier ministers, and was directed against the missionary movement. Daniel Parker, John Taylor, and other rural lay ministers spoke of the virtues of labor, equality, and local autonomy, and brought these ideals to bear in a pair of 1820 tracts denouncing the missions as a corrupt class interest project of the Eastern elite. Their attack in some ways paralleled the contest between Democrats and Whigs for the mantle of American republicanism, but it derived from their Protestantism, and social experience, not from republican political ideology. Jackson's republican nationalism, however, gave frontier revivalists a new grammar, at once an outlet for their grievances and ambitions and an inlet to nationalist politics. In the political landscape of the early republic, Jackson's nationalism and anti-elitism combined for an advantageous profile.[1]

---

1. Harry L Watson, *Liberty and Power: The Politics of Jacksonian America* (New York, 1990), esp. ch. 3; John William Ward, *Andrew Jackson: Symbol for an Age* (New York, 1955), chs. 7–8.

To understand how Andrew Jackson benefited from this contest within Protestantism, it is necessary to grasp the political liabilities of national evangelism. A Mississippi Baptist clarified the political landscape, at least as it appeared to many in rural America, when he alleged: "them missionary men had a bank and Elder Buck was president of it." Similarly, following a mid-1820s missionary tour of Mississippi, a rumor spread that missionary societies were a means of "accumulating a fortune." In contrast, for the national evangelists, contact with frontier society confirmed the threat that it posed to American prospects. After an 1824 tour of Tennessee, Jeremiah Evarts, the secretary of the American Board of Commissioners for Foreign Missions, wrote that Tennessseans exhibit "want of enterprise" and "seldom associate or confer together for any common purpose." Evarts observed "habits of living alone" so deep that "it seems almost impossible to impart to them the. . . principles of social conduct." Without a professionalized ministry, he observed, a ministry that received a regular salary for "valuable services," the prospects of the rural South seemed dim. Not surprisingly, frontier revivalists, and many other rural Protestants, often found these views offensive. They also tended to see the missionaries as agents of a class interest project. Rural Delaware Baptists, for example, voiced a common complaint: missions were not sanctioned in the scriptures, and the "brood of benevolent institutions so called" wrongly united "the church and the world together." The rural Delaware Baptists who, in 1836, refused to admit to fellowship members of missionary groups, which they called "the new-fangled systems of the day," were not unique. One of their lay ministers, from Cow Marsh, Delaware, wrote a tract against the "learned gentry of the day," whom, he alleged, "swarm out of the theological institutions like locusts and are ready to devour the land." In an 1827 letter to the *Holston Messenger*, a Tennessee Methodist characterized the missionaries as "pompous sons of Levi" who live like "fine gentleman. . . on the very fat of the land," then go "eastwardly," where they lie about frontier religion.[2]

The political and economic power of the Southern planters was an obstacle to the nationalization of the frontier in the Yankee model. The

2. Brownlow, *The Baptist Church in the Lower Mississippi Valley*, pp. 73–75; Evarts quoted in Wyatt-Brown, "The Antimission Movement," pp. 518–519; Richard Briscoe Cook, *The Early and Later Delaware Baptists* (Philadelphia, 1880), pp. 92–93; Bertram Wyatt-Brown, *The Shaping of Southern Culture: Honor, Grace, and War, 1760s–1880s* (Chapel Hill, NC, 2001), p. 124.

diversity of many immigrants and migrants to the frontier, their lack of affinity with the New England way, was another. The Yankees themselves, their ability to alienate the people whom they meant to win over, also played a role, engendering among many not emulation but opposition. Despite the achievements of the missions movement, it remained in notable ways a regional and class movement of elite Northeastern Reformed Protestants. The missionaries' scrutiny of nearly every aspect of the lives of settlers and Native Americans, for example, often led to friction. The view that manners lay at the root of society and government, and that manners were inseparable from religion, enjoyed a long history in Anglo-American political thought. In *Leviathan*, Thomas Hobbes, with successive chapters "Of the Difference of Manners" and "Of Religion," explained the link. The problem of men's manners, argued Hobbes, inevitably involved matters of causation, and the investigation of causes either led to monotheism or surrendered en route to sundry superstitions. By "manners," however, Hobbes distinguished between what he called mere "Decency of behaviour; as how one man should salute one another, or how a man should wash his mouth, or pick his teeth before company." Such minor details of comportment he dismissed as "Small Morals." By manners, Hobbes meant "those qualities of man-kind that concern their living together in Peace, and Unity." In a similar spirit, Tocqueville, for example, claimed that manners (*moeurs*), which he called the "sum of the moral and intellectual dispositions of men in society," were the most important force behind the American experiment. Others, however, brought a less capacious apprehension of manners to bear on evaluating the American experiment.[3]

For the Puritans, vigilant attention to the outward signs of grace or degeneration had required scrutiny of one's community and one's self. One scholar has referred to sixteenth- and seventeenth-century Puritans' constant self-disciplining as "holy violence under compression." The national evangelists brought a similar intensity to the practice of correction, but

---

3. Robert F. Berkhofer, *Salvation and the Savage: An Analysis of Protestant Missions and American Indian Response, 1787–1862* (New York, 1972) p. 15. On the Puritans' tendency to bring "vitality and drive into every area. . . whether they were subduing a continent, overthrowing a monarchy, or managing a business," see Roland Bainton's critique of Max Weber's "Protestant ethic" thesis, Bainton, *The Reformation of the Sixteenth Century* (Boston, 1952), p. 255. On the Puritan character, see Alan Simpson, *Puritanism in Old and New England* (Chicago, 1955), pp. 5–6. On the influence of a few New England Federalists on some of Tocqueville's views, see Leo Damrosch, *Tocqueville's Discovery of America* (New York, 2010), esp. chs. 5 and 7.

in contrast to the Puritans, they corrected other people. By the beginning of the nineteenth century, correcting the manners of faraway strangers appeared less like cold-eyed Puritan self-examination than a matter of imposing bourgeois respectability.[4]

The experimental quality of the United States, the newness of modern nationalism, the urgency that many Northeastern missionaries felt to seize the historical moment, all contributed, in the early republic, to, for many, a loss of distinction between manners and "small morals." In her *Domestic Manners of the Americans* (1832), Frances Trollope drew one logical conclusion, observing that the United States was "a continent of. . . distinct nations." Trollope's book, particularly her questioning of American nationality and making fun of American manners, amused some British readers.[5] Trollope's book also passed judgments on a problem that worried members of the American literary class. In his *Letters on Clerical Manners and Habits* (1827), Samuel Miller, a professor at the Princeton Theological Seminary, advised seminary students that small matters of bodily practice would reveal the important truths and nettlesome problems. "If you were to make a blunder in conversation, as to a point of orthoepy, or of history, any common friend might be expected to give you some hint of your delinquency," Miller wrote. In other words, intellectual errors, or gaps in knowledge, were simple matters, whereas if you were to commit "some offence against the delicacy of polished manners," Miller wrote, "not one friend in a hundred that would take the liberty to intimate it to you." Exterior signs, the testing grounds of delicacy in manners, explained William Ellery Channing, signaled the quality of the individual's inner state. American nationalism destroyed some definitive characteristics of Puritanism, but not the Puritan view that society held the right to inspect a man's soul, that a man had the obligation to account for his inner state, to the political community.[6]

---

4. Hobbes, *Leviathan*, quote from p. 160, or Chapter Eleven, "Of the Difference of Manners" and Chapter Twelve, "Of Religion," see pp. 160–183; Norbert Elias, *The Civilizing Process* (London, 2000).

5. William Henry Channing, ed., *Memoir of William Ellery Channing*, (Boston, 1851), p. 513. Trollope's *Domestic Manners of the Americans* excerpted in Rebecca Brooks Gruver, ed., *American Nationalism, 1783–1830: A Self-Portrait* (New York, 1970), p. 83. On how concepts of gentility influenced the nineteenth-century middle class and their domestic life, and gave a cultural character to their "uplift" efforts, see also Richard L. Bushman, *The Refinement of America: Persons, Houses, Cities* (New York, 1992).

6. Samuel Miller, *Letters on Clerical Manners and Habits; Addressed to a Student in the Theological Seminary at Princeton, N.J.* (New York, 1827), p. 15.

To the national evangelists, picayune details of personal comportment could signal political problems meriting public attention. In his *Memoirs of a New England Village Choir*, Samuel Gilman had fretted over the hymnbook doodles of the talented young cobbler and wondered if the unflinching gaze of the gifted maid revealed an arrogance unsuitable for social prominence. William Ellery Channing wrote that if he were to visit a home in a new frontier community, and "see the floor defiled by spittle," it would indicate a lack of the "aspiration for inward purity" necessary in members of a respectable community.[7] In 1823, Channing wrote that "a nation's whole tone of manners" and a "nation's character and modes of living" were not to be found in the structure of any institution, but in the interior life of its individuals. "Is not the interior life," he asked, "the great thing to be inspected?" Tocqueville found the project of making windows into men's souls oppressive, comparing it unfavorably with the bodily torture of absolutist regimes. There, he wrote, "despotism, in order to reach the soul, crudely strikes the body," only to find that "the soul, escaping these blows, rises gloriously above it." In contrast, "in the democratic republics, tyranny does not proceed in this way; it leaves the body alone and goes straight to the soul." What Tocqueville, coming from Catholic France, saw as a new form of democratic despotism was really a Protestant practice of interior inspection, loosed upon a national scale. American society also did rely more on individual character or manners than comparatively statist France. For some watchful American Protestants, this scrutiny of manners raised the loaded question of whether missionaries were promoting salvation by works, which was a crypto-Catholicism. As early as 1804, in a sermon before the Society for Propagating the Gospel Among the Indians, and Others, in North America, John Lathrop, pastor of the Second Church in Boston, addressed this concern. Lathrop's not entirely satisfying explanation was that the changes to outward behavior resulted from a first change in interior knowledge.[8]

The fact that the missionaries tended to be young men of the Northeastern gentry, often graduates of Yale, Andover Theological Seminary, or Williams

---

7. Channing, pp. 511–513.

8. Channing's writings reprinted in William Henry Channing, ed., p. 345; Colin Gordon, "The Soul of the Citizen: Max Weber and Michel Foucault on Rationality and Government," in Sam Whimster and Scott Lash, eds., *Max Weber, Rationality, and Modernity* (London, 1987), pp. 306–307, 297; Alexis de Tocqueville, *Democracy in America*, ed. Hackett, vol. I (New York, 2000) p. 112; John Lathrop, D.D., *A Discourse Before the Society for Propagating the Gospel Among the Indians, and Others, in North America* (Boston, 1804), pp. 5, 11.

College, could contribute to skepticism. They saw themselves as successors to Mark, Matthew, Luke, and John, while others, especially poorer Christians, perceived them more like the Romans of the gospels: privileged, arrogant, imperious. As early as Samuel J. Mills and John J. Schermerhorn's 1813 frontier reconnaissance tour, the missions movement began making enemies. John Taylor, for example, was a yeoman farmer and Baptist lay minister from Franklin County, Kentucky. Taylor's *Thoughts on Missions* (1820) expressed many of the grievances and aspirations, especially those of poor, rural people that would find space under the banner of Jacksonian democracy. Because he was a lay-minister of some renown, Mills and Schermerhorn sought out Taylor, paying him a visit at his Kentucky, farm.[9] Taylor's *Thoughts on Missions* described Mills and Schermerhorn as "respectable looking" and "zealous," but the defining impression they made was of money-hungry Yankees. Taylor wrote in anger of their repeated inquiries about money, about his pay for preaching (they told him it was "very puny indeed"). Taylor also wrote in regret, of his having wanted to impress them. To do so, he showed them copies of minutes from local Baptist meetings. Mills and Schermerhorn asked: If the Kentucky Baptists could meet so often, why were they not raising more money? New Englanders, they told him, were founding missionary societies: "Do you not know when the springs are once opened they will always run?" Once people get "in the habit of giving their money for any religious use," they said, "they will continue to appropriate it for all sacred purposes." Such talk, Taylor wrote, caused him "to smell the *New-England Rat*."[10]

John Taylor's *Thoughts on Missions* contained an implicit, but strong critique of capitalism. Taylor saw capitalism as, in part, a ruse by which rich Yankees fleeced poor country people, and he saw the missions movement as its avant-garde. The missionary societies, he wrote, "had the same taste for money that the horse leech has for blood." Other rural critics described the missionaries as ravenous dogs, beggars, and locusts. One called the whole missionary network a "horse-leach system!" Taylor wrote to warn frontier Christians, in particular Baptists, that the missionaries "are about antipodes with us. . . and in no national connection with us." They were possessed with "folly," not Christians but "aspiring gentlemen." They could not abide "equality in labor" and yearned for "English

9. John Taylor, *Thoughts on Missions* (Franklin County, KY, 1820), p. 5.

10. John Taylor. pp. 6–7.

government." To Taylor, missionary literature announcing support from the British and Foreign Bible Society only confirmed that they wanted their "great machine" to dominate "all over the United States," that they wanted "a large empire."[11]

The matter of money and the missions movement emerged as a major criticism, from multiple perspectives. Like many frontier revivalists, and poorer Christians, Taylor found the missions preoccupation with money un-Christian. Missionary fundraisers, he continued, took advantage of credulous country people. He described attending an 1815 sermon by an ABCFM traveling minister, who, he wrote, told the crowd that angels hovered overhead, ready to bear "our money for the instruction and conversion of the poor Heathens." Warning that the angels were set to depart, the missionary cried, "Stop angels! till you have witnessed the generosity of this assembly." To Taylor's outrage, what Taylor called this "sophistry and Yankee art" extracted "near 200 dollars" from poor frontier settlers. He saw no differences between these practices and the Vatican's notorious "sale of indulgences." One could hardly level a more provocative charge against a New England Congregationalist, and Taylor continued, describing the ABCFM missionary as a "modern Tetzel." Give him money, he warned frontier Baptists, and you would become one of the "adopted daughters of the old mother of Harlots."[12]

Taylor's *Thoughts of Missions* characterized the missionary movement as a program of class exploitation by distant and corrupt interests. Taylor did not cite revolutionary examples, or American ideals, but his views against concentrated power, empire, and aristocracy enjoyed counterparts in republican theories about independence and citizenship. The anti-mission cause found its footing without appeals to the "free born sons of America" or the "citizens of the only republick now existing in the world," such as those with which Andrew Jackson had roused volunteers to join his Tennessee Militia, in 1812. Nonetheless, in spirit and some specifics, the anti-mission cause expressed a strong, consistent view of what was wrong with the world, and how to fix it, which enjoyed a history and a future in American political life. Missions were a problem, but churches were a solution; bankers were a problem, too, but farmers and independent producers were another solution. Another 1820

---

11. Ibid., p. 8; Wyatt-Brown, "The Antimission Movement," pp. 516, 518, 519; Walter Brown Posey, *The Baptist Church in the Lower Mississippi Valley*, p. 74; John Taylor, pp. 8, 10.

12. Ibid., pp. 9–10.

pamphlet, this one more influential, and, coincidentally, also authored by a John Taylor, articulated some of the same views as Taylor's *Thoughts on Missions*. John Taylor of Caroline, a Virginia planter and political intellectual, published *Construction Construed and Constitutions Vindicated*, a critical response to the nationalism of the US Supreme Court's *McCulloch v. Maryland*. Writing from deep within the nationalist tradition ("we have nearly forgotten the principles of our fathers"), John Taylor's *Construction Construed* called for a retrenchment along classical republican principles. John Taylor of Caroline called himself an Old Republican, and John Taylor of Kentucky simply called himself a Christian. One Taylor looked to classical Rome, the other found his ideals in the Reformation, but they both, in 1820, attacked American capitalism while maintaining the superiority of agriculture and local, limited government over the ambition and baroque machinations of commerce and finance.[13]

Paper currency and rights of incorporation constituted important contemporary advances of capitalism, and John Taylor of Kentucky and John Taylor of Caroline paid special attention to them. Taylor of Caroline argued that the Constitution did not allow the government to regulate paper currency, only "coin," or hard money. Taylor warned that federal backing of any bank currency would lead to "corporate despotism over the money or currency of a nation." Granting rights of incorporation to banks, he argued, would create "a power beyond" that of any legislature. Once backed by government, through the "power-amplifying" effect of currency regulation and the rights of incorporation, he wrote, banks would become monsters, at least equals to the "monopoly of the colonial trade" that Americans had "abolished by long war."[14]

John Taylor of Kentucky also offered a brief against Northeastern capitalism. The American Board of Commissioners for Foreign Missions, not the Marshall Court, provoked him, and he thought aspects of capitalism a betrayal not of the republican past, but of Christianity. Even the missionary publications, Taylor wrote, were venal and beggarly, lacking in humility and preoccupied with power. Their constant tallying of the pages published, of publications, of converts, of their manifold local auxiliary societies, wrote Taylor, revealed an impulse to "number Israel." Since the Bible taught, "money and power are two principal members of the

---

13. John Taylor, *Construction Construed, and Constitutions Vindicated* (Richmond, VA, 1820), p. iii.

14. Ibid., pp. 85. 186, 199–189.

old beast," Taylor concluded that the missions movement was a "young beast."[15] He wrote to advise that churches forgo association with such a "motley tribe as the Board of Foreign Missions," to call attention to their imperial ambition, their design to "grasp the whole society." Trying to provoke, Taylor wrote that Christians would do better to make "Masonic friends" than missionary ones. At the moment Taylor was writing, the Masons were becoming the object of popular conspiracy theories alleging that groups of elites were working together in secret to dominate and exploit common people. Taylor warned that these conspiracies would not stop at auxiliaries to missions. With more boards, and more officers, more "vigorous and artful" agents, they who would "create more societies. . . Female Societies, Cent Societies, Mite Societies, Children Societies, and even Negro Societies." At the time Taylor wrote *Thoughts on Missions*, he was 69 years old. He had been a lay minister for 44 years, and had spent 10 years as an itinerant, riding a 200-mile circuit "from the Blue Ridge and the Shenandoah River to the back of Virginia, on the branches of the Potomac and Ohio Rivers." Much like the developing Antimason cause, he and other anti-mission spokesmen meant to call attention to a purported movement of powerful elites using esoteric tools to acquire greater influence.[16]

Daniel Parker, another frontier itinerant, called the missions a class warfare project masquerading as religion. In his 1820 pamphlet, *A Public Address to the Baptist Society and Friends of Religion in General*, Parker wrote that although money and great men backed the missions, decades of reading the scriptures had convinced him that the movement was steeped in "innumerable" errors. Like John Taylor of Kentucky, Parker saw the missions movement as a crypto-Catholic affront, based on "misled zeal and ambition," trying to assert "Popish dominion" and establish a "Popish empire." Parker and Taylor's anti-mission position was not simply theological or religious, but also a critique of the politics and economics of American capitalism.

In 1820, the year Daniel Parker and both John Taylors published, the Panic of 1819 was still fresh in rural America. The West suffered more

---

15. Jackson's 1812 speech to Tennessee Militia quoted in Watson, *Liberty and Power*, pp. 48–49; ibid., pp. 10, 27.

16. Michael F. Holt, "The Antimasonic and Know Nothing Parties," in Arthur M. Schlesinger, Jr., ed. *History of U.S. Political Parties* (New York, 1973), pp. 578–584; Taylor, *Thoughts on Missions*, pp. 11–12, 29–30.

than the East, and debtors and small farmers suffered more than the creditors. One Kentuckian observed, "a deeper gloom hangs over us than was ever witnessed by the oldest man." Thomas Hart Benton later remembered, with some exaggeration, that the Second Bank of the United States became "the engrossing proprietor of whole towns." US Supreme Court Chief Justice John Marshall thought the Panic had thrown the nation into "moral chaos." A combination of corruption and ineptitude at the Second Bank, aggravated by a charter so limited that it hampered a genuine attempt by the Bank to reform itself, worsened the crisis. The Bank, strongly associated with the Northeastern business elite, became a target for widespread public ridicule and, for reasons both right and wrong, took most of the blame for the troubles. The widespread availability of credit, corporate forms of organization, negotiable instruments, equities, and other such abstractions that contributed to the Panic of 1819 would come to be considered factors in the normal vicissitudes of credit markets. In 1819, however, capitalism was new, and few, especially in the North American interior, were prepared for its normalcy. Daniel Parker and both John Taylors, however, suspected that capitalism was going to bring the greatest benefits to the Northeastern elite.[17]

Despite its vulnerability to credit markets and banking policies, the North American interior, in 1820, still in part lay outside the world economic system. Though vulnerable to the fluctuations in a capitalist system beyond their control, farmers in Ohio, Kentucky, and Indiana, for example, bartered for goods and services more often than they used cash, and through the 1820s, they remained dependent on local markets for earning a livelihood. It would not be until the 1830s, for example, that grain grown in Ohio could be sold for a profit in New York City.[18] Paper currency, therefore, signified new economic forces, and was relatively rare on the frontier. The missions movement did many important things, from their publishing campaigns to building schools across North America and around the world, but anti-mission spokesmen paid particular attention

17. Dangerfield, *The Awakening of American Nationalism*, ch. 3, esp. pp. 89–91, wrote, "Jacksonian nationalism was born in the Panic of 1819," quotes from p. 89; Paul E. Johnson, "The Market Revolution," in Mary Kupeic Cayton et al., eds., *The Encyclopedia of American Social History* (New York, 1993), vol. 1, pp. 548, 558–559. For a nuanced description of the political consequences of the Panic of 1819, see Wilentz, *The Rise of American Democracy*, pp. 206–216, 288–298, and Daniel Walker Howe, *What Hath God Wrought*, ch. 4.

18. Robert L. Heilbroner and Alan Singer, *The Economic Transformation of America: 1600 to the Present* (Florence, KY, 1998), ch 3.

to the prominence of money in the movement, and its control by distant boards. Where was the money going, and who was in charge? It was not clear. One might as well, wrote Daniel Parker, "be willing that your brethren should. . . lend it to a gambler" as to donate it to the missions. John Taylor of Caroline spoke for most planters when he allied himself with small farmers, as fellow producers, against banking and commercial interests. It was a claim that would be central to the politics of coalescing Democratic Party.[19]

When he singled out slaveholder support as another reason to oppose the missions, Parker took the class analysis further. A simple look at the planters' slaves, he argued, made a mockery of Christian scruple as the motive of missions. Planters, he wrote, treated "the poor Africans, who have earned" the money slaveholders then donated for Christianization, worse than animals. Missions were run, Parker wrote, by people who deprived Africans of their "natural liberty," violently abused them, and then asked for money to civilize faraway peoples in distant lands. One might as well, wrote Parker, "believe the Devil a saint, as to believe this is the true spirit of religion." He called it "robbery of the darkest shade." In Parker's telling, the planters were neither producers nor benevolent Christian paternalists, but parasites united, in avarice, to an opportunistic merchant class. They placed God in their "long line of trade and traffic." They paid their agents more in a month, plus providing traveling expenses, than most frontier ministers, who paid their own way, earned for several months of labor.[20] Religion, he wrote, was "greater than the merchandize of this world." Anti-mission frontier Christians found the missionaries' claims to be carrying on the work of the original evangelists especially offensive. These missionaries were no modern Matthew, Luke, or John, but "gay gentlemen" and "high flyers." When God sent Paul to the Gentiles, Parker wrote, Paul enjoyed no "established fund to look back at for a support."[21] No salary supported Peter, when God sent him to preach at Cornelius, he noted. The missionaries, however, were "sent on the patrimony of the Board," and on other people's money they lived "in style, in the flourishing towns. . . without any. . . appearance

---

19. Daniel Parker, *A Public Address to the Baptist Society and Friends of Religion in General on the Principle and Practice of the Baptist Board of Foreign Missions for the United States of America* (Vincennes, 1820), pp. 52–54; Paul E. Johnson, "The Market Revolution," p. 550.

20. Parker, pp. 55, 56–58; Taylor, *Thoughts on Missions*, pp. 12, 30–32, 46–47.

21. Parker, *Public Address*, pp. 16–18, 22–23, 41, 30–33.

of self-denial, or abstemious living, or any other anxieties or trouble," yet they were constantly "begging" for money from "poor back-woods people." Like John Taylor, Daniel Parker found little in the scriptures to account for the ways of the national evangelists' version of Christianity. Their established funds, their salaried missionaries, their corporations, were all "without the authority of the bible." If anti-mission writers found the missions' affinity with capitalism an affront, the role of the nation in the missions movement was merely bemusing. Parker noted that many of the missionary organizations used "American" and "United States" in their names because it encouraged, especially abroad, the misapprehension that they represented some sort of "foreign ministry for the United States of America." From the point of view of these frontier itinerants, it was not Christianity, but privilege, greed, conceit, and grasping ambition that distinguished the missionary movement.[22]

To such proud and independent rural men, those for whom anti-mission Christians spoke, Andrew Jackson's call to carry the banner of "common men" against aristocrats and bankers struck these deep chords. Parker, for example, derided the missionary organizations' practice of conferring titles as a form of "heathen idolatry" consistent with their designs to make themselves an aristocracy. The motto of the missions movement, Parker wrote, ought to be " 'God help the rich, and the poor can beg.' " The stand against privilege, and the particular symbol of it in titles, coincided with the republican principle. In 1812 Jackson had rallied prospective Tennessee militia volunteers with the call that the most bedraggled Tennessee frontiersman possessed more dignity than all the "titled Slaves of George the third." In principle, Parker and Taylor found the scriptures alone sufficient authority for their suspicion of titles.[23]

Increasing inequality, the rise of a cash economy, the creation of a dependent labor force, instruments of finance and incorporation, and other targets of the anti-missions came with the rise of capitalism. In their opposition to these changes, artisans from New York and other Northern cities drew on republican principles and the more egalitarian impulses of the American Revolution. Like the artisans of Northern cities, Daniel Parker and John Taylor, frontier itinerants, spoke out on behalf of equality, the legitimacy of wealth derived from labor, and independent, local

22. Taylor, *Thoughts on Missions*, pp. 12–13, 35, 19, finds scriptural evidence against much of the missions movement; see pp. 18–19.

23. Parker, pp. 49–50; Jackson quoted in Watson, p. 49; Taylor, pp. 17–18, 35.

control. Only a local church, Parker and Taylor both believed, not a missionary corporation, had the right to "pay for my labor." Proceeding from some similar presumptions, John Taylor complained that the national evangelists do not know the "worth of property by labouring for it." Their "hands are too delicate either to make tents, or pick up a bundle of sticks, or make a fire to warm themselves as Paul did." Taylor repeatedly came back to the same detail that Samuel Gilman had singled out as the best indication of American class status: white hands. He derided the national evangelists as "white-handed gentry," whose white hands were "always stretched out for money, and like the horse-leech, ever crying *give give!!*" It is probably more accurate to say that they held to a labor theology, rather than theory, of value. Unlike Paul, wrote Taylor, who "laboured with his own hands" to feed himself and others, the national evangelists' were "not fond of digging." He repeated his characterization of their fundraising as "begging."[24]

The missionaries ignored criticism of their movement, as they ignored popular American religion. The missionaries, wrote Taylor, "baptize a few people at St. Louis, and they suppose those waters were never before consecrated to that use from the creation of the world." The published missionary reports tell of a frontier, he wrote, "as destitute, and needing preaching as much as the Empire of Burmah." In fact, he wrote, they knew that local churches filled the frontier.[25] The plan, Parker wrote, was to establish the missionaries' way of life, so they set up "schools and [began] raising family funds and stocks, flocks and herds, of various kinds, all belonging to the missions system."[26]

Daniel Parker and John Taylor's attack on the missions movement advanced many of the grievances and ideals that would drive Andrew Jackson's campaigns for the presidency. Just as anti-missions spokesmen depicted the missions as a front by which a privileged Eastern elite exploited poor Western farmers, so too would Jackson supporters depict the Second Bank of the United States. Moreover, the directors of the Bank

---

24. Parker, pp. 17, 38, 42, 46; Taylor, *Thoughts on Missions*, pp. 18–19, 25. On Northern artisans, see Wilentz, *Chants Democratic*, esp. ch. 2. For an interesting forum on a different version of "whiteness studies" in American history, see "Whiteness Studies and the Historian's Imagination," *International Labor and Working Class History Journal*, vol. 60 (Fall 2001), pp. 1–32.

25. Taylor, p. 14.

26. Parker, *Public Address*, p. 46.

and the missions were often the same men.[27] A strong, and humorous, anti-mission statement came from *The Christian Advocate and Journal*, a Methodist publication, which denounced missionary ecumenism as a front for the advancement of sectarian interests. Charging that "to save appearances" the national societies sang "a song of *union*," but were in fact dominated by Presbyterians, *The Christian Advocate and Journal* called on Methodists to oppose the "dangerous tendency" of the multiplying *"religious national institutions."*[28] Finding the criticism of the editorial too mild, the author of a letter to the editor singled out the missionaries' nationalism and manifold corporations as distinguishing components of a fraud. The letter writer associated the missions movement with the merchant and manufacturing class, and saw a basic difference between the nationalists and the Methodists. His humor, a satirical endorsement, signaled a distance from the national evangelist literature, which could be many things but was not funny. The letter is worth quoting at some length:

> Mr. Editor:—I am a national man, and therefore cannot understand what you mean by complaining of national societies. Sir, it is the order of the day to be national. We have our national theaters, national lottery offices, national hotels, national steamboats, and national grog shops. We have our United States shoe blacks, U.S. corset makers, U.S. infirmaries, and U.S. manufactories of every kind, from our match makers up to our carpet factories. I see no reason why we should not have national societies, since this character gives those societies a popularity and influence they could not otherwise sustain. Besides, sir, to be an officer in a national society sounds abroad like being an officer in a national government, and will, by and by, give those societies an influence with the national government. We have already our American Bible Society, American Tract Society, American Missionary Society, American Temperance Society, American Sunday School Union, American Prison Discipline Society, American Jews' Society, &c &c and we

27. On Jackson as the first truly national political leader, see David Potter, *The Impending Crisis: 1848–1861* (New York, 1977), p. 7; Frederick Jackson Turner, *The Frontier in American History* (Tucson, AZ, 1986), p. 29; George Dangerfield, *The Era of Good Feelings* (New York, 1989), pp. 122–136, 415–425; Arthur M. Schlesinger, Jr., *The Age of Jackson* (Boston, 1945).

28. Editorial, *The Christian Advocate and Journal*, vol. II, no. 32, April 11, 1828, n.p. Italics in original.

are in a fair way to have an American Sabbath Society, and I know not how many more.... The fact is, sir, it is time that some national effort was made to create some religion as the law of the land; and unless you Methodists become "national" too, you will stand a poor chance among so many American societies.

After satirizing the national missionary societies by comparing them to grog shops and carpet manufacturers, the letter writer moved on to threats.[29]

He attributed the Methodists' growth to their newness. The fact that their "engines" had not had to work "all the time," he wrote, accounted for their popularity. He warned the Methodists they risked being crushed: "if the national societies ever raise against you the national arm, you may rely upon it will grind you to powder." He closed by advertising his services. Should "any national society" see fit to provide a "suitable increase of salary" from his current "trifling sum of twelve hundred dollars per year," he noted, he would be willing to act as their secretary. Twelve hundred dollars was far from a trifling sum. The letter writer signed himself "Uncle Sam."[30]

The missions movement began as a committed champion of the incorporation of Native Americans into US society. It acknowledged that earlier Anglo-American missions to the Indians had failed. They had learned, they said, that it was not possible to "*Christianize* the Heathen, before they are in some measure *civilized*."[31] The new missions strategy would emphasize "early education," or civility, before it approached the more nebulous problem of belief. Earlier Anglo-American missions had taken "the most promising children" from many "tribes" and focused on their religious indoctrination. When these purportedly indoctrinated Indians were sent back, as young adults, "to their native tribes," wrote a missionary, they "became *Indians again*." The cultural chauvinism, the presumption that an idealized version of the Anglo-American way of life was God's way, should not obscure the relative optimism

29. "Uncle Sam," *The Christian Advocate and Journal*, vol. II, no. 36, May 9, 1828, n.p.

30. Ibid. Another critic of the national evangelists registered a similar dissent in 1837, when he complained, "we have in our great Metropolitan centers, overseers who are virtually lawgivers to the Church"; see Miller, *The Life of the Mind in America from the Revolution to the Civil War* (New York, 1970), p. 45.

31. Lathrop, pp. 17–18.

inherent in the view of "Indianness" as a social condition, not a racial identity.[32]

The missionary program of early education and civilization led to grand expectations, at least from the missionaries. Still, the ABS acknowledged that the Indians' "repugnance" to Anglo-American ways "must every day grow more inveterate from feeling themselves continually pushed off their grounds." The ABS theorized that if Native Americans could find Christ in their own language, not in "the white man's talk," conversion efforts might bear fruit. As a result, in 1818, the American Bible Society began translating the scriptures in native languages. The ABS conceded, however, that the Indians must also be "able to obtain secure lands." Few things, after all, were as Anglo-American as security of property rights. The ABCFM began with the same commitment. "The doctrine that Indians cannot be civilized," they wrote, "is the. . . slander of men who covet their lands." Again, they too thought that if they could introduce the institution of private property and compel the adoption of Christianity, then they might save the Indians "from extinction."[33]

The missionary organizations undertook Native American nationalization with the best of intentions. In 1823, the United Foreign Missionary Society expressed great optimism about nationalizing Native Americans. They envisioned the "benefits of civilization," blossoming across the Western frontier, accruing to "the red man and the white man." The "savage shall be converted to the citizen. . . the hunter shall be transformed into the mechanic." The "farm, the work shop, the School-House" would "adorn every Indian village" and the "vast country from the Mississippi to the Pacific" would be filled with Europeans and Native Americans, "fellow citizens of the same civil and religious community, and fellow heirs to a glorious inheritance in the kingdom of Immanuel." This is a sharp contrast with earlier Anglo-American approaches to the possibility of Native Americans as members of the same political community. Cotton Mather, for example, had viewed the Indians as "tawney [sic] serpents." Solomon Stoddard had proposed, in 1703, that Massachusetts train dogs "to hunt the Indians as they do Bears." In contrast, in the 1820s, the future of Native Americans in the national political community looked bright to the missionaries. The incorporation of Native Americans into the sacred national project "can no longer

---

32. Ibid., pp. 18–19. Italics in the original.

33. American Bible Society, *Second Annual Report* (New York, 1818), pp. 16–17; Tracy, *HABCFM*, p. 27.

be questioned. The problem has already been solved. Successful experiment has placed the subject beyond doubt." From the Yankee perspective, all the blessed and the brightest stood behind the project of nationalizing Native Americans. The American nation, however, was not built on an idealized version of the New England past: farms, schoolhouses, and workshops.[34]

The Cherokee, Osage, and Creek Indians whose prospective nationalization preoccupied the missions movement lived in the slave society of the nineteenth-century American South, a fact which did not escape their notice. On an 1832 tour of the frontier, Washington Irving witnessed a Cherokee Indian explain to the Rev. John Vail, a Connecticut native and an ABCFM missionary working near St. Louis, why he found Vail's sermon praising the virtues of small-scale, settled agriculture and husbandry less than compelling. The Cherokee told Vail it is better to be a planter, explaining that he preferred to follow the example of Auguste Pierre Chouteau, a rich and powerful descendant of the founder of St. Louis, at whose frontier home many Osage, Creek, and Cherokee gathered to trade. If the United States wants him to follow the missionaries' advice and become a farmer, the Cherokee told Vail, they ought to provide him with some "negroes," like Chouteau has:

'Old Father Vail addressed the Indians on the necessity of industry as a means to happiness. An Indian replied—Father I don't understand this kind of happiness you talk of. You tell me to cut down trees—to lop it—to make fences—to plough—this you call being happy—I no like such happiness. When I go to St. Louis I see Chouteau. . . He says hello—and negro comes in with great plate of cake, wine & he say eat, drink. If you want anything else he say hello—three–four, five, six negro come and do what we want. That I call happy. he no plough. he no work. he no cut wood.'

'Ah, but he has negroes to do all that.'

'Well, father, go to your Great Father,—tell him to find me one, two, three negroes to cut wood and plough for me and I'll be willing to be happy like white man.'[35]

---

34. United Foreign Missionary Board of Managers Annual Report of 1823, quoted in Robert F. Berkhofer, Jr., *Salvation and the Savage*, pp. 11, 153. Discussion of Mather and Stoddard's views found in Frederick Jackson Turner, *The Frontier in American History*, pp. 45–46. James Axtell, "Some Thoughts on the Ethnohistory of Missions," *Ethnohistory* (Winter 1982), vol. 29, pp. 35–41.

35. Washington Irving, *Journals of Washington Irving* (Carlisle, MA, 1919), vol. 3, pp. 128–129.

The exchange between Vail and the Cherokee captured the price the missionary movement had paid for its nationalist commitment. A generation earlier, the founders of the ABCFM had come together, in part, in opposition to the idea that being served by slaves was what it meant to "be happy like a white man."

Another Cherokee told his friends that they had rejected a new missionary because the man was always trying to get his three sons hired (one as a doctor, one as a surveyor, and another as an agent) to the mission. "This man is not for God," said the Cherokee, "not for us, but for himself—he wants to grasp everything." Adoption of Anglo-American civility, and Christianity, could also bring scorn. Pointing out two Indians who had joined the ABCFM mission, Chouteau told Washington Irving, "This one has been twice as long at the Mission as the other and therefore is twice as good for nothing." Irving also told of the response of a Cherokee to the preaching of a new missionary. "An agent newly arrived" to the Cherokee mission, wrote Irving, "was preaching up as usual about their being civilized and happy." An older Indian replied: "What, father, still about that old happiness?—don't talk of that any more. I'll tell you what I call happy—to have my gun—a wide range—to hunt—to kill buffalo—to have plenty to eat—to eat and drink till full—to smoke—to lie down on our backs—beat our bosoms and sing." A history of betrayal by Anglo-Americans, different messages from various parts of the Anglo-American community, and a risk of rejection by their family and community all impeded attempts to Christianize Native Americans. However, the American Indians' attachment to their own way of life probably presented the most consistent challenge to the missionaries' ambitions of conversion and civilization in the Anglo-American manner.[36]

In the way that informed so many poor whites settlers' views of the missionary movement, the commitment to Native American civilization was not only a losing issue, but a counterproductive one. John Taylor, for example, complained about the expenditures on Indian schools and missions. He called it "this *Indian business*" and it was, he wrote, "only another thirsty daughter of the horse-leech thirsting for blood crying give give." Many frontier people suffered from poverty and want, especially

36. Irving, *Journals of Washington Irving*, vol. 3, pp. 130, 156, 129.

after the Panic of 1819, but the missionaries, wrote Taylor, made such "mighty noise" and "pharisaical boast[s]" about the "poor living, and dirt and lice" suffered by their missionaries to the Indians. Taylor claimed that the missionaries perpetrated fraud to raise money for Indian relief. Their missionaries, he wrote, would make a show of donating $10, asking poor frontier people to match the gift, but the Board would later reimburse the missionary his $10. Daniel Parker also wrote that the "extravagant plan of translating the bible and civilizing the Indians" had led the missions movement away from the scriptures. Let the civilizing and translating, wrote Parker, be done "under the direction of our civil government" not "under the sacred name of religion." Taylor and Parker decided that the wayward path of national evangelism could be summed up in the fact that it was a mission, rather than a ministry, and no one was a more conspicuous focus of missionary attention than Native Americans.[37]

Some notable internal criticism echoed the allegations by Taylor and Parker, and the anonymous Cherokees, that the missionary movement was more interested in mammon than God. *An Expose of the Rise and Proceedings of the American Bible Society*, published in 1830, aimed to detail years of systematic corruption at the ABS, to expose it as a profitable ruse. The author presented himself as a disillusioned insider, one "for many years. . . intimately acquainted with the leading operations and designs" of the organization and its allies. Though focused on exposing "internal affairs" at the ABS, the anonymous author also noted that the many "Bible, Missionary, Tract, and Sunday School Societies," he wrote, "are, in the main, one." He began by noting that the constitution of the ABS required two-thirds of its Board of Managers to reside in New York City, that anyone in the city could gain a seat on Board of Managers by donating $150, and that the ABS was an active investor.[38]

The author of *Expose of the Proceedings of the American Bible Society* wanted readers to follow the money, from where it came and to where it went. He reported that in addition to investments in stock in insurance companies, the ABS owned 100 shares, worth $10,000, of stock in the Bank of the United States, $10,500 of stock of "New-York state six per cent stock, 4,500$ of six per cent stock on the Funded Debt of the United States." He explained that in spite of its stated commitment to distribute

37. Taylor, pp. 11, 28, 34; Parker, pp. 13–14.

38. Anonymous, *An Expose of the Rise and Proceedings of the American Bible Society* (New York, 1830), pp. 1–3, 5–7.

Bibles "gratuitously," the ABS pressed its auxiliary branches to contribute to the fund that made possible the dissemination of "the bread of eternal life." Using figures from ABS reports, Anonymous took as an example the East Tennessee Bible Society, showing that it had donated $1,900 and received 1,700 Bibles. The case of East Tennessee Bible Society, he wrote, was typical. The "novelty," professed philanthropic motives, and access to the rich and powerful that the ABS offered led to auxiliary societies "in almost every village, town, and city on this continent." Money, wrote Anonymous, flowed in from each Auxiliary. The ABS gave "gratuitously" 100 Bibles to the Steuben County (Indiana) Bible Society, but the Steuben County Bible Society "returned to this Society 53 dollars. . . and the year following. . . 94 dollars 10 cents." In effect, for their "free" Bibles from the ABS, the Steuben County Bible Society paid over twice the market rate. The measures that auxiliary societies took to raise funds for their donations debased religion, he wrote. The ABS had in effect turned "almost every pulpit in our churches" into a commercial "stall" and had turned "our temples of worship" into "clerical bookstores." The well-intentioned young men who volunteered for the missions were turned into "peddlers and hawkers."[39]

Expose of the Proceedings of the American Bible Society made a case that the philanthropic, ecumenical components of the ABS enabled its fraud. The author claimed that the "donations" that the ABS received from its auxiliary societies more than paid for the cost of printing and distributing Bibles. Averaging ABS costs from the 1817 to 1829 annual reports, he wrote, revealed that the organization printed Bibles at 50 cents per copy. Over the same period, auxiliary societies receiving "gratuitous" Bibles donated $592,478. Having distributed 846,397 books, in 13 years, the exchange left the ABS "the gainers, in profit. . . .. 169,279 dollars and 40 cents," from the distribution of the scriptures alone, as well as owners of a Depository with "about 250,000" Bibles already printed. Another $150,000 of "landed property" had "been bequeathed to the Institution," it had received $287,789.75 from gratuities and investments, and it owned valuable "stereotype plates" and "houses and lands." He calculated the income of the ABS, over the course of 13 years, at $757,068.75. The significant figure, he wrote, made ABS expenditures a matter of interest, and he challenged readers, from using only the Annual Reports of the ABS,

---

39. Ibid, pp. 7–9, 21–22, 11–12.

to ascertain "the amount of money that has been received, and paid out, and whether the Society has made or lost money by its operations." The pursuit, he wrote, "is entirely hopeless." The American Bible Society's reports, he wrote, were meant to conceal financial matters.[40]

If John Taylor, Daniel Parker, and anonymous Cherokees saw the missions movement as too capitalist, Anonymous's *Expose* depicted them, in a sense, as not capitalist enough. Using ABS *Treasurer's Reports*, he cited numerous instances of sloppy and irrational business practices. A typical expenses entry from an ABS *Treasurer's Report* read: "Postages, fuel, lights, stationary, and expenses of Anniversary." Another read: "labour, cartage, repairs and alterations of the building, expenses incurred by visiting Auxiliaries, taxes, stove for Depository, salaries to the General Agent, to his Clerk, to the Acting Secretary, the Recording Secretary, and Keeper of the Depository." A third read: "correcting stereotype plates, labour, cartage, expenses incurred by visiting Auxiliaries, taxes, stove, salaries to the General Agent, Clerk, Secretaries, Porter." The author of the *Expose* mocked the ambiguity of these entries. The imprecision of ABS records, he wrote, would leave any rational businessman "startled and amazed." The ambiguity, he wrote, aimed to conceal the General Agent's $2,500 salary, the Reverend Acting Secretary's $1,500 salary. The ABS meant to mask these salaries not just from the public, but also from the Keeper of the Depository. The man who maintained the grounds of the ABS property, "by the sweat of his brow" and "with full labour. . . earns his wages," the *Expose* reported, did not know that the ABS officers earned several times his salary.[41]

Unlike the frontier itinerants, Anonymous drew on republican principles, wanting readers to see that the ABS sought "privileges. . . incompatible with republican government." Nonetheless, he shared with the frontier itinerants a view of the missions movement as a class interest project of the Northeastern bourgeoisie and its allies, hiding behind a cloak of religion. Taylor, Parker, and Anonymous's work suggests that these grievances and aspirations, which would find welcome in the Jacksonian movement, grew as much out of religion as out of republicanism. All three critics charged that the real ambition of the missions movement was power, influence, and empire. The national evangelists, wrote Anonymous, reveled in the company

---

40. Ibid., pp. 12–15, 22–23.

41. Ibid., pp. 15, 21–24.

of "high dignataries [*sic*] of church and state," and they liked to use money gathered from "the poor and lowly of the world" to pay for the publication of "bespattering flattery and praise" from "arch-bishops and bishops, ministers and prime-ministers, earls, dukes, and lords." The frontier itinerants had also condemned the missionaries' attentiveness to royal and imperial officials. This skepticism of power coincided with republican principles, but it could also derive from a Christian identification with the humble and the meek.

Anonymous charged the missions movement with hostility to labor and exploitation of working men. The organization, he wrote, paid its staff "scanty" wages, while alleging that ABS officers, "by the money they have accumulated" from their supposed philanthropic activities, "have enabled [themselves] to. . . hoard a vast property." At the ABS, he wrote, only "the keeper of the Depository honestly, and with full labour too, earns his wages." Describing a scene worthy of Dickens, Anonymous alleged that ABS officers sent petitions for the Sabbatarian cause to their "manufactories," where they employed a "large number of boys and girls." Noting that these exploited children were often illiterate, the managers asked the children "their names, which were set down for them, or their hands guided while they held the pen." In this sordid manner, alleged Anonymous, the names of illiterate child laborers filled the petitions of their employers' Sabbatarian campaigns.[42]

The grievances that the national evangelist movement sowed pushed critics to reaffirm their commitment to equality, and to sharpen their ideas about legitimate, and illegitimate, sources of wealth. The breadth and scale of mission activity help explain the popularity of the view, especially on the frontier, that corruption and elitism were so common among the Northeastern elite. To critics of the missions, "A Corrupt Bargain," the rallying cry of Jackson supporters that emerged from Jackson's 1824 defeat to John Quincy Adams, made visceral sense. Charges of the Northeastern elite's corruption, elitism, aristocratic ambition, and fraud also characterized the central political event of Jackson's presidency: his war on the Second Bank of the United States. Before these populist charges coalesced against the Bank, the missionary movement brought them to the surface.

---

42. Ibid., pp. 23, 24, 29–30. On Sabbatarianism, see Richard R. John, "Taking Sabbatarianism Seriously: The Postal System, the Sabbath, and the Transformation of American Political Culture," *Journal of the Early Republic*, vol. 10 (Winter 1990), pp. 517–567.

The missionaries' conceit that they represented true Christianity added a measure of insult.[43]

By drawing frontier settlers, especially the revivalists, into this fight, the missions movement would unwittingly change American nationalism. There was a formulaic aspect to the process. As one scholar has observed, the logic of Protestantism does not allow an upper class to impose manners and modes of coexistence from above. On the contrary, Protestantism "not only spreads Truth downward, it elevates the vernacular to a high culture. If the faithful are to read about the path to salvation in their own dialect, that dialect must be given its alphabet." Jackson spoke this dialect. Despite its claim to the party name of Democrat, it was, properly speaking, more anti-elitist than democratic.[44]

In 1813, Jackson himself had brought Samuel J. Mills and John J. Schermerhorn down the Mississippi River on his war-bound steamer, to New Orleans. In spite of this patronage, Jackson would never be the candidate of the Northeastern mission gentry. For one reason, the missions men had devoted time, money, and their religious imaginations to the incorporation of American Indians into the US political community. Indian nationalization would be a casualty of the missionary movement's political weakness, and of Jackson's rise. Like the missions movement, Jackson saw the consolidation of US sovereignty over the frontier as God's work, but they saw God's means, and the Native American role, differently. In March 1814, for example, fighting the Creek Wars, Jackson attacked and destroyed Fort Tallapoosa, the Creek stronghold. He told the victorious Tennessee Militia that the Creeks were "barbarians. . . ignorant of the influence of civilization & of government." He said that God's work was gruesome: it is "lamentable. . . that the path to peace should lead through blood & over the carcases [sic] of the slain," but it was also true that "providence. . . inflicts partial

---

43. As an example of the kind of bitter sense of betrayal that the missions movement could engender among frontier revivalists, John Taylor wrote that the missions represented a "false teacher" who really "loves money, or popularity, or both, more than the religion he professes." They resembled not the evangelists and apostles they liked to cite, he wrote, but the horse-leech, which "is so thirsty for blood. . . that. . . it will suck" on a horse's leg "till it bursts." Did not Judas, continued Taylor, "who loved money as well" as the national evangelists, fall from the gallows and suffer a similar fate when his bowels "burst open" and "gushed out?" The missionaries were not "light" but "darkness," not agents of "Christ" but of "Belial"; see Taylor, pp. 21–22, 24, 26, 34. Daniel Parker and Anonymous also depicted the missionaries not just as misguided, but as artful, diabolical.

44. Gellner, *Nationalism*, pp. 75–76.

evil, to produce general good."[45] In contrast to the "awakening" that the missionary movement sought to precipitate, Jackson saw his campaigns against Native Americans as a forced atonement. He estimated that the Tennessee Militia had killed 850 Indians at the Battle of Tallapoosa, and he told his troops that more Creeks "must be made to atone for their obstinacy & their crimes by still farther suffering." The Creeks' defeat, Jackson said, augured that the obstinate Indians would "disappear from the face of the Earth." The difference from the vision of missionary colonization and civilization was clear.[46]

In 1819, during his invasion of Spanish Florida, Jackson took another opportunity to pursue his plan of eradication. At Fort Tallapoosa, Jackson had told his troops that the Indians must "be made to know that their prophets are imposters." Now, in 1819, in Spanish Florida, on Jackson's order, two captured Seminole prophets were executed. One month later, in the US House of Representatives, Henry Clay attempted to persuade the House to censure Jackson. To justify the invasion of Spanish Florida and subsequent executions, Jackson had pointed to the Treaty of Fort Jackson, the treaty he had imposed upon the Creek after his 1814 victory at Tallapoosa and that had exacted 20 million acres of Creek land.[47] Clay said he had just read the Treaty of Fort Jackson, only to discover that it showed a "more dictatorial spirit" and a more "inexorable spirit of domination" than one could hope to find in the "the most haughty period of Imperial Rome." For republican America to foist such a punitive instrument, "purporting to be a treaty of peace," on opponents, Clay said, caused him "the deepest mortification and regret."[48]

Concerning Jackson's decision to execute his captives, particularly the two Seminole prophets, Clay noted that Jackson's vengeance exceeded that of imperial Rome. "When," he asked, "did the all-conquering and desolating Rome ever fail to respect the altars and the gods of those whom she subjugated?" Anticipating objections to acknowledging

---

45. Harold D. Moser, et al., eds., *The Papers of Andrew Jackson* (Knoxville, TN, 1991), vol. 3, p. 58. Hereafter cited as *PAJ*.

46. Ibid. On the estimate of 850 dead, see Jackson to Rachel Jackson, April 1, 1814, ibid., pp. 54–55.

47. Ibid. Dangerfield, *The Era of Good Feelings*, pp. 124–126. On the figure of 20 million acres, see Jill Norgren, "Lawyers and the Legal Business of the Cherokee Republic in the Courts of the United States," *Law and History Review*, vol. 10, no. 2 (Autumn 1992), p. 258.

48. Calvin Colton, ed., *The Life, Correspondences, and Speeches of Henry Clay* (New York, 1857), vol. V, p. 184. Hereafter cited as *LCSHC*.

pagan religious leaders, Clay added: "They were their prophets; the Indians believed and venerated them, and it is not for us to dictate a religious belief to them." Clay said that Jackson had reverted to the "bloody maxims of barbarous ages" and had committed "revolting cruelties." Jackson, Clay said, had abandoned "every consideration of humanity and justice" and had been driven by mere "vengeance." Clay supporters would soon attribute the end of his presidential prospects to the speech. It was a self-serving explanation, but it was an exceptional speech, and, for the light it casts on the political landscape, a revealing one.[49] Standing with the Indians placed Clay as an ally of the Northern elite, with the missions movement and with the Second Bank of the United States. Both Clay and his 1832 running mate, John Sergeant, worked as lawyers for the Bank; in a gamble that he lost, Clay turned the 1832 presidential election into a referendum on the Bank. His reference to classical ideals of religious toleration also did not find the support it might have, a generation earlier.[50]

Clay did not know it, but Jackson himself had said that vengeance had driven his campaign against the Indians. One month after Tallapoosa, at Fort Williams in the Mississippi Territory, Jackson told his men that the "retaliatory vengeance with which we threatened" the Indians "has been inflicted." He recalled the carnage: we "have seen the ravens & the vultures preying upon the carcases [sic] of the slain," he said. It was satisfactory sight: "our vengeance has been gluted [sic]."[51] There is no entirely satisfactory explanation for the ardor that Jackson brought to war against Native Americans. The zeal, almost pleasure, that Jackson seemed to take in these gruesome endeavors encouraged rumors that he had a drinking problem. In a January 1814 letter to his wife Rachel Jackson, he called those responsible for these rumors "vile slanderous vipers." He swore to Rachel that he had been sober and attributed the rumors to a "fiend. . .

---

49. Ibid., pp. 184, 189; Calvin Colton wrote that Clay's speech "decided the question. . . whether Andrew Jackson or Henry Clay should, from that moment, rise"; see *LCSHC*, vol. V, p. 184.

50. On John Sergeant and the American Sunday School Union, see John Hughes and John Breckenridge, *A Discussion of the Question, Is the Roman Catholic Religion, in Any or in All Its Principles or Doctrines, Inimical to Civil or Religious Liberties* (Philadelphia, 1836), p. 534, and *First Report of the American Sunday-School Union* (Philadelphia, 1825), p. 31. Clay's 1844 running mate, New Jersey's Theodore Frelinghuysen, was one of the great patrons of the national evangelist movement.

51. *PAJ*, vol. 3, p. 65.

not in human shape."[52] Before the Battle of Tallapoosa, he wrote to Rachel, reassuring her that divine protection was "even more conspicuous in the field of Battle" than "there," the Hermitage, their home. Rachel responded that "the same God that Led Moses through the wilderness" would lead him to safety and victory. Jackson replied, calling his critics "reptiles." He taunted them: "I smile with contempt upon those reptiles." He was sure that the "the smiles of heaven" would enable him to "carry into effect the ulterior objects of my government." In brief, Jackson understood himself as a divine agent of a sacred national mission, a view his wife shared.[53]

In the 1828 campaign for the White House, John Quincy Adams attempted to render Jackson's military prowess and charisma as bloodlust and instability. Adams's campaign song, "Little Know Ye Who's Comin,'" mocked Jackson's providential pretensions and portrayed his military campaigns as murderous rampages. The song suggested that Jackson's election would cause destruction of biblical proportions. It depicted Adams as St. Michael, field commander in God's army, with Jackson in the role of Lucifer. "Little Know Ye Who's Comin'" was an early instance of a continuing American tradition: the awkward masquerade, by a member from the Eastern elite, in the clothing of popular culture, in this case popular religious belief.

> *Fire's comin', swords are comin',*
> *Pistols, guns, and knives are comin',*
> *Famine's comin', banning's comin',*
> *If John Quincy not be comin'!*

> *Little know ye who's comin',*
> *Little know ye who's comin',*
> *Little know ye who's comin',*
> *If John Quincy not be comin'*

> *Slavery's comin', knavery's comin',*
> *Plunder's comin', wonder's comin',*
> *Jobbin's comin', robbin's comin'*
> *If John Quincy not be comin'!*

---

52. Two scholarly works that seek to explain Jackson's volatility and the evident pleasure he took in war against Indians do not mention religion. See Michael Paul Rogin, *Fathers and Children: Andrew Jackson and the Subjugation of the American Indian* (New York, 1975), and Andrew Burstein, *The Passions of Andrew Jackson* (New York, 2004); *PAJ*, vol. 3, p. 20.

53. *PAJ*, vol. 3, p. 34, p. 59, 23. For Thomas Jefferson on Jackson's emotional volatility, see Turner, in Allan G. Bogue, ed., *The Frontier in American History* (New York, 2010), p. 253.

Little know ye who's comin',
Little know ye who's comin',
Little know ye who's comin',
If John Quincy not be comin'!

Fears are comin', tears are comin',
Plague and pestilence is comin',
Hatin's comin', Satan's comin',
If John Quincy not be comin'

Little know ye who's comin',
Little know ye who's comin',
Little know ye who's comin',
If John Quincy not be comin'![54]

The song said less about Adams or Jackson than it did about the gulf that had opened between a certain elite and the American people, and how popular religion had filled that space.

For the White House, the missionary movement preferred Daniel Webster. A New Englander, Webster, in *Dartmouth v. Woodward*, was the champion of the "small college" that educated Native Americans. It was also the case that secured the rights of corporations enjoyed by the missionary societies and their patrons. After John Quincy Adams, however, no representative of the New England way would win the White House. At root, the problem was political: a political alliance between Southern planters, laborers, and small farmers, especially in the West, at the expense of the New England merchant and manufacturing class. Jackson was the natural choice of those small Western farmers and settlers aggrieved by the missionaries and the Bank.[55]

When he vetoed Congress's attempt to re-charter the Bank, Jackson characterized it as a means by which the Eastern elite, and their European partners, exploited frontier farmers. The debts that frontiersmen owed

---

54. Oscar Brand, *Presidential Campaign Songs, 1789–1996* (Smithsonian Folkways Recordings, 1999).

55. On Webster, see Dangerfield, *The Awakening of American Nationalism*, p. 92. The disrepute of the bloody Indian campaigns and Jackson's lack of refinement (when in 1833 Harvard awarded him an honorary doctorate, New England patricians mocked Jackson's ignorance of Latin) made the Northeastern elite suspicious of Jackson. Franklin Pierce (1852–1856) was from New Hampshire, but he ran as a friend of the South, even supporting the Confederacy during the Civil War. On the competition between Northern

to the Bank, he said, are "principally a debt to the Eastern and foreign stockholders." With help from Eastern aristocrats, the Bank's foreign stockholders, said Jackson, intended to "place the whole United States in the same relation to foreign countries which the Western States now bear to the Eastern." In this view, it was up to planters, frontiersmen, artisans, and the small farmers to throw off the colonial yoke, just as had the patriots from British monarchists, only this time from an alliance of Anglo-American capitalists. The Bank charter, Jackson explained, served to introduce and perpetuate "artificial distinctions, to grant titles, gratuities, and exclusive privileges, to make the rich richer and the potent more powerful." Jackson pledged to "kill" the Bank and to do so in defense of the integrity of "the humble members of society—the farmers, mechanics, and laborers." He called it a "Monster" and a "hydra of corruption."[56]

Jackson promised that "killing" the Bank would restore control of the republic to common men, laboring men. The United States, he explained, belonged by natural right to such honest, working men. The only people hurt by killing the Bank would be "rich men" who sought to get "richer by act of Congress" and through the trickery of banks. In typically "organic" nationalist language emphasizing the natural body, Jackson explained his veto as fidelity to "the bone and sinew of the country," farmers, mechanics, and laborers.[57] In their anti-missions tracts, a decade earlier, neither John Taylor nor Daniel Parker had mentioned the United States, its revolution, its charter principles, or its constitution. Jackson, however, told frontiersmen that all of these things, as well as a historic, cosmic role for the American nation, stood with them against a corrupt Eastern elite. His veto message was a jeremiad, calling "to review our principles" to reaffirm the those "which distinguished the sages of the Revolution and fathers of our Union." Jackson's anti-Bank platform carried him to re-election.[58]

---

capitalists and Southern planters for the small Western farmers in the nineteenth-century United States, see Barrington Moore, *Social Origins of Dictatorship and Democracy: Lord and Peasant in the Making of the Modern World* (Boston, 1993), ch. 3.

56. Thomas S. Langston, "A Rumor of Sovereignty: The People, Their Presidents, and Civil Religion in the Age of Jackson," *Presidential Studies Quarterly* (Fall 1993), vol. 23, esp. p. 674.

57. Ibid., pp. 674–677.

58. Ibid., pp. 673–675; Robert Remini, *Andrew Jackson and the Course of American Freedom, 1822–1832* (New York, 1981), pp. 382–389; Wilentz, *The Rise of American Democracy*, pp. 202–216, 241–243.

To create support for his veto, to overturn congressional authority, Jackson took his case directly to the American people, as a sovereign whole. "We are in the midst of a revolution," exclaimed Henry Clay. John C. Calhoun compared Jackson, unfavorably, to Caesar. Clay and Calhoun were Jackson's rivals, but it was true that in the brief history of the republic, only nine acts of Congress had met with a presidential veto, and never before for simple political reasons. The veto flouted Congress, the Supreme Court, and Jackson's own Cabinet. One man had never before so dominated the other branches of government. By re-electing him, Jackson told his divided Cabinet, the American people had empowered him to counter the other branches of government. No president had ever claimed that his election had made him, in Jackson's words, "the direct representative of the American people." The political theory invoked to authorize the veto, the claim that in the people, represented by the Executive, "is rightfully placed the sovereignty of the country," was more radical than the veto itself. A popular assembly in Philadelphia announced the arrival of despotism. "*The Republic*," declared the Richmond Whig, "*has degenerated into a Democracy*." Americans disagreed if Jackson was democrat or a despot, but his popularity was undeniable.[59]

The Southeastern Native Americans came to be counted neither Jackson supporters nor opponents, but victims. The Cherokee chief John Ross, speaking of Jackson's repudiation of Native Americans' place in US society, and the punitive course Jackson had visited upon them, gave the line for the ages. "The perpetrator of a wrong," said Ross, "never forgives his victims."[60] Without question, Native Americans were the big losers of Andrew Jackson's rise. By the winter of 1830–1831, the contest between the state of Georgia and the Cherokee over the Indians' federal treaty rights had broken out into open violence. At the same time, the Jackson administration had committed to opposing, by force if necessary, South Carolina's states'-rights position in the Nullification Crisis. South Carolina secessionists were hoping that the Jackson administration would take the same nationalist stance in support of the Cherokees' treaty rights, and thereby push Georgia to secession. With assurances that the administration would look more favorably upon states' rights south of the

59. Harry L. Watson, *Liberty and Power*, pp. 150–156; Wilentz, *The Rise of American Democracy*, pp. 425–436.

60. Quote in Jill Norgren, "Lawyers and the Legal Business of the Cherokee Republic in the Courts of the United States," p. 299.

Savannah River, however, the Georgia Legislature disavowed any intent to join the South Carolinian secessionists. In January 1831, the *Cherokee Phoenix* captured the political nature of the situation, when it observed, "The conduct of the Georgia Legislature is indeed surprising—one day they discountenance the proceedings of the nullifiers of South Carolina— at another, they even out-do the people of South Carolina, and authorize their Governor to hoist the flag of rebellion against the United States!" In the name of federal sovereignty, Jackson forced South Carolina's nulli- fiers to back down. Meanwhile, his administration maintained that state sovereignty allowed Georgia to, in effect, nullify federal treaties with the Cherokee.[61]

The conflict between Jackson and the Cherokee served to clarify the relationship between the federal government and the missions. Missionaries to the Cherokee, working for the American Board of Commissioners for Foreign Missions, had been imprisoned by the state of Georgia for refusing to take an oath swearing that their loyalty to the state of Georgia superseded their loyalty to the Cherokee. On the grounds that they were agents of the federal government, and therefore not required to swear loyalty to the state of Georgia, a sympathetic Georgia judge released the missionaries. The judge's reasoning was based on the facts that federal appropriations made to the missions went through the War Department, and the imprisoned missionaries served as federal postmas- ters. Therefore the missionaries, the judge reasoned, were federal agents. The Jackson administration promptly dismissed Samuel Worcester, the remaining missionary, from his postmaster position. Secretary of War John Henry Eaton wrote to Georgia governor Wilson Lumpkin that, as far as the War Department was concerned, the missionaries were not federal agents. The Jackson administration was forcing the missions movement to choose sides: incorporation of the Indians into Anglo-American society, or loyalty to the Union—that is, their Protestantism and their sense of jus- tice, or their nationalism. The missions movement chose the latter.[62] After suffering imprisonment by defiant Georgia governor Wilson Lumpkin, and, he alleged, torture by the Georgia Militia, Samuel Worcester, at the

---

61. Norgren, "Lawyers and the Legal Business of the Cherokee Republic in the Courts of the United States," pp. 253–314; editorial, *Cherokee Phoenix*, January 8, 1831, reprinted in Perdue and Green, p. 133.

62. Edwin A. Miles, "After John Marshall's Decision: Worcester v. Georgia and the Nullification Crisis," *The Journal of Southern History*, vol. 39 (November 1973), p. 523.

behest of the ABCFM, withdrew his request for a pardon. Worcester wrote to Georgia governor Lumpkin, explaining that he would have persisted but for fear that the attempt to enforce *Worcester v. Georgia*, to recognize the rights of Native Americans, would "be attended with consequences injurious to our beloved country."[63]

The crisis of "Indian removal" brought important change to American nationality, evident in Jackson's 1830 State of the Union Address. The address signaled a remarkable moment in American history, a reformation of American nationality, one that merits comparison with Abraham Lincoln's "Gettysburg Address." In both Lincoln's Gettysburg Address and Jackson's 1830 State of the Union Address, a nineteenth-century US president gave a rationale for the shape of the national political community. Slavery must end, Lincoln explained, because the nation was "dedicated to the proposition that all men are created equal." There are reasons that Lincoln's Address is better remembered than Jackson's 1830 State of the Union. The emancipation of America's slaves and the US Civil War stand as the transformative events of nineteenth-century American history. At Gettysburg, Lincoln also addressed the righting of a wrong.[64] In contrast, Jackson's dispossession of the Cherokee was an act of exclusion. Many would prefer to forget its two original contributions to the ideals of American nationality. It was the first explicitly racist statement on the political community from a sitting US president, and it was also the first time a US president turned to a theological justification for an imperial act. Jackson presented Indian removal as a means by which the Indians would be allowed "to pursue happiness in their own way" and "become an interesting, civilized, and Christian community." Removal, he said, "would reclaim them from their wandering habits." Gesturing to the missions movement, he acknowledged that "[p]hilanthropy had long been busily employed in devising means to avert" removal, but offered the corrective, that "true philanthropy. . .. reconciles the mind to. . . the extinction of one generation to make room for another." Removal, he said, was the Indians' "fate." He asked American citizens to unite in "attempting to open the eyes of those children of the forest to their true condition." How can it be supposed, he asked, "that the wandering savage has a stronger attachment to his home than the settled, civilized Christian?" In one

63. Worcester quote in Edwin A. Miles, "After John Marshall's Decision: *Worcester v. Georgia* and the Nullification Crisis," p. 540.

64. Gary Wills, *Lincoln at Gettysburg: The Words That Remade America* (New York, 2006).

sense, it was a stunning appropriation of the missionaries' language of Christian paternalism, their claim to represent the moral and progressive course, and their jeremiad, in order to repudiate their mission.[65]

Little in Jackson's Address was as it appeared. He characterized the coercion and fraud that informed his and the US Army's campaigns against the Indians as an unfortunate series of "inconveniences and vexations" from which removal would relieve the Southeastern Indians. The pressure and violence unleashed against the Southeastern Indians had precipitated a civil war between pro- and anti-removal tribal factions, but Jackson told Congress that the "tribes have with great unanimity" decided to "avail themselves" of the "liberal offers presented" by the US government "to remove beyond the Mississippi River."[66] What was true, however, was that Indian removal opened territory from Tennessee to Louisiana for white settlement. It relieved much of Alabama and the whole state of Mississippi of Indian occupancy. In these ways, it helped secure for the planter class the balance of power in US politics for a generation and also helped the Southern planter class to become the richest ruling class in the world.[67]

Despite its claim of continuity, specifically that Indian removal represented the "happy consummation" of decades of policy, Jackson's rationale for Indian removal departed from colonial and early national precedents. Nor was it, as he suggested, consistent with the principles of the American Revolution. No one, however, had done more to elevate the authority of the founders than the national evangelists. From the White House, Jackson continued to assert the grounds of exclusion. In his 1833 annual message to Congress, Jackson explained to Congress that the Southeastern Indians "have neither the intelligence, the industry, the moral habits, nor the desire of improvement" that distinguished Anglo-Americans. It was, he said, their misfortune "to be established in the midst of another and

65. Andrew Jackson, "State of the Union Address," December 6, 1830, excerpted in Theda Perdue and Michael D. Green, eds., *The Cherokee Removal: A Brief History with Documents* (New York, 1995), pp. 119–121; Sacvan Bercovitch, *The Rites of Assent: Transformation in the Symbolic Construction of America* (New York, 1992), passim but esp. ch. 5.

66. Andrew Jackson, "State of the Union Address," December 6, 1830; ibid., pp. 120–121.

67. On the legal inadmissibility of heathenism for seizing Indian lands in the colonial era, see Stuart Banner, *How the Indians Lost Their Land: Law and Power on the American Frontier* (Cambridge, MA, 2005), ch. 1. On the Jackson administration's departure from a three-decade-old policy put forth by Washington's Secretary of War Henry Knox, embraced by Washington and subsequent presidents, see Perdue and Green, *The Cherokee Removal*,

superior race." There was no point in conjecture about "the causes of their inferiority." They must, he explained, "yield to the force of circumstances and ere long disappear."[68]

In both his veto of the Bank re-charter and his rationale for Indian removal, Jackson claimed to be conserving the Constitution, to be protecting its sacred place at the root of American nationality. Throughout his second term, including his Farewell Address, Jackson continued to emphasize that popular sovereignty, with the president as the delegate of the people, was merely the fulfillment of a national promise. Jackson's view of the Constitution as a sacred text, honored by faithful preservation, made instinctive sense to people whose historical consciousness was deeply shaped by Protestantism. Justifying his opposition to the Bank, he said, "Each public officer who takes an oath to support the Constitution swears that he will support it as he understands it," Jackson said, "and not as it is understood by others."[69] In a society in which Catholic, or Jewish, concepts of authority and textuality predominated, such an idea would have seemed eccentric, or heretical. In the Catholic and Jewish tradition, the text means what the priest or rabbi says it means. In contrast, Protestantism places the authority of the text above that of any institution while giving every man the right, even the obligation, to arrive at his own relationship to its meaning, its truth. Jackson did not invent the distinctive mixture of democratism and fundamentalism with which Americans typically approach the Constitution. Nor did he bestow to the American nation the notion that cultural preferences, rather than socioeconomic resources, constitute elite status. It was the influence and reach of frontier revivalism and national evangelism, and their Protestant habits of thought, that helped make Jackson's expression of these ideals compelling to the American people.[70]

The contest between national evangelism and frontier revivalism is important to understanding why frontier settlers gave their support

---

esp. pp. 8–10, 119. On the corruption and fraud that marked Jackson's diplomacy with Indians throughout his public career, see Wallace, *The Long, Bitter Trail,* chs. 3 and 4; Adam Rothman, *Slave Country: The Origins of the Deep South,* chs. 4 and 5; Perdue and Green, pp. 119, 121.

68. Quote in Norgren, p. 299.

69. Ibid.

70. Alister McGrath, *Christianity's Dangerous Idea: The Protestant Revolution* (New York, 2008), esp. chs. 1, 9, 12; Ernest Renan, "What Is a Nation?" in Omar Dahbour and Micheline

to Jackson. It also clarifies why the Northeastern elite's opposition to Jackson, and their dedication to the cause of Native American rights, did not run so deep as to insist on the integrity of Worcester v. Georgia, that is, on why the national evangelists, whose movement could claim real anti-racist beginnings, chose nation and empire over equality and law. In other words, this fight within Anglo-American Protestantism helps explain why "Indian removal" happened, when and how it did. The fact that it happened served, most immediately, the interests of the Southern planters. Jackson's rationalizations for the dispossession of Native Americans appealed in different measure to the three basic elements of American political society: Southern planters, the Northeastern elite, and small farmers and producers. The reshaping of the political community is often a crucial moment of self-imagining for a society, one that can come with profound consequences for its political culture. Justifications for exclusions from a political community based on natural rights, such as the United States, also matter. The crisis of "Indian removal," and its rationalizations, brought together and illuminated a mixture of voluntarism, theologizing, anti-elitism, constitutionalism, and racism that remain familiar components of American nationality.[71]

R. Ishay, eds., *Nationalism Reader* (Atlantic Highlands, NJ, 1999), pp. 143–156; Kemp, *The Estrangement of the Past, passim; Sanford Levinson, Constitutional Faith* (Princeton, NJ, 1988), esp. chs. 1–2.

71. Uday Singh Mehta, *Liberalism and Empire: A Study in Nineteenth Century British Liberal Thought* (Chicago, 1999), esp. ch. 1; Barrington Moore, *The Social Origins of Dictatorship and Democracy*, ch. 3.

Index